SELECTED

OF

MARTIN LUTHER

*

1517-1520

*   *

1520-1523

*   *   *

1523-1526

*   *   *   *

1529-1546

SELECTED WRITINGS

OF

MARTIN LUTHER

* * * *

1529-1546

SELECTED WRITINGS
OF
MARTIN LUTHER

* * * *

1529-1546

THEODORE G. TAPPERT

EDITOR

MINNEAPOLIS / FORTRESS PRESS

SELECTED WRITINGS OF MARTIN LUTHER
Volume 4, 1529–1546

Fortress Press 2007 Edition

Selections in this publication were edited and introduced by Theodore G. Tappert and drawn from Luther's Works: American Edition, General Editor, Helmut T. Lehmann, volumes 31-55. Copyright © 1957-1967 Fortress Press. All rights reserved. Except for brief quotations in critical articles or reviews, no part of this book may be reproduced in any manner without prior written permission from the publisher. Visit http://www.augsburgfortress.org/copyrights/contact.asp or write to Permissions, Augsburg Fortress, Box 1209, Minneapolis, MN 55440.

Cover image: Portrait of Martin Luther by Lucas Cranach the Elder, 1533
Germanisches Nationalmuseum, Nuremberg, Germany
Photo © Bettmann / Corbis

Library of Congress Cataloging-in-Publication Data
Luther, Martin, 1483-1546.
[Selections. English. 2007]
Selected writings of Martin Luther / Martin Luther ;
Theodore G. Tappert, editor.
p. cm.
Includes bibliographical references and index.
ISBN 978-0-8006-6226-4 (alk. paper)
1. Theology. 2. Lutheran Church—Doctrines.
I. Tappert, Theodore G. (Theodore Gerhardt), 1904-1973. II. Title.
BR331.E5T32 2007
230'.41—dc22
2007007515

The paper used in this publication meets the minimum requirements of American National Standard for Information Sciences—Permanence of Paper for Printed Library Materials, ANSI Z329.48-1984.
Printed in Canada.

11   10   09   08   07   1   2   3   4   5   6   7   8   9   10

CONTENTS

ABBREVIATIONS

ANF	— *The Ante-Nicene Fathers,* edited by Alexander Roberts and James Donaldson (Buffalo and New York, 1885-1896, American reprint of the Edinburgh edition).
BG	— *Luthers Werke für das christliche Haus,* edited by Georg Buchwald, *et al.* (Braunschweig, 1889-1892).
CIC	— *Corpus Iuris Canonici,* edited by E. Friedberg (Graz, 1955).
CL	— *Luthers Werke in Auswahl,* edited by Otto Clemen, *et al.* (Bonn, 1912-1933; Berlin, 1955-1956).
C. R.	— *Huldreich Zwinglis sämmtliche Werke,* vols. 88 ff. of the *Corpus Reformatorum,* edited by Emil Egli, Georg Finsler, *et al.* (Leipzig, 1905-).
DRTA. JR	— *Deutsche Reichstagsakten unter Kaiser Karl V,* edited by Historische Kommission bei der Bayrischen Akademie der Wissenschaften (Gotha, 1893-).
EA	— *D. Martin Luthers sämmtliche Werke* (Frankfurt and Erlangen, 1826-1857).
EA Var. arg	— *D. Martin Luthers Sämmtliche.* Erlanger Ausgabe: Opera latina varii argumenti ad reformationis historiam imprimis pertinentia (Frankfurt/Erlangen, 1865-1873).
FC	— *Fathers of the Church,* edited by Ludwig Schopp (New York, 1947-).
LW	— American edition of *Luther's Works* (Philadelphia and St. Louis, 1955-).
LWZ	— *The Latin Works of Huldreich Zwingli,* 3 vols., translated and edited by S. M. Jackson, *et al.* (New York, 1912; Philadelphia, 1922, 1929).

GENERAL INTRODUCTION

This selection from the writings of Martin Luther is designed for those who wish to supplement their reading about the Reformer with first hand reading of his own works. It differs from other presently available selections in English translation[1] in that it supplies the need for something between a condensed source book[2] and the large fifty-five volume American edition of *Luther's Works*. Because of limited space the smaller source books are compelled to abridge most of the selections included, and as a rule they present their materials in topical form. In contrast, the present selection aims to reproduce whole works and to arrange these chronologically in their historical setting so as to serve the interests both of the general reader and of students of history, literature, and theology. For the sake of such users the selection was also made with an eye to variety in the types of literature and in the tone—polemical and irenic, satirical and contemplative, academic and devotional. Special consideration was given to writings that have come to be regarded as classics or that illuminate some facet in the career of Luther, the development of his thought, or the course of the Reformation.

Such principles of selection have inevitably led to some repetition insofar as the same basic affirmations appear again and again. This should not be regarded as a defect but rather as an advantage. Although the reader will repeatedly encounter the same convictions and arguments, they are expressed in a variety of ways or

[1] The present collection is intended to replace the six-volume *Works of Martin Luther* (see *PE* in the list of abbreviations above), which has been out of print for several years.

[2] The best of these is John Dillenberger (ed.), *Martin Luther: Selections from his Writings* (Garden City: Doubleday Anchor Books, 1961). Hugh Thomson Kerr, Jr. (ed.), *A Compend of Luther's Theology* (Philadelphia: Westminster Press, 1943), contains excerpts from Luther to illustrate topics of theology. Ewald M. Plass (ed.), *What Luther Says* (3 vols.; St. Louis: Concordia, 1959), is a larger anthology of briefer quotations arranged topically in alphabetical order with little attention to the historical context. Of a different character is Bertram Lee Woolf (trans.), *Reformation Writings of Martin Luther* (2 vols.; London: Lutterworth Press, 1952, 1956), which concentrates on selections from the four years 1517 to 1521.

with different nuances. Besides, it is of great importance to recognize that although Luther was not a "systematic" theologian in one sense of the term, there was a center in his faith and thought.

It should be self-evident that no two persons would make precisely the same selection, and it would be easy to criticize the selection made here. For example, it might have seemed desirable to include some works to illustrate the early development of the Reformer's theology "from Catholicism to Reformation" (to borrow Otto Scheel's phrase), especially because this has occupied the attention of many historians in recent years. Unfortunately, this would have demanded the reproduction of Luther's extensive early lectures or would have required a departure from the principle of including works in their entirety. Some readers will miss Luther's *Small* and *Large Catechisms;* these were omitted despite their vast influence because they are readily available separately, the former in an inexpensive booklet. The omission, with a few somewhat untypical exceptions, of Luther's sermons and letters, not to speak of his Table Talk, may also be criticized. Their exclusion can be justified only on the ground of limitations of space and the fact that such utterances of the Reformer were of a less public character.

After Luther's prefaces to the collected works published in his lifetime, which appropriately stand at the beginning, the present selection begins with the theses of 1517 against scholastic theology and the practice of indulgences. The latter, the *Ninety-five Theses,* brought Luther to public attention. The theses he prepared for the Heidelberg Disputation the following year are even better expressions of his theology at the time. It was in the year 1520 that Luther's break with the theology, piety, and institutions of the Middle Ages became apparent, and six writings of this fruitful year have been included to document the break. The following year Luther defended some of his fundamental views by replying to an able critic, Latomus. In 1522 he directed an attack against Roman attempts to regulate dress, food, drink, and the like, but at the same time he also counseled against a radical overturn of customs in a series of sermons. During the year 1523 Luther dealt with a series of practical problems in a half-dozen writings included in this selection: on civil government, the rights of laymen, organized charity, public worship, celibacy and marriage. The importance of education and malpractices in business were discussed in treatises published in 1524. The following year Luther wrote a long work against those he looked upon as religious extremists on what we call the left. Three pieces also testify to his involvement in the Peasants' War. Further proposals for public worship and some pastoral counsel for soldiers in two works of 1526 are followed by a discussion in 1529 of war against the Turks. An imperial diet was convened in Augsburg in 1530 (it was there that the *Augsburg Confession* was drafted), and Luther addressed a vigorous exhortation to the clergy assembled there. The same year he wrote again on education and published an open letter on the art of translating. Although he remained a prolific writer, what Luther wrote after 1530 seems anticlimactic in many respects. Included in this collection are only his final critical and constructive observations concerning the church in 1539 and, in token of his life-long preoccupation with the Bible, the prefaces of 1545 and 1546 on the Old and New Testaments.

The counsel of Professor Wilhelm Pauck was helpful in making the selection of writings included in this collection.

The translations into English are from those volumes of *LW* which have been published by Fortress Press and its predecessor, Muhlenberg Press. Only two pieces, taken from *PE*, were revised especially for the present collection. The names of the translators are recorded in each instance. The undersigned expresses his thanks to the editors of Fortress Press not only for permission to reproduce the translations but also for other assistance.

T.G.T.

SELECTED WRITINGS

OF

MARTIN LUTHER

* * * *

1529-1546

ON WAR
AGAINST THE TURK

1529

Translated by Charles M. Jacobs
Revised by Robert C. Schultz

INTRODUCTION

For more than three quarters of a century the Ottoman Turks had cast a menacing shadow over Europe. Constantinople had fallen to them in 1453, and by the end of the fifteenth century they had consolidated their power up to the Danube River. To the east and south, Persia, Syria, and Egypt fell under Turkish sway. Under the rule of Suleiman the Magnificent (1520-1566) the Turks turned their attention once more toward Christian Europe. In 1520 they captured Belgrade. The following year Rhodes fell to the Muslims. Then in 1526 King Louis II of Hungary was killed and his troops soundly defeated in the Battle of Mohacs on the Danube.[1] This defeat sent a wave of terror over Europe. Only pressing domestic problems which demanded undivided and immediate attention prevented Suleiman from pursuing his advantage.[2]

The Turkish menace produced a varied and voluminous literature in the West, particularly during the years coinciding with Luther's work of reform. Dark and foreboding prophecies warning of the bloodshed, violence, and terror which the Turks brought found their way into print.[3] One group of writings called for resistance and crusades against the Turks.[4] Another group urged resignation to Turkish conquest and even praised Turkish rule. The authors of these tracts, pamphlets, and books argued that if Europeans did not resist, they would find that the Turks were gentle masters.[5] Following the Turkish victory at Mohacs the literature on the subject mushroomed as books with woodcut illustrations of

---

[1] Cf. below, p. 50, n. 119.

[2] Cf. E. G. Schwiebert, *Luther and His Times* (St. Louis: Concordia, 1950), p. 63, and E. Harris Harbison, *The Age of Reformation* (Ithaca, New York: Cornell University Press, 1955), p. 26.

[3] Cf. *WA* 30[II], 83.

[4] Typical of this group was a pamphlet entitled *A Call for a Crusade Against the Turks and All who Are Opposed to the Christian Faith* (*Das ist ein Anschlag eins zugs wider die Türcken und alle die wider den christlichen glauben sindt*), which was first published in 1518 and then republished in enlarged form in 1522 and addressed to all of Christendom. See *WA* 30[II], 84.

[5] See *WA* 30[II], 85. This point of view was refuted by other publications which related tales of Turkish atrocities and duplicity. The outstanding example of such refutation was the *Turkish Book* (*Türckenbiechlin*), published in 1522.

Turkish atrocities and books by statesmen, popular poets, and humanist thinkers[6] began to be published.

Luther was by no means uninvolved with the Turkish menace.[7] In his *Explanations of the Ninety-five Theses* (1518) Luther had made the statement that "to fight against the Turk is the same as resisting God, who visits our sin upon us with this rod."[8] Now that the Turks were once more on their way westward, Luther's words were recalled and he was held responsible both for the Turkish advance itself as well as for the unwillingness of many to resist the foe of Christendom.[9]

For some time Luther's friends had been urging him to write on the question of war against the Turks,[10] but it was not until 1528 that he actually did so. Even then he wrote not in reply to critics but out of pastoral concern for those who looked to him for guidance.

In 1526 in *Whether Soldiers, Too, Can Be Saved*[11] Luther indicated that he wanted to deal with the Turkish question, but the first hint that such a book was in the offing came in a letter to Nicholas Hausmann[12] dated August 5, 1528.[13] Apparently the actual writing began early in October, but by February, 1529, the book still had

---

[6] See *WA* 30[II], 86-87.

[7] Luther was certainly aware of, if not influenced by, the mass of literature about the Turks, especially Ulrich von Hutten's *Exhortation to the German Princes* (*Ad principes Germaniae ut bellum inuehant. Exhortatoria*) (1518). See *WA* 30[II], 91, and Eduard Böcking (ed.), *Ulrichi Hutteni Opera* (Leipzig, 1861). Cf. also *SW* 3, 476-477.

[8] *LW* 31, 91-92.

[9] Typical of such charges is *Why the Turks Defeated the Hungarians* (*Ein Sendbrief darjnn angetzeigt wird vermeinte ursach warumb der Tuerck widder die Hungern triumphirt un oblegen hab. Antwurt und verlegung obgemelter ursach, durch das rechtgeschaffen wort Gotes und was oder wo dasselbig seye einem jtzlichen Christen zuuoran zu disen getzeiten lustig und nutzlich zu lesen*) (1526). This book attributes the defeat of the king of Hungary at Mohacs to Luther's leading people from the true faith. *WA* 30[II], 92.

[10] Cf. below, p. 9.

[11] Cf. *SW* 3, 427-477.

[12] Hausmann (*ca.* 1478-1538) was a close friend of Luther. As pastor in Zwickau he bore the brunt of the activities of the "Zwickau prophets" and of the city council, which attempted to interfere in the affairs of the church. From 1532 to 1538 he was court chaplain to the dukes of Anhalt. He died in 1538 of a stroke suffered during his inaugural sermon at Freiberg.

[13] *WA*, Br 4, 511.

not appeared. On February 13, 1529, Luther wrote to Hausmann explaining that a number of manuscript pages had been lost and that it had been difficult for him to rewrite the missing sections.[14] The printing was completed by April 23.

In the present treatise Luther does not attempt to lay down a universally binding law or principle. He deals with a specific problem within the context of the moment.[15] At the very outset he defends the position he had taken in 1518[16] on the ground that what he had said then was still essentially true, but that the political circumstances attending his statement were different. Luther makes it clear that a war against the Turks cannot and must not be a crusade or religiously motivated and led by the church. Emphatically he states that it is not the business of church and clergy to promote and wage warfare.[17]

Luther's concern throughout the book is to teach men how to fight with a clear conscience.[18] In so doing he develops two major points. There are, he says, only two men who may properly fight the Turk. The first of these is the Christian, who by prayer, repentance, and reform of life takes the rod of anger out of God's hand and compels the Turk to stand on his own strength.[19] The second man who may wage war is the emperor. The Turk has wrongfully attacked the emperor's subjects, and by virtue of the office to which God has appointed him, the emperor is duty-bound to protect and defend the subjects with whose care God has entrusted him.[20]

The translation is a revision of that by Charles M. Jacobs in PE 5, 79-123, based on the German text, Vom Kriege wider den Türken, in WA 30ᵤ, (81) 107-148.

R. C. S.

---

[14] WA, Br 5, 17-18.
[15] Cf. Heinz Zahrnt, Luther deutet Geschichte (München: Verlag Paul Müller, 1952), p. 119.
[16] Cf. below, p. 10.
[17] Cf. below, pp. 15-16.
[18] Cf. below, p. 17.
[19] Cf. below, p. 18.
[20] Cf. below, p. 32.

ON WAR
AGAINST THE TURK

To the serene, highborn prince and lord, Philip, landgrave of Hesse,[1] count of Katzenellenbogen, Ziegenhain, and Nidda, my gracious lord.

Grace and peace in Christ Jesus our Lord and Savior.

Serene, highborn prince, gracious lord, for the past five years certain persons have been begging me to write about war against the Turks, and to arouse and encourage our people. Now that the Turk is actually approaching,[2] even my friends are urging me to do this, especially since there are some stupid preachers among us Germans (as I am sorry to hear) who are making the people believe that we ought not and must not fight against the Turks. Some are even so foolish as to say that it is not proper for Christians to bear the temporal sword or to be rulers. Furthermore, some actually want the Turk to come and rule because they think our German people are wild and uncivilized—indeed, that they are half-devil and half-man. The blame for this wicked error among the people is laid on Luther and must be called "the fruit of my gospel," just as I am blamed for the rebellion,[3] and for every bad thing that happens anywhere in the world. My accusers know better, but—God and his word to the contrary—they pretend not to know better, and they seek occasion to speak evil of the Holy Ghost and of the truth that is openly confessed, so that they may earn the reward of hell and never repent or receive the forgiveness of their sins.

Therefore it is necessary for me to write about these things for my own sake and that of the gospel to defend ourselves; not be-

---

[1] Philip (1504-1567) had introduced the Reformation into his realm at an early date and was a leader of the Protestant rulers. His bigamous marriage in 1540, to which Luther had consented, was a severe blow to the Protestant cause.

[2] Cf. above, p. 5. The Turkish advance resumed the spring of 1529 when Suleiman the Magnificent began his march to Vienna.

[3] The Peasants' War of 1525.

9

cause of the blasphemers, however. I do not think they are worth my saying a single word to them in my defense, for to them the gospel must always be a stench and savor of death to death [II Cor. 2:16], as they have deserved by their wilful blasphemy. But I must write so that innocent consciences may no longer be deceived by these slanderers and made suspicious of me or my doctrine, and so they may not be deceived into believing that we must not fight against the Turks. I have thought it best to publish this little book under the name of Your Grace, a famous and powerful prince, so that it may be better received and more diligently read. Thus, if it came to a discussion of a crusade against the Turks, the princes and lords would readily recall it. Indeed, I am perfectly willing to point out several passages which ought to be thought about and emphasized. I commend Your Grace to the merciful grace and favor of our God; may he keep Your Grace against all error and against the craft of the devil, and enlighten and strengthen Your Grace for a blessed reign.

> Your Grace's devoted,
> MARTIN LUTHER

Wittenberg, October 9, 1528[4]

Pope Leo X in the bull in which he put me under the ban[5] condemned, among other statements, the following one, "To fight against the Turk is the same as resisting God, who visits our sin upon us with this rod."[6] This may be why they say that I oppose and dissuade from war against the Turk. I do not hesitate to admit that this article is mine and that I stated and defended it at the time; and if things in the world were in the same state now that they were in then, I would still have to hold and defend it. But it is not fair to forget what the situation was then and what my grounds and reasons were, and to take my words and apply them to another situation where those grounds and reasons do not exist. With this kind of skill who could not make the gospel a pack of lies or pretend that it contradicted itself?

---

[4] Cf. above, pp. 6-7.
[5] The bull *Exsurge, Domine* was issued on June 15, 1520.
[6] See *Explanations of the Ninety-five Theses* (1518). *LW* 31, 91-92.

This was the state of things at that time: no one had taught, no one had heard, and no one knew anything about temporal government, whence it came, what its office and work were, or how it ought to serve God. The most learned men (I shall not name them) regarded temporal government as a heathen, human, ungodly thing, as though it jeopardized salvation to be in the ranks of the rulers. This is how the priests and monks drove kings and princes into the corner and persuaded them that to serve God they must undertake other works, such as hearing mass, saying prayers, endowing masses,[7] etc. In a word, princes and lords who wanted to be pious men regarded their rank and office as of no value and did not consider it a service of God. They became real priests and monks, except that they did not wear tonsures and cowls. If they wanted to serve God, they had to go to church. All the lords living at that time would have to testify to this, for they knew it by experience. My gracious lord, Duke Frederick,[8] of blessed memory, was so glad when I first wrote *Temporal Authority*[9] that he had the little book copied and put in a special binding, and was happy that he could see what his position was in God's sight.

And so it was that at that time the pope and the clergy were all in all and through all, like God in the world [Eph. 4:6], and the temporal rulers were in darkness, oppressed and unknown. But the pope and his crowd wanted to be Christians, too, and therefore they pretended to make war on the Turk. It was over those two points that the discussion arose, for I was then working on doctrine that concerned Christians and the conscience,[10] and had as yet written nothing about temporal rulers. The papists called me a flatterer of princes because I was dealing only with the spiritual class,[11] and not with the temporal; just as they call me seditious now that I have written in such glorification of temporal government as no teacher has done since the days of the apostles, except, perhaps, St. Augus-

---

[7] Endowed masses were generally said for the benefit of deceased persons who had made testamentary provision for them.

[8] Elector Frederick the Wise of Saxony had died on May 5, 1525.

[9] *Temporal Authority: To What Extent It Should Be Obeyed* (1523). SW 2, 265-319.

[10] Luther is speaking of the general nature of his work, not of a specific writing.

[11] I.e., the clerical estate or clergy.

tine.[12] I can boast of this with a good conscience, and the testimony of the world will support me.

Among the points of Christian doctrine, I discussed what Christ says in Matthew [5:39-41], namely, that a Christian shall not resist evil, but endure all things, let the coat go and the cloak, let them be taken from him, turn the other cheek, etc. The pope with his universities and cloister schools had made a counsel of this, something which was not commanded and which a Christian need not keep; thus they perverted Christ's word, taught false doctrine throughout the world, and deceived Christians. But since they wanted to be Christians—indeed, the best Christians in the world—and yet fight against the Turk, endure no evil, and suffer neither compulsion nor wrong, I opposed them with these words of Christ that Christians shall not resist evil, but suffer all things and surrender all things. I based the article condemned by Pope Leo upon this. He was eager to condemn it because I took away the cloak covering the Roman knavery.

The popes had never seriously intended to wage war against the Turk; instead they used the Turkish war as a cover for their game[13] and robbed Germany of money by means of indulgences whenever they took the notion.[14] The whole world knew it, but now it is forgotten. So they condemned my article not because it opposed the Turkish war, but because it tore away this cloak and blocked the path along which the money went to Rome. If they had seriously wished to fight the Turk, the pope and the cardinals would have had enough from the pallia,[15] annates,[16] and other unmentionable sources of income so that they would not have needed to practice such extortion and robbery in Germany. If there had

---

[12] Luther is probably speaking in general terms, rather than of a specific writing.

[13] Thiele, *Luthers Sprichwörtersammlung,* No. 88.

[14] Luther had dealt with this point earlier in *To the Christian Nobility of the German Nation* (1520). *SW* 1, 280.

[15] The pallium, or woolen shoulder cape, is the emblem of the archepiscopal office. It had to be secured from Rome. Luther charged that the pallium (and the office it symbolized) was for sale at exorbitant prices. Cf. *SW* 1, 284-285.

[16] Originally the annates were the income received by a bishop from vacant benefices in his diocese. The right to this income was subsequently claimed by the papacy. Cf. *SW* 1, 282-284.

been a general opinion that a serious war was at hand, I could have polished my article somewhat more and made some distinctions.

Nor did I like it that the Christians and the princes were driven, urged, and irritated into attacking the Turk, and making war on him, before they amended their own ways and lived as true Christians. These two points, or either one by itself, were enough reason to dissuade from war. I shall never advise a heathen or a Turk, let alone a Christian, to attack another or begin war. That is nothing else than advising bloodshed and destruction, and it brings no good fortune in the end, as I have written in the book *Whether Soldiers, Too, Can Be Saved*;[17] and it never does any good when one rascal punishes another[18] without first becoming good himself.

But what motivated me most of all was this: They undertook to fight against the Turk in the name of Christ, and taught and incited men to do this, as though our people were an army of Christians against the Turks, who were enemies of Christ. This is absolutely contrary to Christ's doctrine and name. It is against his doctrine because he says that Christians shall not resist evil, fight, or quarrel, nor take revenge or insist on rights [Matt. 5:39]. It is against his name because there are scarcely five Christians in such an army, and perhaps there are worse people in the eyes of God in that army than are the Turks; and yet they all want to bear the name of Christ. This is the greatest of all sins and is one that no Turk commits, for Christ's name is used for sin and shame and thus dishonored. This would be especially so if the pope and the bishops were involved in the war, for they would bring the greatest shame and dishonor to Christ's name because they are called to fight against the devil with the word of God and with prayer, and they would be deserting their calling and office to fight with the sword against flesh and blood. They are not commanded to do this; it is forbidden.

O how gladly Christ would receive me at the Last Judgment if, when summoned to the spiritual office to preach and care for souls, I had left it and busied myself with fighting and with the temporal sword! Why should Christ or his people have anything to do with

---

[17] Cf. *SW* 3, 427-477.
[18] Cf. Wander (ed.), *Deutsches Sprichwörter Lexikon*, I, "*Bube*," No. 14. Cf. also *SW* 3, 332, n. 34; 341, n. 53.

the sword and going to war, and kill men's bodies, when he declared that he has come to save the world, not to kill people [John 3:17]? His work is to deal with the gospel and to redeem men from sin and death by his Spirit to help them from this world to everlasting life. According to John 6 [:15] he fled and would not let himself be made king; before Pilate he confessed, "My kingship is not of this world" [John 18:36]; and in the garden he bade Peter to put up his sword and said, "All who take the sword will perish by the sword" [Matt. 26:52].

I say this not because I would teach that worldly rulers ought not be Christians, or that a Christian cannot bear the sword and serve God in temporal government. Would to God they were all Christians, or that no one could be a prince unless he were a Christian! Things would be better than they now are, and the Turk would not be so powerful. But what I want to do is to keep a distinction between the callings and offices, so that everyone can see to what God has called him and fulfil the duties of his office faithfully and sincerely in the service of God. I have written more than enough about this elsewhere, especially in the books *Whether Soldiers, Too, Can Be Saved*[19] and *Temporal Authority*.[20] In the church, where all should be Christians, Paul will not permit one person to assume another's office, Romans 12 [:4] and I Corinthians 12 [:14-26], but exhorts every member to do his own work so that there be no disorder, rather, that everything be done in an orderly way [I Cor. 14:40]. How much less, then, are we to tolerate the disorder that arises when a Christian abandons his office and assumes a temporal office, or when a bishop or pastor gives up his office and assumes the office of a prince or judge; or, on the other hand, when a prince takes up the office of a bishop and gives up his princely office? Even today this shameful disorder rages and rules in the whole papacy, contrary to their own canons and laws.

Experience shows how well we have succeeded with the Turkish war up to now, though we have fought as Christians until we have lost Rhodes,[21] almost all of Hungary, and much German soil

---

[19] Cf. *SW* 3, 427-477.
[20] Cf. *SW* 2, 265-319.
[21] The Isle of Rhodes had fallen to the Turks in December, 1521.

besides.[22] And to show us clearly that he is not with us in our war against the Turks, God has never put much courage or spirit into the minds of our princes to be able to deal seriously with the Turkish war even once. Though many of the diets,[23] almost all of them in fact, have been called and held on this account, the matter will neither be settled nor arranged, and it seems as though God were mocking our diets and letting the devil hinder them and get the better of them until the Turk comes ravaging on at his leisure and ruins Germany without effort or resistance. Why does this happen? Because my article,[24] which Pope Leo condemned, remains uncondemned[25] and valid. And because the papists reject it, arbitrarily and without Scripture, the Turk must take its side and prove its validity with fist and deeds. If we will not learn from the Scriptures, we must learn from the Turk's scabbard, until we learn from dreadful experience that Christians should not make war or resist evil. Fools should be beaten with rods.[26]

How many wars, do you think, have there been against the Turk in which we would not have suffered heavy losses if the bishops and clergy had not been there? How pitifully the fine king Lassla was beaten with his bishops by the Turk at Varna.[27] The Hungarians themselves blamed Cardinal Julian and killed him for it.[28] Recently King Louis[29] would perhaps have fought with more success if he had not lead a priests' army or, as they call it, a Christian army, against the Turks. If I were emperor, king, or prince and were in a campaign against the Turk, I would exhort my bishops and priests to stay at home and attend to the duties of their office, praying, fasting, saying mass, preaching, and caring for the

---

[22] Cf. above, p. 5.
[23] The diets of Nürnberg (1523 and 1524) and of Spires (1526 and 1529) discussed the Turkish war at length.
[24] Cf. above, p. 6, n. 8.
[25] So far as Luther is concerned, the article is not condemned by God.
[26] Cf. Wander (ed.), *Deutsches Sprichwörter-Lexikon*, II, "Horen," No. 78.
[27] Ladislaus III, king of Poland and Hungary, was killed along with the bishops of Erlau and Grosswardein in the battle of Varna, November 10, 1444.
[28] Julian (Giuliano) Caesarini, papal legate in Hungary who had preached the crusade, was present at Varna and was murdered during the retreat which followed the battle.
[29] Louis II, king of Bohemia and Hungary, fell during the battle of Mohacs, August 29, 1526.

poor, as not only Holy Scripture, but their own canon law teaches and requires. If, however, they were to be disobedient to God and their own law and desire to go along to war, I would teach them by force to attend to their office and not, by their disobedience, put me and my army under the danger of God's wrath. It would be less harmful to have three devils in the army than one disobedient, apostate bishop who had given up his office and assumed the office of another. For there can be no good fortune with such people around, who go against God and their own law.

I have heard from fine soldiers who thought that the king of France,[30] when he was defeated and captured by the emperor before Pavia, had all of his bad fortune because he had the pope's, or, as they boastfully call them, the church's army with him. After they came to his camp with a great cry of "*Ecclesia, ecclesia!* Here is the church! Here is the church!" there was no more good fortune there. This is what the soldiers say, though perhaps they do not know the reason for it, namely, that it is not right for the pope, who wants to be a Christian, and the highest and best Christian preacher at that, to lead a church army, or army of Christians, for the church ought not to strive or fight with the sword. It has other enemies than flesh and blood; their name is the wicked devils in the air [Eph. 6:12]; therefore the church has other weapons and swords and other wars; it has enough to do and cannot get involved in the wars of the emperor or princes, for the Scriptures say that there shall be no good fortune where men are disobedient to God.[31]

And, too, if I were a soldier and saw a priest's banner in the field, or a banner of the cross, even though it was a crucifix, I should run as though the devil were chasing me; and even if they won a victory, by God's decree, I should not take any part in the booty or the rejoicing. Even the wicked iron-eater,[32] Pope Julius,[33] who was half-devil, did not succeed, but finally had to call on Emperor Maximilian and let him take charge of the game, despite the

---

[30] Francis I. Cf. *SW* 3, 430, n. 8.
[31] Cf. I Sam. 12:15.
[32] *Eissenfresser*, literally, "iron-eater." Cf. *SW* 3, 461, n. 72.
[33] Julius II (1503-1513).

fact that Julius had more money, arms, and people. I think, too, that this present pope, Clement,[34] who people think is almost a god of war, succeeded well with his fighting until he lost Rome and all its wealth to a few ill-armed soldiers. The conclusion is this: Christ will teach them to understand my article that Christians shall not make war, and the condemned article must take its revenge,[35] for it refers to Christians and will stand uncondemned. It is right and true, although they do not care and do not believe it, but hardened and unrepentant rush headlong to destruction. To this I say Amen, Amen.

It is true, indeed, that since they have temporal lordship and wealth, they ought to make the same contributions to the emperor, kings, or princes that other possessors of holdings properly make, and render the same services that others are expected to render. Indeed, these "goods of the church," as they call them, ought to be used especially and first of all to serve and help in the protection of the needy and the welfare of all classes, for that is the purpose for which they were given, not for a bishop to give up his office and use these goods for war or battle. If the banner of Emperor Charles or of a prince is in the field, then let everyone run boldly and gladly to the banner to which his allegiance is sworn—more on this will be said later. But if the banner of a bishop, cardinal, or pope is there, then run the other way, and say, "I do not know this coin;[36] if it were a prayer book, or the Holy Scriptures preached in the church, I would rally to it."

Now before I exhort or urge war against the Turk, hear me, for God's sake. I want first to teach you how to fight with a good conscience. For although (if I wanted to give way to the old Adam) I could keep quiet and look on while the Turk avenged me upon the tyrants (who persecute the gospel and blame me for all kinds of misfortune) and paid them back for it, nevertheless, I shall not do this, but rather, shall serve both friends and enemies so that my sun may rise on both bad and good, and my rain fall on the thankful and unthankful [Matt. 5:45].

---

[34] Clement VII (1523-1534).
[35] Cf. above, p. 6, n. 8.
[36] Cf. Wander (ed.), *Deutsches Sprichwörter Lexikon*, III, "Münzen," No. 39.

In the first place, the Turk certainly has no right or command to begin war and to attack lands that are not his. Therefore his war is nothing but an outrage and robbery with which God is punishing the world, as he often does through wicked scoundrels, and sometimes through godly people. The Turk does not fight from necessity or to protect his land in peace, as the right kind of a ruler does; but, like a pirate or highwayman, he seeks to rob and ravage other lands which do and have done nothing to him. He is God's rod and the devil's servant [Isa. 10:5]; there is no doubt about that.

In the second place, we must know who the man is who is to make war against the Turk so that he may be certain that he has a commission from God and is doing right. He must not plunge in to avenge himself or have some other mad notion or reason. He must be sure of this so that, win or lose, he may be in a state of salvation and in a godly occupation. There are two of these men, and there ought to be only two: the one is named Christian,[37] the other, Emperor Charles.

Christian should be there first, with his army. Since the Turk is the rod of the wrath of the Lord our God and the servant of the raging devil, the first thing to be done is to smite the devil, his lord, and take the rod out of God's hand, so that the Turk may be found only, in his own strength, all by himself, without the devil's help and without God's hand. This should be done by Sir Christian, that is, by the pious, holy, precious body of Christians. They are the people who have the arms for this war and they know how to use them. If the Turk's god, the devil, is not beaten first, there is reason to fear that the Turk will not be so easy to beat. Now the devil is a spirit who cannot be beaten with armor, muskets, horses, and men, and God's wrath cannot be allayed by them, as it is written in Psalm 33 [147:10], "His delight is not in the strength of the horse, nor his pleasure in the legs of a man; but the Lord takes pleasure in those who fear him, in those who hope in his steadfast love." Christian weapons and power must do it.

Here you ask, "Who are the Christians and where does one find them?" Answer: There are not many of them, but they are everywhere, though they are spread thin and live far apart, under

---

[37] The name personifies Christian believers.

good and bad princes. Christendom must continue to the end, as the article of the creed says, "I believe one holy Christian church." So it must be possible to find them. Every pastor and preacher ought diligently to exhort his people to repentance and to prayer. They ought to drive men to repentance by showing our great and numberless sins and our ingratitude, by which we have earned God's wrath and disfavor, so that he justly gives us into the hands of the devil and the Turk. And so that this preaching may work the more strongly, they ought to cite examples and sayings from the Scriptures, such as the Flood [Gen. 7:1-24], Sodom and Gomorrah [Gen. 19:24-28], and the children of Israel, and show how cruelly and how often God punished the world and its lands and peoples. And they ought to make it plain that it is no wonder, since we sin more grievously than they did, if we are punished worse than they.

This fight must be begun with repentance, and we must reform our lives, or we shall fight in vain; as the prophet Jeremiah says in chapter 18 [:7-8], "If at anytime I declare concerning a nation or a kingdom that I will pluck up and break down and destroy it, and if that nation concerning which I have spoken turns from its evil, I will repent of the evil that I intended to do it." And again, "And if at any time I declare concerning a nation or a kingdom that I will build and plant it, and if it does evil in my sight, not listening to my voice, then I will repent of the good which I had intended to do it. Now, therefore, say to the men of Judah and to the inhabitants of Jerusalem, Behold I am shaping evil against you and devising a plan against you. Return, every one of you and amend your ways and your doings" [Jer. 18:9-11]. We may apply these words to ourselves, for God is devising evil against us because of our wickedness and is certainly preparing the Turk against us, as he says in Psalm 7 [:12-13], "If a man does not repent, God will whet his sword; he has bent and strung his bow; he has prepared his deadly weapons."

Along with these must be cited the words and illustrations of Scripture in which God makes known how well pleased he is with true repentance or amendment made in faith and reliance on his word—such as the examples of kings David,[38] Ahab,[39] and Manasseh[40] in the Old Testament, and the like; in the New Testament, of St. Peter,[41] the malefactor,[42] the publican in the Gospel,[43] and so forth. Although I know that to the scholars and saints who need no repentance this advice of mine will be laughable for they will consider it a simple and common thing which they have long since passed beyond, nevertheless, I have not been willing to omit it for the sake of myself and of sinners like myself, who need both repentance and exhortation to repentance every day. In spite of it, we remain all too lazy and lax, and have not, with those ninety and nine just persons,[44] got so far as they let themselves think they have.[45]

After people have thus been taught and exhorted to confess their sin and amend their ways they should then be most diligently exhorted to prayer and shown that such prayer pleases God, that he has commanded it and promised to hear it, and that no one ought to think lightly of his own praying or have doubts about it, but with firm faith be sure that it will be heard; all of which has been published by us in many tracts.[46] The man who doubts, or prays for good luck, would do better to let prayer alone because such prayer is merely tempting God and only makes things worse. Therefore I would advise against processions,[47] which are a heathenish and useless practice, for they are more pomp and show than prayer. I say the same thing about celebrating a lot of masses and calling upon the saints. It might, indeed, be of some use to have the people, especially the young people, sing the Litany at mass or vespers or in the church after the sermon, pro-

---

[38] II Sam. 24:10.
[39] I Kings 21:27-29.
[40] II Chron. 33:10-13.
[41] Cf. Mark 14:72; John 21:15-19.
[42] Luke 23:40-42.
[43] Luke 18:10-14.
[44] Luke 15:7.
[45] Wander (ed.), *Deutsches Sprichwörter Lexikon*, I, "Berg," Nos. 29, 65, 104, 109, 113.
[46] Cf. WA 2, 57-65.
[47] Processions were regarded as especially solemn forms of prayer.

vided that everyone, even at home by himself, constantly raised to Christ at least a sigh of the heart for grace to lead a better life and for help against the Turk. I am not speaking of much and long praying, but of frequent brief sighs, in one or two words, such as, "O help us, dear God the Father; have mercy on us, dear Lord Jesus Christ!" or the like.

See, now, this kind of preaching will hit home with Christians and find them out, and there will be Christians who will accept it and act according to it; it does not matter if you do not know who they are. The tyrants and bishops may also be exhorted to stop their raging and persecution against the word of God and not to hinder our prayer; but if they do not stop, we must not cease to pray, but keep on and take the chance that they will have the benefit of our prayer and be preserved along with us, or that we shall pay for their raging and be ruined along with them. They are so perverse and blind that if God gave them good fortune against the Turk they would ascribe it to their holiness and merit and boast of it against us. On the other hand, if things turned out bad, they would ascribe it to no one but us, and lay the blame on us, disregarding the shameful, openly sinful, and wicked lives which they not only lead, but defend; for they cannot teach rightly a single point about the way to pray, and they are worse than the Turks. Oh, well, we must leave that to God's judgment.

In exhorting to prayer we must also introduce words and examples from the Scriptures which show how strong and mighty a man's prayer has sometimes been; for example, Elijah's prayer, which St. James praises [Jas. 5:17]; the prayers of Elisha[48] and other prophets; of kings David,[49] Solomon,[50] Asa,[51] Jehoshaphat,[52] Jesias,[53] Hezekiah,[54] etc.; the story of how God promised Abraham that he would spare the land of Sodom and Gomorrah for

---

[48] Perhaps Luther had in mind passages such as II Kings 4:1-7.
[49] Cf. II Sam. 24:10.
[50] Cf. I Kings 3:6-10.
[51] II Chron. 14:11-12.
[52] II Chron. 20:5-12.
[53] Perhaps Luther meant Josiah or Joash. Cf. II Chron. 34:33 and 24:2.
[54] II Kings 19:14-19.

the sake of five righteous men.[55] For the prayer of a righteous man can do much if it be persistent, St. James says in his Epistle [Jas. 5:16]. They are also to be warned to be careful not to anger God by not praying and not to fall under his judgment in Ezekiel 13 [:5], where God says, "You have not gone up into the breaches or built up a wall for the house of Israel, that it might stand in battle in the day of the Lord"; and in chapter 22 [:30-31], "I sought for a man among them who should build up the wall and stand in the breach before me for the land, that I should not destroy it; but I found none. Therefore I have poured out my indignation upon them; I have consumed them with the fire of my wrath; their way have I requited upon their heads, says the Lord God."

It is easy to see from this that God would have men set themselves in the way of his wrath and stave it off, and that he is greatly angered if this is not done. That is what I meant when I spoke above about taking the rod out of God's hand.[56] Let him fast who will. Let him go down on his knees and bow and fall to the ground if he is in earnest, for the bowing and kneeling that has been practiced up to now in the chapters and monasteries was not in earnest; it was, and still is, sheer nonsense. It is not for nothing that I exhort pastors and preachers to impress this upon the people, for I see plainly that it rests entirely with the preachers whether the people shall amend their ways and pray or not. Little will be accomplished by preaching in which men call Luther names and blaspheme, and do not touch upon repentance and prayer; but where God's word is spoken, it is not without fruit [Isa. 55:11]. They, however, must preach as though they were preaching to saints who had learned all that there was to know about repentance and faith, and they, therefore, have to talk about something higher.

The great need of our time should have moved us to this prayer against the Turk, for the Turk, as has been said, is the servant of the devil,[57] who not only devastates land and people with the sword, as we shall hear later, but also lays waste the

---

[55] Gen. 18:22-32.
[56] Cf. above, p. 18.
[57] Cf. above, p. 18.

Christian faith and our dear Lord Jesus Christ. For although some praise the Turk's government because he allows everyone to believe what he will so long as he remains the temporal lord, yet this reputation is not true, for he does not allow Christians to come together in public, and no one can openly confess Christ or preach or teach against Mohammed. What kind of freedom of belief is it when no one is allowed to preach or confess Christ, and yet our salvation depends on that confession, as Paul says in Romans 10 [:9], "To confess with the lips saves," and Christ has strictly commanded us to confess and teach his gospel.[58]

Since, therefore, faith must be stilled and held in secret among this wild and barbarous people and under this severe rule, how can it exist or remain alive in the long run, when it requires so much effort and labor in places where it is preached most faithfully and diligently?[59] Therefore it happens, and must happen, that those Christians who are captured or otherwise get into Turkey fall away and become altogether Turkish, and it is very seldom that one remains true to his faith, for they lack the living bread[60] of the soul and see the abandoned and carnal life of the Turks and are obliged to adapt themselves to it.

How can one injure Christ more than with these two things, namely, force and wiles? With force they prevent preaching and suppress the word. With wiles they put wicked and dangerous examples before men's eyes every day and draw men to them. So in order not to lose our Lord Jesus Christ, his word and faith, we must pray against the Turks as against other enemies of our salvation and of all good, indeed, as we pray against the devil himself.

In this connection the people should be told about the Turk's dissolute life and ways so that they may the better feel the need of prayer. To be sure, it has often disgusted me, and still does,

---

[59] Matt. 10:32. Christians under Turkish rule were not permitted to organize congregations. The use of bells was prohibited and conversion to Christianity was punishable by death. BG 7, 454, n. 2.

[59] Luther devoted the last part of his 1529 Army Sermon Against the Turk (Heerpredigt wider den Türken) to prisoners and other Christians in this situation. Cf. WA 30[II], 160-197.

[60] Cf. John 6:35.

that neither our great lords nor our scholars have taken any pains to give us any certain knowledge about the life of the Turks in the two estates, spiritual and temporal; and yet the Turk has come so near to us.[61] It is said that the Turks, too, have chapters and monasteries. Some, indeed, have invented outrageous lies about the Turks to incite us Germans against them, but there is no need for lies; there is enough truth. I will tell my dear Christians a few things, so far as I know the real truth, so that they may the better be moved and stirred to pray earnestly against the enemy of Christ our Lord.

I have some parts of Mohammed's Koran which in German might be called a book of sermons or doctrines of the kind that we call pope's decretals. When I have time I must translate it into German so that everyone may see what a foul and shameful book it is.[62]

In the first place, he greatly praises Christ and Mary as being the only ones without sin, and yet he believes nothing more of Christ than that he is a holy prophet, like Jeremiah or Jonah, and denies that he is God's Son and true God. Furthermore, he does not believe that Christ is the Savior of the world who died for our sins, but that he preached to his own time and completed his work before his death, just like any other prophet.

On the other hand, Mohammed highly exalts and praises himself and boasts that he has talked with God and the angels, and that since Christ's office of prophet is now complete, he has been commanded to bring the world to his faith, and if the world is not willing, to compel it or punish it with the sword; there is much glorification of the sword in it. Therefore the Turks think that their

---

[61] Cf. above, p. 5.

[62] In 1542 Luther published *Brother Richard's Refutation of the Koran, Translated into German by Dr. M. Luther* (*Widerlegung des Alkoran Bruder Richardi; verdeutscht durch Dr. M. Luther*) (*WA* 53, [261] 271-396). In the preface Luther expressed amazement that the Koran had not been translated into Latin. He went on to say that as recently as Shrove Tuesday 1542 he had seen such a translation for the first time, but that it was a very poor one. Later that year a new Latin version was published in Basel, but it was banned by the magistrate. Luther urged the lifting of this ban. Cf. Julius Köstlin, *Martin Luther. Sein Leben und Schriften,* ed. and rev. by Gustav Kawerau (5th ed.; 2 vols.; Berlin: Alexander Duncker, 1903), II, 603.

Mohammed is much higher and greater than Christ, for the office of Christ has come to an end and Mohammed's office is still in force.

From this anyone can easily see that Mohammed is a destroyer of our Lord Christ and his kingdom, and if anyone denies the articles concerning Christ, that he is God's Son, that he died for us and still lives and reigns at the right hand of God, what has he left of Christ? Father, Son, Holy Ghost, baptism, the sacrament, gospel, faith, and all Christian doctrine and life are gone, and instead of Christ only Mohammed with his doctrine of works and especially of the sword is left. That is the chief doctrine of the Turkish faith in which all abominations, all errors, all devils are piled up in one heap.

And yet the world acts as though it were snowing[63] pupils of the Turkish faith, for it is extraordinarily pleasing to reason that Christ is not God, as the Jews, too, believe, and especially is reason pleased with the thought that men are to rule and bear the sword and get ahead in the world. The devil is behind that. Thus the Turk's faith is a patchwork of Jewish, Christian, and heathen beliefs. He gets his praise of Christ, Mary, the apostles, and other saints from the Christians. From the Jews he gets abstinence from wine and fasting at certain times of the year, washing like the Nazirites [Num. 6:1-21], and eating off the ground. And the Turks perform the same holy works as some of our monks and hope for everlasting life at the Judgment Day, for, holy people that they are, they believe in the resurrection of the dead, though few of the papists believe in it.[64]

What pious Christian heart would not be horrified at this enemy of Christ when he sees that the Turk allows no article of our faith to stand, except the single one about the resurrection of the dead? Then Christ is no redeemer, savior, or king; there is no forgiveness of sins, no grace, no Holy Ghost. Why should I say

---

[63] Cf. Thiele, *Luthers Sprichwörtersammlung*, No. 71.
[64] See the text of the decree affirming the immortality of the soul, *Apostolici regiminis*, adopted by the Fifth Lateran Council (December 19, 1513) in H. J. Schroeder, *Disciplinary Decrees of the General Councils* (St. Louis: B. Herder Book Co., 1937), pp. 487-488 (English) and pp. 630-631 (Latin).

more? In the article that Christ is beneath Mohammed, and less than he, everything is destroyed. Who would not rather be dead than live under such a government, where he must say nothing about his Christ, and hear and see such blasphemy and abomination against him? Yet this article takes such a powerful hold when the Turk wins a land that people even submit to it willingly. Therefore let everyone pray who can that this abomination not become lord over us and that we not be punished with this terrible rod of God's anger.

In the second place, the Turk's Koran or creed teaches him to destroy not only the Christian faith, but also the whole temporal government. His Mohammed, as has been said, commands that ruling is to be done by the sword, and in his Koran the sword is the commonest and noblest work. Thus the Turk is really nothing but a murderer or highwayman, as his deeds show before men's eyes. St. Augustine[65] calls other kingdoms, too, a great robbery; Psalm 76 [:4] also calls them "the mountains of prey" because an empire seldom has come into being except by robbery, force, and wrong; or, at the very least, it is often seized and possessed by wicked people without any justice, so that the Scriptures, in Genesis 10 [:9], call the first prince upon earth, Nimrod, a mighty hunter. But never has any kingdom come into being and become so mighty through murder and robbery as that of the Turk; and he murders and robs every day, for robbing and murdering, devouring and destroying more and more of those that are around them, is commanded in their law as a good and divine work; and they do this and think that they are doing God a service. Their government, therefore, is not a godly, regular rulership, like others, for the maintenance of peace, the protection of the good, and the punishment of the wicked, but a rod of anger and a punishment of God upon the unbelieving world, as has been said. The work of murdering and robbing pleases the flesh in any case because it enables men to gain high place and to subject everyone's life and goods to themselves. How much more must the flesh be pleased when this is a commandment, as though God would have it so and is well pleased by it! So it is among the

---

[65] *The City of God (De civitate dei)*, IV, 4, 6.

Turks that the most highly regarded are those who are diligent to increase the Turkish kingdom and constantly murder and rob those around them.

This second thing must follow from the first,[66] for Christ says in John 8 [:44] that the devil is a liar and murderer. With lies he kills souls and with murder he kills bodies. If he wins with a lie, he does not take a holiday and delay; he follows it up with murder. Thus when the spirit of lies had taken possession of Mohammed, and the devil had murdered men's souls with his Koran and had destroyed the faith of Christians, he had to go on and take the sword and set about to murder their bodies. The Turkish faith, then, has not made its progress by preaching and the working of miracles, but by the sword and by murder, and its success has been due to God's wrath, which ordered that since all the world has a desire for the sword, robbery, and murder, one should come who would give it enough of murder and robbery. As a rule, fanatics, when the spirit of lies has taken possession of them and led them away from the true faith, have not been able to stop there, but have followed the lie with murder and taken up the sword, as a sign that they were children of the father of all lies and murder. Thus we read how the Arians[67] became murderers and how one of the greatest bishops of Alexandria, Lucius by name, drove the orthodox out of the city, and went into the ship and held a naked sword in his own hand until the orthodox were all on board and had to go away.[68] And these tender, holy bishops committed many other murders even at that time, which is almost twelve hundred years ago. Again, in St. Augustine's time, almost eleven hundred years ago, the holy father abundantly shows in his books how many murders the Donatists committed.[69] In such an utterly worldly way did the clergy conduct

---

[66] I.e., the murdering and robbing comes from Turkish doctrine.

[67] The Arians, followers of Arius (ca. 250-336), maintained that the Son was not divine by nature, but was a creature. The issue caused widespread controversy in the early church but despite condemnation of this doctrine by the Council of Nicaea (325), Arianism persisted—particularly among Germanic tribes—until the early sixth century.

[68] These events took place in 374 during the reign of the Arian emperor Valens. The orthodox bishop was Peter.

[69] Cf. Augustine, *Against Gandentius* (*Contra Gandentium*), I, 22. MPL 43, 720.

themselves! They had only the name and guise of bishops among the Christians; but because they had fallen away from the truth and become subject to the spirit of lies, they had to go forward in his service and become wolves and murderers. What was Münzer[70] seeking in our own times, but to become a new Turkish emperor? He was possessed by the spirit of lies and therefore there was no holding him back; he had to take on the other work of the devil, take the sword and murder and rob, as the spirit of murder drove him, and he created a rebellion and such misery.

And what shall I say of the most holy father, the pope? Is it not true that he and his bishops have become worldly lords, and, led by the spirit of lies, have fallen away from the gospel and embraced their own human doctrine, and thus have committed murder down to the present hour? Read the histories and you find that the principal business of popes and bishops has been to set emperors, kings, princes, lands, and people against one another, and they themselves have fought and helped in the work of murder and bloodshed. Why? Because the spirit of lies never acts any other way. After he has made his disciples teachers of lies and deceivers, he has no rest until he makes them murderers, robbers, and bloodhounds. Now who has commanded them to bear the sword, to wage war, and to incite and arouse men to murder and war, when their duty was to attend to preaching and prayer?

They call me and my followers seditious; but when have I ever coveted the sword or urged men to take it, and not rather taught and kept peace and obedience, except when I have instructed and exhorted the regular temporal rulers to do their duty and maintain peace and justice?[71] One knows the tree by its fruits [Matt. 7:16]. I and my followers keep and teach peace; the pope, along with his followers, wages war, commits murder, and robs not only his enemies, but he also burns, condemns, and persecutes the innocent, the pious, the orthodox, as a true Antichrist.[72] And he does this while sitting in the temple of God [II Thess. 2:4], as head of the church;

---

[70] Thomas Münzer, radical religious leader, executed for his part in the Peasants' War of 1525. Cf. SW 3, 305, n. 3.
[71] Cf. *Against the Robbing and Murdering Hordes of Peasants* (1525). SW 3, 352.
[72] The term Antichrist is used to designate the prince of Christ's enemies. Cf. I John 2:18, 22; 4:3; II John 7. According to II Thess. 2:3-10 he would appear after great apostasy and set himself up in the sanctuary and claim to be God. Luther had long identified the papacy with the Antichrist.

the Turk does not do that. But just as the pope is the Antichrist, so the Turk is the very devil incarnate. The prayer of Christendom against both is that they shall go down to hell, even though it may take the Last Day to send them there; and I hope that day will not be far off.[73]

Summing up what has been said, where the spirit of lies is, there also is the spirit of murder, though it may not get to work or may be hindered. If it is hindered, it still laughs and is jubilant when murder is done, and at least consents to it, for it thinks murder is right. But good Christians do not rejoice over any murder, not even over the misfortunes of their enemies.[74] Since, then, Mohammed's Koran is such a great spirit of lies that it leaves almost nothing of Christian truth remaining, how could it have any other result than that it should become a great and mighty murderer, liar, and murderer under the appearance of truth and righteousness? Now just as lies destroy the spiritual order of faith and truth, so murder destroys all temporal order which has been instituted by God; for there can be no good, praiseworthy temporal government where murder and robbery are rampant. Because they cannot think more highly of peace than of war and murder or attend to the pursuits of peace, as one can see in soldiers,[75] the Turks do not regard the work of agriculture highly.

The third point is that Mohammed's Koran has no regard for marriage, but permits everyone to take wives as he will. It is customary among the Turks for one man to have ten or twenty wives and to desert or sell any whom he will, so that in Turkey women are held immeasurably cheap and are despised; they are bought and sold like cattle. Although there may be some few who do not take advantage of this law, nevertheless, this is the law and anyone who wants to can follow it. That kind of living is not and cannot be marriage, because none of them takes or has a wife with the intention of staying with her forever, as though the two were one body, as God's word says in Genesis 3 [2:24], "Therefore a man cleaves to his wife and they become one flesh." Thus the marriage of the Turks closely resembles the chaste life soldiers lead with their

[73] On Luther's belief that the Last Day was near, cf. SW 3, 318, n. 3.
[74] See Luther's comments in WA 15, 71-72.
[75] Cf. SW 3, 474-475.

harlots; for the Turks are soldiers and must act like soldiers; Mars and Venus, say the poets, must be together.[76]

These are the three points I wanted to mention. I am sure of them from the Koran of the Turks. I will not bring up what I have heard besides because I cannot be sure about it. Suppose, then, that there are some Christians among the Turks. Suppose that some of them are monks. Suppose that some are honorable laymen. Now supposing all this, what good can there be in the government and the whole Turkish way of life when according to their Koran these three things rule among them, namely, lying, murder, and disregard of marriage, besides the fact that everyone must be silent about Christian truth and dare not rebuke or try to reform these three points, but must look on and consent to them (as I fear), at least to the point of keeping silent? What could be a more horrible, danger- ous, terrible imprisonment than life under such a government? As I said, lies destroy the spiritual estate; murder, the temporal; disre- gard of marriage, the estate of matrimony. Now if you take out of the world *veram religionem, veram politiam, veram oeconomiam,* that is, true spiritual life, true temporal government, and true home life, what is left in the world but flesh, world, and devil? It is like the life of the "good fellows" who live with harlots.

It is said that among themselves the Turks are faithful, friend- ly, and careful to tell the truth. I believe that and I think that they probably have more fine virtues in them than that. No man is so bad that there is not something good in him. Now and then a woman of the streets has more good qualities than do ten honorable matrons. The devil would have a cloak and be a handsome angel of light, so he hides behind certain works that are works of light. Murderers and robbers are more faithful and friendly to each other than neigh- bors are, even more so than many Christians. For if the devil keeps the three things—lies, murder, and disregard of marriage—as the real foundation of hell, he can easily tolerate, even help, carnal love and faithfulness being built upon it, as though they were precious gems (though they are nothing but hay and straw), though he knows well that nothing will remain of them in case of fire.[77] On the other

---

[76] Mars was the classical god of war; Venus, the goddess of love. Luther may have had in mind Ovid's *Tristia,* II, 295-298.
[77] Cf. I Cor. 3:11-15.

hand, where there is true faith, true government, true marriage, he strives earnestly to keep a little love and fidelity from appearing and being shown so that he can put the foundation to shame and have it despised.

What is more, when the Turks go into battle their only war cry is "Allah! Allah!" and they shout it till heaven and earth resound. But in the Arabic language[78] Allah means God, and is a corruption of the Hebrew *Eloha*. For they have been taught in the Koran that they shall boast constantly with these words, "There is no God but God." All that is really a device of the devil. For what does it mean to say, "There is no God but God," without distinguishing one God from another? The devil, too, is a god, and they honor him with this word; there is no doubt of that. In just the same way the pope's soldiers cry, "*Ecclesia! Ecclesia!*"[79] To be sure, the devil's *ecclesia!* Therefore I believe that the Turks' Allah does more in war than they themselves. He gives them courage and wiles; he guides sword and fist, horse and man. What do you think, then, of the holy people who can call upon God in battle, and yet destroy Christ and all God's words and works, as you have heard?

It is also part of the Turks' holiness to tolerate no images or pictures, and they are even holier than are our iconoclasts.[80] For our iconoclasts tolerate and are glad to have images on gulden, groschen, rings, and ornaments; but the Turk tolerates none of them and stamps nothing but letters on his coins. He is entirely Münzerian,[81] too, for he exterminates all rulers and tolerates no gradations of government such as princes, counts, lords, nobles, and others. He alone is lord over all in his own land, and what he gives out is only pay, never property or rights of rulership.[82] He is also a papist, for

---

[78] Luther was aware that Arabic was not the language of the Turks. Cf. *WA* 30[II], 128, n. 2.

[79] Cf. above, p. 16.

[80] Cf. *Against the Heavenly Prophets in the Matter of Images and Sacraments* (1525). *SW* 3, 151-302.

[81] Cf. above, p. 28, n. 70; *SW* 3, 305, n. 3.

[82] Cf. *SW* 3, 467-468. The Turkish Sultan, however, invested members of his select troops with small estates upon which they could live as lords. Upon their death the estate reverted to the Sultan. The favored soldiers were known as Timars, and among their ranks were the captured children of Christian parents. Cf. Schwiebert, *op. cit.*, p. 62.

he believes that he will become holy and be saved by works. He does not think it a sin to overthrow Christ, lay government waste, and destroy marriage. The pope also works at all these things, though in other ways—with hypocrisy, while the Turk uses force and the sword. In a word, as has been said, the Turk's holiness is the very dregs of all abominations and errors.

I have wanted to tell all this to the first man, namely, Christian,[83] so that he may know and see how much need there is for prayer, and how he must first smite the Turk's Allah, that is, his god the devil, and overcome his power and divinity; otherwise, I fear, the sword will accomplish little. Now this man is not to fight physically with the Turk, as the pope and his followers teach; nor is he to resist the Turk with the fist, but he is to recognize the Turk as God's rod and wrath which Christians must either suffer, if God visits their sins upon them, or fight against and drive away with repentance, tears, and prayer. Let whoever will despise this counsel despise it; I will watch to see what damage he will do the Turk.

The second man who ought to fight against the Turk is Emperor Charles, or whoever may be emperor; for the Turk is attacking his subjects and his empire, and it is his duty, as a regular ruler appointed by God, to defend his own. I repeat it here: I would not urge or bid anyone to fight against the Turk unless the first method, mentioned above, that men had first repented and been reconciled to God, etc., had been followed. If anyone wants to go to war in another way, let him take his chances. It is not proper for me to say anything more about it other than to point out everyone's duty and to instruct his conscience.

I see clearly that kings and princes are taking such a foolish and careless attitude toward the Turk that I fear they underestimate God and the Turk too greatly, or perhaps they do not know that the Turk is such a mighty lord that no kingdom or land, whatever it is, is strong enough to resist him alone, unless God performs a miracle. Now I cannot expect any miracle[84] or special grace of God for Germany unless men amend their ways and honor the word of God

---

[83] Cf. above, p. 18, n. 37.
[84] Luther regarded the lifting of the siege of Vienna in October, 1529, as a miracle. Cf. the letter to Nicholas Amsdorf, October 27, 1529. WA, Br 5, 167.

differently than they have before. But enough has been said about that for those who will listen. Now we want to speak of the emperor.

In the first place, if there is to be war against the Turk, it should be fought at the emperor's command, under his banner, and in his name. Then everyone can be sure in his conscience that he is obeying the ordinance of God, since we know that the emperor is our true overlord and head and that whoever obeys him in such a case obeys God also, whereas he who disobeys him also disobeys God. If he dies in this obedience, he dies in a good state, and if he has previously repented and believes in Christ, he will be saved. I suppose everyone knows these things better than I can teach him, and would to God they knew them as well as they think they do. Yet we will say something more about them.

In the second place, this fighting under the emperor's banner and obedience to him ought to be true and simple. The emperor should seek nothing else than simply to perform the work and duty of his office, which is to protect his subjects; and those under his banner should seek simply to do the work and duty of obedience. By this simplicity you should understand that you are not fighting the Turk for the reasons the emperors and princes have been urged to go to war for, such as the winning of great honor, glory, and wealth, the extension of territory, or wrath and revenge and other such reasons. By waging war for these reasons men seek only their own self-interest, not what is right or to obey, and so we have had no good fortune up to now, either in fighting or planning to fight against the Turk.

Therefore the urging and inciting with which the emperor and the princes have been stirred up to fight against the Turk ought to cease. He has been urged, as head of Christendom and as protector of the church and defender of the faith, to wipe out the Turk's religion, and the urging and exhorting have been based on the wickedness and vice of the Turks. Not so! The emperor is not the head of Christendom or defender of the gospel or the faith. The church and the faith must have a defender other than emperor and kings. They are usually the worst enemies of Christendom and of the faith, as Psalm 2 [:2] says and as the church constantly laments. That kind of urging and exhorting only makes things worse and angers

God deeply because it interferes with his honor and his work, and would ascribe it to men, which is idolatry and blasphemy.

And if the emperor were supposed to destroy the unbelievers and non-Christians, he would have to begin with the pope, bishops, and clergy, and perhaps not spare us or himself; for there is enough horrible idolatry in his own empire to make it unnecessary for him to fight the Turks for this reason. There are entirely too many Turks, Jews, heathen, and non-Christians among us with open false doctrine and with offensive, shameful lives. Let the Turk believe and live as he will, just as one lets the papacy and other false Christians live. The emperor's sword has nothing to do with the faith; it belongs to physical, worldly things, if God is not to become angry with us. If we pervert his order and throw it into confusion, he too becomes perverse and throws us into confusion and all kinds of misfortune, as it is written, "With the crooked thou dost show thyself perverse" [Ps. 18:26]. We can perceive and grasp this through the fortune we have had up to now against the Turk. Think of all the heartbreak and misery that have been caused by the *cruciata*,[85] by the indulgences,[86] and by crusade taxes.[87] With these Christians have been stirred up to take the sword and fight the Turk when they ought to have been fighting the devil and unbelief with the word and with prayer.

Here is what should be done. The emperor and the princes should be exhorted concerning their office and their bounden duty to give serious and constant thought to governing their subjects in peace and to protecting them against the Turk. This would be their duty whether they themselves were Christians or not, though it would be very good if they were Christians. But since it is and remains uncertain whether they are Christians, and it is certain that they are emperors and princes, that is, that they have God's command to protect their subjects and are duty bound to do so, we must let the uncertain go and hold to the certain,[88] urge them with continual preaching and exhortation, and lay it heavily upon their

---

[85] I.e., the Crusades.
[86] Luther is probably referring to the indulgence granted to crusaders by Pope Urban II. Cf. SW 1, 280, n. 59.
[87] Cf. Schwiebert, *op. cit.*, pp. 62, 264.
[88] Cf. Thiele, *Luthers Sprichwörtersammlung*, No. 33.

consciences that it is their duty to God not to let their subjects perish so terribly, and that they commit serious sin when they are not mindful of their office and do not use all their power to bring counsel and help to those who should live, with body and goods, under their protection and who are bound to them by oaths of homage.

For I think (so far as I have observed the matter in our diets) that neither emperor nor princes themselves believe that they are emperor and princes. They act as though it were up to them whether to rescue and protect their subjects from the power of the Turk or not; and the princes neither care nor think that they are bound and obligated before God to counsel and help the emperor in this matter with body and goods. Each of them passes it by as though it were no concern of his and as though he were forced neither by command nor necessity, but as though it were left up to him to do it or not. They are just like the common people who do not think they have a responsibility to God and the world when they have bright sons, to send them to school and have them study; but everyone thinks he has the right to raise his son as he pleases regardless of God's word and ordinance. Indeed, the councilmen in the cities and almost all the rulers act in the same way and let the schools go to ruin, as though they had no responsibility for them, and had an indulgence besides. No one remembers that God earnestly commands and desires bright children to be reared to his praise and for his work. This cannot be done without the schools. On the contrary, everyone is in a hurry to have his children make a living, as though God and Christendom needed no pastors, preachers, physicians of souls, and as though the worldly rulers needed no chancellors, counselors, or secretaries—but more of this another time.[89] The pen must remain empress, or God will show us something else.

Emperor, kings, and princes act the same way. They do not stop to think that God's commandment requires them to protect their subjects; they think that it is a matter for them to decide if they get the notion or if they have leisure for it. Dear fellow, let us all do that! Let none of us attend to that which is commanded him

---

[89] Cf. *A Sermon on Keeping Children in School* (1530), below, pp. 115-166.

and which God orders him to do; let all our actions and duties depend on our own free will, and God will give us good grace and fortune, and we shall be plagued by the Turk here and by the devil yonder in eternity.

Perhaps, then, some worthless prattler—I should say a legate—will come from Rome and exhort the estates of the empire and stir them up against the Turk by telling them how the enemy of the Christian faith has done such great harm to Christendom, and that the emperor, as guardian of the church and defender of the faith, should do this and that; as though they themselves were great friends of the Christian faith![90] But I say to him: You are a base-born scoundrel, you impotent chatterer! All you accomplish is to make the emperor feel that he should do a good Christian work, one that he is not commanded to do, and one that is a matter of his own free choice. His conscience is not touched at all by that, and he is not reminded of the duty laid upon him by God, but the whole thing is left to his free choice.

This is how a legate ought to deal with the estates of the empire at the diet. He should hold God's commandment before them and make it an unavoidable issue, and say, "Dear lords, emperor, and princes, if you want to be emperor and princes, then act as emperor and princes, or the Turk will teach you with God's wrath and disfavor. Germany, or the empire, is given and committed to you by God for you to protect, rule, counsel, and help, and you not only should but must do this at the risk of losing your soul's salvation and God's favor and grace. But now it is evident that none of you believes or takes this seriously; you take your office as a jest, as though it were a Shrove Tuesday mummery.[91] You abandon the subjects God has committed to you to wretched harassment, to being taken captive, put to shame, plundered, slain, and sold by the Turk. Are you not aware that since God has committed this office to you, and has even given you money and people for you to do good to them, he will hold you accountable for all the subjects

---

[90] In 1518 Pope Leo X (1513-1521) sent cardinals Allesandro Farnese, Egidio Canisio, Antonio Bibbiena, and Lorenzo Campeggio as papal legates to the imperial court, Spain, France, and England to lay the groundwork for a crusade.
[91] I.e., as though it were part of the masquerading in the customary carnival on Shrove Tuesday, the day before Ash Wednesday, the first day of Lent.

whom you so shamefully deserted while you danced, reveled in pomp, and gambled? If you seriously believed that God appointed and ordained you to be emperor and princes, you would leave your banqueting and rivalry for seats of honor[92] and other unprofitable displays for a while, and give conscientious consideration to how to discharge your office, fulfil God's commandment, and rescue your consciences from all the blood and misery which the Turk inflicts upon your subjects. How can God, or any godly heart, think otherwise of you than that you hate your subjects or have a secret covenant with the Turk or, at least, regard yourselves as neither emperor nor princes, but as dolls and puppets for children to play with? If you seriously regarded yourselves as overlords appointed by God and did not discuss and take counsel about these matters differently than before, your consciences could not possibly give you any peace. In this you see that you are steadily becoming Turks to your own subjects.

"Why, you even take up the case of Luther and discuss in the devil's name whether one can eat meat in the fasting seasons, whether nuns can take husbands, and things of that kind which are not your business to discuss and about which God has given you no commandment. Meanwhile the serious and strict commandment of God, the commandment by which he has appointed you protectors of poor Germany, hangs in the air; and you become murderers, betrayers, and bloodhounds to your own good, faithful, obedient subjects, and abandon them—no, you cast them into the Turk's jaws, as a reward for the bodies and money, wealth and honor that they stake on you and extend to you."

A good orator can see well what I would like to say here if I were skilled in the art of oratory, and what a legate should aim for and expound at the diet, if he would discharge his office honestly and faithfully.

This is why I said above that Charles, or the emperor, should be the man to fight against the Turk, and that the fighting should be done under his banner. "Oh, that is easy! Everyone knew that a long time ago. Luther is not telling us anything new, but only

---

[92] Rivalry for prominent seats played a sorry role at the imperial diets. Cf. BG 7, 471, n. 3.

worn-out old stuff." But, my dear fellow, the emperor must truly see himself with other eyes than before, and you must see his banner with other eyes. You and I are talking about the same emperor and the same banner, but you are not talking about the eyes I am talking about. You must see on the banner the commandment of God that says, "Protect the good; punish the wicked." Tell me, how many can read this on the emperor's banner, or really believe it? Do you not think that their consciences would terrify them if they saw this banner and had to admit that they were most guilty before God because of their failure to help and protect their faithful subjects? Dear fellow, a banner is not simply a piece of silk; there are letters on it, and he who reads the letters will lose his taste for luxury and banqueting.

It is not difficult to show that up to now the banner has been regarded as a mere piece of silk, for otherwise the emperor would long ago have unfurled it, the princes would have followed it, and the Turk would not have become so mighty. But because the princes called it the emperor's banner with their lips and were disobedient to it with their fists, and by their deeds treated it as a mere piece of silk, things have come to the state we now see with our own eyes. God grant that all of us are not too late in coming—I with my exhortation and the lords with their banner—and that it may not happen to us as it did to the children of Israel, who would not fight against the Amorites when God commanded them; afterward, when they would have fought, they were beaten because God would not be with them [Deut. 1:19-46]. Nevertheless, no one should doubt that repentance and right conduct always find grace.

So when emperor and princes realize that by God's commandment they owe this protection to their subjects, they should be exhorted not to be presumptuous and undertake this work defiantly, or to rely upon their own might or action; for there are many foolish princes who say, "I have right and authority; therefore I will do it!" Then they pitch in with pride and, boasting of their might, ultimately meet defeat. If they had not felt their power, the matter of right would have little effect on them, as is proved in other cases in which they had little regard for what was right. It is not enough for you to know that God has committed this or that to you; you should do it with fear and humility, for God commands no one to do anything on the basis of his own wisdom or strength. He, too, wants to have a part in it and be feared. He wants to do it through us and wants us to pray to him so that we will not become presumptuous or forget his help, as the Psalter says, "The Lord takes pleasure in those who fear him, and in those who hope in his steadfast love" [Ps. 147:11]. Otherwise we would persuade ourselves that we could do things and did not need God's help, and would claim for ourselves the victory and honor that belong to him.

An emperor or prince ought to learn well that verse of the Psalter, in Psalm 44 [:6-7], "For not in my bow do I trust, nor can my sword save me. But thou hast saved us from our foes and hast put to confusion those who hate us," as well as the rest of what that Psalm says. And Psalm 60 [:10-12], "Thou dost not go forth, O God, with our armies. O grant us help against the foe, for vain is the help of man! With God we shall do valiantly; it is he who will tread down our foes." These and similar words have had to be fulfilled by many kings and great princes from the beginning down to the present day. They have become examples, though they had God's commandment, authority, and right. Emperor and princes, therefore, should not treat these words as a jest. Read the apt illustration given in Judges 20 [:18-25] of how the children of Israel were beaten twice by the Benjaminites, despite the fact that God bade them fight and that they had the best of right. Their boldness and presumption were their downfall, as the text itself says, *"Fidentes fortitudine et numero."*[93] It is true that one should have horses and men and weapons and everything that is needed for battle, if they are to be had, so that one does not tempt God. But when one has them, one must not be bold because of it lest God be forgotten or despised, since it is written, "All victory comes from heaven" [I Macc. 3:19].

If these two things are present, God's commandment and our humility, then there is no danger or need so far as this second man, the emperor, is concerned. Then we are strong enough for the whole world and must have good fortune and success. But if we do not have good fortune, it is certainly because one of the two things

---

[93] "Trusting in bravery and numbers." This version is from the Latin text of Judg. 20:22.

is lacking; we are going to war either without God's commandment, or in our own presumption, or the first soldier, Christian, is not there with his prayers.[94] It is not necessary here to warn against seeking honor or booty in war; for he who fights with humility and in obedience to God's command, with his mind fixed solely upon the simple duty of protecting and defending his subjects, will forget about honor and booty; they will come to him without his seeking, more richly and gloriously than he can wish.

At this point someone will say, "Where are we going to find such pious warriors who will act this way?" Answer: The gospel is preached to all the world, and yet very few believe; nevertheless, Christendom[95] believes and abides. I am not writing this instruction with the hope that it will be accepted by all; indeed, most people will laugh and scoff at me. I will be content if I am able to instruct some princes and their subjects with this book, even though their number may be small; numbers do not matter to me; there will be victory and good fortune enough. And would to God that I had instructed only the emperor, or whoever is to conduct the war in his name and at his command; then I would be of good hope. It has often happened, indeed, it usually happens, that God bestows good fortune and success upon a whole land and kingdom through one single man; just as on the other hand he brings a whole land into all sorts of distress and misery through one scoundrel at court, as Solomon says in Ecclesiastes [9:18], "One sinner destroys much good."

We read of Naaman, the captain of the king of Syria, that through this one man God gave the whole land good fortune and success [II Kings 5:1-27]. Through the holy Joseph God gave good fortune to the whole kingdom of Egypt [Gen. 39:5], and in II Kings [3:14] Elisha says to Jehoram, "Were it not that I have regard for Jehoshaphat the king of Judah, I would neither look at you nor see you." Thus the godless kings of Israel and Edom had to be helped for the sake of one godly man, when otherwise they would have been ruined in all kinds of distress. And in the book of Judges one can see the good that God did through Ehud [Judg. 3:15-30], Gid-

---

[94] Cf. above, pp. 20-21.
[95] I.e., the totality of Christians.

eon [Judg. 6:11–8:28], Deborah [Judg. 4:4–5:31], Samson [Judg. 13:2–16:31], and other individuals, though the people were not worthy of it. See, on the other hand, what great harm Doeg did at the court of King Saul, I Samuel 22 [:18], and what Absalom accomplished against his father David with the aid and counsel of Ahithophel, II Samuel 16 [:22–17:23].

I say this so that we will not be frightened or moved in any way if the great majority who fight under the emperor's banner are unbelieving and have an un-Christian mind. We must also remember that Abraham, all by himself, was able to do much—Genesis 14 [:17; 18:24-33]. It is also certain that among the Turks, who are the army of the devil, there is not one who is a Christian or who has a humble and right heart. In I Samuel 14 [:6], the godly Jonathan said, "Nothing can hinder the Lord from saving by many or by few," and he himself inflicted a great slaughter on the Philistines such as Saul with his whole army could not do. It does not matter, then, if the entire crowd is not good, provided only that the head and some of the chief men are upright. Of course, it would be good if all were upright, but that is scarcely possible.

Moreover, I hear it said that in Germany there are those who desire the coming of the Turk and his government because they would rather be under him than under the emperor or princes.[96] It would be hard to fight against the Turk with such people. I have no better advice to give against them than that pastors and preachers be exhorted to be diligent in their preaching and faithful in instructing such people, pointing out to them the danger they are in, the wrong they are doing, and that by holding this opinion they make themselves a party to serious and innumerable sins in God's sight. It is dreadful enough to have the Turk as overlord and to endure his government; but willingly to submit oneself to it, or to desire it when one need not and is not compelled—well, the man who does that ought to be shown what kind of sin he is committing and how terrible his conduct is.

In the first place, these people are disloyal and are guilty of perjury to their rulers, to whom they have taken oaths and done homage. In God's sight this is a great sin which does not go un-

---

[96] Cf. above, p. 5.

punished. The good king Zedekiah perished miserably because of such perjury; he did not keep the oath he gave to the heathen emperor at Babylon [Jer. 21:7]. Such people may think or persuade themselves that it is within their own power and choice to go from one lord to another, as though they were free to do or not to do whatever they pleased, forgetting God's commandment and not remembering their oath, by which they are bound to be obedient until they are compelled by force to abandon that loyalty or are put to death because of it. This is what the peasants wanted to do in the recent rebellion, and this is why they were beaten.[97] For just as a man may not slay himself, but must submit to being slain by the violence of others, so no one should evade his obedience or his oath unless he is released from it by others, either by force or by favor and permission.

This is what the preachers must diligently impress on such people; indeed, their office of preaching compels them to do so, for it is their duty to warn their parishioners and to guard them against sin and harm to their souls. No one who willingly turns from his lord and submits to the Turk can ever remain under the Turk with a good conscience; his own heart will always accuse and rebuke him this way, "See, you were disloyal to your overlord and deprived him of the obedience you owed him, and robbed him of his right to rule you; now, no sin can be forgiven unless stolen goods are restored." But how will you make restitution to your lord when you are under the Turk and cannot make restitution? One of two things, then, must happen. Either you must toil and labor forever, trying to get away from the Turk and back to your overlord; or your conscience must forever suffer compunction, pain, and unrest (God grant that it does not result in despair and everlasting death) because you submitted to the Turk willingly and without necessity, contrary to your sworn duty. In the latter case you must be among the Turks physically, but with your heart and conscience yearn to be over on this side. What have you gained then? Why did you not stay on this side from the first?

In the second place, besides all that, such faithless, disloyal, and perjurious people commit a still more horrible sin. They make

---

[97] Cf. *Against the Robbing and Murdering Hordes of Peasants*. SW 3, 350.

themselves a party to all the abominations and wickedness of the Turks; for he who willingly goes over to the Turks is their comrade and accomplice in all they do. Now we have heard above what kind of man the Turk is, that he is a destroyer, enemy, and blasphemer of our Lord Jesus Christ, a man who instead of the gospel and faith sets up his shameful Mohammed and all kinds of lies, ruins all temporal government and home life or marriage, and his warfare, which is nothing but murder and bloodshed, is a tool of the devil himself. See, then! He who consorts with the Turk has to be a party to this terrible abomination and brings down on his own head all the murder, all the blood the Turk has shed, and all the lies and vices with which he has damaged Christ's kingdom and led souls astray. It is dreadful enough if one is forced against his will to be under this bloodhound and devil and to see, hear, and put up with these abominations, as the godly Lot had to do in Sodom, as St. Peter [II Pet. 2:7-8] writes; it is not necessary to desire or to seek them of one's own accord.

Indeed, a man ought far rather die twice over in war, obedient to his overlord, than, like a poor Lot, have to be brought by force into such Sodoms and Gomorrahs.[98] Still less ought a godly man desire to go there of his own accord, in disobedience and against God's commandment and his own duty. That would mean not only becoming a party to all the wickedness of the Turk and the devil, but strengthening and furthering them; just as Judas not only made himself a party to the wickedness of the Jews against Christ, but strengthened and abetted it; Pilate did not act as wickedly as Judas did, as Christ testifies in John 17 [19:11].

In the third place, the preachers must impress upon the people that if they do go over to the Turks, they will not have bettered themselves and that their hopes and intentions will not be realized. For it is characteristic of the Turk not to let those who are anything or have anything stay in the place where they live, but to put them far back in another land, where they are sold and must be servants. Thus they fulfil the proverbs about "running out of the rain and falling in the water," "lifting the plate and breaking the dish," and

---

[98] Cf. Gen. 13:10-13.

"bad becomes worse."[99] It scarcely serves them wrong. For the Turk is a real warrior who has other ways of treating land and people, both in getting and keeping them, than our emperor, kings, and princes have. He does not trust and believe these disloyal people and he has the force to do as he will; so he does not need these people as do our princes.

The preachers and pastors, I say, must impress this upon such disloyal people, with constant admonition and warning, for it is the truth, and it is needed. But if there are some who despise this exhortation and will not be moved by it, let them go to the devil, as St. Paul did with the Greeks and St. Peter with the Jews;[100] the others should not mind. Indeed, if it were to come to war, I would rather that none of these people were under the emperor's banner, or stayed under it, but were all on the Turk's side. They would be beaten all the sooner and they would do the Turk more harm in battle than good, for they are out of favor with God, the devil, and the world, and they are surely condemned to hell. It is good to fight against such wicked people, for they are plainly and surely damned both by God and the world. There are many depraved, abandoned, and wicked men; but anyone with any sense will certainly heed such exhortation and be moved to remain obedient and not throw his soul so carelessly into hell to the devil, but rather fight with all his might under his overlord, even though he is slain by the Turks in so doing.

But then you say, "If the pope is as bad as the Turk—and you yourself call him Antichrist, together with his clergy and his followers—then the Turk is as godly as the pope, for he acknowledges the four Gospels and Moses, together with the prophets. Ought we not, then, fight the pope as well as the Turk, or, perhaps, rather than the Turk?" Answer: I cannot deny that the Turk esteems the four Gospels as divine and true, as well as the prophets, and that he also speaks very highly of Christ and of his mother. But at the same time, he believes that his Mohammed is superior to Christ and that

---

[99] These expressions are found in Thiele, *Luthers Sprichwörtersammlung*, No. 478; cf. also Nos. 276 and 477.

[100] Cf. I Cor. 1:22-25 and Gal. 2:7-8. It is unlikely that Luther had specific passages in mind. The point is that neither apostle effected the conversion of the entire people to whom his mission was directed.

Christ is not God, as we said above.[101] We Christians acknowledge the Old Testament as divine Scripture, but now that it is fulfilled and is, as St. Peter says in Acts 15 [:10-11], too hard without God's grace, it is abolished and no longer binding upon us. Mohammed treats the gospel the same way. He declares that the gospel is indeed correct, but that it has long since served its purpose and that it is too hard to keep, especially in those points where Christ teaches that one is to leave all for his sake [Matt. 19:29], love God with his whole heart [Matt. 22:37], and the like. This is why God has had to give another new law, one that is not so hard and one which the world can keep. And this law is the Koran. But if anyone asks why the Turk performs no miracles to confirm this new law, he says that that is unnecessary and of no use, for people had many miracles before, when Moses' law and the gospel arose, and did not believe. This is why his Koran does not need to be confirmed by wasted miracles, but by the sword, which is more persuasive than miracles. This is how it has been and still is among the Turks: everything is done with the sword instead of with miracles.

On the other hand, the pope is not much more godly than Mohammed and resembles him extraordinarily; for he, too, praises the gospel and Holy Scripture with his lips, but he holds that many things in it are too hard, and these are the very things Mohammed and the Turks also consider too hard, such as those contained in Matthew 5 [:20-44]. So he interprets them and makes them *consilia,* that is, "counsels," which no one is bound to keep unless he desires to do so, as Paris and other universities, schools, and monasteries have brazenly taught. Therefore, he, too, does not rule with the gospel, or word of God, but has made a new law and Koran, namely, his decretals, and these he enforces with the ban[102] just as the Turk enforces his Koran with the sword. He even calls the ban his spiritual sword, though only the word of God is that and should be called that (Ephesians 6 [:17]). Nevertheless, he also uses the temporal sword when he can, or at least he calls upon it and urges and incites others to use it. And I am confident that if the pope could use the temporal sword as mightily as the Turk, he would do

---

[101] Cf. above, p. 24.
[102] The sentence of excommunication, which often carried with it a variety of civil punishments and disabilities.

so with less goodwill than the Turk, and indeed, he has often tried it.

God visits them with the same plague, too, and smites them with blindness so that it happens to them as St. Paul says in Romans 1 [:28] about the shameful vice of the dumb sins, that God gives them up to a perverse mind because they pervert the word of God. Both the pope and the Turk are so blind and senseless that they commit the dumb sins shamelessly, as an honorable and praiseworthy thing. Since they think lightly of marriage, it serves them right that there are dog-marriages (and would to God they were dog-marriages), indeed, also "Italian marriages" and "Florentine brides"[103] among them; and they think these things good. I hear one horrible thing after another about what an open and glorious Sodom Turkey is, and everybody who has looked around a little in Rome and Italy knows very well how God revenges and punishes the forbidden marriage,[104] so that Sodom and Gommorah, which God overwhelmed in days of old with fire and brimstone [Gen. 19:24], must seem a mere jest and prelude compared with these abominations. On this one account, therefore, I would very much regret the rule of the Turk; indeed, his rule would be intolerable in Germany.

What are we to do, then? Ought we to fight against the pope as well as against the Turk, since the one is as godly as the other? Answer: Treat the one like the other and no one is wronged; like sin should receive like punishment. This is what I mean: If the pope and his followers were to attack the empire with the sword, as the Turk does, he should receive the same treatment as the Turk; and this is what was done to him by the army of Emperor Charles outside of Pavia.[105] God's verdict is, "He that takes the sword shall perish by the sword" [Matt. 26:52]. I do not advise men to wage war against the Turk or the pope because of false belief or evil life, but because of the murder and destruction which he does. The best thing about the papacy is that it does not yet have the sword, as the Turk does; otherwise it would certainly undertake to subject the

---

[103] These expressions were current names attached to perversions and vices usually identified with Italy. Cf. *BG* 7, 482, n. 3.

[104] I.e., homosexuality.

[105] Cf. *SW* 3, 430, n. 8. Cf. also below, p. 47, n. 108.

whole world, although it would accomplish no more than to bring it to faith in the pope's Koran, the decretals. For the pope pays as little heed to the gospel or Christian faith as the Turk, and knows it as little, though he makes a great pretense of Turkish sanctity by fasts (which he himself does not observe); thus they deserve the reputation of being like the Turk, though they are against Christ.

The first man, Sir Christian,[106] has been aroused against the papacy because of its errors and wicked ways, and he attacks it boldly with prayer and the word of God. And he has wounded it, too, so that they feel it and rage. But raging does not help; the axe is laid to the tree and the tree must be uprooted, unless it bears different fruit.[107] I see clearly that they have no intention of reforming, but the further things go, the more stubborn they become, the more they want to have their own way, and the more they boast, "All or nothing, bishop or drudge!" They are so godly I know that rather than reform or turn from their shameful ways (both they themselves and the whole world admit that it is not to be endured) they would rather go over to their comrade and brother, the holy Turk. Oh well! May our heavenly Father soon hear their own prayer and grant that, as they say, they may be "all or nothing, bishop or drudge." Amen! This is what they want. Amen! So be it; let it happen as God pleases!

But you say further, "How can Emperor Charles fight against the Turk now, when he has against him such hindrances and treachery from kings, princes, the Venetians,[108] indeed, from almost everybody?" This is my reply: A man should let lie what he cannot lift.[109] If we can do no more, we must let our Lord Jesus Christ counsel and aid us by his coming, which cannot be far off.[110] For the world has come to its end; the Roman Empire is almost gone; it is torn asunder; it is like the kingdom of the Jews when Christ's birth was near. The Jews had scarcely anything of their kingdom; Herod was

---

[106] Cf. above, p. 18, n. 37.
[107] Cf. Matt. 3:10.
[108] The Venetian republic, through the influence of Pope Clement VII, had supported the French king Francis I against the emperor. Along with Francis, Venice broke the terms of the Treaty of Madrid.
[109] Cf. Thiele, *Luthers Sprichwörtersammlung*, No. 488.
[110] Cf. SW 3, 318, n. 3.

the token of the end.[111] So I think that now that the Roman Empire is almost gone, Christ's coming is at the door, and the Turk is the empire's token of the end, a parting gift to the Roman Empire. And just as Herod and the Jews hated each other, though both stood together against Christ, so Turk and papacy hate each other, but stand together against Christ and his kingdom.

Nevertheless, the emperor should do whatever he can for his subjects against the Turk, so that even though he cannot entirely prevent the abomination, he may nonetheless try to protect and rescue his subjects by checking the Turk and holding him off. The emperor should be moved to do this not only by duty, his office, and God's command, nor only by the un-Christian and vile government the Turk brings, as has been said above,[112] but also by the misery and wretchedness that befalls his subjects. Doubtlessly they know better than I how cruelly the Turk treats those whom he takes captive. He treats them like cattle, dragging, towing, driving those that can move, and killing on the spot those that cannot move, whether they are young or old.

All this and more like it ought to move all the princes, and the whole empire, to forget their own causes and quarrels, or to put them aside for awhile, and earnestly unite to help the wretched so that things may not go as they went with Constantinople[113] and Greece.[114] They quarreled with one another and looked after their own affairs for a long time until the Turk overwhelmed both of them, as he has already come very near doing to us in a similar case. But if this is not to be, and our unrepentant life makes us unworthy of any grace, counsel, or support, we must put up with it and suffer under the devil; but that does not excuse those who could help and do not.

I wish it clearly understood, however, that it was not for nothing that I called Emperor Charles the man who ought to go to war against the Turk.[115] As for other kings, princes, and rulers who despise Emperor Charles, or are not his subjects, or are not obedi-

---

[111] *Die letze*, i.e., a farewell banquet, the end.
[112] Cf. above, pp. 25-27.
[113] Constantinople fell to the forces of Mohammed II on May 29, 1453.
[114] Mohammed II completed the conquest of Greece in 1461.
[115] Cf. above, p. 18.

ent, I leave them to take their own chances. They shall do nothing because of my advice or admonition; what I have written here is for Emperor Charles and his subjects; the others do not concern me. I know quite well the pride of some kings and princes who would be glad if it were not Emperor Charles, but they, who were to be the heroes and victors who win honor against the Turk. I grant them the honor, but if they are beaten, it will be their own fault. Why do they not conduct themselves humbly toward the true head and the proper ruler? The rebellion among the peasants was punished, but if the rebellion among the princes and lords were also to be punished, I think that there would be very few princes and lords left.[116] God grant that it may not be the Turk who inflicts the punishment! Amen.

Finally, I would have it understood as my kind and faithful advice that if it comes to war against the Turk, we should arm and prepare ourselves, and not underestimate the Turk and not act as we Germans usually do, and come on the field with twenty or thirty thousand men. And even though good fortune is bestowed upon us and we win a victory, we have no power in reserve,[117] but sit down again and carouse until another danger comes along. And although I am not qualified to give instruction on this point, and they themselves know, or ought to know, more about it than I, nevertheless, when I see people acting so childishly I must think either that the princes and our Germans do not know or believe the strength and power of the Turk, or that they have no serious intention of fighting against the Turk, but just as the pope has robbed Germany of money under the pretense of the Turkish war and by indulgences,[118] so they, too, following the pope's example, would swindle us out of money.

My advice, then, is that we not insufficiently arm ourselves and send our poor Germans off to be slaughtered. If we are not going to make an adequate, honest resistance that will have some reserve power, it would be far better not to begin a war, but to yield lands and people to the Turk in time, without useless bloodshed, rather

---

[116] When the Peasants' War ended in 1525 many peasants were executed. Cf. *SW* 3, 359-360.

[117] I.e., manpower in reserve.

[118] A complaint raised in *To the Christian Nobility* (1520). *SW* 1, 280.

than have him win anyhow in an easy battle and with shameful bloodshed, as happened in Hungary with King Louis.[119] Fighting against the Turk is not like fighting against the king of France, or the Venetians, or the pope; he is a different kind of warrior. The Turk has people and money in abundance; he defeated the Sultan twice in succession,[120] and that took people! Why, dear sir, his people are always under arms so that he can quickly muster three or four hundred thousand men. If we were to cut down a hundred thousand, he would soon be back again with as many men as before. He has reserve power.

So there is no point in trying to meet him with fifty or sixty thousand men unless we have an equal or a greater number in reserve. Just count up the number of lands he controls, dear sir. He has Greece, Asia, Syria, Egypt, Arabia, etc. He has so many lands that if Spain, France, England, Germany, Italy, Bohemia, Hungary, Poland, and Denmark were all counted together, they would not equal the territory he has. Besides, he is master of all of them and commands effective and ready obedience. And, as has been said, they are constantly under arms and are trained in warfare so that he has reserve power and can deliver two, three, four heavy battles, one after another, as he showed against the Sultan. This Gog and Magog[121] is a different kind of majesty than our kings and princes.

I say this because I fear that my Germans do not know it or believe it, and that perhaps they think they are strong enough by themselves and that the Turk is a lord like the king of France, whom they would easily withstand. But I shall be without blame and shall not have wet my tongue and pen with blood if a king takes on the Turk by himself. It is tempting God to set out with a smaller force against a stronger king, as Christ shows in the Gospel of Luke

---

[119] At the battle of Mohacs, August 29, 1526, Louis II of Hungary with thirty thousand troops was opposed by a Turkish army of more than one hundred thousand. It has been estimated that in this engagement the Hungarians lost twenty thousand men, including their king.

[120] The victories of the Ottoman Turks at Aleppo (1516) and Reydaniya (1517) secured their supremacy in the Muslim world. Cf. A. W. Ward *et al.* (eds.), *The Cambridge Modern History* (New York: The Macmillan Company, 1903), I, 90-91.

[121] Cf. Ezek. 38:2.

[14:31], especially since our princes are not the kind of people for whom a divine miracle is to be expected. The king of Bohemia[122] is a mighty prince now, but God forbid that he match himself alone against the Turk! Let him have Emperor Charles as his captain and all the emperor's power behind him. But then, let whoever will not believe this learn from his own experience! I know how powerful the Turk is, unless the historians and geographers—and daily experience, too—lie; I know that they do not lie.

I do not say this to frighten the kings from waging war against the Turk, but to admonish them to make wise and serious preparation, and not to go about this matter so childishly and lethargically, for I would like, if possible, to prevent useless bloodshed and lost wars. The best preparation would be if our princes would wind up their own affairs and put their heads and hearts and hands and feet together and make one body out of the great crowd from which one could make another army if one battle were lost, and not, as before, let individual kings and princes set upon him—yesterday the king of Hungary,[128] today the king of Poland, and tomorrow the king of Bohemia—until the Turk devours them one after another and nothing is accomplished except that our people are betrayed and slaughtered and blood is shed needlessly.

If our kings and princes were to agree and stand by one another and help each other, and the Christian man were to pray for them, I should be undismayed and of good hope. The Turk would stop his raging and find his equal in Emperor Charles. Failing that, if things go as they are going now, and no one is in agreement with another or loyal to another, and everyone wants to be his own man and takes the field with a beggarly array, I must let it go at that. Of course, I will gladly help by praying, but it will be a weak prayer, for because of the childish, presumptuous, and short-sighted way in which such great enterprises are undertaken, I can have little faith that it will be heard, and I know that this is tempting God and that he can have no pleasure in it.

---

[122] Ferdinand of Austria, brother of Emperor Charles V, was elected king of Bohemia in 1526. Luther did not regard him very highly. Cf. WA 30^{II}, 146, n. 3.
[128] Cf. above, p. 50, n. 119.

What do our dear lords do? They treat it as just a joke. It is a fact that the Turk is at our throat,[124] and even if he does not decide to march against us this year, he is still there, always armed and ready to attack us when he will. Meanwhile, our princes consult about how they can harass Luther and the gospel: It is the gospel which is the Turk! Force must be used against it! The gospel must be put to rout! That is what they are doing right now at Spires,[125] where the most important matters are the eating of meat and fish and foolishness like that. May God honor you,[126] you faithless lords of your poor people! What devil commands you to deal so vehemently with spiritual things concerning God and matters of conscience which are not committed to you, and to be so lax and slothful in things that God has committed to you and that concern you and your poor people now in the greatest and most pressing need, and thereby only hinder all those whose intentions are good and who would gladly do their part? Yes, go on singing and hearing the Mass of the Holy Ghost.[127] He is greatly pleased with that and will be very gracious to you disobedient, stubborn fellows because you neglect those things that he has committed to you, and work at what he has forbidden you! Yes, the Evil Spirit may hear you!

With this I have saved my conscience.[128] This book shall be my witness concerning the measure and manner in which I advise war against the Turk. If anyone wishes to proceed otherwise, let him do so, win or lose. I shall neither enjoy his victory nor pay for his defeat, but I shall be innocent of all the blood that will be shed in

---

[124] Cf. above, p. 5.

[125] The Second Diet of Spires was in session at the time Luther wrote. At this diet Charles V, fresh from his victory over the League of Cognac (an alliance of France, England, the pope, Venice, and Milan), commanded the estates to execute the terms of the Edict of Worms (1521), which, in effect, had been suspended by the First Diet of Spires (1526).

[126] The implication is that Luther cannot honor them.

[127] The Mass of the Holy Ghost is a votive mass, i.e., a mass celebrated not in conformity with the office of the day, but according to the wish (*votum*) of the celebrant, his superior, or of the person for whom the mass is offered. The mass is celebrated on Thursdays. See J. O. O'Connell, *The Celebration of Mass* (London: Burns, Oates & Washbourne, Ltd., Publishers to the Holy See, 1941), I, 63-113.

[128] Cf. Ezek. 3:19; 33:9.

vain. I know that this book will not make the Turk a gracious lord to me should it come to his attention;[129] nevertheless, I have wished to tell my Germans the truth, so far as I know it, and to give faithful counsel and service to the grateful and the ungrateful alike. If it helps, it helps; if it does not, then may our dear Lord Jesus Christ help, and come down from heaven with the Last Judgment and strike down both Turk and pope, together with all tyrants and the godless, and deliver us from all sins and from all evil. Amen.

---

[129] A few years after the publication of this book a member of the ambassadorial party in Turkey reported that the Sultan had inquired about Luther. When told that Luther was forty-eight years old, the Sultan replied, "I wish he were younger; he would find me a gracious lord." Cf. Köstlin, *op. cit.*, I, 283.

EXHORTATION TO ALL CLERGY ASSEMBLED AT AUGSBURG

1530

Translated by Lewis W. Spitz

INTRODUCTION

In October, 1529, the brave defenders of Vienna turned back massive Turkish forces from the walls of the city. The victory relieved the empire of immediate danger from a Turkish invasion and insured the success of Charles V over his opposition in northern Italy. On his birthday, February 24, 1530, Charles was crowned emperor in Bologna by Pope Clement VII,* the last crowning of a German emperor by a pope. With great confidence Charles summoned the imperial diet to convene in Augsburg.† The diet was to supply further aid against the Turks and by reconciling differences was to bring religious unity to Germany. Charles spoke of setting discord aside and called on all the estates to be ready to express their views on religious questions. But behind these conciliatory words lay his strong determination to proceed against the Protestants with fire and sword, should they not yield to his kindness, that is, to the extent that his other political plans allowed.

In 1521 at Worms only one heretic stood before him, but now a large number faced him, including many of the most powerful princes of the empire. The Elector of Saxony arrived at Coburg on April 15 with his entourage including his theological advisers Luther, Philip Melanchthon, Justus Jonas, Georg Spalatin, Johann Agricola, and Anton Musa of Jena. A week later they moved on to Augsburg, leaving Luther behind, for he was under the ban of the empire and could not safely attend the diet. On the morning of April 23 Luther took up residence in the castle, the fortress at Coburg, from where he kept in close touch with the proceedings. On June 20 Emperor Charles presided over the festive opening of the Diet of Augsburg, from which the evangelicals expected so much.

On June 25 the evangelicals presented their statement of faith,

---

* Clement VII (Giulio de' Medici), cousin of Leo X (Giovanni de' Medici), reigned as pope from 1523 to 1534.
† Cf. B. J. Kidd (ed.), *Documents Illustrative of the Continental Reformation* (Oxford, 1911), pp. 257-258, where an excerpt is given from the "Imperial Summons to the Diet, 21 January 1530."

the Augsburg Confession. Already, in March,‡ Luther, Johann Bugenhagen, Justus Jonas, and Melanchthon had met at Torgau to prepare articles on faith and ecclesiastical practices which served as a guideline for writing the confession. But the confession itself was essentially the work of Melanchthon, Luther's young lieutenant. When Luther heard that the confession had been read, he exulted, "I rejoice mightily that I have experienced this hour, when Christ is publicly proclaimed through this glorious confession by such men in such an assembly!"§ The evangelicals did not want to emphasize differences any more than necessary, for they, too, wished for reconciliation, but on the basis of the Word of God. Long negotiations followed in which conciliatory Melanchthon yielded to the opposition step by step until he finally even offered the return of the evangelicals to episcopal jurisdiction. He appealed to the kindness and understanding of the pope and conceded, "We honor the authority of the apostolic see."|| Finally on August 3, the Roman Catholics read their *Confutation*, prepared by some twenty theologians including Eck, Faber, Cochlaeus, and Wimpina.# The emperor thereupon declared the Augsburg Confession refuted and threatened as "overseer and protector of the church" to proceed against the disobedient.

Meanwhile from Coburg Luther watched the proceedings with misgiving. He wrote almost daily letters to Melanchthon, Jonas, and

---

‡ On March 14, 1530, Elector John of Saxony wrote a letter to Luther and his colleagues, summoning them to Torgau on March 20. Cf. WA, Br 5, 264-265; Preserved Smith and Charles M. Jacobs (eds. and trans.), *Luther's Correspondence and Other Contemporary Letters* (2 vols.; Philadelphia: The Lutheran Publication Society), II (1918), 522-524.

§ Walter Goetz, Paul Joachimsen *et al.* (eds.), *Das Zeitalter der religiösen Umwälzung: Reformation und Gegenreformation 1500-1660, Propyläen Weltgeschichte*, V (Berlin, 1930), 148.

|| Karl Brandi, *Deutsche Reformation und Gegenreformation*, Vol. I (Leipzig, n.d. [1927]), p. 236.

Johann Eck (1486-1543), theologian at Ingolstadt, was one of Luther's principal opponents. For further details, cf. *The Leipzig Debate* (1519) in LW 31, 307-325; WA 2, 158-161; WA, Br 1, 420-424. Johann Faber (1478-1541), originally friendly with Erasmus and Zwingli, became a very active antagonist of the Reformation in Switzerland and southern Germany. Johann Cochlaeus (1479-1552) had written a number of treatises against Luther. To the vexation of Cochlaeus, Luther replied to him in a single work, *Adversus armatum virum Cocleum* (1523). Cf. WA 11, 295-306. Konrad Wimpina (*ca.* 1460-1531), professor of philosophy and theology at the University of Leipzig, entered into the religious controversy at an early date by rallying to the defense of Johann Tetzel. Cf. SW 1, 49.

occasionally to Spalatin and Agricola. "Act manly!" he admonished. On June 29 he wrote Melanchthon that more than enough concessions had been made.** He had gone through the Bible again and again, but was always strengthened further in his teaching, so that he would now no longer let them take anything away, no matter how things went. "I would sooner fall with Christ," he vowed, "than stand with the emperor." On July 15 he exclaimed, "In God's name I free you from this diet, go home again! home again! If the emperor wants to send out an edict, let him do it. He did it at Worms, too. We take the emperor as emperor and nothing more, nothing further! Home, home—the Lord protect you!"†† Such was the mood of the reformer during the proceedings.

During his enforced idleness Luther had the leisure to write, and the first work which he undertook was his *Exhortation to All Clergy Assembled at Augsburg*. Already, on April 29, he wrote to Melanchthon that the *Exhortation* was growing under his hands in content and force so that he had to repress many aggressive thoughts which kept suggesting themselves to him.‡‡ On May 12 he wrote his friend that he had finished it and sent it to the printer in Wittenberg.§§ "If judgments concerning my little book vary," he encouraged Melanchthon on June 5, "let nothing move you." ‖ ‖ When on June 7 a bookdealer brought the first five-hundred copies to Augsburg, they were quickly sold.## Although the Augsburg city council a few days later upon the earnest demand of the imperial government forbade republishing and selling the book, sales continued. "Your truly prophetic book is read by all the pious . . ." wrote Justus Jonas from Augsburg on June 12.*** This treatise might be considered Luther's own Augsburg Confession. Spirited and outspoken, it deals with many of the subjects treated in the confession, drawing especially in matters of ceremonies and abuses in the church upon a common source, notes on the discussions, and the articles of Torgau.

In the *Exhortation* Luther looks back to the time when the

** *WA*, Br 5, 405-408.
†† *WA*, Br 5, 479-480.
‡‡ *WA*, Br 5, 297-298.
§§ *WA*, Br 5, 316-317.
‖ ‖ *WA*, Br 5, 350-351.
WA, Br 5, 361.
*** *WA*, Br 5, 358.

papacy had been unchallenged and gives an account of all the changes that had been effected by the Reformation in the past ten years. Beginning on a humble note, he rises to a triumphant tone which belies the uncertainty of the historical moment, for he trusts God who is above all empires. His goal was to win over the bishops, as the winsome appeals interspersed throughout the treatise clearly show. Moreover, some bishops and especially the ecclesiastical princes were irresolute and hesitant and had to be held in line by their theologians. With this aim in mind Luther uses the approach not of surface conciliation, but of a frontal assault on abuse and false teaching designed to shake the very foundations of the episcopal edifice. Thus aroused, he believed, the bishops could surely see the right and join the evangelical cause. Cardinal Campeggio was impressed and commanded a secretary in his service to turn the *Exhortation* into Latin. The man whom he commissioned to make the translation wrote to a friend on June 21, "It is a summary of all Lutheranism. If you wish to see the whole of Luther, you ought to buy it. . . ."†††

The basis for this English translation is the original German text published by Hans Lufft in Wittenberg in 1530. The manuscript, *A155, Blätter 1-40,* last reported as in the Königliche Öffentliche Bibliothek in Dresden, is reproduced in WA 30ᴵᴵ, 268-356; cf. also the introduction, 237-267. Other editions of Luther's works containing this selection are *EA*¹ 24, (329) 330-379, *EA*² 24, (356) 358-407; *CL* 4, 104-143; Johann Georg Walch (ed.), *D. Martin Luthers sämmtliche Schriften* (1st ed., 24 vols.; Halle, 1740-1753), XVI, 1120-1179; *St. L.* 16, (945) 946-992; and *PE* 4, 325-382. I have made use of C. M. Jacobs' sentences and notes where they seemed adequate and thank Muhlenberg Press, holders of the copyright, for permission to do so. WA, Br 5, contains Luther's correspondence of 1530. Karl Förstemann, *Urkundenbuch zu der Geschichte des Reichstags zu Augsburg im Jahre 1530* (2 vols.; Halle, 1833-1835) supplies relevant documents.

L.W.S.

---

††† WA 30ᴵᴵ, 238.

EXHORTATION TO ALL CLERGY ASSEMBLED AT AUGSBURG

An Exhortation of Martin Luther to All the Clergy Assembled at Augsburg for the Diet of 1530

Grace and peace from God our Father and the Lord Jesus Christ! It is not suitable for me to appear personally at this diet, dear sirs. Even if I had to or should appear, nothing useful could come of it, since amid such pomp and activity nothing of consequence would thereby be accomplished. Nevertheless, in addition to my spiritual presence (which I wish to prove with my whole heart with God's help diligently and sincerely through prayer and entreaty to my God), I have undertaken to be among you also in writing with this mute and weak message of mine.

The reason for this is that my conscience drives me to entreat, implore, and admonish you all in a friendly and cordial way not to let this diet slip by or use it in vain. For God gives you grace, opportunity, time, and cause through our most gracious Emperor Charles to do and accomplish much and great good through this diet, if you only want to. He now certainly speaks as St. Paul says, II Corinthians 6 [:1-3], "We entreat you not to accept the grace of God in vain. For he says, 'At the acceptable time I have listened to you, and helped you on the day of salvation.' Behold, now is an acceptable time and a day of salvation," for you above all. We see and hear how the hearts of all people watch and wait upon this diet with great expectation that good will come of it.

Should, however, this diet (may God graciously favor it!) adjourn without result and nothing worthwhile be accomplished, after the whole world has been appeased and teased along for so long a time with diets and councils and all hope has been false and in vain, it is to be feared that despair will result. Everyone will become far too tired of the false hope and waiting, and the vain staring in expectation will produce impatience and make bad blood. For the situation cannot and may not remain any longer as it now is, especially with you and your estate and system. That you know and feel better than I can tell you. Therefore I, too, am now doing what I do for your own good and for the sake of peace and unity.

Some will perhaps look acidly upon my boldness and assert, "Who needs you? Who ever demanded your exhortation or writing? There are so many learned and pious people here who can give better advice than a fool like you." All right! That I will gladly believe and may God grant that it all be true. I am truly willing to have my audacity punished and condemned. But still it is also true that one cannot do too much of a good thing and a fool has often given better advice than many wise men. On the other hand, wise people have generally done the greatest harm on earth, especially when they depended on their own wisdom and did not act in the fear of God and with humble hearts pray for divine help and grace.

All the histories are replete with examples of this, both in and outside the Scriptures. Even though there would be no other example at hand, one could well find it in your own example. For you have indeed tried your wisdom in this affair for ten years now[1] with so many deliberations, with so many tricks and machinations, with so many fair words and false hopes, yes, also with force and wrath, with murder and punishment, so that I have seen in you occasion for wonder and woe. Yet nothing went the way you wanted it to go. That is just it! Wisdom has wanted to control such lofty and great matters by itself without fear of God and humble prayer and has thereby come to shame in its arrogance. If you still do not come to fear God and humble yourself before him, so that you give up threatening and vengefulness and earnestly beg God for help and counsel, you will surely achieve nothing, even though you would be all at once as wise as King Solomon. For there the Scriptures stand, I Peter 5 [:5], "God opposes the proud, but gives grace to the humble."

As for us, we pray with zeal and, by God's grace, also know the right way to pray. We are also certain that our prayer is acceptable and is heard for us, which, I fear, few of your party are able to do. We have now also begun to pray earnestly for you, that almighty

---

[1] That is, ten years had elapsed since the Diet of Worms was held in 1521.

God may for once enlighten and move your hearts to fear his Word
and act humbly toward him. Such prayer is accepted for us, that we
know, but may God grant that you do not set yourselves stubbornly
against it, so that our prayer must return again into our bosom, as
lost and scorned by you [Matt. 10:13]. For we see that the devil
wants to move in with the Turk,[2] excites one uproar after another
besides, and would gladly pound everything to the ground. If you
also, then, were still to remain as obdurate and headstrong as before,
that would certainly be too much and absolutely unbearable.

First of all, you need not deal with me or my kind, for the true
Helper and Counselor has brought us and our cause so far and has
established it where it should remain and where we also wish to
leave it. In this matter we for our part need no diet, no counsel, no
control; nor do we want any of these things from you, for we know
that you are unable to do any better, no, not so well as we. Whether
we fall prey to Turks or Tartars, pope or devil, no matter, our cause
stands secure. Thus we know how we should believe and live, how
we should teach and act, how we should suffer and pray, how we
should recover and die, where we should look for, get, and find
everything, and where we are finally to remain, according to the
word of St. Paul, Romans 8 [:28], "In everything the Spirit works
things out for the best of those who are elect." God has richly bestowed this upon us through Christ Jesus our Lord and it has already
been proclaimed and established through the blood and martyrdom
of many pious people put to death by your party. Not that we are
perfect or have attained all things. But we have the right rules, as
St. Paul [Phil. 3:16] puts it, the right way, the right beginning in our
favor. Indeed our teaching is lacking in nothing at all no matter how
things are in life.

We are concerned about you, however, and the poor people still
under you who are entirely uninstructed or always uncertain. We
would always gladly help in this respect at any time with prayer and
exhortation, the best we can. For I fear very much that you have
forgotten your office and humility toward God and will draw the

---

[2] The Turks had been driven back from Vienna only by fierce fighting in October, 1529. Emperor Charles urged the diet to provide. for defense against
invasion by the Turks. Cf. Kidd, *op. cit.*, "Imperial Summons to the Diet, 25
June 1530," pp. 257-258.

reins too tight and ride the docile steed too hard, so that an uproar will again arise and we and you together will come to grief and misery, as happened once before.[3] For you doubtless still well remember how, before the revolt, the diet at Spires was summoned with such glorious, consoling hope that the whole world looked to it with great eagerness and heartily expected good to come of it. But there your counsel was full of wisdom and succeeded in getting that diet called off ungraciously, insultingly, and shamefully.[4] Then quickly thereafter came the whip, namely, Münzer with revolt, and gave you a blow from which you still have not recovered and from which we unfortunately suffered even greater damage.[5] That is what comes of always acting with force and according to your own notion.

Thus at Worms that noble lord, our dear Emperor Charles, had to do what you wanted and condemn me and my whole teaching,[6] many parts of which you yourselves had before then secretly adopted and used. Your preachers even now would have nothing to preach, if it were not for Luther's books. For they slyly leave their sermon book under the bench and whatever else the shouting in the pulpit was formerly about, and begin to preach to us again about faith and good works and the like, about which one never used to hear or know anything. What is more, at that time you forced through a decree for the slaying of Lutherans so gruesome that you yourselves could not hold to it or tolerate it, and it had to be altered at the Diet of Nürnberg.[7] Some of the princes had to forbid it of their own accord, if they did not want to endanger themselves together with their land and people.

I recount this not for your derision or ridicule (for I have been too strongly avenged on you already without this), but in order to beseech you heartily and to exhort you faithfully to learn from your own experience and misfortune hereafter to give up defiance and threatening, force and boasting, and to act toward God with fear

---

[3] The reference is to the Peasants' War in 1525.

[4] The Diet of Nürnberg, 1524, decided that a church council should be held and called for a meeting at Spires that fall to arrange for such a council, but this meeting was never held.

[5] Thomas Münzer, one of the "Zwickau prophets," led a mob of over six thousand peasants against the princes in 1525.

[6] In the Edict of Worms, 1521. Cf. Kidd, *op. cit.*, pp. 87-89.

[7] The Diet of Nürnberg declared the enforcement of the Edict of Worms to be impossible.

and humility and, after putting aside your arrogance, to seek his help and grace with earnest prayer. Truly, truly, the stakes are too high! Human wisdom and power are much too inadequate. God must help or evil will become even worse, that is certain. For if you wish to persist in your insolence and bragging, you shall learn that Münzer's spirit still lives on and is, I fear, mightier and more dangerous than you believe or can now conceive. It concerns you more than us, although he is more hostile to us than to you. But, God be praised in all eternity, we have a defense against him! Would God that you also had the same, that is, the pure Word and righteous prayer.

You know, too, how faithfully and firmly we have held out against all factious spirits. If I dared boast, I might almost say that we were your protectors and that it was our doing that you have remained until now what you are. Had it not been for us,[8] I truly fear, your scholars would have been too weak for the problem and the enthusiasts and sects would have shortly taught you something quite different. For this reason they are more hostile to us than to you and accuse us of knuckling under and recanting. We must suffer this and experience the truth of the proverb, "If you help someone down from the gallows, he would gladly put you on it." The factious rascals would not have known how to attack the pope at a single point. Now that they have been freed through our help and eat our bread, they lift their heel against us, as Christ says of his betrayer, Judas.[9]

But some will here say, "Yes, it is all your fault: You started it and these are the fruits of your teaching." All right, I must bear it, knowing very well that it is said of me! On the other hand, I know many pious people among you who know that is not true. The work stands there in broad daylight, my strong evidence that the fanatics have always scorned and persecuted my teaching more than yours. I have also had to oppose them more strongly and defend myself against them more rigorously than I ever did against the pope. How, then, could it have come from my teaching? Or why did not such a disturbance originate among my followers, where I myself daily

---

[8] The original reads, "Vnd hetten wir gethan." Otto Clemen thinks this means "Wären wir nicht dagewesen." Cf. CL 4, 108.
[9] John 13:18. Luther says, ". . . they step on us with their feet."

preached and taught, and where things should surely have gone wrong first and foremost, if such mischief were to result from my teaching?

But have you forgotten that at Worms the German nobility presented His Imperial Majesty with around four hundred articles in which they complained about the grievances against the clergy and declared openly that if His Imperial Majesty did not wish to abolish such abuses, they would do so themselves, for they could no longer endure them?[10] What do you think about this? If that had once begun (as the rebels started it afterward), and if just one preacher had arisen who would have advised it, where would you clergy be now? In hell.[11] Yet at that time my teaching was in full swing and had begun no revolt and was not running in that direction. Rather, it was teaching the people nicely to maintain the peace and to obey the authority. If it had not been for that, the grievances against the clergy would certainly have given rise to a suitable sport. Now it must be my teaching which has done it. But such is the thanks due me and I also hanker after none other. Thus it went with all the prophets and apostles and with Christ himself.

Likewise, have you also forgotten how my teaching was at first so precious to almost all of you? Then all the bishops were very glad to see the tyranny of the pope restrained a little, since he handled the endowed foundations too severely. Then they could watch me politely, listen, sit quietly, and be on the lookout how they might regain once more their entire episcopal authority. Then Luther was an excellent teacher who attacked indulgences so honestly. At that time bishops and parish priests had to put up with a monk or an intruding rascal in their chapters and parishes who with letters of indulgences carried on a thoroughly scandalous trade and no one dared to utter a sound against it. There was no doctor in all the universities or monasteries who could have known how or dared to oppose such filth. Luther was the "dear boy." He swept the chapters and parishes clean of such huckstering, held the stirrups for the bishops to enable them to remount, and threw a stumbling block

---

[10] A commission composed of members of both the spiritual and secular estates prepared a report on the grievances (*Gravamina*) of the German nation in March, 1521, in Worms.

[11] *In bus Correptam* is a euphemistic expression for hell derived from Latin grammar. Cf. WA 30[II], 714.

into the road for the pope. Why did you not consider that revolt as well?

I heard no weeping from bishop or parish priest when afterward I attacked the monastic life and the monks became fewer. I know that no greater service was ever done the bishops and priests than freeing them from the monks. Indeed, I fear there will now be at Augsburg hardly anyone who will take the monks' side and ask that they return again to their former position. No, the bishops will not allow such bedbugs and lice to be put back in their fur again. They are happy that I deloused their fur so thoroughly, although, to tell the truth, the monks had to govern the church under the pope and the bishops contributed nothing to that end except to permit themselves to be addressed as lords. However, I have not destroyed the monks with revolt but with my teaching and the bishops were well pleased. They could not have done it even with the force of all the kings or with the learning of all the universities. Why, then, did they not consider that revolutionary, too? Ah, they are too pleased that the monks are down and that the pope has thereby almost lost an entire hand. Still they give no thanks to Luther, whose teaching they exploit so gloriously at this point.

Since I now come to the point that people have forgotten how things stood in the world before my teaching began and no one now wants to admit to having ever done wrong, I must drag out the old skeletons[12] and place before the eyes of the clergy their forgotten virtue so that they may see or reflect once more on what conditions would be like in the world if our gospel had not come. We, too, may see for our comfort what manifold glorious fruits the Word of God has produced. We wish to begin precisely at the point where my teaching began, that is, with indulgences.[13]

---

[12] *Larven.*

[13] According to Roman Catholic teaching, the guilt of sin and the eternal punishment were remitted at the time of confession, but temporal punishment remained to be borne either on earth or after death in purgatory. The church had available the treasury of the merits of Christ and the saints from which it could grant satisfaction for temporal punishment in whole or in part upon the performance of specified good works or, in time, the gift of money. A letter of indulgence certified the remission of temporal punishment. It was in opposition to the sale of indulgences that Luther posted his *Ninety-five Theses* in 1517, inadvertently precipitating the Reformation. Cf. SW 1, 43-59.

Concerning Indulgences

If our gospel had accomplished nothing else than to redeem consciences from the shameful outrage and idolatry of indulgences, one would still have to acknowledge that it was God's Word and power. For the whole world must acknowledge that no human wisdom could have accomplished this, since no bishop, no chapter, no monastery, no doctor, no university, not even I myself at that time, in short, no reason understood or saw through this abomination. Much less did anyone know how to control or attack it, but everyone had to sanction all and let it pass for good wholesome doctrine. Also the dear bishops and popes took out their cut without blinking an eyelash and allowed it to go on full-scale, namely:

1. They sold the indulgence as the divine grace which forgives sin. Thereby Christ's blood and death were denied and blasphemed together with the Holy Spirit and the gospel.

2. They falsely sold souls out of purgatory through it, to the great shame of the Divine Majesty, but it brought in lots of money.

3. They thereby put the pope in heaven as a god who could command the angels to carry to heaven the souls of pilgrims who died on their trip to Rome.

4. The gospel, which is, after all, the only true indulgence, had to keep silence in the churches in deference to the indulgence.

5. Through it they defrauded and fleeced the whole world out of immeasurable sums of money with shameless greed and lies, as though they wanted to make war against the Turks.

6. They always declared earlier letters of indulgences void in favor of new ones and always abrogated the old indulgences in the churches for the sake of new ones, and played with the golden year,[14] according as they wanted money. Yes, even against the Turks!

7. Also the swindle of the golden year is sheer fiction and a spurious lie to corrupt the faith of Christ and Christ's daily golden year. Yet, countless thousands of souls have been misled by it and the people shamefully duped into running to Rome, cheated of money and goods, with pains and expense lost besides.

8. In the indulgence they sold good works to all of Christendom and absolution, too, as something special, which, however, the gospel

---

[14] During the jubilee year special indulgences were granted. Cf. SW 1, 46-47.

forever gives the whole world free of charge. Thus consciences were led astray from the gospel and from Christ to the works of men.

9. They praised the indulgence more highly than all works of love.

10. They deposited the merit of the saints, beyond what they needed for themselves, as a treasure of indulgence, as though Christ's suffering were not sufficient for the forgiveness of all sins. This again corrupts faith in Christ.

11. They finally exalted indulgence so high that they taught if someone had even slept with the mother of God, through indulgence it would be forgiven.[15]

12. They taught that when the penny rang in the money box, the soul rose to heaven.[16]

13. One need have neither contrition nor sorrow to receive the indulgence. It was enough that one now deposit the money.

14. St. Peter himself could not grant a greater grace than the indulgence represented.

15. What has now become of the immeasurable amount of money, treasure, and wealth stolen through indulgence so long ago and acquired so shamefully?

In short, who wants to relate all the outrages that the indulgence alone brought on, as a truly mighty idol, in all the chapters, monasteries, churches, chapels, cells, altars, pictures, panels, yes, in almost all houses and chambers and wherever there was money? One would have to read anew the books that were written against it for about ten years. Now speak up, dear sirs! All of you clergy bear the guilt for this unspeakable thievery and robbery of money, for such an inconceivable multitude of misled hearts and consciences, for such a most horrible outrageous lie and blasphemy of the suffering of Christ, of the gospel, of grace, and of God himself, perpetrated through indulgence. This is true not only of you who accepted money from it, but also of you who kept silent about it and willingly looked on at such raging of the devil. You speak of revolt, of expropriation of monasteries, of the Turks! Yes, what are all such things

---

[15] Cf. *Ninety-five Theses* (or *Disputation on the Power and Efficacy of Indulgences*, 1517), Thesis 75, in *SW* 1, 58; *Explanations of the Ninety-five Theses* (or *Explanations of the Disputation Concerning the Value of Indulgences*, 1518), Thesis 75, in *LW* 31, 240-241.
[16] Cf. Theses 27. *SW* 1, 53-54; *LW* 31, 175-176.

together compared with you indulgence hawkers, if one only wants to think of it? It was a real Turkish army against the true Christian faith.

But who among all of you would ever have repented for such frightful abomination, would ever have sighed, or would ever have moistened an eye? Yes, now, like hardened, unrepentant men you want to pretend that you never did any evil. You now come to Augsburg, therefore, and want to persuade us that the Holy Spirit is with you and will accomplish great things through you (although in your whole lifetime you have done Christendom nothing but harm) and that he will thereafter lead you straight to heaven with all such abominations, unrepented and defended besides, as though he had to rejoice over you who have served your god-belly so gloriously and laid waste his church so miserably. For this reason you have no success and also shall have none until you repent and mend your ways.

Well, that is one of the pretenses! That is the way things stood and went in this matter before my teaching came. That it is now that way no longer is the fault of my rebellious gospel. It is appropriate for that other trade fair called confessionals to follow the indulgence.

Concerning Confessionals

These were the butter letters in which the pope sold liberty to eat butter, cheese, milk, and eggs, and gave authority to hear mass at home, to marry within forbidden degrees, and to choose a father-confessor to release, as often as he wished, from agony and guilt in life or in perils of death and the like. My dear man, was not this, too, a blasphemous trade fair, invented in every respect for the sake of money? As if God had not before through the gospel given all such things freely to all the world, or as if God had forbidden these things, and they were the mighty men who could sell the commandments of God for money. The gospel must be nothing and God must be their merchandise. Also this swindling, bargaining, and blaspheming has been overthrown by the rebellious gospel, but now all is forgotten and there is no bishop or cleric whom it grieves or who needs forgiveness for it before God. Here, too, there was no bishop or doctor who would have condemned such matters, but all were silent and acquiesced. All right, we shall see whether, as they suppose, God will let them make a monkey of him.

Concerning Confession

Your books are still extant in which you have set down your teaching concerning confession, which I consider one of the greatest plagues on earth whereby you have confused the conscience of the whole world, caused so many souls to despair, and have weakened and quenched all men's faith in Christ. For you have said nothing at all to us about the comfort of absolution, the chief article and the best part in confession, which strengthens faith and trust in Christ. But you have made a work out of it, extorting it by force with commands from unwilling hearts to strengthen your tyranny. Afterward you let them suffer pangs, torture and torment themselves with recounting all sins. That is, you have disturbed forever their rest and peace of mind with an impossible task. But when will you bring all such souls back again and make good the deadly, baseless damage you have done? My gospel has brought to justice this kind of confession also, and strengthened once more the timid consciences. Then no bishop, doctor, or university knew anything about this and now they feel neither contrition nor sorrow for such misery.

Concerning Penance[17]

That is the very worst and hell itself! If one were to forgive and remit all abominations, one can never forgive you for this one. This doctrine has filled hell and has troubled the kingdom of Christ more horribly than the Turk or the whole world could ever do. For you taught us that we should by our own works make satisfaction for sin, even against God. And that was called repenting of sin. You have nowhere given so much emphasis to contrition and confession, although you have made works of them also. Now what else does it mean to say, "You must make satisfaction for your sins," than to say, "You must deny Christ, renounce your baptism, blaspheme the gospel, reproach God for lies, disbelieve the forgiveness of sins, tread

---

[17] In Roman Catholic teaching the confessor could impose works of penance upon the confession of sin by a layman. Luther learned from the New Testament that repentance (*metanoia*) meant not to do penance, but to repent, that is, to sorrow for sin and look in faith to Christ for forgiveness.

underfoot Christ's blood and death, dishonor the Holy Spirit, and go to heaven by your own effort with such virtues"? Alas, where are the tongues and voices which can say enough about this?

What else is such a faith than the faith of the Turks, heathen, and Jews? All of them, too, want to make satisfaction through their works. How is it possible, however, for a soul not to despair, if it has no other solace against sin than its own works? You cannot deny all this. Your books are extant in which nothing is taught about faith either in the treatment of confession or penance, but solely about our own works. Yet there is no bishop or cleric here who sheds a tear for such a monstrous, hellish blasphemy of Christ. On the contrary, they are pure and safe, while they reproach us as rebels, murder married priests,[18] even contrary to their own law,[19] and are annoyed because the Lutherans make no pretense of fasting, as they do, and do not wear tonsures. Moreover, they defy the eternal God with all their inhuman wickedness.

From this abomination have come all the other outrages (they had to come from it, too, and there was no way of warding them off), namely, the self-righteousness of so many of the monasteries and chapters, with their worship service, the sacrificial masses, purgatory, vigils, brotherhoods, pilgrimages, indulgences, fasts, veneration of saints, relics, poltergeists, and the whole parade of the hellish proces-

---

[18] In 1527, George Winkler, a pastor in Halle, was tried by an ecclesiastical court at Aschaffenburg, charged with administering the sacrament in both kinds. It was known at the trial that he was not only guilty of this offense but had also taken a wife. He was released by the archbishop of Mainz, but on the way home was set upon and murdered. Circumstances pointed to the archbishop as the instigator of the deed. Luther wrote a letter of sympathy *To the Christians at Halle. WA* 23, 402ff.; *PE* 4, 341, n. 1.

[19] Cf. *Decretalium D. Gregorii Papae IX,* lib. iii, tit. III: *De clericis coniugatis,* including provisions in canon law for deposition and excommunication in force in Luther's day. Aemilius Friedberg (ed.), *Corpus Iuris Canonici* (Graz, 1955), II, cols. 457-460. For the initial demands for celibacy, cf. *Decreti Magistri Gratiani Prima Pars,* dist. XXXI-XXXIV. *Corpus Iuris Canonici,* I, cols. 111-130; *Secunda Pars,* causa XXVII, ques. 1. *Corpus Iuris Canonici,* I, cols. 1047-1062. Perhaps Luther here has in mind also the canonical injunctions to mercy and forbidding violence to clergy, *Decreti Prima Pars,* dist. XLV, *I. Pars: Sequitur: "non percussorem." Corpus Iuris Canonici,* I, cols. 160-167. Luther had recently written a brief preface to Lazarus Spengler's little book demonstrating that some parts of the canon law conformed to God's Word, *Ein kurczer auszuge, aus den Bebstlichen rechten der Decret und Decretalen, Ynn den artickeln, die ungeferlich Gottes wort und dem Euangelio gemes sind, odder zum wenigsten nicht widderstreben. Mit einer schönen Vorrhede. Mart. Luth. Wittemberg.* (1530). *WA* 30^II, 215-219.

sion of the cross.[20] For what else is possible? If a conscience is to rely and build on its own works, it stands on loose sand which moves to and fro and continually sinks away. It must always seek works, one after the other. The longer it looks, the more it needs. At last they put cowls on the dead in which they should ascend to heaven. Dear Lord God, how were poor consciences to act? They had to build on works. Therefore, they also had to seek them so miserably and snatch whatever they could find and fall into such deep folly.

What is more, through such shameful doctrines all the legitimate good works instituted and ordered by God were despised and even reduced to nothing, such as the work of a ruler, subject, father, mother, son, daughter, servant, and maid. They were not called good works and did not belong to penance either, but were known as a "secular existence," a "perilous estate," and "lost works." Thus this doctrine entirely trod under foot both the Christian and secular life and gave neither God nor Caesar his due. It invented instead a new and special life which is neither this nor that. They themselves do not know what it is, since there is no word of God for it. As Moses says, they serve gods whom they know not. That was not surprising, for at that time no one knew how to preach even the gospel in a way other than that one ought to learn from it examples and good works. None of us ever heard a gospel that was designed for the comfort of the conscience, for faith and trust in Christ, as it properly should be and, God be praised, as it is now again being preached. The world was thus in the gospel, yet was without the gospel.

If they had only wisely made a distinction with respect to satisfaction for sins, namely, that it may be made in relation to men and not God, as Christ shows in Matthew 7 [:12] and 18 [:15]. In the past the holy fathers, too, made use of it in this way by having Christians who had sinned make satisfaction before the congregation and the brethren, as the words suggest, and imposing two, three, or seven years of penance.[21] Thus Christ with his satisfaction for us would still have remained in heaven. But in this way the services in the chapters and monasteries and indulgence, as I said above, would not have arisen and not so much would have gotten to the great god-

---

[20] It was customary to carry the cross in procession from church to church in Easter Week, sometimes three days in a row. Cf. WA 30^II, 261, n. 43.

[21] Luther is here referring to the penitential canons.

belly. Therefore, they had to mix it all together and at last elevate satisfaction as availing only before God.[22] This error, to be sure, assailed[23] Christendom from the beginning, even through important men like Origen, St. Jerome, and St. Gregory,[24] but it never reached so completely into the government of the church and to God's very throne, as happened under the pope. For this error has been the oldest from the beginning of the world. It will also probably remain the youngest until the end of the world. We now wish to relate some practices which followed from the same.

Firstly, Concerning the Sale of Masses or Private Masses.

On this point, dear sirs, you know yourselves what a shameful huckstering and bargaining you have made of the sacrament. That has been the common handiwork of all of you, that every day in the whole world you bought and sold so many thousand masses for money, the one for a groschen, one for eight pennies, another for six pennies, etc. And no excuse or denial helps here. For though you have not called it trade, nevertheless, you know that in actual fact it was nothing else but trade. For money it was done and if there was no money there, the masses remained unsaid. This sin alone is so terrible that it would be no wonder if God had let the whole world become Turks or sink into an abyss because of it. That God could tolerate it so long is one of the things at which I greatly wonder. It is an inconceivable patience, although anger was not slow in

---

[22] I.e., penance came to be viewed as satisfaction for sins before God, not merely a sign of sorrow for sins before men.

[23] *Angefochten.*

[24] Origen (d. *ca.* A.D. 254), a leading theologian and church father of Alexandria, named penance among the remedies for sin. Cf. *In Leviticum Homilia 2,* Migne, *Patrologiae cursus completus, Series Graeca,* XII, 418-419. Cf. also *Homilia 3* in *ibid.,* 429; *Homilia 15* in *ibid.,* 560-561; *Selecta in Psalmos: Homilia 2 in Psal. 37* in *ibid.,* 1386.

Jerome (d. A.D. 420), translator of the Vulgate and renowned western church father, in recounting the penitence of Fabiola wrote, "What sins would such a penance fail to purge away? What ingrained stains would such tears be unable to wash out?" *Epistola 77, Ad Oceanum.* Migne 22, 692. Cf. also *Epistola 122, Ad Rusticum, De Poenitentia.* Migne 22, 1038ff.

Gregory (d. A.D. 604), the "father of the medieval papacy" and one of the four great doctors of the Latin church, introduced many Semi-Pelagian elements into the tradition and affords many examples of Luther's point. *Cf. Moralium,* lib. viii, cap. 21 in Migne 75, 822-823; *40 Homiliarum in Evangelia,* lib. ii: *Homilia 26* in Migne 76, 1200-1201; on confession, *In Primum Regum Expositiones,* lib. vi, cap. 2, par. 4.

coming. Well, that's what you have done and that was your practice before our gospel came. You cannot put on airs. It is so very plain that you yourselves at that time shuddered at it. Yet for all that you let it go on and were not obliged to call it an innovation.

Now your scholars want to clean themselves up and bring out the old canons and sayings of the fathers to prove that they called the mass a sacrifice. Shine yourself up, dear pussy, you need to! What help is it when you adduce lengthy canons and quotations? We are here speaking of the sale of masses and private masses[25] and the canons speak of the common or communicants' masses and they emphasize strongly the communing. That the private masses do not do. They compare with the common or communicant masses as a priest's secret mistress compares with a pious, honest, acknowledged wife. So very artfully these learned scholars know how to cite the canons! And what is even much more clever is that whereas the ancient canons distinguish neatly between the sacrifice and the communion, they mix it all together still more slyly. For in the early days of the church, when they wished to hold mass, they held it in the manner of the old law in that the Christians brought to the altar all kinds of first fruits, milk, honey, apples, pears, etc. [Lev. 23:10, 18, 24; Deut. 26:2-4], and these the priest then offered as Moses commanded the Jews. For this reason the service was for a long time thereafter called a sacrifice. After that followed the communing or celebration of the sacrament, which they did not call sacrifice, but communing. But our private masses make a sacrifice out of the sacrament and let communing go.

I must here speak with those of you, dear sirs, who shout that no innovations should be allowed. Tell me, is not the private mass a scandalous innovation? Why, then, have you allowed it to arise and even now defend it? Yes, if you had allowed no innovations, my dear sirs, what and how much would one now still find among you that is contained in the ancient canons and fathers? I could almost get it in a nutshell, while your innovations in comparison have filled the world. I intend to say even more. What was the condition of your churches before our gospel came but a series of daily innovations rushing in one after another, in great number, like a cloudburst?

---

[25] *Winkelmessen* were masses said for the benefit of individuals, usually for the souls of the dead.

One set up St. Anne,[26] another St. Christopher,[27] another St. George,[28] another St. Barbara,[29] another St. Sebastian,[30] another St. Catherine,[31] another perhaps the Fourteen Helpers in Need.[32] Who alone wants to recount the new kinds of saint veneration? Are not these innovations? Where were bishops and shouters who should not permit such innovations? Let us continue. One set up the rosary,

---

[26] Although the gospels do not give the names of Mary's parents, tradition gave them as Joachim and Anne. St. Anne's cultus appeared in some Eastern liturgies in the sixth century. The first mention of the cultus in the West was in 1378 in a letter of Urban VI to the English prelates, but it did not become general until the late fourteenth century and was on the increase in Germany in the late fifteenth and early sixteenth centuries. Cf. Sabine Baring-Gould, *The Lives of the Saints* (Edinburgh, 1914), VIII, 564-570; *The Book of the Saints* (New York, 1947), p. 55. Willy Andreas, *Deutschland vor der Reformation* (5th ed.; Stuttgart, 1948), pp. 173-175, describes the increase of the veneration of Anne in Germany during these decades.

[27] A martyr of Lycia under Decius in the third century. Though little that is factual is known of him, one of the most popular legends recounts how he carried the Christ child, bearing the weight of the world, across a stream. Relics of the saint abounded in western Europe and in the Middle Ages it was common to represent St. Christopher outside churches and city gates. Cf. Baring-Gould, *op. cit.*, VIII, 553-559; *The Book of the Saints,* p. 140.

[28] Probably a martyr under Diocletian in Palestine. He was venerated in the West, particularly after the crusades, as a model of knighthood and the avenger of women. He was the acknowledged patron saint of Germany as well as of other lands. Cf. Baring-Gould, *op. cit.,* IV, 301-310; *The Book of the Saints,* p. 259.

[29] One of the most popular saints in the late Middle Ages. She was reported in legend to have been imprisoned in a tower and put to death by her own father for being a Christian. She was the patron saint of such artisans such as the firework-makers, artillery-men, architects, founders, and the like. The relics of St. Barbara were particularly numerous in Germany. Cf. Baring-Gould, *op. cit.,* XV, 25-28; *The Book of the Saints,* p. 86.

[30] An officer in Diocletian's army, St. Sebastian became one of the most famous Roman martyrs. When it was discovered that he was a Christian he was tied to a tree, pierced with arrows, and then beaten to death. Cf. Baring-Gould, *op. cit.,* I, 300-305; *The Book of the Saints,* p. 529.

[31] Catherine of Sienna· (d. 1380) heroically worked for healing the papal schism, rallying Italy around Pope Urban VI. She left many letters and a mystical dialogue and was canonized in 1461. Cf. Baring-Gould, *op. cit.,* I, 377ff.; *The Book of the Saints,* pp. 132-133.

[32] Especially in Germany a collective festival was celebrated in honor of the Fourteen Holy Helpers, each offering help in a special form. The customary fourteen were Achatius, Barbara, Blaise, Catherine, Christopher, Cyriacus, Dionysius, Erasmus, Eustace, George, Margaret, Pantaleon, Vitus, and Giles. Cf. *The Bock of the Saints,* p. 241. Willy Andreas, *op. cit.,* pp. 176-178, describes their functions and their popularity in Germany during these decades.

another the crown of Mary,[33] that one the Psalter of Mary,[34] this one ten Pater Noster stones on the doors,[35] another prayers to St. Bridget,[36] one this prayer, another that prayer, and all that without number and measure, and all the books are full of it. Where was there a bishop or doctor who would have looked even a little askance at these innovations?

Thus it was with the pilgrimages. New ones arose daily, to Grimmenthal, to Eicha, to Birnbaum, to Regensburg, and so many "Our Dear Ladies."[37] There was hardly a chapel or altar that did not blossom into a place of pilgrimage. The people ran to them, as if they were mad, neglecting their employment and obedience as though, if one could grasp it, it were the devil's delusion. Yet bishops, monasteries, and universities kept silence. If our gospel had not come, there would have been no more room or place left for a pilgrimage. And was that not a remarkably masterful fraud with our Lord's mantel at Trier, which was later exposed as a shameful lie?[38] What have all the Lutheran innovations done compared with this single instance of humbug and roguery? Here again, there was no one who could decry or even point out innovation. But Luther, who exposes and chastises such innovation, is an innovator!

Again, how is the indulgence alone daily and diversely renewed?

---

[33] The crown of Mary was a form of the rosary consisting of thirty-three Pater Nosters (Lord's Prayer) in commemoration of the thirty-three years of Christ's life on earth and five Ave Marias (Hail, Mary) for the five wounds of Christ. Cf. *WA* 30[II], 296, n. 1.

[34] The Psalter of Mary or Dominican Rosary consisted of fifteen decades (ten Ave Marias each) with a Pater Noster after each decade. *WA* 30[II], 296, n. 2.

[35] The Pater Noster beads of the rosary which the Franciscans and others hung at the church doors. Worshipers who recited the prayers as they entered the church received special indulgence.

[36] St. Bridget of Sweden (d. 1373) in her widowhood instituted the Order of the Most Holy Savior, known as the Bridgettines. She died in Rome on returning from a pilgrimage to Jerusalem and was canonized in 1391. She composed a book of prayers on the sufferings and love of Christ which show her to have been a woman of pious heart. Cf. Baring-Gould, *op. cit.,* XI, 182-189; *The Book of the Saints,* p. 116.

[37] Grimmenthal was a pilgrimage center three to four miles from Meiningen in Thuringia; Eicha was not far from Naunhof, and Birnbaum was not far from Rötha, both near Leipzig in Saxony; and the pilgrimage to the beautiful Mary in Regensburg or Ratisbon was one of the most popular of the day.

[38] The Holy Coat of Trier, alleged to be the seamless garment of Christ, was exposed for adoration in 1512 and was exhibited with special splendor in 1515. Cf. also Luther's *Warnung an seine lieben Deutschen* (1531). *WA* 30[III], 315; *EA* 2, 25, 44.

77

How do the priests and monks establish various new brotherhoods[39] through all guilds in the names of all saints? They daily sold letters of brotherhood and gave their good works and holy life for money. They sold vigils, anniversary masses, masses for the dead, with pageantry around the bier.[40] Some invented the golden masses,[41] others the five masses,[42] still others masses of this or that kind without number. Nothing, to be sure, is found in the ancient fathers about this. I shall at this point be silent about the relics. God help us, how one new one followed another! Among them were crude and palpable lies about the holy cross, about many whole bodies of one and the same saint, about many fingers of a single saint, until they even venerated St. Francis' underclothing[43] and woman's hair for the hair of St. Catherine. In short, there was neither end nor limit, so that you yourselves finally made a joke of it. Yet it continued unpunished and no bishop saw here anything new.

Were I to speak of what goes on in pulpits, however, then things would really become boundless. The monks daily preached their new visions, dreams, and notions, new miracles and examples, and that without moderation. There was scarcely a monk who, when he had been a preacher for two or three years, did not publish a new sermon book which was to rule the pulpit for a time. Though the world was full of such books there was still nothing in them about Christ and faith, but all about our works, merits, and devotion with many false and scandalous illustrations. Even when they did their best therein, it was still only about the invocation of the saints, not forgetting their own orders, to be sure, until they at last depicted to all the world that holy and noble woman, the virgin Mary, as a

---

[39] Brotherhoods were sodalities or associations of laymen who devoted themselves to charitable and devotional purposes. Luther offered his estimate of these organizations as early as 1519 in connection with his *Blessed Sacrament of the Holy and True Body of Christ, and the Brotherhoods* (1519). *LW* 35, 67-73; *WA* 2, 754-758.

[40] Masses for the dead at which a bier was placed in the church and a procession made around it. *PE* 4, 346, n. 2.

[41] Masses for the dead held on Golden Sunday, the first Sunday after Pentecost; sometimes the Saturday mass of the week following the festival of St. Michael and All Angels. *PE* 4, 346, n. 3.

[42] The five masses said on Christmas Day. *PE* 4, 346, n. 4.

[43] The undergarment of St. Francis was kept in Frederick the Elector's relic collection in Wittenberg. *WA* 30[II], 265, n. 91.

mediator for poor sinners, even for her Son, Christ himself. For we all know, and I was as deep in it as all the rest, that we were plainly taught to hold Mary in Christ's place and office. We held Christ to be our angry judge and Mary to be our throne of grace, where all our comfort and refuge lay, if we did not wish to despair.[44] Was that not a horrible innovation? Where were the bishops who rebuked such new blasphemers and betrayers of Christ who took away Christ's office and gave it to Mary, who taught us to flee from Christ and fear him as a whipmaster, and directed elsewhere our confidence which we owe to him as the true divine service? We have learned nothing but idolatry from these traitors!

Even at that, the doctors in the universities helped along. They had nothing else to do than to devise new "opinions," one after another. One could not be a doctor with special honors unless one had brought forth something new. They were at their very best, however, in that they despised the Holy Scriptures and let them lie under the bench. "What? The Bible? The Bible?" they said, "The Bible is a heretics' book! You must read the doctors! There you find what is what." I know that I am not lying on this point, for I grew up among them and have observed and heard all such things among them. Scotus writes that one cannot prove from the Scriptures this article: He descended into hell.[45] Occam, my dear master, writes that one cannot prove from the Scriptures that God's grace is necessary for a man to do a good work.[46] These two are the best, so what should the others do? Transcending all these, Thomas Aquinas,

---

[44] Cf. Luther's *Warnung an seine lieben Deutschen* (1531) (*WA* 30[III], 312), where he expresses a similar view.

[45] John Duns Scotus (d. 1308), scholastic philosopher, wrote, "Whatever is in the Apostles' Creed, even though the gospel does not teach it, as the descent into hell, must be held as an article of faith. . . ." I, dist. XI, ques. 1, 5, cited in Reinhold Seeberg, *Die Theologie des Johannes Duns Scotus* (Leipzig, 1900), p. 119.

[46] William of Occam (d. 1349 or 1350) was the founder of scholastic nominalism in which Luther was trained. Luther frequently charged Occam with denying the necessity of grace for the performance of good works. Cf. *WA*, TR 4, 679, No. 5135; *WA* 30, 160; *WA* 39[I], 419-420. In emphasizing free will, Occam did deny the necessity of habitual grace for good works. This did not, however, render him a Pelagian, since these works did not avail for man's salvation, which depended on God's free choice. Cf. Erwin Iserloh, *Gnade und Eucharistie in der philosophischen Theologie des Wilhelm von Ockham* (Wiesbaden, 1956), pp. 77-133.

"teacher of teachers" (if the "preaching monks"[47] rightly call him that), says frankly that to become a monk is as good as to be baptized.[48] That is the way to honor Christ's blood and death! Still, that is no innovation! And he is canonized besides by the pope and all the bishops.

In short, preaching and teaching were in a lamentable and pitiful state. Still all bishops kept silence and saw nothing new, though they can now see a new gnat in the sun.[49] Everything was so confused and upside-down with sheer discordant doctrines and strange new opinions that no one could know any longer what is certain or uncertain, what it means to be a Christian or not a Christian. The old doctrine of faith in Christ, of love, of prayer, of the cross, of comfort in affliction lay trodden under. Indeed, there was no doctor in the whole world who would have known the whole Catechism, that is, the Lord's Prayer, the Ten Commandments, and the Creed, to say nothing of understanding and teaching it, as it is now taught and learned, praise God, even by young children. For proof of this I refer to all the books of both theologians and jurists. If you can learn from them correctly one part of the Catechism, I will let myself be put on the wheel and be shredded. Yet there can have been nothing new in all that, but this must be a novelty.

"Yes," you say, "these things have now been accepted and are in daily use, but your teaching is entirely new." My dear sir, tell me, how old then is the idol, St. Anne?[50] How old is the rosary or the crown of Mary?[51] How old are the barefoot monks' Pater Noster stones on the doors and gates and in all the corners?[52] How old is the pilgrimage to Grimmenthal, Regensburg, the mantel of Trier,[53]

---

[47] The Order of Preaching Monks, title of the Dominican Order, was given papal confirmation in 1216-1217.

[48] Thomas Aquinas (d. 1274), scholastic philosopher, valued the contemplative life more highly than the active life of the baptized Christian. Cf. *Summa Theologica*, 2, I, ques. 182.

[49] The original reads, ". . . *die doch jtzt eine newe mucken jnn der sonnen sehen können.*" WA 30[II], 301, n. 1, incorrectly takes this to refer to the difficulty of seeing. CL 4, 118, correctly interprets the statement to refer to being sharp-sighted or quick-eyed (*scharfsichtig*).

[50] Cf. above, p. 76, n. 26.

[51] Cf. above, p. 77, n. 33.

[52] Members of many orders, especially the stricter ones, went about barefooted in obedience to Matt. 10:10. On Pater Noster stones, cf. p. 77, n. 35.

[53] Cf. above, p. 77, nn. 37, 38.

and many more like it? Were they not new ten, twenty, forty years ago? But who then stood up against innovations? Let my gospel go that long, and what will you bet, it, too, will become old. "Indeed, your new gospel may well be right, but it has a special novelty about it which is insufferable!" "What is that?" "Alas, it harms the purse and kitchen," say the canons in Magdeburg. "That rings true"[54] says the servant. That would at least be good German for once, that one could understand. If I had only known that before! Why then have we been wasting so many words up to now? Well, then, let us conclude here in privy council that "new doctrine" means whatever hurts the purse and kitchen and "old doctrine" means whatever fills the purse and kitchen. O my dear man, now write and seal it. We want to send it to the diet in Augsburg and hear what the lords say to it!

God knows I do not say this to dishonor you. I would gain nothing by your ruin. I would prefer it, if your situation were better. But you yourselves can well bear in mind that if you want to forget such abominations and, beyond that, you want to adorn and cleanse yourselves, people will be at hand who do not forget and will perhaps deal with the matter in an unadorned way. For such shameless violation is not to be tolerated that whatever you choose must be known as an innovation and what you do not so choose must not be called an innovation. You are suppressing the truth against your own consciences. This would bring us back to the beginning of the problem and hereafter we will become more severe with you than before. It is wretched for one to undertake to conceal such misery and even justify himself for it, and defame and persecute others. That will be a sign of an obdurate, impenitent heart and that you must soon go to ruin, since no other sin offends and grieves God more than to deny, decorate, and conceal open wickedness, as Cain and Saul did [Gen. 4:9; I Sam. 15:13ff.]. Not so, dear sirs, do not do so! At least some of you should give honor to God! Confess that in such things you have done evil. Humble yourselves and he will exalt you. Ask and he will forgive you. Mend your ways and he will help you.

If, however, you will not humble yourselves, but wish rather to hide these wrongs, keep them silenced, have them unrepented and

---

[54] On the meaning of the original, *das laut*, cf. Ernst Thiele, *Luthers Sprichwörtersammlung*, No. 202.

unpunished, and persecute the poor Lutherans for it besides and contemplate suppressing them, well, we shall keep an eye on you. If a scourge falls upon you, as cannot fail to come, remember that you have been warned enough. You shall not be the first to overcome God with defiance, that I know for sure. My intention is kindly and sincere in still trying to move a few of you, because I hope that there may still be a Lot or two in your Sodom. The others who remain unrepentant will not only not acknowledge such abominations for which they have indeed deserved death more than a thousandfold; but, on the contrary, they will, because of them, choke, drown, hang, and burn also the innocent (who will not praise such depravity and shame), as they even now are openly doing.

Too many things are now coming to my mind! I would like to come back to the private masses and pass over the abominations which occur to me at this point until I see how you wish to improve yourselves or adorn and whitewash[55] yourselves at this diet, then we shall show you what you really are and drink to your health,[56] if God wills. Let this suffice for the present about the trade in paid masses. Even when they are not sold but are kept at their best and are held for God's sake, nevertheless, you teach and hold them to be a sacrifice and a work by which one serves God and makes satisfaction for sin, both for us and others, be they living or dead, and most of all for the dead, as we all know that the mass must almost fight for the dead against purgatory. My suffragan bishop, when he made me a priest and put the cup in my hand, spoke these very words, "Receive power to sacrifice for the living and the dead."[57] That the earth did not then swallow us both was unjust and due to God's all too great patience! The living had this advantage from it that they believed whoever saw daily mass was made well, secure, and blessed. This was the best and most common use of the mass. That you cannot deny. Ask all the merchants about it—at least about the Rorate

---

[55] *Weis börnen.* Cf. Thiele, *Luthers Sprichwörtersammlung,* p. 163, n. 151.

[56] The original reads, *So wollen wir denn komen mit ewr rechten farbe, und euch proficiat bieten.* On the meaning of this sentence as given in the translation above, cf. WA 30^{II}, 305, nn. 3 and 4.

[57] *Accipe potestatem sacrificandi pro vivis et mortuis.* According to J. S. M. Lynch, *The Rite of Ordination according to the Roman Pontifical* (4th ed.; New York, 1912), p. 65, the bishop says to the newly ordained priest, "Receive power to offer sacrifice to God and to celebrate mass, as well for the living as for the dead, in the name of the Lord."

mass[58]—and men who must travel, and the pious burghers and ladies in the cities.

Is that not a terrible innovation? Do not your ancient *Canons of the Apostles* say, "No one shall be present at the mass who does not want to commune or receive the sacrament"?[59] Did Christ not institute it so that it might be received, that he might be remembered through it, and faith in him be strengthened, when he says, "Do this in remembrance of me"? You, however, keep silence about this remembrance, allow people neither to remember nor to receive it, do not teach and admonish to faith, as Christ has ordained. Satisfied that the bystander has seen the mass which you meanwhile secretly offer, you leave it at that. You thus allow lies and false confidence to remain in the heart of the poor onlooker, as if he had done well by being an onlooker, though he in no way partook of the sacrament either physically or spiritually, as Christ surely wants it and his apostles after him. I say it again! You complain that the endowments and monastic properties are being taken away. Because of such abomination and blasphemous misuse of the masses, the endowments and monasteries should be dealt with as Josiah, the king of Judah, handled the altars at Bethel, so that not one stone remained on another [II Kings 23:15]. That would be fair and right, if you will not mend your ways in this respect.

You cry, "What good has come of Luther's new teaching?" I must ask you in turn, "Tell me, what good has remained among you?" You have not left one thing incorrupt. You have, as you heard, disgraced the mass, our unique and highest treasure, with countless idolatries and abominations and crushed underfoot the right Christian usage, disturbed the faith, and silenced the Word. Baptism has remained for the children, though used clumsily and indolently

---

[58] *Rorate Coeli* ("Drop down, ye heavens," Isa. 45:8) is the text used frequently at mass and in the divine office during Advent as introit, antiphon, and versicle. Votive masses in honor of the Virgin Mary during Advent (December 18-24) used the text consistently. Cf. *The Catholic Encyclopedia* (New York), XIII (1912), 183; *CL* 4, 120, note to l. 22.

[59] Luther possibly has regulation ten in mind, "All those of the faithful that enter into the holy church of God, and hear the sacred Scriptures, but do not stay during prayer and the holy communion, must be suspended, as causing disorder in the church." A. Roberts and J. Donaldson (eds.), *The Ecclesiastical Canons of the Same Holy Apostles* ("The Ante-Nicene Fathers," Vol. VII [Grand Rapids, 1950-1951]), p. 501; original text in Carl Joseph von Hefele, *Conciliengeschichte,* Vol. I (Freiburg im Breisgau, 1873), p. 805.

enough. But as soon as the child has grown up and come to the age of reason, you have straightway strangled him, worse than the Turk does, and have taken his baptism away again through your damnable doctrine of penance and works whereby he learns to scorn his baptism, as now lost through sin and become of no value and henceforth to seek salvation through his own works. It is exactly as though baptism had been a temporary human work, just as the Anabaptists teach, and not an everlasting covenant of God. Tell me here, what good is left among you? I will not ask what good would have come of it, if we also could not have maintained against you our baptism, sacrament, gospel, faith, and Christ. For you have taught nothing right, but have taught everything contrary to baptism, sacrament, and penance. That is clear.

Among the Turks, however, there is the advantage that if someone is baptized, he is certainly not instructed in what is contrary to his baptism. Rather, the evil Turkish life and example is dangerous and offensive. And if someone were to teach directly against baptism, it would be easy to resist, because the Turk is no Christian and is scorned by a Christian, along with his doctrine. But here among you not only the example and life are dangerous, but you also teach against baptism and storm against it with words and works and do that in the name of Christ, as the dear fathers of souls and friends of baptism. That cuts like a sharp razor, as the Psalm [52:2] says. St Peter, too, complains about you in II Peter 2 [:18], "For, uttering loud boasts of folly, they entice with licentious passions of the flesh men who have barely escaped from those who live in error.[60]

The good, however, which has come from my doctrine is that this abomination and blasphemy of yours has all been brought to light and condemned. This is a great good and more than enough, though still more good comes of it daily, as will appear later. Among you, however, all good is spoiled and nothing has remained.

Concerning the Ban[61]

To begin with, you know it is great robbery and an outrage that you have usurped for yourself the great ban called *Excommunicatio*

---

[60] Luther renders the final phrase, "and now must live in error."

[61] For other discussions of the ban by Luther, cf. *Ein Sermon von dem Bann*

major, which properly belongs to the secular authorities. It has gone so far that popes even have undertaken to depose emperors, kings, and princes and make themselves secular emperors. Let me tell you, dear sirs, that this is not right! Your ban should be called the small ban, which closes not earth, but heaven, and severs from Christendom and sacrament, as Christ says in Matthew 18 [:17], "Let him be to you as a Gentile," and St. Paul in I Corinthians 5 [:12], "For what have I to do with judging outsiders?" If other matters should be reformed, this, too, should be corrected, for God is not pleased with any sacrifice or service that comes from robbery, as Isaiah [61:8] says.

In addition, this is and should be the use of the ban: it should be for the punishment of public offenses such as robbery, adultery, fornication, murder, hate, usury, drunkenness, also heresy, blasphemy, and the like, for our Lord Christ teaches in Matthew 18 [:17] that the ban should be put upon those who will not obey the church or his congregation. Thus the church truly teaches nothing else than God's Word. Now tell me, what good and ancient features of the ban are left to you? What new harmful abuses have not arisen here? I shall not mention that you have banned, cursed, damned, and strangled innocent, pious people as heretics. The ban is used for nothing else than to enforce payment of taxes and debts and cause much misery for poor people.[62] You know in part what kind of wantonness the scamps, officials, and commissaries have practiced in this matter. And if you do nothing about it at this diet, we shall hereafter put out for you a catalogue[63] of these virtues so that you

---

(1520) in *WA* 6, (61) 63-75; *The True Christian Ban* in *LW* 40, 311-313; *LW* 40, 340, 371-372; *Vom Bann* in *WA*, Br 6, (338) 339-342, No. 1949; *Luther über Bann und Exkommunikation* (1539) in *WA* 47, 666-671; *Sermo de virtute excommunicationis* (1518) in *WA* 1, (634) 638-643.

[62] The Diet of Worms in 1521 among the one hundred and one *Gravamina* or grievances of the German nation against the papal curia included also this abuse of the ban and the financial exploitation of the people. Cf. Anton Störmann, *Die städtischen Gravamina gegen den Klerus am Ausgange des Mittelalters und in der Reformationszeit* (Münster in Westfalen, 1916), "Die Abgaben an den Klerus," pp. 4-97, especially pp. 32, 39, and 41. Cf. also Bruno Gebhardt, *Die Gravamina der deutschen Nation gegen den römischen Hof* (2nd ed.; Breslau, 1895), p. 113; Adolf Wrede (ed.), *Deutsche Reichstagsakten unter Kaiser Karl V* (3rd ed.; 1901), pp. 645-688.

[63] *Kalender* in the original. On the meaning of the word, cf. *WA* 30II, 311, n. 1.

may comprehend that we have understood your abuse of the ban and announce it to the whole world.

But in the place where the ban should have its proper power and use, there it has been indulgent altogether and an empty blessing. It has not been able to cut at all, that is to say among the bishops and canons, yes, also among the popes and cardinals themselves. I would like to hear a doctor of canon law on this point who would show me how often, according to the canons and spiritual laws, the pope, cardinals, bishops, priests, foundations, and monasteries have been condemned and cursed under the ban because of simony[64] and other vices. Who holds them subject to the ban? The declaration supports them and reads as follows: "He is under the ban whom we want to have under the ban; whom we do not want to have under the ban, he is not under the ban." Carry on, dear sirs! If your will is to be called law, then the church can well dispense with such bishops and popes.

I would like to know what we are to take you for anyhow. You do not want to be Christians, for you do not want to endure Christ's Word and ordinance. You also do not want to be papist, for you want to keep the canons and spiritual laws much less, since they are also much harder to keep than the gospel. Now isn't that a strange bit of news that papists do not wish to be papist? And still they will give themselves out as papists, want to have the government and property of the church, solely for their wantonness and not for the use of the church. These things do not jibe! Well, then, continue being Epicurean and Turkish,[65] for that is certainly what you are. But because you are truly Epicurean and now complain so miserably that the goods of the monasteries and endowments are being seized,

---

[64] In the Middle Ages simony became a technical term referring to the practice of securing ecclesiastical office or preferment with money. The term is derived from Simon the Magician, who offered the apostles money for the gift of the Holy Spirit (Acts 8:9-24). Gregory VII (1073-1085) defined as simony the acceptance of a clerical appointment from the hands of a layman. Cf. *LW* 31, 201, n. 75.

[65] The philosophy of Epicurus (341-270 B.C.), the chief representative of hedonism among the Greeks, who interpreted pleasure negatively as the "absence of pain from the body and trouble from the mind," was at this time popularly understood as allowing license, material pleasure, and free reign to passion. Similarly the Turks, who were threatening the empire throughout the reign of Suleiman and after, were thought of as fierce but licentious and pleasure-loving conquerors fond of booty.

I must on this account have a friendly private talk with you.

It is true, and it doesn't please me either, that such goods are seized and scattered. The non-Lutherans do this the most and also profit from it more than those who are reproached for being Lutheran, as can easily be proved. I am displeased especially when wicked rascals get hold of these goods (as I well know), who do not deserve them. For I will raise no scruples, if those who work and serve faithfully get some of them. But there is one question which I would dearly love to have answered, because there are obviously two kinds of endowment thieves and monastery robbers, namely, some on the outside and some on the inside. Which of these two should by right be called the worst? Those on the outside are the evil and unworthy of whom I spoke above. Those on the inside are the bishops, canons, and the monks themselves, who sit inside. They misuse such properties for all kinds of vice and unchastity and shamelessly overstep their established estate. They send away great sums to Rome to still greater knaves and thereby plunder the endowments so shamefully! Do you not think that if the emperors, kings, princes, and lords, who have endowed these bishoprics and monasteries, would have wanted to endow brothels or churches for the Romans to rob, they would have acted differently and would not have handed over their money and property to harlots and rascals, to Roman thieves and robbers? But such fellows sit in endowed houses and monasteries and people use these properties whom the founders never had in mind or did not want. These fellows, therefore, hold them contrary to the founders' will and endowment, disgracefully consume and shamefully ruin them, and are consequently under the ban and accursed as "irregulars"[66] in the highest degree. Tell me, now, who are the worst endowment robbers and church thieves? You will see the pope sitting at the head together with cardinals, bishops, canons, abbots, and monks. For nowhere do they keep and do that for which they have been endowed, but precisely the reverse, like the mad. For all that, they take and use the properties as they wish. Ah, my dear sir, if you can see the splinter in another's eye [Matt. 7:3] and cry out about the extortion of eccle-

---

[66] *Irregulares* in this instance were persons who, having received Holy Orders, were barred from carrying out specific religious functions because of crime (*ex delicto*).

siastical properties, then you must be shown the beams in your own eyes which you do not want to see. If you can say the one, you must also hear the other, so that you may know that other people also have eyes, also feel, smell, and hear.

Now you claim that what is yours should not be taken from you. To be sure, what is yours should not be taken from you. Nevertheless, I want to play off your canon law against you.[67] Canon law judges, bans, curses, and deposes you and says, "It is not yours." It is called *Deponatur*.[68] For you do not keep your endowment and law and have thus deposed yourselves. Therefore, according to your own law, you lost your properties long ago, but you have insolently held them until now like damned robbers. For if one were to decline and conjugate the word *Deponatur* through all its persons, where would the pope, cardinal, bishop, and canons remain? It would certainly become an impersonal verb which would retain no person. But if you think it proper that people have patience with you, because you do not keep your own law, then you should in turn let yourselves consider it proper to have patience with those who, like unrepentant simonists and banned robbers, have taken your goods or have not let you succeed to them, because here they have your own law called *Deponatur*. May your request be granted that one leave to you what is yours, namely, the harlotry and rascality. But may what is not yours, that is, the taxes and goods, not be left to you but taken again as from robbers and thieves.

I do not wish this to be a defense for anyone. Let each one see for himself for what service or purpose he needs such properties. But against those who cry out, I make a distinction in the use of ecclesiastical properties. I say that if the goods of the foundations and monasteries are to be wickedly stolen for Rome and shamefully consumed by harlots and rascals, with the intention of the founders

---

[67] *Ewrs geistlichen Rechts mit euch spielen.* On the meaning as rendered above, cf. *WA* 30^{II}, 314, n. 2.

[68] *Deponatur*, i.e., deposed. Cf. *Decretalium D. Gregorii Papae IX*, lib. v, tit. III: *De Simonia, et ne aliquid pro spiritualibus exigatur vel promittatur. Corpus Iuris Canonici*, II, cols. 749ff. On the care of prebends and benefices, cf. *Decretalium D. Gregorii Papae IX*, lib. iii, tit. V: *De Praebendis et dignitatibus;* tit. VIII: *De concessione praebendae et ecclesiae non vacantis. Corpus Iuris Canonici*, II, cols. 465, 488. On the alienation of ecclesiastical properties, cf. *Decreti Secunda Pars*, causa X, ques. 2: [*An res ecclesiarum episcopis usurpare liceat*]. *Corpus Iuris Canonici*, I, cols. 617ff.

so completely absent, I would much prefer to have the emperors, kings, princes, and lords keep them and put them to better use. For it is certain that the founders wanted to entrust them to pious, chaste, Christian persons, not to men who would stand there and bleat or carry falcons, but to those who studied, read, and prayed, so that learned men could be chosen from among them to become bishops, pastors, preachers, school teachers, chancellors, secretaries, etc., as actually happened in the beginning, long ago. Now, however, they neglect and despise these offices and works—yes, even mock and persecute that sort of thing under the ban many times over. Therefore, I would not weep over it, even if they were to lose also wages and taxes. There is a saying that an ecclesiastical benefice is granted for carrying out official duty: kindness is not granted in return for wrong-doing.[69] Your own law teaches that and punishes it most cruelly with the ban and calls it simony.

Tell me, now, what pope, bishop, chapter, or monastery has up to now ever experienced sorrow and repentance, because they have allowed the offices to go to ruin or afterward endeavored to have them restored again? Nevertheless, they have used such "livings" [*beneficia*]. So they lived on them, twofold church-thieves and double monastery-robbers. For they not only possessed the properties that were endowed for other kinds of people than they are, but they also have stolen and robbed from the whole church and have prevented it from having pious, learned, Christian bishops, pastors, preachers and similar, necessary persons, who cannot be spared and whom they should have provided according to the intention and will of the founders. My dear sir, the founders did not intend the "duties of office" to mean that you should wear a long mantel, a surplice, and a tonsure, or put on chasubles and consecrated clothes. Sticks and stones could wear them just as well. They wished to have people trained for the comfort and salvation of Christendom.

If you now wish arrogantly to demand that the endowments and monasteries should be returned to you and everything given up again,[70] the proper reply to you is: Dear sirs, first make good your

---

[69] *Beneficium propter officium*, but not *beneficium propter maleficium*. The play on the double meaning of the word *beneficium* is not translatable.

[70] Cf. Melanchthon's letter to Luther, July 8, 1530. *WA*, Br 5, 446, No. 1629, ". . . the emperor commands that we restore all things to the original state until a council is convened."

twofold robbery, namely of persons and goods. You have robbed the church of the persons. You have stolen the goods from the foundations. Give them back again so that the "duties of office" may thrive once again, then indeed, the "livings" are justly yours. Such persons are more essential to the church than all the properties and the splendor of the entire clergy. If not, it will not be nice reckoning for you to give an account only of the expenditure and to suppress the income. You must be asked to keep account differently and see to your labors better. You have received the lords' goods in order to support and educate people. Where are they? Give account! Yes, you are the ones who have let the poor boys'-schools go to ruin, so that through you Christendom is truly everywhere corrupted thoroughly, just so that your Epicurean belly may fare well. I wanted to say this so that it may be seen what the cavilers stand to gain when they do their muckraking. Therefore, remember God and beseech him to help you accomplish some good at this diet. The affairs are great and weighty and unfortunately lie deeply submerged and wasted so that human power and ingenuity can here accomplish nothing. The ban is necessary, to be sure, but Lord God, it must not strain out gnats and swallow camels [Matt. 23:24] or nothing will come of it!

The subjects of penance, mass, baptism, faith, and works are, I fear, too lofty for you. Therefore, I have little hope that you will arrive at any pure conclusions about them, for your scholars themselves understand nothing about them. Such articles must be maintained and exercised only through Christ himself and his Holy Spirit without human assistance. Then, too, aside from the first council, Acts 15 [:4-29], hardly one or two have dealt with them. For this reason I shall further beg, implore, and admonish only about the subjects in which the special enlightenment of the Holy Spirit is not needed, but which are comprehensible and certain for all Christians, and which can almost be known by reason. And first:

Concerning Both Kinds in the Sacrament

On this point, you know full well that communion in one kind is a vexatious innovation contrary to the clear, distinct words of Christ and against the long, ancient custom of all of Christendom, as has been powerfully demonstrated to you through much Scripture. Nevertheless, you great foes of all innovation have not only accepted and maintained this blasphemous novelty, but out of sheer mischievousness you have even defended it with frightful ragings and persecutions. You have thereby tempted God to the uttermost, blasphemed and damned his Word. God grant that you may truly repent and subject your mind to his Word. You could support it with no Scripture and if you maintain it with sheer wantonness and force against the Scriptures, that will not turn out well in the end. It does not help you to pretend that one should do nothing new or change anything, for you have heard that this article is a novelty and that it is you who have unceasingly introduced false innovations and changes in Christendom. What is changed according to God's Word is no innovation. All customs must yield to it, no matter how good they may be, your own law says.[71] God and his Word are older than you are. They will also be younger and newer than we and you are, since they are eternal. Therefore, the Word must alter and rule both old and new and must not let itself be altered and ruled by either what is new or old.

You allege that nothing should be changed or modernized without the consent of the church. Who, then, is the church? Are you? Then show the seals and credentials or prove it another way with deeds and fruits. Why are not also we the church, since we are baptized as well as you, teach, preach, have the sacraments, believe, pray, love, hope and suffer more than you? Or are you the church because you introduce nothing but novelties and thereby change, blaspheme, persecute, and murder God's Word and, in addition, occupy the foundations and monasteries like church robbers? Yes, you are the devil's church![72] She is a liar against God's Word and a murderess, for she sees that her god, the devil, is also a liar and a murderer.[73] For the right church must surely be the one which holds to God's Word and suffers for it, as we do, praise God, and murders no one or leads no one away from God's Word. You should, therefore, not say to us so much, "Church, church, church." You should rather make us certain that you are the church. That is the

---

[71] *Decreti Prima Pars*, dist. VIII, C. VII: *Consuetudo rationi frustra opponitur;* C. IX: *Dei ueritatem, non hominum consuetudinem sequi oportet;* dist. IX, C. V: *In scripturis canonicis mendacia non admittuntur;* C. VIII: *Litteris omnium episcoporum sacra scriptura preponatur. Corpus Iuris Canonici,* I, cols. 15-17.
[72] Cf. Rev. 2:9.
[73] Cf. John 8:44.

crux of the matter! The devil can also say, "I am God, worship me,"
Matthew 4 [:9]. The wolf can also say, "I am a shepherd," Matthew
7 [:15], John 10 [:1]. We know very well ourselves that we ought to
obey the church, but we ask, who and where is it?

God help you to a reformation in this point. If you do not
improve, we shall nevertheless with God's grace act as we have done
up to now. I intend to say still more. If God grants that at this diet
you yield anything, we shall not accept it with the thought that
through your yielding all is now made right which up to now has
been wrong. No, you are much too trifling for us to think that it lies
in your discretion and power to say when and for how long God is
truthful or a liar, and when or for how long his Word is right or
wrong. That would be too highhanded! It would be elevating you
above God and his Word with the arrogance of the Antichrist and
retracting all our teachings and action. Rather, we want you to be
forced to it by God's Word and have you worn down like blasphemers, persecutors, and murderers, so that you humble yourselves
before God, confess your sins, murder, and blasphemy against God's
Word and reform, as men who have up to now done wrong, persecuted God's Word, and shed innocent blood. We want such sins and
depravity to be unconcealed and do not wish to agree to them by
keeping quiet and glossing them over, thus making ourselves parties
to such outrages. We are willing to stake everything on this and
fight it out with you on the basis of God's Word, which you persecute. For, as I said at the beginning, in no way do we need your
diet and resolutions. We stand where we stand without your assistance, yes, even against your blustering and raging. But we are doing
what we do for your sake and for the sake of the poor people, on the
chance that we may help you or perhaps some of you and give the
people counsel to the honor of God and the welfare of Christendom.

Concerning the Unmarried State

Celibacy, that is, the unmarried state or prohibited marriage, as
you know, is also one of your papal innovations contrary to God's
eternal Word and contrary to the ancient blessed custom of Christendom, contrary also to all living creatures and the creation of God
himself. Thereby the prophecy of Daniel 11 [:37] is fulfilled where
he speaks of your king, "He shall give no heed to any god or the

desire of women."[74] Not to love women must be a great vice, since the prophet here points it out as a special abomination of Antichrist, next after idolatry. The old translation[75] reads, "he will follow the lust of women," he will have desire for women. But that would not be an anti-Christian "virtue." Rather, it must read thus, "he shall follow the lust of men,"[76] though that is just what he means when he says, "he will not care for feeling towards women," which is the correct text.[77]

Now, dear sirs, if you want to be pious and do well, constrain yourselves to repentance in this matter for all the dissolute and in-expressible misery of all kinds of unchastity in the whole world which has grown out of this accursed papal innovation. It also hangs around the necks of all of you and will remain there, unless you do something about it and change it. You hear that it is an anti-Christian outrage and plague to despise the love of women, that is, to forbid marriage. For God has created women to be held in honor and as helpers for man and for this reason he does not wish to have such love forbidden and despised. The flesh and the devil teach men to use women only for dishonor so that one after another is put to shame, as your new, highly lauded marriageless (I nearly said honor-less)[78] state has done up to now and still does.[79] That is not to love women, but to love and seek unchastity and shame in women, treating and regarding them not as women but as harlots, so that hence-forth no one wants to love or respect them. But God wills that they be valued and esteemed as women and that this be done gladly and with love. That is to say, one should take them in marriage and re-

---

[74] RSV reads, "He shall give no heed to the gods of his fathers, or to the one beloved by women."

[75] I.e., the Vulgate. *Erit in concupiscentiis feminarum.* The English rendering is that of the Douay-Challoner text.

[76] *Erit in concupiscentiis masculorum.*

[77] *Affectum erga mulieres non curabit.*

[78] A play on the German words *ehelos* and *ehrlos: eheloser (ich hätte schier gesagt ehrloser) stand.*

[79] Luther here adds the marginal note, "In former times the canons vigorously opposed the pope in this matter, especially those at Mainz, so that those at Erfurt would almost have slain their bishop." Luther's reference is apparently to the *Chronicle* of Lambert of Hersfeld. The incident occurred in 1075, when Pope Gregory VII undertook to enforce celibacy on the clergy. Erfurt belonged to the archdiocese of Mainz. *WA* 30[II], 324, n. 1; *CL* 4, 128, note to l. 36. The *Augsburg Confession* (1530), Art. XXIII, also refers to this incident.

main with them in conjugal love. That pleases God, but it requires skill and grace.

Do you also know that the sixth commandment reads, "You shall not commit adultery"?[80] This commandment, like all the others, makes no distinction of persons, whether spiritual or secular, clergy or laymen. They should not break the marriage vow, that is, not touch the wife of another. Since, however, it forbids everyone another's wife, it is certain that it permits everyone a wife of his own. Indeed, so that no one touches the wife of another, it constrains one to have a wife of his own. Now if it were true, as the dear canons blasphemously declare,[81] that a pastor with a wife of his own cannot serve God, then this sixth commandment would really have to be repealed and would not apply generally to all kinds of persons and allow them their own wives.

I would accordingly like to speak at once about other commandments also, as, "You shall have no money or property of your own, otherwise you cannot serve God." Yet the seventh commandment, "You shall not steal," permits one to have one's own money and property and only forbids one the property of another. Indeed, so that one may not steal, it commands each to have his own property. So I do not yet know whether the danger of sin is greater in connection with one's own money or one's own wife. Greed, mammon, and company are truly mighty. But, briefly, it is a great knavery of canon law that it alleges one cannot serve God while having one's own wife and can still serve God well while having one's own mammon, money, property, castles, and cities. The opposite is true! It is better to serve God having one's own wife than having one's own property, although neither prevents one from being a Christian. For a wife one has already, and the worry about how to get her is over, and she can take care of herself. But one can never get enough money and one worries continually without ceasing how to increase and keep it. Such worry and love are the real obstacles to the service of God, of which a wife can free the pastor by doing the worrying herself and letting him simply serve God.

---

[80] Luther's argument turns on the German *ehebrechen*, which means to break the marriage vow.

[81] *Decreti Prima Pars*, dist. XXXI, C. II: *Sacerdotibus semper castitas obseruanda precipitur. Corpus Iuris Canonici*, I, col. 111, *passim*.

Likewise, one might also make sport of the fifth commandment and say, "You can not have weapons, guns, and other arms and serve God at the same time, for you might kill, injure, or be hindered thereby." And yet the fifth commandment merely forbids one to kill, but at the same time permits weapons and arms. Yes, it commands having weapons and arms in order that murder may be prevented. Why do our marriageless saints have both their own money and weapons, build and battle confidently? Does that not hinder them in the service of God? No, but a little wife must hinder them. It must have been a good-for-nothing who contrived this canon and a ne'er-do-well the other. Still, he has blinded all the world, even all the great scholars.

With this canon, however, the devil wanted so to arrange things that his celibates would not have their own wives, but instead the wives, daughters, and maids of everybody else, and in addition sodomy[82] as well, which in the state of marriage they would not have done. He wanted them also, instead of having their own property (for it is difficult to acquire), to swallow up the goods of the whole world and dissipate it with slothfulness. This would not be done, if they had to seek and earn what is their own. They have likewise forbidden weapons so that they might move the swords of all kings and do with them what they wanted. This, too, would not be done, if they had to have only their own swords. But wonder of wonders, these three vices, namely, all kinds of open unchastity, all kinds of greed and pomp, all kinds of weapons and war, do not hinder these celibate saints in serving God. Yet one pious wife hinders them.

If everything were to fail, so that pope, bishops, canons, and the people as well wanted to remain in their celibate condition like harlots and rascals, since even the heathen poet[83] acknowledges that philanderers and procurers take wives unwillingly, I hope, nevertheless, that you will take pity on the poor pastors and clergymen[84] and allow them to marry. And I hope that you will no longer be such shameful, murderous, senseless canonists or jurists as you have been up to now. For your canons decree that a married priest must be suspended, that is, deposed from office, and so you with your crude

---

[82] Cf. *WA* 30[II], 715; *Nachträge und Berichtigungen* to p. 323, ll. 30ff.

[83] Cf., for example, Horace, *Satires*, lib. i, 4, 48-50.

[84] *Seelsorger.*

asses and blockheads have expounded thus: they should be hanged, drowned, stabbed, murdered, and expelled.[85] So completely bloodthirsty and murderous are you bloodhounds that you are not ashamed to rage with all wantonness even contrary to and beyond your own law. If you will not have mercy, as I fear—so much innocent blood, so many horrible vices, and such monstrous evil hang around your neck and press in on you so hard that God will hardly grant you grace to do otherwise than you are doing, except to bring your own destruction on yourselves, as St. Peter says, II Peter 2 [:18-20]— well, then, God's will shall nevertheless be done and not what pleases you.

I do not know what to ask for the monks. For it is well known that you would just as soon see them all with the devil (God grant it), whether they take wives or not. Not without reason, for two roosters on a dunghill cannot tolerate each other. They want the kind of life you have and would like to have to yourselves. That you cannot permit. Therefore, let them go, the scoundrels! They must not lead the lives of bishops or canons. That befits only the church and the servants of God, such as you are. May God almighty graciously do more and better than you intend and than we expect of you. Amen! Otherwise, I fear, the devil will become an abbot and his mother an abbess. All the same, this is my hope and comfort that since you cannot live here forever and new pastors and clergymen must always be educated, the young fellows, God willing, who press forward in the future will not allow themselves to be tied up with your senseless, blasphemous vows and obligations to the honorless state[86] and other abominations. Should, however, the parishes become desolate because of it and the people be left without the Word, and the monks be passed by, then you shall see how long bishops and canons, endowments and monasteries will last. There must be pastors, even if there were no longer bishops, canons, or monks.

Christendom has been sustained for many hundreds of years without such endowment bishops and canons and it can well be maintained without them in the future. At the last judgment, cer-

---

[85] Cf. above, p. 72, n. 19.
[86] A play on the words *ehrlos*, "honorless," and *ehelos*, "unmarried." The original reads *ehrlos*, the Wittenberg and Jena editions of Luther's works read *ehelos*. Cf. WA 30[II], 715: *Nachträge und Berichtigungen* to p. 338, ll. 2 and 16.

tainly no Christian soul will be able to boast or testify that in so many hundreds of years anyone ever heard or learned from his endowment bishop the Lord's Prayer, Ten Commandments, the Creed, or a Gospel or ever felt or benefited by a single episcopal duty or work. "We ourselves formerly lived, before Luther, as though we had no bishops and must still live that way." I know for sure that all the world must say that prior to Luther's teaching they received no more benefits from their bishops than now, and now no less than before, except for the extortion and tax assessments. They can neither feel nor notice whether they had bishops formerly or have none now, so little have the workings of the episcopal offices and duties affected them. That is called zealously attending to souls! This is the way they now seek to attend to them again!

"Yes," they say, "but we consecrate and ordain others to do these things in our place." They do not even do that, but the suffragan bishop does it, and he, too, has no episcopal manner or nature about him, for he ordains only for the sacrifice of the mass and does not ask at all about how and what one should preach and what the people need to learn. He is, therefore, even satisfied if the priests can hardly read a requiem, accordingly quickly smears the un-learned asses with his chrism, and lets them go [into the priesthood]. If they really are preachers, God himself makes them so, and he thereby preserves his church. If it were left up to the endowment bishops and suffragran bishops, the church would long since have perished a hundred thousand times. Whose fault is it that up to now the church has been and still is in such an evil condition, if not that of the endowment bishops who sit in the seat of the apostles and in the episcopal office and do none of their duties, and let every-thing go to ruin? For all that, they now shout that they should be allowed to return to their former rule, because they seek the salvation of souls. In other respects, it has been an excellent government and they truly seek the salvation of souls! Yes indeed, the devil on their heads (for he rides them), and the bad luck of all of us around our necks, as we formerly experienced. It is a matter of princely "mine" and "thine." The bishop's office will, I daresay, remain with the pastors and preachers.

They allege further, "But we let people study in the universities who learn to preach ably and after that are ordained by the suffragan bishop on our command." That is true! You unfortunately just let them study. Turks and Jews do that, too. But what help do they give them? You, too, what do you give from your mammon of endowments to help anyone study, as you are deeply obligated to do? Indeed, it grieves you that there are universities. But here you do crave for something.[87] You are now free of the monks or in any case have them under control; that part of the gospel you accept gladly. You would also like to be rid of the theologians and scholars, who are still lying in your way. If they were gone, well, then you would be completely the powerful lords of the pastors. You could then once more climb above kings and princes. Yes, you could even command the pope himself, who cannot prosper without you, and you bishops alone could become the gods and lords on earth. That is the way you want to go, dear sirs. Is it not true that the secret conference of Mainz,[88] which I could not attend, moved stealthily along this course? We would then have the world full of asses and the churches would hardly have either Word or pastoral office any longer. Oh, you should let them study. But the prebends which in the chapters have been incorporated with the universities are given to no one unless he has first studied beforehand with the help of other people. And if they are to become his, he must first buy them and pay with a sum of money. When he has then paid, he is bound to howl and babble in the chapter, so that his studies and skill in no case benefit the preaching or teaching office. That is how you help Christendom!

I now assume that you ordain others in your stead (which, however, you do not do), who should preach and be bishops in your behalf; then listen very carefully: I am now speaking of bishops and am not speaking of men who make appointments. A peasant or village judge, a city, a prince, can also appoint a preacher, but he is

---

[87] The text reads, *Sondern da stinckt euch der odem nach*, pointing toward the sentence following. Jacob and Wilhelm Grimm, *Deutsches Wörterbuch*, VII (Leipzig, 1889), col. 1147, *odem* 2, cites from Luther, *"der odem stinkt inen nach der heiden golt (sie sind darnach begierig)."*

[88] Cf. WA 19, 252ff.: *Wider den rechten auffrührischen, verrätherischen und mordischen Rathschlag der ganzen Mainzischen Pfafferei Unterricht und Warnung* (1526). The resolution called for the exclusion of all Lutherans from secular or spiritual office. The secret conference to which Luther refers took place in November, 1525. Cf. CL 4, 132, note to l. 23.

not for that reason a bishop. A bishop is one who shall feed God's people. For there in Acts 20 [:28] is St. Paul's instruction to the bishops, "Take heed to yourselves and to all the flock, in which the Holy Spirit has made you bishops,[89] to feed the church of God, which he obtained with his own blood." If you were bishops, as your name and office demand, your hair would stand on end at this saying. You would be as loathe to be endowment bishops as I am to be a preacher and doctor, since you would not have it much better than I and men like me. St. Paul also says, "A bishop must be *didacticus*," I Timothy 3 [:2], Titus [1:9], that is, an apt teacher, who always perseveres in teaching. He does not, however, mean prince bishops or castle bishops, but church bishops, who carry the work forward, as praise God, many excellent pastors now do, even though they do not wear pointed hats,[90] which blockheads and "Nicholas bishops"[91] can also wear. For it is laughable that you as bishops should attend to what is correct teaching without yourselves knowing what it is. No, unfortunately, it is not a laughing matter, for till now we have experienced what good your supervision accomplishes, as the articles mentioned above show.

I have had to remind and admonish you of all this, dear sirs, because I see how you do not fear God and seek neither contrition nor repentance for your atrociously perverted conduct and do not even have pangs of conscience about it, for God is most deeply angered by this. For since we poor Lutherans have taken wives, you let yourselves imagine that for once you have a little point on which you can lay hold, because you could find nothing else. You thought that you would turn it to your advantage and so abuse and oppress us with it that thereby all your shameful, unchaste, whoring lives, all robbing of monasteries and thieving of endowments, together with all the rubbish of your abominations and perverted, unbishoplike abuses, shame, depravity, injury, and the ruination of the church, all would be concealed, covered up, silenced, and become nice and honored. Thereafter you, as pure and innocent men who never muddied up the water, might dare to assume all power, even above

---

[89] RSV renders the Greek *episkopous* as "guardians." The Vulgate has *episcopos.*

[90] Miters.

[91] Nicholas went from house to house in the garb of a bishop, giving presents to good children. He is an ancestor of the modern Santa Claus.

the apostles themselves. Easy now, dear sirs! See to it that you make no mistakes. Do not say, "Hurrah!" You are not yet over the hill. You have now seen how you can deck yourselves out and adorn yourselves, but you have not yet seen how we can strip the pretty hide off you and picture you in such a way that you will have to spit at yourselves. Only do not brag and be haughty; your case is not as good as you imagine!

Though you can reproach us for our wives, whom we acknowledge before God and before the world with a good conscience not as our whores but as our wives, you would never believe how masterfully we will picture for you your harlots and stolen wives, whom we both know you have without a good conscience, and whom you do not acknowledge before the world as anything but your whores. You must let yourselves be styled and judged before God and the world as procurers and harlot keepers. We shall depict for you in addition your Roman sodomy, Italian marriage, Venetian and Turkish brides, and Florentine bridegroom, so that you shall see and comprehend that our marriage has taken honest vengeance on your honorless chastity.[92] The fact that perhaps some of you are not guilty of all such wrongs is none of our concern. The protector, defender, comrade, and accomplice should be considered the same as those who are themselves guilty, because they do not punish, ban, and shun such vices, as the gospel and your own law teach,[93] but help these evildoers, back them, and join them in raging against us. By such support they make themselves partakers of all such outrages and are therefore no better than the guilty, Romans 2 [:1-2].

Never has a heathen, never a Turk, never a pope, never an emperor, and never any human being on earth made or enforced a law that anyone should be put to death because of marriage.[94] It is a new, unheard-of thing, begun by you new bishops, who are the greatest endowment robbers, harlot keepers, and whore hunters on earth in your chapters.[95] Nor do you do it for the sake of chastity,

---

[92] The unchastity of Venice and Florence was proverbial. In *WA*, TR 2, 138-139, No. 1575, Luther refers to the incestuous celibacy of the papists, impious abominations, and Italian weddings. The Florentine bridegroom is a reference to Pope Clement VII (1523-1534), bastard of Giuliano de' Medici of Florence.
[93] *Decreti Prima Pars*, dist. LXXXIII. *Corpus Iuris Canonici*, I, cols. 293-294.
[94] Cf. above, p. 72.
[95] Luther is here probably referring to Archbishop Albrecht of Mainz, who con-

but all because others will not practice harlotry and unchastity, as you do, for you let them go unpunished. No one can believe that you conscientiously intend chastity with this penalty, since there are no greater enemies of chastity anywhere than you are, for you pursue it in your own bodies with all lewdness most shamefully, without letup.

To be sure, this is a small matter compared with the great general abomination that you are the kind of bishops described above and, in time, if you do not improve, you will be pictured differently. For truly, if we must have godless procurers and enemies of God as bishops, we want to show them very frankly in which church[96] they belong, as you will assuredly be told. For as long as you will not let our marriage alone, you shall also not have much pleasure and honor from your harlotry and anti-Christian "bishopry."[97] If I die for it, there are others who can do it better! To be brief, we both know that you are living without God's Word, but that we have God's Word. It is therefore our deepest desire and humblest request that you will give honor to God, acknowledge yourselves for what you are, repent, and mend your ways. If not, do away with me. If I live, I shall be your plague. If I die, I shall be your death. For God has set me on you. I must be, as Hosea says, a bear and a lion in the way of Assur.[98] You shall have no rest in the presence of my name until you reform yourselves or go to ruin!

We, therefore, offer you a choice. In the first place, since you cannot or will not perform the episcopal office and work, since you together with all your scholars are verily, verily, not fit to preach and to comfort and judge consciences, then let us exercise your office for which you are responsible. Allow us to teach the gospel freely and let us serve the poor people who desire to be pious. Do not persecute and resist that which you cannot do and are nevertheless obligated to do and which others want to do for you.

---

ducted "an ingeniously dissolute petticoat government" at Moritzburg in Halle, his favorite residence, which the Reformation, in fact, forced him to abandon. Cf. WA 30[II], 338, n. 3; Otto Hintze, *Die Hohenzollern und ihre Werke* (Berlin, 1915), p. 125.

[96] I.e., the pretended church.

[97] *Bisschofferey.*

[98] Hos. 13:7-8. The mighty empire of Assyria scourged sinful Israel and in 722 B.C. led the northern ten tribes into captivity.

In the second place, we wish to demand nothing further of you or take any pay from you. On the contrary, if God supports us otherwise, we expect to work, so that you will thus be spared both labor and pay, care and cost. Not that we take such great delight in preaching, because, speaking for myself, I would rather hear no other news than that I had been deposed from the preaching office. I am so very tired of it, as a result of the great ingratitude of the people,[99] but much more because of the unbearable hardships which the devil and the world deal out to me. But the poor souls will not let me [stop preaching]. Besides, there is a man, named Jesus Christ, who says "No" to my resignation. I rightly follow him to whom I am even more indebted. You yourselves all know now, praise God, that the Lutheran preachers are upright and do you no harm, but are more useful to you than all your scholars and the pope's. More godly heretics you have never had nor will you ever get them any more pious. Entreat God that they may remain with you!

In the third place, we wish to let you remain what you are and teach (as we have done in the past) that you should be allowed to be princes and lords, for the sake of peace, and that your properties should be left alone. The Hussites and Wyclifites surely did not do this and even now the enthusiasts and factious spirits are not willing to do so. Thus you see after all that in us you have not foes, but great friends, yes, even protectors. For what harm does it do us, if you are lords and princes? If you do not want to do what is right for yourself, and your estate and office, well, then, it is not we, but you who will give account for that. Only keep the peace and do not persecute us! We do not ask for more, and have never asked for anything else, than that the gospel be free. You could help us and we could help you to peace. If you do not do so, then we retain the honor, and you lose both peace and honor.

In the fourth place, you could restore the episcopal jurisdiction[100] again, as long as you left us free to preach the gospel. For my part, I will readily give help and counsel so that you may have something of the episcopal office after all. Thus you would have

---

[99] At the end of a sermon preached on January 1, 1530, the Nürnberg Codex Solger adds the note, "At this point Dr. Luther discontinued the delivery of his sermons on account of the ingratitude and disobedience of the people." WA 32, 4.

[100] On the rendering of *zwangk* as "jurisdiction," cf. CL 4, 136, note to l. 4.

two parts of the episcopal office: the one, that we and the preachers teach the gospel in your place; the other, that you would assist such administration with episcopal jurisdiction. Your person, life, and princely demeanor we leave to your conscience and God's judgment. Up to now we have never taken such jurisdiction from you. You yourselves have let it fall. For when you were unable to maintain indulgences and other unbearable abuses with it, you let it fall entirely, and were not willing to protect our gospel or even to tolerate it. But you turned this authority against us and against the gospel. Then it had to bump itself, indeed, and become blunted. For God did not ordain it against his Word but for his Word.

We truly cannot accommodate you with anything more or anything loftier, except daily prayer, good will, and service which we owe to all enemies anyway. The offer is this: we will perform the duties of your office; we will support ourselves without cost to you; we will help you remain as you are; and we will counsel that you have authority and are to see to it that things go right. What more can we do? Truly we carry a heavy burden, having loaded ourselves down with you, the factious spirits, and the whole world, yes, and all the devils, and no one helps us. If you, too, will not want to help, but continually suppress us, see to it that you do not break our backs in two and try our patience too far. If you are going to suppress the upright heretics who are carrying you along, take care what becomes of you. Unfortunately the game is no longer in our hands, as it was before, for the devil has taken it away from us. We can assuredly help you no longer. Now help yourselves and do not consider yourselves, but the common multitude and precious peace. It is high time! We too will do our best. If there is any upright heart at all among you, he can certainly tell from this whole treatise that I speak the truth and must speak it, and that I intend it sincerely from the heart for you and everyone. More I cannot do, for your affairs are too utterly wicked.

But someone might at this point think it silly to hear that the endowment bishops should rule the churches, since it is well known that they cannot and will not learn how, as St. Paul says, "If a man does not know how to manage his own household, how can he care for God's church?" [I Tim. 3:5]. And one can see before his very eyes how the bishops administer their chapters and maintain discipline, namely, by letting them be dens of unpunished rapaciousness and robberies.[101] Answer: I know well, sad to say, that it is true. But in order that the wicked people may see that we seek peace and that nothing is lacking in us, I can put up with their providing parishes and pulpits with clergymen and thus help to administer the gospel. I would sooner have the fault be theirs than ours, and God has before now ruled and done good by means of wicked rogues. One must think it is now the time when Herod in Jerusalem is selling the priestly office and the Romans are doing the same.[102] Nevertheless, the service and Word of God remain. If, however, they want to suppress the gospel or remain so completely unrepentant, they may do so at their own risk. We shall still preach what we want to. They are also not so securely established that if they are eager for misfortune, God cannot quickly raise up another Münzer, who will completely overthrow them. If they do not want to be bishops in God's name, let them be bathhouse keepers[103] in the devil's name. Nor are we to blame or the cause for it. The Lutherans remain masters because Christ is with them and they remain with him, even though hell, the world, devil, princes, and all should go mad.

To deal with more topics now would be too much and take too long. God help you to act at the diet in such a way that it will not be necessary for us to start in all over again from the beginning. For that is not good for you, and we would rather be spared the trouble. But in order that you do not think that these are merely threatening words which I now speak, I will here list as many points and articles as occur to me offhand which are being discussed by both sides.

The topics[104] with which it is necessary to deal in the true

---

[101] The text reads *impunita Lupanaria und Latrocinia*. Cf. p. 100, n. 95.

[102] For an account of Herod's abolition of the hereditary tenure of the high priesthood, cf. H. Graetz, *History of the Jews* (Philadelphia, 1893), II, 90ff. Luther's reference most likely is to Werner Rolevink, *Fasciculus temporum* (Cologne: H. Quentell, 1481) (Hain 6929), in which immediately after a reference to Herod, the author says of the Procurator Valerius Gratus, "*Iste palam vendit sacerdocium.*" Herod installed seven high priests, Ananel of Babylon, twice. Cf. WA 30[II], 715: *Nachträge und Berichtigungen* to p. 344, n. 2.

[103] The bathhouse keeper was also the barber and bloodletter of the time. PE 4, 373, n. 1.

[104] For a more detailed and complete listing of topics by Luther, cf. WA 30[II], 249-255, as reprinted from an appendix in Chancellor Brück's *Geschichte der Religionsverhandlungen auf dem Reichstag zu Augsburg* (1530).

Christian church and about which we are concerned:

What law is	What a deacon is
What gospel is	What the preaching office is
What sin is	The true catechism, namely, the
What grace is	Ten Commandments, the
What the gift of the Spirit is	Lord's Prayer, the Creed
What true repentance is	True prayer
How true confession is made	The litany
What faith is	The reading and interpretation
What forgiveness of sins is	of the Scriptures
What Christian liberty is	What good works are
What free will is	Instruction of married people,
What love is	children, manservants, and
What the cross is	maids
What hope is	Respecting authority
What baptism is	Children's schools
What the mass is	Visitation of the sick
What the church is	Providing for the poor and hos-
What the keys are[105]	pitals
What a bishop is	Ministering to the dying[106]

No bishop has ever dealt with such topics and besides your people have never thoroughly understood or been taught them and a large part has become utterly meaningless.[107] You cannot deny this. We have been educated in your schools, and your books, which testify to it, are still extant. The whole world gives evidence that these things were formerly never preached. Now it is certain that all depends upon these points, that the Christian Church is cared for through them, and does not need your superfluous additions at all.

With this I will not tell of the German hymns, the blessing of

---

[105] The office of the keys by which Christ empowered the church to remit or retain sins, Matt. 18:18. Cf. Luther's discussion, *The Keys* (1530). LW 40, (321) 325-377; WA 30[II], 465-507.

[106] *Die sterbenden berichten*, i.e., to comfort the dying and administer the sacraments to them. Cf. WA 30[II], 346, n. 1; CL 4, 138, note to l. 16[b].

[107] *Gar verblichen*, i.e., *ganz bedeutungslos geworden*. Cf. CL 4, 138, note to l. 19.

the bride,[108] and many good wholesome books. Nor will I now relate how many outrages we have leveled with them and rooted out from among us. Enough is indicated to show how many points we could still speak about, if we wanted to take the time and space for it.

The things which have been practice and custom in the pretended church.

1. Indulgences
2. Sacrificial masses and the innumerable ways of doing them
3. Abuse of the ban
4. Purgatory
5. Poltergeists
6. Innumerable pilgrimages
7. Vigils
8. Masses for the dead
9. Anniversary masses
10. Masses at four weeks[109]
11. Soul-baths[110]
12. Veneration of saints, some of whom were never born
13. Saints' days without measure
14. Mary made a common idol with countless services, celebrations, fasts, hymns, and antiphons
15. Butter letters[111]
16. Countless relics, with fraud
17. Innumerable brotherhoods
18. Celibate life
19. Dedications of churches
20. Dedications of altars
21. Dedications of images with indulgences
22. Baptism of bells with two-hundred godfathers on one rope
23. Distinctions of foods ⎫
24. Distinctions of days ⎬ made obligatory
25. Distinctions of dress ⎭

---

[108] Probably a reference to Luther's own formula of marriage, the *Traubüchlein. PE* 4, 375, n. 1.
[109] Masses for the souls of the dead said on the thirtieth day after the death.
[110] The endowment of free baths as a good work for the benefit of souls in purgatory. *CL* 4, 139, note to l. 4ᵃ.
[111] Cf. above, p. 70.

26. The compulsory seven, or canonical hours
27. Sunday procession, a spectacle
28. Extreme unction, for death, not for health
29. Sacrament of marriage
30. Sacrament of priesthood
31. Sacrament of confirmation
32. Acolytes ⎤
33. Tonsurists ⎟ their consecration not for office,
34. Lectors ⎟ but for liberty[112]
35. Subdeacons ⎦
36. Prayers to St. Bridget[113]
37. The same kind of prayers without number, and all types of prayer books replete with blasphemous, shameful dishonors to God

Tonsures	Candles	
Chasubles	Flags	
Albs	Censers	
Surplices	Fonts	
Cowls	Monstrances	
Churches	Pyxes	All of these beyond necessity,
Chapels	Chalices	purely as a special service to
Altars	Organs	God, which is contrary to
Altar cloths	Bells	faith
Lights	Holy water	
Candlesticks	Holy salt[114]	
Images	Incense	
Tablets	And all sorts of	
Crucifixes	food	

In Lent:
    Ash Wednesday
    Hunger cloths[115]

---

[112] Acolytes and lectors belong to the lower orders of clergy. All of the lower orders were included in one consecration, known as "the first tonsure." Through it they received immunity and became tax-exempt. *CL* 4, 136, note to l. 2ᵇ.
[113] Cf. above, p. 77, n. 36.
[114] Used in baptism.
[115] The purple or violet altar cloths used in the fast seasons, Advent and Lent. *PE* 4, 377, n. 2.

Veiling of images

Keeping fasts, except for the clerics[116]

Litany of the saints

Hymns to Mary of an evening[117]

Confession torture[118]

Penance and satisfaction

Long prayers[119]

Palm-ass[120]

Palm-shooting[121]

Palm-swallowing[122]

Palm crosses[123]

Compulsory confession

Compulsory communion

Kissing and idolizing the cross[124]

Burying the cross

Half-mass on Good Friday

Singing psalms at the [holy] grave

Dark-mass[125]

Not ringing, but clattering of bells

Passion sermons eight hours long

Consecrating the fire[126]

---

[116] *Pfaffen.*

[117] Customary especially in the month of May. *PE* 4, 377, n. 3.

[118] The plenary confession, demanded once a year, usually before the Easter communion. *PE* 4, 377, n. 4.

[119] *Preces*, a name referring to suffrages and supplications in the form of versicles and responses.

[120] A wooden dummy with an image of Christ mounted on it was drawn in procession to commemorate the entry into Jerusalem on Palm Sunday.

[121] This is a reference to the custom of throwing green twigs representing palms after the palm-ass.

[122] Swallowing bits of consecrated palms distributed on Palm Sunday was regarded as a preventive for throat infections.

[123] Parts of consecrated palm fastened together in the form of a cross were used by the peasants for blessing the fields.

[124] This and the six items following were part of the Holy Week observances, especially on Good Friday.

[125] *Finster Metten*, i.e., holding mass while the altar lights are extinguished. *CL* 4, 140, note to l. 23ª.

[126] This and the two items following were customs on the Saturday before Easter.

Easter candles

Lifting the cross out of the grave and carrying it as in a play[127]

Consecrating cakes on Easter Day

Procession on St. Mark's Day[128] ⎫
Cross weeks[129]   ⎬ both good for all unchastity
                                        ⎭

Ascension at nones[130]

The Holy Ghost on Pentecost[131]

Corpus Christi procession[132]

The Assumption of the Blessed Virgin[133]

Church dedications

Festivals of patron saints

Community weeks[134]

St. Burkart's Day[135]

Ember days

All Saints' Day

All Souls' Day

St. Martin's goose[136]

Advent, more to serve Mary than Christ

The Rorate mass[137]

The Conception of the Blessed Virgin[138]

Three Christmas masses

The *Apparuit* and music[139]

---

[127] I.e., carrying it in procession. Cf. *CL* 4, 140, note to l. 2ᵇ.

[128] The great procession of the year (April 25).

[129] The cross week was the week after Rogate Sunday, observed with processions and prayers for the crops.

[130] The hour of nones (3 P.M.) was said to be the time of the Ascension and the chief service on Ascension Day was held at that hour.

[131] The dramatic representation of the Pentecost miracle.

[132] The procession took place in the week after Trinity Sunday.

[133] The Assumption was celebrated on August 15.

[134] The week following the Sunday after St. Michael's Day. The masses of that week were usually for the dead.

[135] October 14.

[136] It was an ancient custom to eat a goose on St. Martin's Day (November 11).

[137] Cf. above, p. 83, n. 58.

[138] March 25.

[139] *Apparuit*, "He has appeared." U. J. Chevalier, *Repertorium Hymnologicum* (Louvain, 1892), I, 76, Nos. 1244-1247, lists four hymns of which the *inicipit* is

Oats on St. Stephen's Day[140]
St. John's draught[141]
Candlemas and wax market[142]
St. Agatha's lights[143]
St. Blasius' lights[144]

I shall stop here, for who can count up everything in such a brief space? However, if they do not want to have peace, I can easily enumerate further, or someone else can do it even better, so that the dear canons and bishops will not think that only the monks have sinned and that they are the clean kitten. Not so! For the time being I wished to point out nothing more than what has been customary in the parish churches, although they are the least part of your government and have been despised beyond all measure, and you have even trampled them underfoot. Were I to get around to the chapter churches, cathedrals, official houses, monasteries, and endowed pulpits and after that to the mendicants, the stationaries,[145] and finally to the sophists in the universities, God help us! It does not surprise me that you forget such boundless outrages and now try to spruce up. Did not I myself forget (by the dear God!) and not imagine that you would sit there where I now see you sitting? Oh, now for God's sake be silent and reform, otherwise, things will go bad with you.

It is certainly true that there are some among the practices listed above which should not be discarded. And some of these

---

apparuit. The text of the first, *Apparuit benignitas* (*XV saec.*), is to be found in F. J. Mone, *Lateinische Hymnen des Mittelalters* (Freiburg im Breisgau, 1853), I, 66-68, No. 51: *De nativitate domini hymnus.*

[140] On the festival of St. Stephen's Day (December 26) oats and fodder were consecrated.

[141] On the festival of St. John the Evangelist (December 27) wine was consecrated and drunk.

[142] Candlemas (February 2) was the day on which candles to be used throughout the year were consecrated, leading to a great sale of candles on that day.

[143] On St. Agatha's Day (February 5) candles on which prayers to the saint had been inscribed were burnt.

[144] On St. Blasius' Day (February 3) the priest held two candles in his left hand in the form of a Greek cross before his throat. Candles burned to Blasius were thought to help ward off throat infections.

[145] Relic venders.

have declined which I did not want to see decline, but which can easily come back into use again. Among them the very best to remain are the fine Latin songs, *de tempore*,[146] although they have been almost drowned out by the new saint-songs and also count almost for nothing. We retain them, nevertheless, and they truly please us from the heart.

To express my opinion briefly, this is the sum total of it. If these things had been left as child's play for youth and young pupils, so that they would have had a childlike image of Christian teaching and life, as one must give children dolls, puppets, hobby-horses, and other kinds of children's toys, if things had gone no further than the custom by which one teaches the children to fast for St. Nicholas and the Christ child, so that they may give them presents on their respective nights,[147] as our ancestors apparently intended, then it would be possible to tolerate the palm-ass, Ascension, and many similar things, and let them go on and take place, for then they would confuse no consciences. But that we old fools march around in bishops' hats and with clerical pageantry and take it seriously, yes, not only seriously but as an article of faith, so that it must be a sin and must torment the conscience of anyone who does not venerate such child's play—that is the devil himself!

From this it follows that all the practices named above, no matter how childish and laughable they are, nevertheless seriously storm against and corrupt the Christian faith and the truly necessary things referred to above, as though there were no help unless one has kept them. For we have unfortunately had the experience up to now that such child's play and fool's play has been, and still is, practiced more often and more seriously than the really important things. We are of the opinion, then, that if we can help retain such children's games as are tolerable for the sake of the young without any disadvantage to the really serious important matters, we shall gladly do so. But that we should hold them as articles of faith and even play the fool in bishops' hats, nothing will come of that, let him be angry or laugh who will!

I have pointed out these things to you at this time, dear sirs, as

---

[146] For the seasons of the church year. *PE* 4, 380, n. 2.
[147] On the Eve of St. Nicholas (December 5) and Christmas Eve.

a friendly and faithful admonition, begging most zealously that you will join us in calling on God that he may grant you grace and wisdom so to act and deal in these important matters that it may be to his honor and for the salvation of us all. And may he keep you from adorning yourselves, or excusing, defending, or continuing by force your former misconduct. For what good does it do for you to create still more bad blood among the people? Men's hearts are already much too embittered, and not without good reasons. This makes it necessary to soothe, mollify, and quiet them with humble confession and solemn reformation and not to jolt and irritate them further. For you know that, even if there were no gospel, your organization and estate have fallen so far out of bounds and lie so corrupted, even judged by your own laws, that it would be intolerable if you want to force your way through.

You also know that Pope Adrian himself confessed through his legate at Nürnberg[148] that the Roman See was the cause of much misery and offered himself to improve it. Why should you then be ashamed to confess this and in addition still persist so obstinately in your pride, yield nothing or admit nothing, but carry off everything with force regardless of whether the result is better or worse? For you know, or ought to know, that Christian government or power has been instituted by God not for tearing down but for building up, as St. Paul says [II Cor. 13:10], and should not be a tyranny, but a service. Grant this and we could then help to raise you again in the eyes of the people. For I maintain that you will not very well be able to do without the Lutherans, the pious heretics, least of all their prayers, if you want to achieve anything lasting. But if you are going to proceed with force and want to go through stiffly and stubbornly (may God forbid it!), then, I, together with all who believe with me, hereby testify before God and the whole world that it is not our fault, if your pride fails you so that you go to rack and ruin. Your blood be upon your own head! We are and want to be innocent of your blood and damnation, since we pointed out to you sufficiently your wrongs, faithfully admonished to repentance, prayed

---

[148] This document of November 25, 1522, presented by Chieregati to the estates at Nürnberg on January 3, 1523, is found in Smith and Jacobs, *op. cit.*, II, 141-148.

sincerely, and offered to the uttermost all that could serve the cause of peace, seeking and desiring nothing else than the one comfort for our souls, the free, pure gospel. Therefore, we may boast with a good conscience that the fault has not been ours.

But may the God of peace and comfort give you his Spirit, to direct and lead you to all truth, through our Lord Jesus Christ, to whom be praise and thanks for all of his unspeakable grace and gifts in all eternity. Amen.

A SERMON ON KEEPING
CHILDREN IN SCHOOL

1530

Translated by Charles M. Jacobs
Revised by Robert C. Schultz

INTRODUCTION

Education was generally held in contempt and derision by the masses during the early decades of the sixteenth century. To a large extent this negative attitude was fostered by a spirit of materialism which went hand-in-hand with the rapid expansion of trade and commerce. Unless a youth was destined for a learned profession in law, medicine, or theology, parents and children saw little if any value in learning which was not obviously and directly related to the world and work of commerce. Time spent in school, they reasoned, could be spent more profitably in earning a living. Indeed, the spirit of the age was so averse to formal education that the derisive saying was widespread in Germany, "The learned are daft."[1]

But the spirit of materialism was not the sole factor responsible for the anti-education attitude of the masses. A second and perhaps even more significant factor is to be found in the popular reaction to the Reformation. One of the early results of the Reformation movement had been the large-scale abandonment of monasteries and cloisters by monks and nuns won over to the evangelical point of view. For practical, religious, and economic reasons, the secular authorities confiscated the properties and endowments of the abandoned monasteries and cloisters. Although not so intended, these actions of the monastics and of the secular authorities caused the collapse of existing monastic and other church-dominated schools which were staffed by monks and nuns and supported by the endowments of their religious communities.[2]

Further, there were those who interpreted the doctrine of the spiritual priesthood of believers to mean that the ministerial office required no formal education. They held that the inner word, prompted by the Holy Spirit, was all sufficient, and that formal education and academic degrees were dispensable vanities and even offensive to God.[3]

---

[1] *Gelehrte sind verkehrte.* See below, p. 140. See also *SW* 3, 33-34, and Preserved Smith, *The Life and Letters of Martin Luther* (Boston and New York: Houghton Mifflin Company, 1911), p. 185.
[2] Cf. *SW* 3, 34; Smith, *op. cit.,* pp. 185-186.
[3] Cf. *SW* 3, 34.

Most important of all, however, was the common reaction of the masses to the Reformation contention that many of the church's doctrines, teachings, and practices were not only permeated by error, but were actually dangerous to salvation. If such were actually the case, parents reasoned, why should they send their children to schools where such errors were inculcated?[4] Their negative conclusions were reflected in the sharp decline in enrolment at educational institutions, including the University of Wittenberg where Luther was the star of the faculty.[5]

It was under the pressure of this anti-education attitude and the collapse of many schools that Luther, in 1524, issued his appeal *To the Councilmen of All Cities in Germany that They Establish and Maintain Christian Schools.*[6] In this treatise Luther offered the authorities practical advice and replied to current popular arguments against schooling. This appeal had some measure of success, for in that very year the cities of Magdeburg, Nordhausen, Halberstadt, and Gotha took action. Eisleben and Nürnberg followed suit in 1525 and 1526 respectively.[7] Territorial church orders also stressed the matter of providing schools.[8]

Despite these and other efforts, however, little actual progress was made, for the problem of persuading parents to send their children to school and to keep them there still remained. Luther announced his intention of setting himself to this task in the spring of 1529 when he wrote a preface for a book[9] by his friend Justus Menius. The book dealt with the duties of married people and the Christian training of children. In this preface Luther wrote, "Thus, even in worldly government, you can serve your lord or your city better by training children than by building him castles and cities and gathering the treasures of the whole world;

---

[4] Cf. SW 3, 34.
[5] See below, p. 142, n. 39.
[6] SW 3, 31-70.
[7] SW 3, 36.
[8] Schwiebert cites particularly the *Hallische Kirchenordnung* of 1526, the *Braunschweig'sche Kirchenordnung* of 1528, and the *Hamburger Kirchenordnung* of 1529. See Schwiebert, *Luther and His Times,* pp. 677-678.
[9] The book was entitled *Oeconomia Christiana.* See the text of Luther's preface in WA 30[II], 60-63.

for what good does all that do if there are no learned, wise, and godly people? I shall say nothing of the temporal gain and eternal reward that accrue to you before God and the world, how in this way your child will be even better fed than by raising him in the shameful, despicable, hoggish way you had intended. But I shall deal with this matter more fully another time in a separate book, God willing, in which I shall really go after the shameful, despicable, damnable parents who are no parents at all but despicable hogs and venomous beasts, devouring their own young."

Luther carried out this intention in the summer of 1530. With the diet in session at Augsburg, a period of enforced idleness at the Coburg Castle was imposed upon him. It was there that the sermon began to grow on him.[10] He was already hard at work on the manuscript by July 5 when he remarked both candidly and humorously concerning it in a letter to Melanchthon, "I was never so verbose as I seem now to have become; perhaps it is the garrulity of old age."[11] The manuscript was completed by the middle of July and sent to Nickel Schirlentz in Wittenberg for printing. On August 15 Luther wrote to his wife that if the printing still was not even begun she should "take the manuscript from Schirlentz and give it to George Rau."[12] By August 20 Luther had received at least a portion of the printed text from Schirlentz.[13] On August 24 and 25 he sent his only copies of the full text to Melanchthon and to Lazarus Spengler,[14] to whom—on the suggestion of Veit Dietrich—he had dedicated the work.

Whereas Luther's 1524 appeal *To the Councilmen of All Cities in Germany that They Establish and Maintain Christian Schools* argues for the establishment and maintenance of schools, the present treatise argues for the use of the schools thus established. Together these treatises give a clear conception of Luther's ideas on education.

---

[10] Cf. below, p. 121.
[11] *WA*, Br 5, 439. At the time Luther was approaching his forty-seventh birthday.
[12] *WA*, Br 5, 546.
[13] *WA*, Br 5, 552.
[14] *WA*, Br 5, 560-561.

The translation by Charles M. Jacobs was based on *CL* 4, 144-178. Our revision was made on the basis of the text, *Eine Predigt, dass man Kinder zur Schulen halten solle,* in *WA* 30ᴨ, 517-588.

C. M. J.
R. C. S.

A SERMON ON KEEPING
CHILDREN IN SCHOOL

To the honorable and wise Lazarus Spengler, syndic of the city of Nürnberg, my especially dear sir and friend: grace and peace in Christ, our dear Lord and faithful Savior. Amen.

Honorable and wise dear sir and friend, I have composed a sermon[1] to the preachers here and there to the effect that they should exhort people to keep their children in school. It has grown on me to the point where it has almost become a book, though I have forcibly restrained myself to keep it from becoming altogether too big, so full and rich is this subject. I hope that it may do much good, and I have published it under your name[2] with the sole thought that it may thereby receive greater attention and, if worthy, be read by the people of your city. For although I can well believe that your preachers will be diligent enough in this matter—they have been endowed by God with great gifts—to understand and promote the cause without any need, thank God, of admonition or instruction on my part, still it does no harm to have many people agreeing with one another and opposing the devil the more strongly.

For it is hardly likely that in so great a city with such a large population the devil will not try his arts and tempt some to despise the word of God and the schools. This is true particularly because there are many things there (especially trade and commerce)[3] to turn the children away from the schools to the service

---

[1] On the sense in which many of Luther's treatises were and may be called "sermons," see *LW* 51, xiii.

[2] On the suggestion of Veit Dietrich the treatise was dedicated to Lazarus Spengler (1479-1534), a leader of the reform movement in Nürnberg. Spengler first met Luther in 1518 when the Reformer was on his way to Augsburg. His published defense of Luther's doctrines in 1519 led to his being included in the bull *Exsurge, Domine*. Spengler represented Nürnberg at the diets of Worms (1521) and Augsburg (1530). Cf. *SW* 3, 7, n. 7.

[3] On the evils Luther saw in trade and commerce, see his 1524 treatise on *Trade and Usury*. *SW* 3, 71-150.

of Mammon. The devil undoubtedly thinks that if he could cause the word and the schools to be despised in Nürnberg, his purpose would in large measure have been accomplished, for he would have set an example that would carry great weight throughout Germany and be a real blow to the schools in all the other cities. For Nürnberg truly shines throughout all Germany like a sun among the moon and stars, and what is practiced there has a powerful influence on other cities.

But praise and thanks be to God, who has long since countered the devil's intentions and put it into the heart of an honorable and wise council to found and equip such a splendid and excellent school.[4] They spare no expense to find and secure the very finest people, so that it can be said without boasting that no university, not even Paris, has ever been so well provided with teachers. (Everyone who has ever studied in the universities as I have will have to say the same thing, for I know what they are and have learned what they teach; I still know them only too well!)[5] This is indeed a magnificent achievement. It is a credit to your distinguished city and a fitting honor to its widely renowned council. For in this they have shown generous Christian consideration of their subjects, contributing faithfully to their eternal salvation as well as to their temporal well-being and honor. God will assuredly strengthen such a work with ever increasing blessings and grace, though the devil must strive against it for a while since he cannot be happy when so excellent a tabernacle is built to the Lord in this sun.[6] He must assemble clouds and mist and dust, trying in every way to keep such glory from shining too far, or at least to dim its splendor. What else could he do?

For this reason I hope that the citizens will recognize the fidelity and love of their lords, and help earnestly to support this work by keeping their children in school, since without cost to themselves their children are so bountifully and diligently cared

---

[4] In 1526 the city of Nürnberg had Melanchthon dedicate its new school among whose teachers were such distinguished scholars as Joachim Camerarius in Greek and Eobanus Hess in poetry. Cf. WA 30^II, 518, nn. 1 and 2.
[5] See Luther's critique of university curriculum in *To the Christian Nobility* (1520). SW 1, 336-343.
[6] Cf. Mark 9:5-7.

for, with everything provided for them. This will happen only if the preachers get behind it. If they do not urge it, the common man will be beset and overcome by thoughts from Satan, and he will easily give up. Other responsibilities will keep him from thinking the matter through, as a preacher can, and seeing how important it is, how much is to be gained—or lost. This is why we must be patient with such people as long as they are not obdurate or wicked. I know Nürnberg well enough to know that it has, thank God, many fine Christian people who gladly and from the heart do that which they ought to do, provided they know or are told what that is. They have a reputation for this, not only with me, but far and wide, and there is no reason to fear that they will fail in this matter. There may, of course, be an occasional idolater, a servant of Mammon [Matt. 6:24], who will take his son out of school and say, "If my son can read and do arithmetic, that is enough; we now have books in German, etc." Such a person sets a bad example for all the other good citizens. With the best of intentions they imitate him, thinking it the right and only thing to do, without realizing the harm involved. The preachers can be of real help in such a situation.

Every community, and especially a great city, must have in it many kinds of people besides merchants. It must have people who can do more than simply add, subtract, and read German. German books are made primarily for the common man to read at home. But for preaching, governing, and administering justice, in both spiritual and worldly estates, all the learning and languages in the world are too little, to say nothing of German alone. This is particularly true in our day, when we have to do with more than just the neighbor next door. But these idolaters forget all about this matter of governing. They do not realize that without preachers and rulers they could not serve their idol a single hour.

Of course, I can understand that among so many people there may be an occasional idolater who would not care whether honor or shame came to the noble city of Nürnberg, so long as he got his two cents.[7] But then people ought not to care about such a

---

[7] Pfennig.

despicable idolater either. They should ignore him and his bad example, figuring that the greater the reputation that comes to our city when our honorable council deals so earnestly and faithfully with the schools, the greater would be the shame if our citizens were to despise the faithfulness and generosity of our lords, and the greater would be their share in the bad example and offense we give to all the other cities, which could then say, "Well, if that is what they do at Nürnberg—and they have fine people there too—why should we do any better?"

You idolater, if you will give no thought to what God and honor require, and will think of nothing but Mammon, God will find others who will give thought. Thank God that I have known several cities where although the council cared nothing for the word or the schools, there were many upright citizens who by daily persistence compelled the council to found schools and churches. God willing, therefore, Nürnberg will not come to such a sorry pass on account of you that the citizens follow your example and despise the schools which an honorable council has faithfully established and maintained at such great cost, while in much smaller cities the citizens have secured schools for themselves, even though their councils thought nothing of them.

But here I am talking on and on, dear sir and friend. I suppose it lies in the nature of these things that there has to be much talk about them. In this case what I have been trying to do is to speak in your name to all the citizens of your city, and I hope that you will not take offense. Indeed, I hope you will continue to push and promote this matter, as you have been doing anyway all along. God knows, I mean it well.

May Christ our Lord strengthen and preserve you until that day when, God willing, we shall see each other with joy and in another form. For he who has given you so much to do for his work and word as you have done till now, will also go on and complete it all. To him be praise and thanks forever. Amen.

Your obedient servant,
MARTIN LUTHER

From Martin Luther to all my dear friends, pastors, and preachers who truly love Christ: Grace and peace in Christ Jesus, our Lord.

My dear sirs and friends, you see with your own eyes how that wretch of a Satan is now attacking us on all sides with force and guile. He is afflicting us in every way he can to destroy the holy gospel and the kingdom of God, or, if he cannot destroy them, at least to hinder them at every turn and prevent them from moving ahead and gaining the upper hand. Among his wiles, one of the very greatest, if not the greatest of all, is this—he deludes and deceives the common people so that they are not willing to keep their children in school or expose them to instruction. He puts into their minds the dastardly notion that because monkery, nunning, and priestcraft no longer hold out the hope they once did,[8] there is therefore no more need for study and for learned men, that instead we need to give thought only to how to make a living and get rich.

This seems to me to be a real masterpiece of the devil's art. He sees that in our time he cannot do what he would like to do; therefore, he intends to have his own way with our offspring. Before our very eyes he is preparing them so that they will learn nothing and know nothing. Then when we are dead, he will have before him a naked, bare, defenseless people with whom he can do as he pleases. For if the Scriptures and learning disappear, what will remain in the German lands but a disorderly and wild crowd of Tartars or Turks,[9] indeed, a pigsty and mob of wild beasts? But he does not let them see this now. He blinds them in masterly fashion so that, when it comes to the point where their own experience compels them to see it, he can laugh up his sleeve at all their weeping and wailing. However much they may wish it, they will then be able to do nothing about it; they will have to admit that things have gone on too long. Then they will be will-

---

[8] Luther makes the same point at the beginning of his 1524 appeal *To the Councilmen of All Cities in Germany That They Establish and Maintain Christian Schools. SW* 3, 40-41.

[9] On the menace to Europe posed by the Turks, see *On War Against the Turk* (1529), above, pp. 3-53.

ing to give a hundred gulden for half a scholar, where today they will not give ten gulden for two whole scholars.

And it will serve them right. Because they are not now willing to support and keep the honest, upright, virtuous schoolmasters and teachers offered them by God to raise their children in the fear of God, and in virtue, knowledge, learning, and honor by dint of hard work, diligence, and industry, and at small cost and expense, they will get in their place incompetent substitutes,[10] ignorant louts such as they have had before, who at great cost and expense will teach the children nothing but how to be utter asses, and beyond that will dishonor men's wives and daughters and maidservants, taking over their homes and property, as has happened before. This will be the reward of the great and shameful ingratitude into which the devil is so craftily leading them.

Now because it is a part of our duty as pastors to be on guard against these and other wicked wiles, we must not shut our eyes to a matter of such great importance. On the contrary, we must advise, exhort, admonish, and nag with all our power and diligence and care, so that the common people may not let themselves be so pitifully deceived and deluded by the devil. Therefore let each of us look to himself and remember his office so that we do not go to sleep in this matter and allow the devil to become god and lord. For if we are silent about this and shut our eyes to it, and the young people are neglected and our offspring become Tartars or wild beasts, it will be the fault of our own silence and snoring, and we shall have to render full account for it.

I know very well that many of you, without any exhortation on my part, are acting in this matter and would do so anyway better than I can advise. Moreover, I have already published a message to the councilmen in the cities.[11] Nevertheless, because some may have forgotten this, or would be more persistent as a

---

[10] Luther specifically refers—with customary contempt—to the *Locaten*, classroom helpers and overseers who lacked the educational requirements for a full-fledged teaching position of their own, and *Bachanten*, upperclassmen assigned to supervise classes in some lower grades during the absence of a teacher. *MA*³ 5, 439, n. 265, l. 8.

[11] See Luther's 1524 treatise *To the Councilmen of All Cities in Germany That They Establish and Maintain Christian Schools. SW* 3, 31-70.

result of my example, I have sent you this sermon of mine, which I have preached more than once to our people. From it you can observe that I am working faithfully with you in this matter, and that we are doing our best everywhere and are guiltless before God in the conduct of our office. The case is truly in our hands because we see that even the clergy, who are called spiritual, appear to take the view that they would let all schools, discipline, and teaching go by the board, or themselves even help to destroy them, simply because they cannot have their own way with them as they once did. This too is the devil's doing, through them. God help us. Amen.

A Sermon on
Keeping Children in School

Dear friends, the common people appear to be quite indifferent to the matter of maintaining the schools. I see them withdrawing their children from instruction and turning them to the making of a living and to caring for their bellies. Besides, they either will not or cannot think what a horrible and un-Christian business this is and what great and murderous harm they are doing everywhere in so serving the devil. For this reason I have undertaken to give you this exhortation, on the chance that there may be some who still have at least a modicum of belief that there is a God in heaven and a hell prepared for unbelievers, and that by this exhortation they might be led to change their minds. (Actually, almost everybody is acting as if there were neither a God in heaven nor a devil in hell.) I propose, therefore, to take up the question of what is at stake in this matter in the way of gains and losses, first those that are spiritual or eternal, and then those that are temporal or worldly.

I hope, indeed, that believers, those who want to be called Christians, know very well that the spiritual estate[12] has been established and instituted by God, not with gold or silver but with the precious blood and bitter death of his only Son, our Lord Jesus Christ [I Pet. 1:18-19]. From his wounds indeed flow the sacra-

---

[12] *Der geistliche stand* refers to the clergy or the ministry.

ments[13] (they used to depict this on broadsides).[14] He paid dearly that men might everywhere have this office of preaching, baptizing, loosing, binding, giving the sacrament, comforting, warning, and exhorting with God's word, and whatever else belongs to the pastoral office. For this office not only helps to further and sustain this temporal life and all the worldly estates, but it also gives eternal life and delivers from sin and death, which is its proper and chief work. Indeed, it is only because of the spiritual estate that the world stands and abides at all; if it were not for this estate, the world would long since have gone down to destruction.

I am not thinking, however, of the spiritual estate as we know it today in the monastic houses and the foundations with their celibate way of life, for it has long since fallen from its glorious beginning and is now nothing more than an estate founded by worldly wisdom for the sake of getting money and revenues.[15] There is nothing spiritual about it except that the clergy are not married (they do not need marriage for they have something else in its place); except for this, everything about it is merely external, temporal, perishable pomp. They give no heed to God's word and the office of preaching—and where the word is not in use the clergy must be bad.

The estate I am thinking of is rather one which has the office of preaching and the service of the word and sacraments and which imparts the Spirit and salvation, blessings that cannot be attained by any amount of pomp and pageantry. It includes the work of pastors, teachers, preachers, lectors, priests (whom men call chaplains), sacristans, schoolmasters, and whatever other work belongs to these offices and persons. This estate the Scriptures

---

[13] In his *Lectures on the Gospel According to St. John* (Tractate 120), Augustine comments on how the Evangelist in John 19:34 significantly says that Jesus' side was not pierced "but 'opened,' that thereby, in a sense, the gate of life might be thrown open, from whence have flowed forth the sacraments of the Church." *PNF*[1] 7, 434.

[14] Some of the one-page tracts or book pages frequently illustrated with woodcuts which Luther may have had in mind are suggested in *WA* 30[II], 527, n. 1, and *MA*[3] 5, 439, n. 266, l. 21. The scene of Christ's blood dripping from his wounded feet into a sacramental chalice at the base of the cross was a common theme in art.

[15] *Zins;* for an explanation of this term, see *SW* 3, 75-78.

highly exalt and praise. St. Paul calls them God's stewards and servants [I Cor. 4:1]; bishops [Acts 20:28]; doctors, prophets [I Cor. 12:28]; also God's ambassadors to reconcile the world to God, II Corinthians 6 [5:20]. Joel calls them saviors.[16] In Psalm 68[17] David calls them kings and princes. Haggai [1:13] calls them angels,[18] and Malachi [2:7] says, "The lips of the priest keep the law, for he is an angel of the Lord of hosts." Christ himself gives them the same name, not only in Matthew 11 [:10] where he calls John the Baptist an angel, but also throughout the entire book of the Revelation to John.

This is why the ancients greatly avoided this estate.[19] Because of its great dignity and honor they so dreaded to take the office upon them that they had to be forced and driven into it. To be sure, there have been many since then who have praised this estate highly, though more because of the saying of mass than because of the preaching. This praise and glorification grew to the point where the office and estate of the priesthood (that is, of the sacrificing of the mass) was placed above Mary and the angels because the angels and Mary could not say mass but a priest could. A new priest and his first mass were glorious, and blessed was the woman who bore a priest [Luke 11:27]. The office of preaching the word, however, which is the highest and chief of all, was not regarded so highly. In a word, a priest was a man who could say mass, even though he could not preach a word and was an unlearned ass. Such in fact is the spiritual estate even to the present day.

Now if it is true and certain that God himself has established

---

[16] *Heilande,* which may have reference to Joel 2:23, where Luther followed the Vulgate (*doctorem justitiae*) in his 1545 German Bible by rendering the ambiguous Hebrew *hammoreh litsedaqah* ("early rain for your vindication" in the RSV) as *Lehrer zur gerechtigkeit* ("teachers unto righteousness"). *WA,* DB 11[II], 221.

[17] Luther consistently understood the "kings" of Ps. 68:12 as "the host of those who bore the tidings" in the preceding verse. In his German Psalter he translated the verse, "The kings of the armies are friends with one another," and in a marginal gloss he noted that "[kings] are the apostles whose teaching is in harmony." *WA,* DB 10[I], 312-313.

[18] Etymologically the term "angel" means "messenger." The Hebrew *malak* is translated both ways in German as in English.

[19] Gregory of Nazianzus is an example. Cf. *WA* 30[II], 529, n. 1.

and instituted the spiritual estate with his own blood and death, we may conclude that he will have it highly honored. He will not allow it to be destroyed or to die out, but will have it maintained until the Last Day. For the gospel and the church must abide until the Last Day, as Christ says in the last chapter of Matthew [28:20], "Lo, I am with you always, to the close of the age." But by whom then shall it be maintained? Oxen and horses, dogs and swine will not do it; neither will wood and stone. We men shall have to do it, for this office is not committed to oxen and horses, but to us men. But where shall we get men for it except from those who have children? If you will not raise your child for this office, and the next man will not, and so on, and no fathers or mothers will give their children to our God for this work, what will become of the spiritual office and estate? The old men now in the office will not live forever. They are dying off every day and there are no others to take their place. What will God finally say to this at last? Do you think he will be pleased that we shamefully despise his office, divinely instituted to his honor and glory and for our salvation and won at such a price—so despise it that we ungratefully let it fade away and die?

He has not given you your children and the means to support them simply so that you may do with them as you please, or train them just to get ahead in the world. You have been earnestly commanded to raise them for God's service, or be completely rooted out—you, your children, and everything else, in which case everything you have done for them is condemned, as the first commandment says, "I visit the iniquities of the fathers upon the children to the third and fourth generation of those who hate me" [Exod. 20:5]. But how will you raise them for God's service if the office of preaching and the spiritual estate have fallen into oblivion?

And it is your fault. You could have done something about it. You could have helped to maintain them if you had allowed your child to study. And where it is possible for you to do this but you fail to do so, where your child has the ability and the desire to learn but you stand in the way, then you—and mark this well!—you are guilty of the harm that is done when the spiritual estate disappears and neither God nor God's word remains in the world.

To the extent that you are able you are bringing about its demise. You refuse to give one child—and would do the same if all the children in the world were yours. So far as you are concerned, the serving of God can just die out altogether.

It does not help your case to say, "My neighbor keeps his son in school, so I don't need to." For your neighbor can say the same thing, and so can all the neighbors. Meanwhile, where is God to get people for his spiritual office? You have someone you could give, but you refuse—as does your neighbor. The office simply goes down to destruction so far as you are concerned. But because you allow the office instituted and established by your God and so dearly won to go to ruin, because you are so horribly ungrateful as to let it be destroyed, you yourself will be accursed. You will have nothing but shame and misery both for yourself and for your children, or be so tormented in other ways that both you and they will be damned, not only here on earth but eternally in hell. This will happen so that you may learn that your children are not so wholly yours that you need give nothing of them to God. He too will have what is rightfully his—and they are more his than yours!

And lest you think I am being too severe with you in this matter, I shall lay before you a partial statement of the gains and losses you are effecting—for who can recount them all?—such that you will have to admit yourself that you indeed belong to the devil and rightly deserve to be damned eternally in hell if you acquiesce in this fault and do not amend your ways. On the other hand, you may rejoice and be glad from the heart if you find that you have been chosen by God to devote your means and labor to raising a son who will be a good Christian pastor, preacher, or schoolmaster, and thereby to raise for God a special servant, yes (as was said above), an angel of God, a true bishop before God, a savior of many people, a king and prince in the kingdom of Christ, a teacher of God's people, a light of the world—indeed, who can recount all the distinction and honor that a good and faithful pastor has in the eyes of God? There is no dearer treasure, no nobler thing on earth or in this life than a good and faithful pastor and preacher.

Just think, whatever good is accomplished by the preaching office and the care of souls is assuredly accomplished by your own son as he faithfully performs this office. For example, each day through him many souls are taught, converted, baptized, and brought to Christ and saved, and redeemed from sin, death, hell, and the devil. Through him they come to everlasting righteousness, to everlasting life and heaven, so that Daniel [12:3] says well that "those who teach others shall shine like the brightness of the firmament; and those who turn many to righteousness shall be like the stars for ever and ever." Because God's word and office, when it proceeds aright, must without ceasing do great things and work actual miracles, so your son must without ceasing do great miracles before God, such as raising the dead, driving out devils, making the blind to see, the deaf to hear, the lepers clean, and the dumb to speak [Matt. 11:5]. Though these things may not happen bodily, they do happen spiritually in the soul, where the miracles are even greater, as Christ says in John 14 [:12], "He who believes in me will also do the works that I do; and greater works than these will he do." If the single believer can accomplish these things working independently with individuals, how much more will the preacher accomplish working publicly with the whole company of people? It is not the man, though, that does it. It is his office, ordained by God for this purpose. That is what does it— that and the word of God which he teaches. He is only the instrument through which it is accomplished.

Now if he accomplishes such great things spiritually, it follows that he also does bodily works and miracles, or at least gets them started. For how does it happen that Christians will rise from the dead at the Last Day, and that all the deaf, blind, lame, and other sufferers of bodily ills must lay aside their ailments? How does it happen that their bodies will not only become healthy, sound, and beautiful, but even shine as bright and fair as the sun [Matt. 13:43], as Christ says? Is it not because here on earth, through God's word, they have been converted, become believers, been baptized and incorporated into Christ? Thus Paul says in Romans 8 [:11] that God will raise up our mortal bodies because of his Spirit which dwells in us. Now how are men helped to this faith and to this beginning of the resurrection of the body except through the office of preaching and the word of God, the office your son performs? Is this not an immeasurably greater and more glorious work and miracle than if he were in a bodily or temporal way to raise the dead again to this life, or help the blind, deaf, dumb, and leprous here in the world, in this transitory life?

If you were sure that your son would accomplish even one of these works in a single human being, that he would make one blind man to see or one dead man to rise, snatch one soul from the devil or rescue one person from hell, or whatever else it might be, ought you not with utmost joy devote all your means to train him for this office and work? Ought you not leap for joy that with your money you are privileged to accomplish something so great in the sight of God? For what are all the foundations and monastic houses of our day with their self-appointed works in comparison with one such pastor, preacher, or schoolmaster? To be sure, they were originally founded long ago by pious kings and lords precisely for this precious work of training such preachers and pastors. But now, sad to say, the devil has brought them to such a wretched state that they have become death traps, the very ramparts of hell, to the hurt and detriment of the church.

Now just look at what your son does—not just one of these works but many, indeed, all of them! And he does them every day. Best of all, he does them in the sight of God who, as we have said, looks upon them so highly and regards them as precious, even though men may not recognize or esteem them. Indeed, if all the world should call your son a heretic, deceiver, liar, and rebel, so much the better. That is a good sign that he is an upright man, like his Lord Christ. For Christ too had to be a rebel, a murderer, and a deceiver, and be condemned and crucified with the murderers. What would it matter to me as a preacher if the world were to call me a devil, so long as I knew that God calls me his angel? Let the world call me a deceiver as much as it pleases, so long as God calls me his faithful servant and steward, the angels call me their comrade, the saints call me their brother, believers call me their father, souls in anguish call me their savior, the ignorant call me their light, and God adds, "Yes, it is so," and the angels and all creatures join in. Ah! How prettily the world, with the devil, has deceived me with its slanders and scoffing! How the dear world has hurt me and gained at my expense!

I have spoken so far about the works and miracles which your son does for individual souls, helping them against sin, death, and the devil. Beyond that, however, he does great and mighty works for the world. He informs and instructs the various estates on how they are to conduct themselves outwardly in their several offices and estates, so that they may do what is right in the sight of God. Every day he can comfort and advise those who are troubled, compose difficulties, relieve troubled consciences, help maintain peace and settle and remove differences, and countless other works of this kind. For a preacher confirms, strengthens, and helps to sustain authority of every kind, and temporal peace generally. He checks the rebellious; teaches obedience, morals, discipline, and honor; instructs fathers, mothers, children, and servants in their duties; in a word, he gives direction to all the temporal estates and offices. Of all the good things a pastor does these are, to be sure, the least. Yet they are so high and noble that the wisest of all the heathen have never known or understood them, much less been able to do them. Indeed, even to the present day no jurist, university, foundation, or monastery knows these works, and they are not taught either in canon law or secular law. For there is no one who regards these offices as God's great gifts, his gracious ordinances. It is only the word of God and the preachers that praise and honor them so highly.

Therefore, to tell the truth, peace, the greatest of earthly goods, in which all other temporal goods are comprised, is really a fruit of true preaching. For where the preaching is right, there war and discord and bloodshed do not come; but where the preaching is not right, it is no wonder that there is war, or at least constant unrest and the desire to fight and to shed blood. We can see even now how the sophists[20] can do nothing but cry bloody murder and spit fire. They shed the blood of innocent priests who get mar-

---

[20] *Sophisten* was Luther's favorite term for the scholastic theologians. Cf., for example, SW 3, 55; 2, 272.

ried,[21] even though the pope and their own canon law in punishing such clerical marriages at most merely suspend the priest from office,[22] without so much as touching his person or property or Christian honor, much less condemning him to hell or regarding him as a heretic. This the jurists and everybody else will have to concede. It was even made a law at the Diet of Nürnberg.[23] But these blind bloodhounds have given up preaching and betaken themselves to lies, and this is why they cannot desist from murder. The devil their god does the same; according to John 8 [:44] he was "from the beginning" and still is "a liar and a murderer."

A true pastor thus contributes to the well-being of men in body and soul, in property and honor. But beyond that see how he also serves God and what glorious worship and sacrifice he renders. For

---

[21] George Winkler, a priest in Halle, was tried by an ecclesiastical court at Aschaffenburg for administering the sacrament in both kinds. It was known at the time that he was also guilty of having taken a wife. He was released by Archbishop Albrecht of Mainz, but on the way home was set upon and murdered on April 23, 1527. Suspicion fixed upon the archbishop as the instigator of the crime. Cf. Luther's letter of sympathy *To the Christians at Halle* in *WA* 23, 402-430; cf. especially his reference to the archbishop on pp. 407-408.

[22] See Luther's *Articles Against the Whole Synagogue of Satan and All the Gates of Hell*, written about the same time, in which the last ten of forty articles deal specifically with the marriage of priests, the punishment of which is said to be limited to suspension from office (*WA* 30^{II}, 423-424). See also the second of Luther's nine articles prepared about the same time for his colleagues at the Diet of Augsburg, in which he makes the same point (*WA*, Br 5, 431). The applicable canon laws (listed above, p. 72, n. 19) had recently been brought to Luther's attention again in a little book written by Lazarus Spengler in which Spengler recounts the instances in which canon law conformed to God's word (the book was published early in 1530 with a preface by Luther; the text of Luther's preface is given in *WA* 30^{II}, 219). In 1089 Pope Urban II had prescribed removal from priesthood and benefice for any member of the higher orders of clergy who took a wife; see *Decreti Magistri Gratiani Prima Pars*, dist. XXXII, C. X. *CIC* 1, 120.

[23] The Diet of Nürnberg rejected papal demands for strict enforcement of the Edict of Worms, declaring specifically on March 6, 1523, "Since the extant laws of the temporal authority provide no punishment for priests who marry or for monks and nuns who leave the cloister none shall be inflicted beyond that stipulated in the canon law. The spiritual authorities are not to be hindered but protected in their enforcement of such penalties as may apply, the loss of rights, privileges, benefices, etc. Where such priests, monks, and nuns offend in other ways, however, they are to be punished according to established law." A. Kluckhohn and A. Wrede (eds.), *Deutsche Reichstagsakten unter Karl V* (4 vols.; Gotha: Perthes, 1893-1905), III, 451; and *St. L.* 15, 2145.

by his work and word there are maintained in this world the kingdom of God, the name and honor and glory of God, the true knowledge of God, the right faith and understanding of Christ, the fruits of the suffering and blood and death of Christ, the gifts and works and power of the Holy Spirit, the true and saving use of baptism and the sacrament, the right and pure teaching of the gospel, the right way of disciplining and crucifying the body, and much more. Who could ever adequately praise any one of these things? And what more can still be said? How much he accomplishes by battling against the devil, the wisdom of this world, and the imaginations of the flesh; how many victories he wins; how he puts down error and prevents heresy. For he must strive and fight against the gates of hell [Matt. 16:18] and overcome the devil. This too is not his own doing; it is accomplished by his office and his word. These are the innumerable and unspeakable works and miracles of the preaching office. In a word, if we would praise God to the uttermost, we must praise his word and preaching; for the office and the word are his.

Now even if you were a king, you should not think you are too good to give your son and to train him for this office and work, even at the cost of all that you have. Is not the money and the labor you expend on such a son so highly honored, so gloriously blessed, so profitably invested that it counts in God's sight as better than any kingdom or empire? A man ought to be willing to crawl on his hands and knees to the ends of the earth to be able to invest his money so gloriously well. Yet right there in your own house and on your own lap you have that in which you can make such an investment. Shame, shame, and shame again upon our blind and despicable ingratitude that we should fail to see what extraordinary service we could render to God, indeed, how distinguished we could be in his sight with just a little application of effort and our own money and property.

The sophists accuse us Lutherans of not teaching good works. Isn't that great! They know so much about good works! Are not these things we have been speaking of good works? What are all the works of the foundations and monasteries compared with these glorious miracles? They are like the cawing of jackdaws and ravens, though not as good. For the daws at least like to caw; they do so gladly. But the sophists take no pleasure in their croaking; they caw reluctantly, like the hoopoes and owls. Now if it was formerly the custom to think highly of new priests and their first masses, and if fathers and mothers and all their friends were glad that they had raised a son to be an idle, lazy, useless mass-priest or glutton[24] who puts God to shame with his blasphemous sacrifice of the mass and his wasted prayers and scandalizes and defrauds the world with his unchaste life, how much more should you rejoice if you have raised a son for this office of preaching in which you are sure that he serves God so gloriously, helps men so generously, and smites the devil in such knightly fashion? You have made of your son such a true and excellent sacrifice to God that the very angels must look upon it as a splendid miracle.

You ought also to know the harm that you are doing if you take the opposite course. If God has given you a child who has the ability and the talent for this office, and you do not train him for it but look only to the belly and to temporal livelihood, then take the list of things mentioned above and run over the good works and miracles noted there, and see what a pious hypocrite and unproductive weed[25] you are. For so far as it is up to you, you are depriving God of an angel, a servant, a king and prince in his kingdom; a savior and comforter of men in matters that pertain to body and soul, property and honor; a captain and a knight to fight against the devil. Thus you are making a place for the devil and advancing his kingdom so that he brings more souls into sin, death, and hell every day and keeps them there, and wins victories everywhere; the world remains in heresy, error, contention, war, and strife, and gets worse every day; the kingdom of God goes down to destruction, along with Christian faith, the fruits of the suffering and blood of Christ, the work of the Holy Spirit, the gospel, and all worship of God; and all devil worship and unbelief get the upper hand. All of this need not have happened and could have been prevented, things could even have been improved, if your son had been trained for this work and entered it.

---

[24] *Messpfaffen oder fresspfaffen.*
[25] *Kreutlein;* cf. WA 33, 162, n. 1.

Suppose God were to address you on your deathbed, or at the Last Judgment, and say, "I was hungry, thirsty, a stranger, naked, sick, imprisoned, and you rendered me no service. For in that you have not done it to people on earth and to my kingdom or gospel, but have helped put them down and allowed men's souls to perish, you have done this to me. For you could have helped. I gave you children and material means for this purpose, but you wantonly allowed me and my kingdom and the souls of men to suffer want and pine away—and you thereby served the devil and his kingdom instead of me and my kingdom. Well, let him be your reward. Go with him now into the abyss of hell. You have not helped to build but to weaken and destroy my kingdom in heaven and on earth; but you have helped the devil to build and increase his hell. Live, therefore, in the house that you have built!"[26]

How do you think you will stand then? You will not be tainted by little drops of sin, but inundated by whole cloudbursts of it—you who now give no heed but just go nonchalantly along as if you were doing well in keeping your child from an education. But then you will have to say that you are justly condemned to the abyss of hell as one of the most odious and vile men who ever lived. Indeed, if you were to consider these things even now, while you are living, you would be truly horrified at yourself. For no conscience can bear to be found guilty of even one of the things that have been mentioned; how much less can it bear it if suddenly all these things, more than can be numbered, fall on it all at once? Your heart will then have to cry out that your sins are more than the leaves and the grass, indeed, greater than heaven and earth; and you will say with Manasseh, king of Judah, "The sins I have committed are more in number than the sands of the sea; my transgressions are multiplied" [Pr. of Man. 9]. Even the law of nature tells you that he who is able to prevent injury but does not do so is guilty of the injury because he certainly desired and willed it and would have inflicted it himself if he had had occasion or opportunity. These people, therefore, are certainly no better than the devil himself because they are so angry with both God and the world that they help to ruin both heaven and earth, and serve the devil faithfully. In a word, if we cannot adequately

---

[26] Cf. Matt. 25:42-43.

denounce the devil, neither can we adequately denounce these people who hinder the work and office of God, for they are the devil's servants.

In saying this I do not mean to insist that every man must train his child for this office, for it is not necessary that all boys become pastors, preachers, and schoolmasters. It is well to know that the children of lords and other important people are not to be used for this work, for the world also needs heirs, people without whom the temporal authority would go to pieces.[27] I am speaking of the common people, who used to have their children educated for the sake of the livings and benefices but now keep them away from learning to earn a livelihood. Even though they need no heirs they keep their children out of school, regardless of whether the children have the ability and talent for these offices and could serve God in them without privation or hindrance. Boys of such ability ought to be kept at their studies, especially sons of the poor, for all the endowments and revenues of the foundations and monasteries are earmarked for this purpose. In addition, though, other boys as well ought to study, even those of lesser ability. They ought at least to read, write, and understand Latin, for we need not only highly learned doctors and masters of Holy Scripture but also ordinary pastors who will teach the gospel and the catechism[28] to the young and ignorant, and baptize and administer the sacrament. That they may be incapable of doing battle with heretics is unimportant. For a good building we need not only hewn facings but also backing stone. In like manner we must also have sacristans and other persons who serve and help in relation to the office of preaching and the word of God.

Even though a boy who has studied Latin should afterward learn a trade and become a craftsman, he still stands as a ready reserve in case he should be needed as a pastor or in some other service of the word. Neither will such knowledge hurt his capacity to earn a living. On the contrary, he can rule his house all the better because of it, and besides, he is prepared for the office

---

[27] The temporal government which Luther knew best was the hereditary feudal lordship.

[28] I.e., the Ten Commandments, the Creed, and the Lord's Prayer.

of preacher or pastor if he should be needed there. It is especially easy in our day to train persons for teaching the gospel and the catechism because not only Holy Scripture but also knowledge of all kinds is so abundant [29] what with so many books, so much reading, and, thank God, so much preaching that one can learn more now in three years than was formerly possible in twenty. Even women[30] and children can now learn from German books and sermons more about God and Christ—I am telling the truth!—than all the universities, foundations, monasteries, the whole papacy, and all the world used to know. Ordinary pastors, however, must be able to use Latin. They cannot do without it any more than scholars can do without Greek and Hebrew,[31] as St. Augustine says[32] and canon law even prescribes.[33]

But you say, "Suppose things turn out badly and my son becomes a heretic or a knave? As they say, 'The learned are daft.' "[34] Well, you have to take that chance. Your diligence and labor will not be lost. God will have regard for your faithful service and count it as though it had turned out well. You simply have to

---

[29] By this time Luther had already published his translation of the New Testament (1522), the Pentateuch (1523), Joshua—Esther (1524), Job—Song of Solomon (1524), Jonah (1526), Habakkuk (1526), Zechariah (1527), and Isaiah (1528). Complete Bibles translated by Protestants had appeared in German in 1529 at Zurich and Worms. Cf. *LW* 35, 227-229.

[30] For instances of Luther's repeated advocacy of education for girls, see *SW* 1, 341-342; *SW* 2, 351 and 364-365; *SW* 3, 36, n. 12; *SW* 3, 60-63.

[31] See Luther's fuller argument for the study of classical languages in *To the Councilmen of All Cities in Germany* (1524). *SW* 3, 48-69.

[32] "Men who know the Latin language . . . have need of two others in order to understand the Sacred Scriptures. These are Hebrew and Greek, by which they may turn back to the originals if the infinite variances of Latin translators cause any uncertainty." *Christian Instruction* (*De doctrina Christiana*), Book II, chap. 11. *FC* 4, 73; cf. *MPL* 34, 42.

[33] The eleventh canon of the Council of Vienna (1312) directed that in the interests of scriptural exposition and world mission Greek, Hebrew, Syriac, and Arabic be taught at the principal universities of Paris, Oxford, Bologna, and Salamanca, as well as in the curriculum for curial studies—though not general studies—at Rome. Berthold Altaner, "Die Durchführung des Vienner Konzilsbeschlusses über die Errichtung von Lehrstühlen für orientalische Sprachen," *Zeitschrift für Kirchengeschichte*, LII (1933), 227. The text of the decree as altered and promulgated by Pope John XXII on October 25, 1317, is given in *Clementis papae V. Constitutiones*, lib. v, tit. I: *De Magistris*, C. I. *CIC* 2, 1179.

[34] *Die Gelehrten, die Verkehrten.*

take the chance as you would in any other occupation for which you might train your son. How was it with the good Abraham? His son Ishmael did not turn out well; neither did Isaac's son Esau, or Adam's son Cain. Should Abraham therefore have given up training his son Isaac, or Isaac his son Jacob, or Adam his son Abel for the service of God? How many bad kings and people there were among the holy and chosen nation of Israel! With their heresies and idolatries they brought on all kinds of trouble and killed all the prophets. Ought Levi the priest to have let the whole nation go on that account, and no longer trained anyone for the service of God? How many bad priests and Levites were there among the tribe of Levi, which God himself had chosen for the priesthood? How many people has God on earth who misuse all his kindness and all his creatures? Ought he on that account to desist from his kindness and let no man live? Ought he cease to do good?

Moreover, that you may not worry too much about where your son's living will come from if he gives himself to learning and to this divine office and ministry, God has not left you or forgotten you in this matter either, so you need not worry or lament. He has promised through St. Paul in I Corinthians 9 [:14] that "those who proclaim the gospel should get their living by the gospel"; and Christ himself says in Matthew, "The laborer deserves his wages; eat and drink what they have."[35] Under the Old Testament, so that his office of preaching might not perish, God chose and took the whole tribe of Levi, that is to say, one-twelfth of the whole nation of Israel, and gave them the tithe from the whole nation, besides the first-fruits, all kinds of sacrifices, their own cities and pasture lands,[36] fields and meadows, cattle, and all that goes with them. Under the New Testament, see how in former times emperors, kings, princes, and lords gave to this office rich possessions, which the foundations and monasteries now have in more abundance than even the kings and princes themselves. God will not and cannot fail those who serve him faithfully, for he has bound himself by the promise given in Hebrews 13 [:5], "I will never fail you nor forsake you."

---

[35] Luke 10:7-8; cf. Matt. 10:10.
[36] *Vorstedte;* cf. Num. 35:1-8.

Think, too, how many parishes, pulpits, schools, and sacristan-ships there are. Most of them are sufficiently provided for,[37] and vacancies are occurring every day. What does this mean except that God has provided kitchen and cellar for your son in advance? His living is ready for him before he needs it; he does not have to scrape it together for himself. When I was a young student I heard it said that in Saxony there were (if I remember rightly) about eighteen hundred parishes.[38] If that is true, and every parish required at least two persons, a pastor and a sacristan (except that in the cities there are preachers, chaplains, assistants, schoolmasters, and helpers), then in this one principality about four thousand educated persons are needed, of whom about one-third die off every ten years. I would wager that in half of Germany today there are not four thousand pupils in the schools. Now I estimate that there are scarcely eight hundred pastors in Saxony; how many will that make for the whole of Germany? I would like to know where we are going to get pastors, schoolmasters, and sacristans three years from now. If we do nothing about this, and if the princes especially do not try to see that the boys' schools and the universities are properly maintained, there will be such a scarcity of men that we shall have to give three or four cities to one pastor and ten villages to one chaplain, if indeed we can get even that many men.

The universities at Erfurt, Leipzig, and elsewhere, as well as the boys' schools here and there, are so deserted that it is distressing to behold; little Wittenberg now does better than any of them.[39] The foundations and the monasteries, I suppose, will also

---

[37] I.e., by endowments.

[38] If the reference is limited to Electoral Saxony, Luther's memory—or information—could be wrong, for the 1528-1529 visitation disclosed that apart from Wittenberg there were only one hundred forty-five pastoral positions. C. A. H. Burckhardt, *Geschichte der sächsischen Kirchen- und Schulvisitation* (Leipzig: Grunow, 1879), pp. 30-36.

[39] When Luther entered Erfurt as a student in 1501 the enrolment was about two thousand (Schwiebert, *Luther and His Times*, p. 131), but by 1529 the enrolment had dropped to twenty. The enrolment at Leipzig dropped from a five-year average (1526-1530) of 175 to 93 in 1529. Enrolment at the University of Wittenberg, which was founded later than the universities of Erfurt and Leipzig and had been a much smaller school, dropped from 250 to 173 in the same period. Cf. WA 30[II], 550, n. 2.

feel the scarcity, but who cares?[40] Cocky as they are, they are going to have to come down off their high horse[41] and accept—even recruit—people into their chapters whom they formerly would not have looked at twice. Let your boy go on with his studying, therefore, and do not worry; perhaps if the world lasts a while longer[42] and God gives the princes and the cities grace to act, the property of the foundations and monasteries will be restored to the use for which is was originally intended. And why worry anyway about the belly? Christ stands there and says, "Do not be anxious about what you shall eat and drink. Your heavenly Father knows well that you need all this. Seek first the kingdom of God and his righteousness, and all these things shall be yours as well" [Matt 6:31-33]. If anyone does not believe Christ, he can just go on worrying—and die of hunger too!

Although it is true that a few years ago many pastors did suffer great want, and many still do, that is due to the convulsions[43] of our time: people are so wicked, ungrateful, and avaricious that they even persecute the gospel. By this God is trying us to see whether we are upright and sincere. We must think of our time as being like that of the martyrs, for then, too, godly teachers suffered great want and poverty, as Paul himself boasts [II Cor. 11:27], and Christ also prophesied in Matthew 9 [:15], "When the bridegroom is taken away from them, then they will fast." This is the fasting that is true to the gospel. Then, too, whenever God's word has come forth hard times have almost always come with it. In the days of Abraham [Gen. 12:10], Isaac [Gen. 26:1], Jacob and Joseph [Gen. 41:56], Elijah [I Kings 18:2], and

---

[40] *Solten sie ein gut jar haben.* Thiele, *Luthers Sprichwörtersammlung,* No. 186; *WA,* Br 5, 370, n. 7; Jacob and Wilhelm Grimm, *Deutsches Wörterbuch,* IV², 2232-2233.

[41] *Nicht so hoch hinaus singen, wie sie es angefangen haben* refers to the embarrassment of the vocalist whose voice must crack before he finishes because he foolishly pitched his song too high at the beginning. Cf. Thiele, *Luthers Sprichwörtersammlung,* No. 159.

[42] Luther anticipated the imminent coming of the Last Day. Cf. SW 3, 318, n. 3.

[43] The term *paroxysmus,* which recurs in several of Luther's letters during this same period, has reference to that part of Greek drama which is called the epitasis, the extreme or climactic stage which follows the protasis and precedes the catastrophe. *WA,* Br 5, 459, n. 3; cf. also 417, n. 9; 471, n. 1; 473, n. 4.

Elisha [II Kings 4:38] there was, besides the great light of truth, cruel famine. And in the beginning of the gospel there was a great famine throughout the world [Acts 11:28]. This of course has to be blamed on the dear gospel and the word of God, not on the world's former misdeeds and present obstinate ingratitude! Thus did the Jews blame all their misery on the teaching of Jeremiah [Jer. 44:16 ff.]. And the Romans, when they were overthrown by the Goths, knew nothing to blame it on except the fact that they had become Christians. Indeed, it was to refute this charge that St. Augustine wrote a great book, *De civitate dei.*[44]

Well, they can say what they please—the world is still the world. As in those days the liars were exposed and destroyed, so shall it be today, so that Christ and his word may yet abide. He sits exalted and immovable, as it is written, "The Lord said to my Lord, 'Sit at my right hand' " [Ps. 110:1]. There he sits; if anyone is wicked and wants to pull him down, let him do so! But as long as he remains seated there, we too shall remain; and that is that! To put it in a word, your son can easily get as good a living from the preaching office as from a trade—unless of course you are thinking of great wealth and of making your son a great lord in the eyes of the world, such as the bishops and canons are. If that is what you are after, then what I am saying does not concern you. I am speaking here only to believers, who respect and honor the preaching office above all riches as being, next to God himself, the greatest treasure ever given to men. I would have them know how great is the service they can and ought to render God in this matter, as men who would rather participate in this work, even though the material rewards be few, than to have this world's goods and be without this work. Such men will recognize that the soul is more than the belly, and that though the belly be surfeited it will still be obliged to leave everything else behind at death. But those who seek [true] riches will take all their goods with them, leaving nothing behind; that is for sure!

So much then for the first part of this sermon, a brief and cur-

---

[44] Augustine wrote *The City of God* in the years 413-426 to refute the pagan charge that the fall of Rome to Alaric in 410 was due to the abolition of heathen worship. Cf. SW 2, 300, n. 68.

sory account of the spiritual gains and losses which accrue from the maintenance and neglect of the schools.

The second part will deal with the temporal or worldly gains and losses. And in the first place, it is true that the office of temporal authority cannot at all be compared with the spiritual office of preaching, as St. Paul calls it [Col. 1:25]; for it is not purchased at so dear a price as the preaching office, by the blood and dying of the Son of God. Neither can it therefore do such great wonders and works as the preaching office. For all the works of this estate belong only to this temporal, transient life. They protect body, wife, child, house, property, and honor, and whatever else pertains to the needs of this life. As far, then, as eternal life surpasses this temporal life, so far does the preaching office exceed the temporal office—even as the substance surpasses the shadow. For worldly lordship is an image, shadow, or figure of the lordship of Christ. The office of preaching—where it exists as God ordained it—brings and bestows eternal righteousness, eternal peace, and eternal life; thus does St. Paul extol it in II Corinthians 4. Worldly government, on the other hand, preserves peace, justice, and life, which is temporal and transient.

Nevertheless, worldly government is a glorious ordinance and splendid gift of God, who has instituted and established it and will have it maintained as something men cannot do without. If there were no worldly government, one man could not stand before another; each would necessarily devour the other, as irrational beasts devour one another. Therefore as it is the function and honor of the office of preaching to make sinners saints, dead men live, damned men saved, and the devil's children God's children, so it is the function and honor of worldly government to make men out of wild beasts and to prevent men from becoming wild beasts. It protects a man's body so that no one may slay it; it protects a man's wife so that no one may seize and defile her; it protects a man's child, his daughter or son, so that no one may carry them away and steal them; it protects a man's house so that no one may break in and wreck things; it protects a man's fields and cattle and all his goods so that no one may attack, steal, plunder, or damage them. Protection of this sort does not exist among the beasts, and if it were not for worldly government there would be none of it among men either; they would surely cease to be men and become mere beasts. Do you not think that if the birds and beasts were to see the worldly government that exists among men they would say—if they could speak—"O men! Compared with us you are not men but gods! What security you have, both you and your possessions, while among us no one is safe from another regarding life, home, or food supply, not even for a moment! Shame upon your ingratitude—you do not even see what a splendid life the God of us all has given you compared with us beasts!"

It is certain, then, that temporal authority is a creation and ordinance of God, and that for us men in this life it is a necessary office and estate which we can no more dispense with than we can dispense with life itself, since without such an office this life cannot continue. That being true, it is easy to understand that God has not commanded and instituted it only to have it destroyed. On the contrary, he wills to have it maintained, as is clearly stated by Paul in Romans 13 [:4], and in I Peter 3 [2:13-14], to protect those who do good and to punish those who do wrong. Now who will maintain this office except us men to whom God has committed it, and who truly need it? The wild beasts will not maintain it, nor will wood and stone. And what men are capable of doing it? Certainly not those who would rule only with the fist, as many now think to do. For if men were to rule solely by the fist, the end result would surely be a bestial kind of existence: whoever could get the better of another would simply toss him into the discard pile. We have enough examples before our eyes to see what the fist can accomplish apart from wisdom or reason.

This is why Solomon says in Proverbs 8 [:14-15] that wisdom, not force, must rule. He speaks of wisdom this way, "I, Wisdom, have counsel and sound wisdom. I have insight, I have strength. By me kings reign, and rulers decree what is just." And Ecclesiastes 10 [9:18, 16] says, "Wisdom is better than weapons of war"; and again, "Wisdom is better than might." All experience proves this and in all the histories we find that force, without reason or wisdom, has never once accomplished anything. Indeed, even murderers and tyrants, if they are not clever enough to adopt for themselves and among themselves some kind of laws and regulations to control and limit the power of the fist (even though these be equally wicked), will not be able to continue; they will fall out among themselves and perish by each other's hand. Briefly, then, it is not the law of the fist but the law of the head that must rule—not force but wisdom or reason—among the wicked as well as among the good.

Accordingly, since the government in our German lands is supposed to be guided by the imperial law of Rome,[45] and this law is our government's wisdom and reason, given it by God, it follows that this government cannot be maintained and will inevitably perish unless this law is maintained. Now who will maintain it? Not fist and weapons; heads and books must do it. Men must learn and know the law and wisdom of our worldly government. It is a fine thing, to be sure, if an emperor, prince, or lord is by nature so wise and able that he can instinctively hit upon what is right, as could two men I knew, Duke Frederick of Saxony[46] and Sir Fabian von Feilitzsch,[47] to speak only of men no longer living. Such rulers are pretty rare birds.[48] It would be dangerous to make an example of them because others may not have this power by nature. In ruling it is better to stick to the written law, which carries with it greater recognition and respect and obviates the need for special gifts or charisms.

Thus the jurists and scholars in this worldly kingdom are the persons who preserve this law, and thereby maintain the worldly kingdom. And just as in the kingdom of Christ, a pious theologian

---

[45] Cf. SW 1, 339, n. 219, and SW 3, 315, n. 29.

[46] Known as Frederick the Wise, the elector of Saxony (1486-1525) remained officially neutral toward the Reformation faith until shortly before his death; he was, however, staunch in his defense of the person of his subject Luther and of Luther's rights to freedom and justice. Cf. LW 36, 227, n. 91.

[47] Fabian von Feilitzsch, counselor at the court of Frederick the Wise, was a defender of the Reformation. He died shortly after Luther had dedicated his 1520 Defense of All the Articles of Martin Luther Condemned by the Recent Bull of Pope Leo X (Assertio omnium articulorum M. Lutheri per bullam Leonis X novissimam damnatorum) to him; though the treatise had not yet actually been published at the time of Fabian's death, Luther refused to change the dedication, in which he refers to Fabian as a Christian "layman," one of "the new generation of clergy" (WA 7, 95). Cf. MA³ 5, 441, n. 280, l. 38. See also Luther's later laudatory reference to both Fabian and Frederick in his 1534 Exposition of Psalm 101 (LW 13, 157).

[48] Cf. Wander (ed.), Deutsches Sprichwörter Lexikon, IV, "Vogel," No. 599.

and sincere preacher is called an angel of God, a savior, prophet, priest, servant, and teacher (as has been said above),[49] so a pious jurist and true scholar can be called, in the worldly kingdom of the emperor, a prophet, priest, angel, and savior. Again, just as in the kingdom of Christ a heretic or false preacher is a devil, thief, murderer, and blasphemer, so in the emperor's house or realm a false and faithless jurist is a thief and a knave, a traitor, scoundrel, and devil for the whole empire. Now when I speak of the jurists I mean not only the doctors but the whole profession, including chancellors, clerks, judges, lawyers, notaries, and all who have to do with the legal side of government; also the counselors at the court, for they too work with law and exercise the function of jurists. And just as the word "counselors" is not far from the word "traitors,"[50] so the deeds of the two are not far apart. These bigwigs[51] sometimes "counsel" their lords so effectively that no traitor could do a better job of deceiving them.

You see, then, how much good a pious jurist or legal scholar can produce. Indeed, who can recount it all? For any ordinance and work of God constantly produces so much great fruit that it cannot be counted or comprehended. For one thing, the jurist with his law book (by God's ordinance) maintains and helps to further the whole worldly government—emperor, princes, lords, cities, land, and people, as was said above; for all these must be preserved by wisdom and law. But who is able adequately to praise this work alone? By it you receive protection of life and limb against neighbors, enemies, and murderers. Then, too, you have peace and tranquillity for your wife, daughter, son, house and home, servants, money, property, lands, and everything that you have. For all of this is comprehended in, encompassed by, and hedged about with law. What a great thing this is can never be fully told in any book; for who can adequately describe what an unspeakable blessing peace is, and how much it both gives and saves even in a single year?

---

[49] Cf. above, pp. 128-129.
[50] An untranslatable play on the words *Rethe* and *Verrether* which has to do with the "advisor" who gives "bad advice."
[51] *Die grossen Hansen;* cf. SW 2, 300, n. 69; SW 2, 311; and LW 36, 246.

All these great works your son can do. He can become such a useful person if you will hold him to it and see him educated. And you can have a share in all this, and invest your money that profitably. It ought to be a matter of great honor and satisfaction for you to see your son an angel in the empire and an apostle of the emperor, a cornerstone and bulwark of temporal peace on earth, knowing for a certainty that God so regards it and that it really is true. For although such works do not make men righteous before God or save them, nevertheless, it is a joy and comfort to know that these works please God so very much—and the more so when such a man is a believer and is in the kingdom of Christ, for he thereby thanks God for his benefits, bringing to him the finest thankoffering, the highest service.

You would have to be a gross, ungrateful clod, worthy of being numbered among the beasts, if you should see that your son could become a man to help the emperor preserve his empire, sword, and crown; to help the prince rule his principality; to counsel and help cities and lands; to help protect so many men's bodies, wives, children, property, and honor—and yet would not risk enough on it to let him study and come to such a position. Tell me, what do all the foundations and monasteries do that can begin to compare with this? I would take the work of a faithful, pious jurist and clerk over the holiness of all the priests, monks, and nuns, even the very best. And if these great and good works do not move you, then you ought at least to be moved by the honor and good pleasure of God, knowing that by this means you thank him so gloriously and render him such great service, as has been said. We shamefully despise God when we begrudge our children this glorious and divine work and stick them instead in the exclusive service of the belly and of avarice, having them learn nothing but how to make a living, like hogs wallowing forever with their noses in the dunghill, and never training them for so worthy an estate and office. Certainly we must either be crazy, or without love for our children.

But listen still further. Suppose God means to have his way with you and demands your son for this office! For you surely owe it to your God to help maintain this estate if you can. Yet it cannot possibly be maintained unless people keep their children studying and in school; there is no doubt about that. Indeed, there is need in this office for abler people than are needed in the office of preaching, so it is necessary to get the best boys for this work; for in the preaching office Christ does the whole thing, by his Spirit, but in the worldly kingdom men must act on the basis of reason—wherein the laws also have their origin—for God has subjected temporal rule and all of physical life to reason (Genesis 2 [:15]). He has not sent the Holy Spirit from heaven for this purpose. This is why to govern temporally is harder, because conscience cannot rule; one must act, so to speak, in the dark.

Now if you have a son who is able to learn, and you are in a position to keep him at it, but do not do so, if you go your way without even asking what is to become of worldly government and law and peace, then you are doing all in your power to oppose worldly authority, like the Turks, indeed, like the devil himself. For you are taking from empire, principality, land, and city, a savior, comforter, cornerstone, helper, and deliverer. So far as you are concerned the emperor will lose both sword and crown, the land will lose its peace and tranquillity. And you will be the one who is responsible when—as much as it is up to you—no man will have any security for his person, his wife, child, house, home, and property. You blithely hack them all to pieces,[52] causing men to become mere beasts who devour one another in the end. This is what you assuredly are doing, especially if you knowingly keep your son from this wholesome estate for the sake of the belly. Now are you not a fine, useful man in the world? Every day you use the empire and its peace, and in return, by way of thanks, you rob it of your son and stick him in the service of avarice. In so doing you are striving as best you can to see to it that there will be no one to help maintain the empire and law and peace, and that everything will go down to destruction, even though it is only by this empire that you have and maintain your own life and limb, property and honor.

What do you think you have deserved by this? Are you even worthy to dwell among men? But what will God, who has given you child and property with which to serve him by keeping your

---

[52] *Opffert . . . auff die fleissch banck;* see WA 18, 94, n. 1; SW 3, 188-189; and WA 17¹, 369, n. 1.

son in his service, say to this? Is it not a service of God to help maintain his ordinance of worldly government? Now you neglect that service as if it were no concern of yours, or as if you were more free than other men and did not have to serve God but could do just as you please with your child and property, even though God and both his worldly and spiritual kingdoms should fall into the abyss. Yet at the same time you want to make daily use of the empire's protection, peace, and law; you want to have the preaching office and the word of God ready for you and at your service. You want God to serve you free of charge both with preaching and with worldly government, so that you can just calmly turn your child away from him and teach him to serve Mammon alone. Do you not think that God will some day pronounce a benediction[58] over your avarice and concern for the belly such as will destroy you both here and hereafter together with your child and all that you have? Dear fellow, is not your heart terrified at this abominable abomination—your idolatry, despising of God, and ingratitude, your destruction of both these institutions and ordinances of God, yes, the injury and ruin that you inflict on all men? Well, I have told you and warned you. Now you see to it! Having heard both the gains and the losses that are involved, you can just do as you please: God will reward you accordingly.

I shall say nothing here about the pure pleasure a man gets from having studied, even though he never holds an office of any kind, how at home by himself he can read all kinds of things, talk and associate with educated people, and travel and do business in foreign lands; for there are perhaps very few people who are moved by this pleasure. But since you are so bent on the pursuit of Mammon and the making of a living, see what great wealth God has put at the disposal of the schools and scholars so you will have no need to despise learning and knowledge for fear of attendant poverty. Just look, emperors and kings must have chancellors and clerks, counselors, jurists, and scholars. There is no prince who does not need to have chancellors, jurists, counselors, scholars, and clerks. All the counts, lords, cities, and castles must have syndics, city

---

[58] *Benedicite;* "benediction" is used in the sense of saying the last word or bringing to an end. *MA*[a] 5, 441, n. 283, l. 38.

clerks, and other scholars. There is not a nobleman who does not need a clerk. And to speak also about men of ordinary education, there are also the miners, merchants, and businessmen. Just count the number of kings, princes, counts, lords, cities, villages, and other places. Where shall we be getting the educated men three years from now, when here and there the shortage is already beginning to be felt? I really believe that kings will have to become jurists, princes chancellors, counts and lords clerks, and mayors sextons.

Unless something is done about this quickly, we must all become Tartars or Turks—either that or incompetent schoolmasters[54] will become doctors and counselors at court. This is why I hold that there was never a better time to study than right now, not only because knowledge is so abundant and cheap, but also because of the great wealth and honor to which it leads. Those who study in these times will become so highly prized that two princes and three cities will yet compete for one scholar. For whether you look above you or about you, you find that in these next ten years countless offices will be waiting for educated men; yet very few are being trained to fill them. And not only has God appointed such great wealth for schools and scholars, but it is honorable and divine wealth, earned in a divine and honorable estate by many glorious, good, and useful works which please God and are a service to him. The avaricious man, on the contrary, earns his wealth with spite (even though his works are not godless and sinful) and with hateful works, about which he cannot have a glad conscience or say that they are a service of God. For my part, I would rather earn ten gulden by a work that is a service of God, than a thousand gulden by a work that is not a service of God but serves only self and Mammon.

Beyond this honestly gotten wealth, there is also the honor which accrues to them. Chancellors, city clerks, jurists, and the people who hold such offices also sit in high places and help to counsel and rule, as has been said. They are in actual fact lords upon earth, even though they are not that by virtue of their own person, birth, or estate. For Daniel says that he had to do the king's

---

[54] *Locat oder bacchant;* cf. above, p. 126, n. 10.

work [Dan. 8:27]. And that is true: a chancellor must go about the work or business of the emperor, king, or prince; a city clerk must do the work of the council or the town. And they do this with God and with honor, to which God adds blessing, good fortune, and success. And when an emperor, king, or prince is not at war but simply goes about the business of ruling in accordance with the law, what is he but a clerk or jurist, so far as his works are concerned? He is dealing with the law, and that is the work of a clerk or jurist. And who actually rules the land and people in time of peace? Is it the fighting men or their officers? I think it is the pen that does it. And what is the avaricious man doing in the meantime with his Mammon? He attains no such honor but defiles himself all the while with his rust-eaten money [Matt. 6:19].

The Emperor Justinian[55] himself declares, "*Oportet maiestatem imperatoriam non solum armis decoratam, sed etiam legibus armatam esse.*"[56] "Imperial majesty," he says, "must not only be adorned with arms, but also armed with laws." See how marvelously this emperor turns his words about. He calls the laws his armor and weapons, and he calls arms his decoration and adornment; he would make his clerks his knights and fighting men. That is excellently put, for the laws are indeed the true armor and weapons which maintain and protect land and people, yes, the empire and worldly government itself, as has been sufficiently stated above.[57] Wisdom is indeed better than might [Eccles. 9:16], and pious jurists are the true knights who defend the emperor and the princes. One could cite many passages to this effect from the poets and the histories, but it would take too long. Solomon himself declares in Ecclesiastes 9 [:15] that a poor man by his wisdom delivered a city from a mighty king.

By this I do not mean to say that we should despise, reject, or do away with soldiers, fighting men, and those whose business is war. They too, when they are obedient, help with their fist to main-

---

[55] Justinian, emperor of Rome from 527 to 565, was the great consolidator of Roman law, which was the basis of the German legal system of Luther's day.

[56] The sentence which Luther here quotes almost verbatim is the opening sentence in the Preface to the *Institutes of Justinian* in the *Corpus iuris civilis*.

[57] Cf. above, pp. 145-148.

tain peace and protect things. Every occupation has its own honor before God, as well as its own requirements and duties. For once, though, I must also praise my own—because my neighbors have fallen out with it and there is danger that it may come into contempt—even as St. Paul also praises his office so constantly that some think he goes too far and is guilty of pride. Whoever wants to praise and honor soldiers and the fist will find ground enough for doing so, as I myself have—I hope—intentionally and extensively done in another little book.[58] For the jurists and pen-pushers do not please me either when they so praise themselves as to despise or ridicule other estates, as if they were everything and no one else in the world amounted to anything except themselves, as the "shavelings" and indeed the whole papacy used to do. All the estates and works of God are to be praised as highly as they can be, and none despised in favor of another. For it is written, *"Confessio et magnificentia opus ejus,"* "What God does is fine and beautiful";[59] and again in Psalm 104 [:31], "God rejoices in his works." These ideas ought to be impressed particularly by the preachers on the people from their youth up, by schoolmasters on their boys, and by parents on their children, so that they may learn well what estates and offices are God's, ordained by God, so that once they know this they will not despise or ridicule or speak evil of any one of them but hold them all in high regard and honor. That will both please God and serve the cause of peace and unity, for God is a great lord and has many kinds of servants.

We find, too, some swaggers who fancy that the name "writer" is scarcely worth either speaking or hearing. Well, do not let that worry you! Remember that these guys occasionally have to have their little jokes; well, let them enjoy it! You are still a writer in the eyes of God and of the world. However much they swagger, you notice that they still pay the highest honor to the quill:[60] they put it atop their hats and helmets as if to confess by this very act that the pen is indeed supreme in the world and that without it they

---

[58] Cf. *Whether Soldiers, Too, Can Be Saved* (1526). SW 3, 427-477.
[59] Luther's free rendering of Ps. 111:3 does not correspond either to that of his earlier or later Psalters (*WA*, DB 10[I], 478-479) or to the Latin of the Vulgate he had just quoted.
[60] *Fedder*, which means both "pen" and "plume."

would be neither equipped for battle nor able to walk about in peace, much less swagger so boldly. For they too must make use of the peace which the emperor's preachers and teachers, that is, the jurists, teach and maintain. You see, therefore, that they put the tool of our trade, the good quill, on top, and rightly so, whereas the tool of their trade, the sword, they gird about their loins where it hangs handsomely for their purposes. On their heads it would not be becoming—there the feather must wave. So if they have sinned against you, this is their penance, and you should forgive them.

But that brings me to this, that there are many bigwigs for whom the business of writing is a hateful thing because they do not know, or do not consider, that it is a divine office and work. They do not see how necessary and useful it is to the world. And if they were to see it—God forbid!—their knowledge in any case would have come too late. This, therefore, is what you ought to do. Pay no attention whatever to them. Instead just look around at such fine, pious noblemen as Count George of Wertheim,[61] Baron Hans von Schwarzenberg,[62] Baron George von Frundsberg[63] and others

---

[61] Count George of Wertheim (1509-1530) was a member of the special commission appointed at the 1521 Diet of Worms to plead with Luther privately and in a friendly way to recant his writings (WA 7, 843-844); Luther names the count himself in reporting the affair on May 3 to Albrecht of Mansfeld (WA, Br 2, 322). The following year the count introduced the Reformation into his territory by asking for and receiving from Luther an evangelical pastor for Wertheim (WA, Br 2, 597, n. 14; EA 4, 3, n. 11). In a Table Talk of 1531 Luther refers to Count George of Wertheim and Duke George of Saxony as illustrative of the "righteous man who perishes" and the "wicked who prolongs his life" spoken of in Eccles. 7:15 (WA, TR 1, No. 44).

[62] Baron Johann von Schwarzenberg II (1463-1528), friend of Albrecht Dürer and patron of learning, learned a good deal of what he knew about Luther from his cousin and close friend George of Wertheim, whose daughter married his son Friedrich in 1527. Working in close collaboration with Hans von der Planitz, von Schwarzenberg—who served as imperial chamberlain in 1521—was instrumental in blocking papal efforts to implement the Edict of Worms at the Diet of Nürnberg (cf. SW 2, 340, n. 15). As the chief deputy of Margrave George of Brandenburg/Ansbach he was instrumental in establishing the 1528 church visitation which consolidated the Reformation in that area (cf. below, p. 333, n. 374). See the popularized biography by Johannes von Wagner, *Johann von Schwarzenberg* (Berlin: Bücherfreunde, 1893), especially pp. 268-269, 293, 298-301, 364, 368; cf. also Willy Scheel, *Johann Freiherr von Schwarzenberg* (Berlin, 1905).

[63] Baron George von Frundsberg (1473-1527) was a professional soldier who instilled pride of calling into the foot soldiers of the emperor, demonstrated

of blessed memory—not to mention those who are still living—and take comfort in such men. Remember that for the sake of one man, Lot, God honored the whole land of Zoar [Gen. 19:21]; for the sake of a single Naaman, the whole land of Syria [II Kings 5:1]; for the sake of one Joseph, the whole kingdom of Egypt [Gen. 41:53-56]. Why should not you also, for the sake of the many honest noblemen whom you doubtless know, honor all the nobility? And when you look at them you must think that there is not a bad one left. How could it be that untimely fruit should not fall from the fair tree of the nobility, and that some of the fruit should not be wormy and warty? That does not necessarily make the tree bad and worthy of condemnation.

This is how the children of God look at things, for God himself spares the whole human race for the sake of one man, whose name is Jesus Christ; if he were to look at men alone, he would have nothing but wrath. The preaching office and temporal authority of course cannot do this; they cannot ignore or shut their eyes to evil. For they must punish the bad, one with the word, the other with the sword. In saying all this I am speaking to individual Christians. I am saying that they should learn to distinguish between God's work and men's wickedness. In all of God's offices and estates there are many wicked men; but the estate itself is good and remains good no matter how much men misuse it. You find many bad women, many false servants, many unfaithful maids, many despicable officials and counselors; nevertheless, the estates themselves—wife, servant, maid, and all the offices—are God's institution, work, and ordinance. The sun remains good, even though everyone misuses it, one to rob and another to kill, one to do this kind of evil and another that. And who could do any evil at all if he did not have the sun to light his way, the earth to hold him up and nourish him, and the air to keep him alive—in short, God himself to sustain him? The saying remains true, "The whole creation was subjected to futility, but not of its own will" (Romans 8 [:20]).

---

the decisive role of the infantry in military conflict, and insisted on subordination of the military to the duly constituted authority. His acquaintance with both the peasant soldiers and the ruling nobility enabled him to mediate in the Peasants' War and bring peace in Swabia and Salzburg. *Allgemeine Deutsche Biographie*, VIII, 154-159.

Some think that the office of writer is simple and easy, that real work is to ride in armor and suffer heat, cold, dust, thirst, and other discomforts. It is always the same old story: no one sees where the other's shoe pinches; everyone is aware only of his own problems and thinks the other fellow has it made. True, it would be hard for me to ride in armor; but on the other hand I would like to see the horseman who could sit still with me all day and look into a book— even if he had nothing else to care for, write, think about, or read. Ask a chancery clerk, preacher, or speaker whether writing and speaking is work! Ask a schoolmaster whether teaching and training boys is work! The pen is light, that is true. Also there is no tool of any of the trades that is easier to get than the writer's tool, for all that is needed is a goose feather, and you can pick them up anywhere free of charge. But in writing, the best part of the body (which is the head) and the noblest of the members (which is the tongue) and the highest faculty (which is speech) must lay hold and work as never before. In other occupations it is only the fist or the foot or the back or some other such member that has to work; and while they are at it they can sing and jest, which the writer cannot do. They say of writing that "it only takes three fingers to do it"; but the whole body and soul work at it too.

I have heard it said of the noble and illustrious Emperor Maximilian[64] that when bigwigs complained that he was using so many writers in ambassadorial and other posts he said, "What else can I do? You cannot be used, so I have to take writers." He is also supposed to have said, "I can make knights, but I cannot make doctors." I once heard too of a fine nobleman who said, "I want my son to study. It takes no great skill to hang two legs over a horse and become a knight; in fact I taught him that myself already." That was very well put. Once more, I do not want this to be understood as though I were speaking against the knight's estate, or any other estate. I am speaking only against the worthless swaggerers who despise all learning and wisdom and can boast of nothing except wearing armor and hanging two legs over a horse—though they are seldom actually called upon to do so and in return have enough of comfort, pleasure, joy, honor, and wealth the whole year

---

[64] Maximilian I, Holy Roman emperor, 1493-1519. Cf. SW 3, 448, n. 39.

round.[65] It is true, as they say, that learning is easy to carry but armor is heavy. On the other hand, though, the wearing of armor is easily learned whereas learning is not easily acquired, nor easily put to work.

To bring all this talk to an end, we ought thus to know that God is a wonderful lord. His business is to take beggars and make them into lords, even as he makes all things out of nothing, and no one can disrupt him in his work. He has the whole world sing of him, in Psalm 113 [:5-8], "Who is like the Lord our God, who is seated on high, who looks far down? He raises the poor from the dust and lifts the needy from the dunghill, to make them sit with princes, with the princes of his people." Look about you at the courts of all the kings and princes, at the cities and the parishes, and see whether they do not contain many striking examples of the fulfilment of this psalm. There you will find jurists, doctors, counselors, writers, preachers, who for the most part were poor and who have certainly all attended school, and who by means of the pen have risen to where they are lords—as this psalm says—helping to rule land and people like princes. It is not God's will that only those who are born kings, princes, lords, and nobles should exercise rule and lordship. He wills to have his beggars among them also, lest they think it is nobility of birth rather than God alone who makes lords and rulers. They say, and rightly so, that the pope too was once a schoolboy. Therefore do not look down on the fellows who come to your door saying, "Bread for the love of God,"[66] and singing for a morsel of bread; you are listening—as this psalm says—to the singing of great princes and lords. I too was such a crumb collector[67] once, begging from door to door, especially in my beloved city of Eisenach[68]—though afterward my dear father lovingly and faith-

---

[65] Cf. *Whether Soldiers, Too, Can Be Saved.* SW 3, 468-470.

[66] *Panem propter deum* was the beggars' cry, the reference to God being intended as an appeal to greater generosity. *MA*³ 5, 442, n. 289, l. 16.

[67] *Partekenhengst,* derived from the Greek term for something given over or laid out (*paratheke*), had reference to the students who sang and begged for alms. *WA* 33¹, 4, n. 7, l. 22.

[68] Prior to enrolling at the University of Erfurt in the spring of 1501, Luther spent four years in the St. George's school at Eisenach, where he enjoyed participating in the popular practice of student begging though he was by no means financially dependent upon it. Schwiebert, *op. cit.,* p. 127.

fully kept me at the University of Erfurt, by his sweat and labor helping me to get where I am.[69] Nevertheless, I was once a crumb collector, and I have come so far by means of the writer's pen—as this psalm says—that I would not now change places with the Turkish sultan, giving up my knowledge for all his wealth. Indeed, I would not exchange what I know for all the wealth in the world multiplied many times over. Without any doubt, I should not have come to this if I had not gone to school and become a writer.

Therefore go ahead and have your son study. And even if he has to beg bread for a time, you are nonetheless giving to our Lord God a fine bit of wood out of which he can carve you a lord. That is the way it will always be: your son and my son,[70] that is, the children of the common people, will necessarily rule the world, both in the spiritual and the worldly estates, as this psalm testifies. For the rich misers cannot and will not do it; they are the Carthusians[71] and monks of Mammon, whom they must serve day and night. The born princes and lords cannot do it alone; they are particularly unable to understand anything at all about the spiritual office. Thus both kinds of government on earth must remain with the middle class of common people, and with their children.

And do not be disturbed because the run-of-the-mill miser despises learning so deeply and says, "Ha, if my son can read and write German and do arithmetic, that is enough. I am going to make a businessman of him." They will soon quiet down; indeed, they will be glad to dig twenty feet into the earth with their bare hands just to get a scholar. For if preaching and law should fail, the businessman will not be a businessman for long; that I know for sure. We theologians and jurists must remain or everything else will go down to destruction with us; you can be sure of that. When the theologians disappear, God's word also disappears, and nothing but heathen remain, indeed, nothing but devils. When the jurists dis-

---

[69] Luther takes the occasion to pay this tribute to his father, who had died less than two months earlier, on May 29, 1530. WA 30[II], 576, n. 3.

[70] At the time Luther had only one son. Of the three sons ultimately born to him and Katherine, Hans (born 1526) became a lawyer and was later employed in the chancellory of Weimar; Martin (born 1531) studied theology but never occupied a pulpit; and Paul (born 1533) became an able and distinguished physician.

[71] I.e., the strictest devotees.

appear, then the law disappears, and peace with it; and nothing but robbery, murder, crime, and violence remain, indeed, nothing but wild beasts. But what earnings and profits the businessman will have when peace is gone, I shall let his ledger tell him; and what good all his wealth will do him when the preaching comes to an end, his conscience will surely show him.

It is particularly vexing that such rude and un-Christian words are spoken by those who claim to be so thoroughly evangelical. They know how to get the better of everyone and shout down their opponents with Scripture; yet they begrudge both God and their own children the honor and the material means that would be involved in sending their children to school so that they may attain to these splendid and divine estates in which they can serve God and the world—even though it is plain and certain that these estates are established and ready and well provided with both wealth and honor. On the contrary, they turn their children away from such estates and push them instead into the service of Mammon, in which nothing is plain and certain, which is necessarily full of danger to body, soul, and property, and which in addition is not and cannot be a service of God.

At this point I should also mention how many educated men are needed in the fields of medicine[72] and the other liberal arts.[73] Of these two needs one could write a huge book and preach for half a year. Where are the preachers, jurists, and physicians to come from, if grammar[74] and other rhetorical arts are not taught? For such teaching is the spring from which they all must flow. To speak of this here in detail would be too big a task. I will simply say briefly that a diligent and upright schoolmaster or teacher, or anyone who faithfully trains and teaches boys, can never be ade-

---

[72] *Ertzney*, i.e., all the medical arts, which in the academic situation of Luther's time were taught in connection with the liberal arts. *MA*[3] 5, 443, n. 290, l. 28.
[73] The liberal arts were traditionally seven in number. Grammar, rhetoric, and dialectic comprised the trivium of the medieval elementary schools; music, arithmetic, geometry, and astronomy comprised the quadrivium of the secondary schools. SW 3, 48, n. 15.
[74] *Grammatica*, the most basic of the liberal arts, included much more than we understand by the term "grammar" today. It included, besides the rules of a language, such things as vocabulary, reading, interpretation, and creative expression. SW 3, 68, n. 56.

quately rewarded or repaid with any amount of money, as even the heathen Aristotle says.[75] Nevertheless, this work is as shamefully despised among us as if it amounted to nothing at all. And still we call ourselves Christians! If I could leave the preaching office and my other duties, or had to do so, there is no other office I would rather have than that of schoolmaster or teacher of boys; for I know that next to that of preaching, this is the best, greatest, and most useful office there is. Indeed, I scarcely know which of the two is the better. For it is hard to make old dogs obedient and old rascals pious; yet that is the work at which the preacher must labor, and often in vain. Young saplings are more easily bent and trained, even though some may break in the process. It surely has to be one of the supreme virtues on earth faithfully to train other people's children; for there are very few people, in fact almost none, who will do this for their own.

We can see with our own eyes that the physicians are lords; experience teaches clearly that we cannot do without them. It is not the practice of medicine alone, however, but Scripture too that shows it to be a useful, comforting, and salutary estate, as well as a service acceptable to God, made and founded by him. In Ecclesiasticus 38 [:1-8] almost an entire chapter is devoted to praise of the physicians, "Honor the physician, for one cannot do without him, and the Lord created him; for all healing comes from God. The skill of the physician lifts up his head, and in the presence of great men he is admired. The Lord created medicines from the earth, and a sensible man will not despise them. For as in the time of Moses the bitter water was made sweet with a tree,[76] so it was his will to make known to men thereby what medicine can do. And he gave skill to men that he might be glorified in his marvelous works. For by them the physician can take away all kinds of pain, and make many sweet and good confections, and prepare salves whereby the sick become well; and of these works of his there shall be no end." But I have

---

[75] In his *Large Catechism* of 1529 (I:130) Luther quotes the full Latin proverb, ascribing it to the "wise men of old": *"Deo, parentibus, et magistris non potest satis gratiae rependi."* Cf. WA 30[I], 151; cf. also Theodore G. Tappert (ed.), *The Book of Concord* (Philadelphia: Muhlenberg Press, 1959), p. 383.

[76] Cf. Exod. 15:23-25.

already said too much about this; the preachers will be able to expand upon these points more fully, and show the people better than I can write about it the gains and losses they can effect in this matter for the whole world, and for our descendants.

Here I will leave the matter, faithfully exhorting and urging everyone who can to help in this cause. Only think for yourself how many good things God has given and still gives to you each day free of charge: body and soul, house and home, wife and child, worldly peace, the services and use of all his creatures in heaven and on earth; and besides all this, the gospel and the office of preaching, baptism, the sacrament, and the whole treasure of his Son and his Spirit. And all of this not only without any merit on your part, but also without cost or trouble to you; for you do not now have to support either schools or pastors,[77] as you would be bound to do according to the gospel.[78] Yet you are such an accursed, ungrateful wretch that you will not give a son into training for the maintenance of these gifts of God. You have everything, all of it free of charge; yet you show not a particle of gratitude. Instead you let God's kingdom and the salvation of men's souls go to ruin; you even help to destroy them.

Ought not God to be angry over this? Ought not famine to come? Ought not pestilence, flu,[79] and syphilis[80] find us out? Ought not blind, fierce, and savage tyrants come to power? Ought not war and contention arise? Ought not evil regimes appear in the German lands? Ought not the Turks and Tartars plunder us? Indeed, it would not be surprising if God were to open the doors and windows of hell and pelt and shower us with nothing but devils, or let brimstone and hell-fire rain down from heaven and inundate us one and all in the abyss of hell, like Sodom and Gomorrah [Gen. 19:24]. If Sodom and Gomorrah had had or seen or heard as much as we, they would surely have remained until this day [Matt. 11:23]. For they were not one tenth as wicked as Germany is today, for they did not

---

[77] Cf. above, p. 122.
[78] Cf. above, p. 130.
[79] *Schweis* probably refers to the so-called "English sweat," an influenza which had reached epidemic proportions just a year earlier. *MA*[3] 5, 443, n. 292, l. 4.
[80] *Frantzosen;* see *LW* 45, 44, n. 44.

have God's word and the preaching office. We have both, free of charge, yet act like men who want God, his word, and all discipline and honor to go to ruin. Indeed, the fanatics have actually begun to suppress the word of God, and the nobles and the rich too have attacked it to overthrow discipline and honor—so that we may become the kind of people we have deserved to be!

For we have the gospel and the preaching office only by the blood and sweat of our Lord. He won them by his anguished, bloody sweat. He earned them by his blood and cross, and gave them to us. We have them without any cost to ourselves, having done nothing and given nothing for them. Ah, God! How bitter it was for him! Yet how kindly and gladly he did it! How greatly the dear apostles and all the saints suffered that these things might come to us! How many have been put to death for them in our own time!

To boast a bit myself, too, how many times have I had to suffer—and will yet suffer—the pains of death for them, that I might thereby serve my countrymen! But all this is nothing compared with what Christ, God's Son and our dear heart, has given for them. Yet by all this suffering he will have earned from us only this, that some men persecute, condemn, blaspheme, and consign to the devil this dearly-bought office of preaching the gospel, while others keep hands off, supporting neither pastors nor preachers and giving nothing toward their maintenance. Besides this, they turn the children away from this office, so that it will soon go to destruction, and Christ's blood and agony will be in vain. Still, they go their way undisturbed, having no qualms of conscience, no repentance or regret, for this hellish and more than hellish ingratitude, this unspeakable sin and blasphemy. They show neither fear nor awe of God's wrath, neither desire nor love for the dear Savior in return for his bitter pain and agony. Instead, with these terrible abominations they still claim to be evangelicals and Christians!

If this is the way things are to go in the German lands, then I am sorry that I was born a German, or ever wrote or spoke German; and if I could do it with a good conscience, I would give my aid and counsel to have the pope come back to rule over us, and with all his abominations to oppress and shame and ruin us worse than before. Formerly, when people served the devil and put the blood of Christ to shame, all the purses stood wide open. There was no limit to men's giving to churches, schools, and all sorts of abominations. Children could be driven, pushed, and forced into monasteries, churches, foundations, and schools at unspeakable cost—all of which was a total loss. But now when men are to establish real schools and real churches—no, not establish them but just maintain them in a state of good repair, for God has established them and also given enough for their maintenance—and we know that in so doing we keep God's word, honor Christ's blood, and build the true church, now all the purses are fastened shut with iron chains. Nobody can give anything. And besides, we tear the children away. We will not allow them to be supported by the churches (to which we give nothing) and to enter these salvatory offices in which, without any effort on their part, even their temporal needs are met. We will not allow them to serve God and to honor and preserve Christ's blood, but push them instead into the jaws of Mammon while we tread Christ's blood underfoot—and yet are good Christians!

I pray that God will graciously let me die and take me from here, that I may not see the misery that must come over Germany. For I believe that if ten Moseses stood and prayed for us [Exod. 17:11], they would accomplish nothing. I feel, too, when I would pray for my beloved Germany, that my prayer rebounds; it refuses to ascend as when I pray for other things. For it simply must be so: God will save Lot and inundate Sodom [Gen. 19:29]. God grant that in this matter I must be lying, a false prophet! This would be the case if we were to reform and honor our Lord's word and his precious blood and death differently from what we have been doing, and if we were to help and train our young people to fill God's offices, as has been said.

But I hold that it is the duty of the temporal authority to compel its subjects to keep their children in school, especially the promising ones we mentioned above. For it is truly the duty of government to maintain the offices and estates that have been mentioned, so that there will always be preachers, jurists, pastors, writers, physicians, schoolmasters, and the like, for we cannot do without them. If the government can compel such of its subjects as are fit for military service to carry pike and musket, man the ramparts, and do other kinds of work in time of war, how much more can it and should it compel its subjects to keep their children in school. For here there is a worse war on, a war with the very devil, who is out to secretly sap the strength of the cities and principalities, emptying them of their able persons until he has bored out the pith and left only an empty shell of useless people whom he can manipulate and toy with as he will. That is, indeed, to starve out a city or a land and destroy it without a battle, before anyone is even aware of what is going on. The Turk has quite a different approach. He takes every third child in his whole empire and trains it for what he will.[81] How much more ought our lords, then, to take some boys for schooling, since that would not be to take the child away from his parents, but to train him for the benefit of the whole community—and the good of the parents too—and for an office in which enough is given him.

Therefore let everyone be on his guard who can. Let the government see to it that when it discovers a promising boy he is kept in school. If the father is poor, the resources of the church should be used to assist. Let the rich make their wills with this work in view, as some have done who have established scholarship funds. This is the right way to bequeath your money to the church, for this way you do not release departed souls from purgatory[82] but, by maintaining God's offices, you do help the living and those to come who are yet unborn, so that they do not get into purgatory, indeed, so that they are redeemed from hell and go to heaven; and you help the living to enjoy peace and happiness. That would be a praiseworthy Christian testament. God would have delight and pleasure in it, and would bless and honor you in return by giving you pleasure and joy in him.

Well, then, my beloved Germans, I have told you enough.

---

[81] On Luther's knowledge of the Turks, cf. above, pp. 5-7.

[82] Luther's reinterpretation of the traditional doctrine of purgatory began with the *Ninety-five Theses* of 1517 (*SW* 1, 52-54) and the *Explanations of the Ninety-five Theses* the following year (*LW* 31, 114-118), and led finally to an explicit refutation of the arguments supporting purgatory in his 1530 *Disavowal of Purgatory* (*Widerruf vom Fegefeuer*) (*WA* 30[II], 367-390).

You have heard your prophet.[83] God grant that we may obey his word, in praise and thanksgiving to our dear Lord for his precious blood so freely offered for us; and may he preserve us from the abominable sin of ingratitude and forgetfulness of his blessings. Amen.

---

[83] In his *Warning to His Dear Germans* (*Warnung an seine lieben Deutschen*) of less than a year later, Luther refers to himself as "the German prophet" who out of faithfulness is obliged to warn and instruct his people concerning the peril in which they stand; *WA* 30^II, 290; cf. *SW* 3, 40.

ON TRANSLATING:
AN OPEN LETTER

1530

Translated by Charles M. Jacobs
Revised by E. Theodore Bachmann

INTRODUCTION

During the sessions of the imperial diet at Augsburg Luther was lodged at Coburg castle nearly seventy miles north of Nürnberg, both for safekeeping and for possible consultation, since Coburg was relatively more accessible to Augsburg than was Wittenberg. Like the Wartburg earlier, the Coburg castle—which Luther called "The Wilderness"—became his temporary home from April 23 to October 4, 1530.

Understandably anxious and apprehensive about the outcome of the evangelical cause at Augsburg, Luther kept characteristically busy. His correspondence was weighty and voluminous, and his writings included a number of longer works in addition to what he had set as his foremost task while at the Coburg, that of translating. On the day of his arrival he wrote to Melanchthon, "Out of this Sinai we shall make a Zion and build three tabernacles: One to the Psalter, one to the Prophets, and one to Aesop."[1]

Luther set to work immediately on the Prophets, first of all—in view of the continuing threat of the Turks against the empire—translating and preparing for special publication chapters 39 and 40 of Ezekiel, in which he interpreted Gog and Magog to be the Turks, hoping that all the faithful might thereby draw courage and comfort from this passage.[2] In the same letter of May 12, 1530, in which Luther announced his treatise on Ezekiel 38–39 concerning Gog, he also told of his intention of finishing the Prophets by Ascension and how it had been thwarted by severe illness.[3] By June 10 he was finished with Jeremiah and working on Ezekiel which proved—with the recurrent headaches—impossible to complete while at the Coburg. Meanwhile he had taken up Hosea and completed all the Minor Prophets by early September. His wife Kate had heard

---

[1] Margaret A. Currie (trans.), *The Letters of Martin Luther* (London: Macmillan, 1909), p. 208.
[2] See the text of this brief treatise in *WA* 30[II], (220) 223-236.
[3] Currie, *op. cit.*, pp. 211-212.

that he was ill, and his letter of September 8 reassured her that he was well, had finished all the Prophets except one, and was working on Ezekiel again.[4]

Meanwhile doctrinal issues central to the Reformation kept coming into his thoughts and writing, giving added pertinence to his task of translating. What was on his mind needed telling. Resorting to an open letter, Luther formulated his thoughts on translating and sent them to his friend, Wenceslaus Link, at Nürnberg on September 12 to have them published. Link turned the letter over to the Nürnberg printer, Johann Petreius,[5] together with his own brief introduction[6] dated September 15, 1530, indicating that this was a letter of Luther which Link had received "through a good friend."

Luther used this open letter to answer two questions which had apparently been put to him by some other "friend." Who that friend may have been we do not know. Nor does it matter, for the letter itself may well have been merely a literary device[7] for airing two doctrinal issues: the matter of justification by faith alone and the question of intercessory prayer by the saints. Both issues had again come to the fore during the summer at Augsburg, notably in Melanchthon's encounter with Johann Eck on the *sola fides*.[8] Luther's treatment of the second question is here so cursory (see page 190 where he announces his intention of treating it more fully elsewhere) that we have omitted mention of it in the title altogether.

His treatment of the first issue involved him in a direct discussion of a basic principle of translation. Luther readily admits that at times it is necessary for the translator to depart from the literal meaning of the words of the original in order to clarify in

---

[4] *Ibid.*, pp. 246-247. *WA*, DB 2, xii-xiii.
[5] *MA*³ 6, 431. *WA* 30^II, 632, incorrectly names Johann Stüchs as the printer.
[6] We have here included in our translation Link's own introduction, which was omitted at *PE* 5, 10.
[7] This interpretation is suggested by the editors in both *WA* 30^II, 627, and *CL* 4, 179.
[8] See Eck's *Four Hundred and Four Articles for the Diet in Augsburg*, Michael Reu, *The Augsburg Confession* (Chicago: Wartburg, 1930), pp. 58ff., °97-°121. On the saints, see the *Augsburg Confession*, Art. 21.

the new language their actual sense, and that a careful translation will sometimes therefore convey a meaning quite different from the one conventionally held.[9] His much criticized translation of Rom. 3:28 is defended as being both theologically and linguistically just and necessary. By way of illustrating and buttressing this claim Luther also touches on the problems of relinquishing the letters and rendering the sense of Matt. 12:34, 26:8, and the angelic salutation to Mary in Luke 1:28.

Ever since its first publication in 1522 Luther's translation of the New Testament had been drawing not only wide approval but also certain narrow and often envious criticism. Among his sharpest critics was the notorious Jerome Emser (1478-1527), theologian, lawyer, and for over twenty years secretary to Duke George of Saxony. Like certain other rulers in the empire, Duke George had forbidden the circulation of Luther's German New Testament in his territory. However not to be left without a New Testament in German, the Duke had commissioned Emser to provide a reliable Roman version. Emser obliged and, in the year of his death, lived to see the publication of his traditionalist version of the New Testament in German.

Outwardly it looked almost identical with the folio edition of Luther's translation, even down to some of the Cranach woodcuts. But its introductions and glosses were all designed to cancel out those which accompanied Luther's version. The text of Emser's New Testament was based not on the original Greek text of Erasmus, which Luther had used, but on the Latin Vulgate and the late medieval German Bible. With these traditional sources as his base, Emser proceeded to "correct" the errors in Luther's German New Testament; he did not claim to offer wholly a "new" version.

Emser's translation, however, was not as traditional as might be supposed. Actually he had plagiarized much of Luther's translation and then palmed off the finished product as his own. Hence

---

[9] Cf. *Defense of the Translation of the Psalms* in LW 35, 209, 216, 222, where the principle here enunciated with respect to translation of the New Testament is further illustrated in terms of the Old Testament.

the deep scorn and hostility which surges through Luther's open letter, here before us.

The following is a revision of the translation by Charles Michael Jacobs in *PE* 5, 10-27, in which he had followed *CL* 4, 180-193. Ours is based on the original text as given in *WA* 30^{II}, (627) 632-646: *Ein sendbrieff D. M. Luthers. Von Dolmetzschen und Fürbit der heiligenn.*

E.T.B.

ON TRANSLATING:
AN OPEN LETTER

Wenceslaus Link:[1] *to all Believers in Christ*

God's grace and mercy. Solomon the Wise says, in Proverbs 11[:26], "The people curse him who holds back grain, but a blessing is on the head of him who sells it." This verse should really be understood to apply to everything that can serve the common good and well-being of Christendom. This is why the master in the gospel scolds the unfaithful servant as a slothful rogue for having buried and hidden his money in the ground [Matt. 25:25-26]. In order to avoid this curse of the Lord and of the whole church, I just had to publish this letter which came into my hands through a good friend. I could not hold it back. For there has been much talk about the translation of the Old and New Testaments.[2] The enemies of the truth charge that in many places the text has been modified or even falsified, whereby many simple Christians, even among the learned who do not know the Hebrew and Greek languages, have been startled and shocked. With this publication it is devoutly to be hoped that, at least in part, the slander of the godless will be stopped and the scruples of the devout removed. Perhaps it may even give rise to further writing on questions and matters such as these. I therefore ask every lover of the truth to take this work seriously to

---

[1] Wenceslaus Link (1483-1547), formerly dean of the theological faculty at Wittenberg and successor to Staupitz as vicar-general of the Augustinian Order, as a close friend of Luther, was acting on Luther's instruction in releasing this open letter for publication. We have here included the brief foreword appended to it by Link himself, which was omitted at *PE* 5, 10. See the Introduction, p. 170.

[2] Having published the first German New Testament in 1522 and promptly begun on the Old Testament—which he published serially in instalments—Luther's work of translating the entire Bible was by this time far advanced; he was almost finished with the Prophets. See the Introduction, pp. 169-170; see also *LW* 35, 228-229.

heart and faithfully to pray God for a right understanding of the divine Scriptures, to the improvement and increase of our common Christendom. Amen.

Nürnberg, September 15, 1530.

To the honorable and worthy N., my esteemed lord and friend.

Grace and peace in Christ, honorable, worthy, and dear lord and friend. I have received your letter with the two questions, or inquiries, to which you ask my reply. First you ask why in translating the words of Paul in Romans 3[:28], *Arbitramur hominem justificari ex fide absque operibus,*[3] I rendered them thus: "We hold that a man is justified without the works of the law, by faith alone."[4] You tell me, besides, that the papists are making a tremendous fuss, because the word *sola* (alone) is not in Paul's text, and this addition of mine to the words of God is not to be tolerated. Second you ask whether the departed saints too intercede for us, since we read that angels indeed do intercede for us?

With reference to the first question, you may give your papists the following answer from me, if you like.

First if I, Dr. Luther, could have expected that all the papists taken together would be capable enough to translate a single chapter of the Scriptures correctly and well, I should certainly have mustered up enough humility to invite their aid and assistance in putting the New Testament into German.[5] But because I knew—and still see with my own eyes—that none of them knows how to translate, or to speak German, I spared them and myself that trouble. It is evident, indeed, that from my German translation they are learning to speak and write German, and so are stealing from me my language, of which they had little knowledge before. They do not thank me for it, however, but prefer to use it against me. How-

---

[3] In Jerome's Vulgate the Latin actually was: *per fidem sine operibus legis.* Luther retained this reading unembellished in his 1529 revision of the Vulgate. *WA, DB* 5, 636.

[4] Luther inserted the word "alone" in his 1522 (and his 1546) translation, even though it did not originally appear in either the Latin or the Greek texts. *WA, DB* 7, 38-39.

[5] Luther regularly availed himself of the best technical consultants he could assemble for assistance in the work of translating. See, for example, *LW* 35, 206.

ever I readily grant them this, for it tickles me[6] that I have taught my ungrateful pupils, even my enemies, how to speak.

Second you may say that I translated the New Testament conscientiously and to the best of my ability. I have compelled no one to read it, but have left that open, doing the work only as a service to those who could not do it better. No one is forbidden to do a better piece of work.[7] If anyone does not want to read it, he can let it alone. I neither ask anybody to read it nor praise anyone who does so. It is my Testament and my translation, and it shall continue to be mine. If I have made some mistakes in it—though I am not conscious of any and would certainly be most unwilling to give a single letter a wrong translation intentionally—I will not allow the papists [to act] as judges. For their ears are still too long, and their hee-haws[8] too weak, for them to criticize my translating. I know very well—and they know it even less than the miller's beast[9]—how much skill, energy, sense, and brains are required in a good translator. For they have never tried it.

There is a saying, "He who builds along the road has many masters."[10] That is the way it is with me too. Those who have never even been able to speak properly, to say nothing of translating, have all at once become my masters and I must be the pupil of them all. If I were to have asked them how to put into German the first two words of Matthew's Gospel, *Liber Generationis*,[11] none of them would have been able to say Quack![12] And now they sit in judgment

---

[6] *Es thut mir doch sanfft.*

[7] Cf. below, pp. 389-391; cf. also *LW* 35, 221-223.

[8] *Ycka, ycka:* the braying of an ass.

[9] The ass.

[10] The sense of the proverb is that whoever undertakes to do anything publicly will have everybody looking on to judge and instruct. Cf. Wander (ed.), *Deutsches Sprichwörter-Lexikon*, IV, 1851, "Weg," No. 228.

[11] Matt. 1:1, "The book of the genealogy" (RSV), was rendered by Luther both in 1522 and in 1546, "This is the book of the birth [of Jesus Christ]." *WA*, DB 6, 14-15. Emser's itemized critique of Luther's New Testament began with this very verse. His point, however, was that Luther's translation introduced a new idea in making David—rather than Jesus Christ—to be "the son of Abraham." *Annotationes Hieronimi Emsers vber Luthers Newe Testament* (4th edition; 1529), p. XVIII.

[12] *Gack* is the cackle of the mother hen which has just laid an egg. It represented the simplest nonsense syllable that could be uttered by those fowl generally regarded to be models of stupidity. Grimm, *Deutsches Wörterbuch*, IV, 1128.

on my whole work! Fine fellows! That is the way it was with St. Jerome too when he translated the Bible. Everybody was his master. He was the only one who was totally incompetent. And people who were not worthy to clean his shoes criticized the good man's work.[13] It takes a great deal of patience to do a good thing publicly, for the world always wants to be Master Know-it-all.[14] It must always be putting the bit under the horse's tail,[15] criticizing everything but doing nothing itself. That is its nature; it cannot get away from it.

I should like to see a papist who would come forward and translate even a single epistle of St. Paul or one of the prophets without making use of Luther's German translation. Then we should see a fine, beautiful, praiseworthy German translation! We have seen the Dresden scribbler[16] who played the master to my New Testament. I shall not mention his name[17] again in my books as he has his Judge now,[18] and is already well known anyway. He admits that my German is sweet and good.[19] He saw that he could not im-

---

[13] In about the year 382 Jerome was commissioned by Damasus, the bishop of Rome (d. 384), to prepare an authoritative revision of the Latin Bible. In accepting the task Jerome spoke of the harsh criticism he anticipated both of himself and of his work. His expectations were fulfilled. Jerome's Vulgate version drew criticism even from Augustine, Rufinus, and others, criticism which had ceased, however, by the time of his death in 420. Jackson (ed.), *The New Schaff-Herzog Encyclopedia of Religious Knowledge*, II, 123-124; Hauck (ed.), *Realencyklopädie für protestantische Theologie und Kirche*, III, 36-40.

[14] *Meister Klüglin* is a favorite expression of Luther for someone who always knows everything better than the next fellow.

[15] Cf. Wander (ed.), *Deutsches Sprichwörter-Lexikon*, III, 579, "*Meister*," No. 8; "The real Master Know-it-all is the one who can bridle the horse at the rear and ride it backward."

[16] *Sudler* was a choice bit of invective. Derived from the term to "dirty" or "deal in dirt" and "handle dirty things," it had come to be used of any craftsman—even an author—whose work was poor, clumsy, unreliable, and superficial. Grimm, *Deutsches Wörterbuch*, X, 972.

[17] Jerome Emser. . . .

[18] Jerome Emser had died November 8, 1527, after nearly a decade of literary hostility against Luther which called forth little response from Luther subsequent to his bitter polemical treatises of 1521. *PE* 3, (277) 282-401. See also the Introduction, pp. 171-172.

[19] Emser had admitted that Luther's translation "was nicer and sounded better" than the old version, but added, "This is why the common folk prefer to read it, and amid the sweet words they swallow the hook before they know it." Arnold E. Berger, *Luthers Werke* (Leipzig: Bibliographisches Institut [no date]), III, 172, n. 2.

prove on it. But eager to discredit it, he went to work and took my New Testament almost word for word as I had written it. He removed my introductions and explanations, inserted his own, and thus sold my New Testament under his name. Oh my, dear children, how it hurt me when his prince,[20] in a nasty preface, condemned Luther's New Testament and forbade the reading of it; yet commanded at the same time that the scribbler's New Testament be read, even though it was the very same one that Luther had produced!

That no one may think I am lying, just take the two Testaments, Luther's and the scribbler's, and compare them; you will see who is the translator in both of them. He has patched and altered it in a few places. And though not all of it pleases me, still I can let it go; it does me no particular harm, so far as the text is concerned. For this reason I never intended to write against it either. But I did have to laugh at the great wisdom that so terribly slandered, condemned, and forbade my New Testament, when it was published under my name, but made it required reading when it was published under the name of another. What kind of virtue that is, to heap slander and shame on somebody else's book, then to steal it and publish it under one's own name—thus seeking personal praise and reputation through the slandered work of somebody else—I leave that for his Judge to discover. Meanwhile I am satisfied and glad that my work (as St. Paul also boasts [Phil. 1:18]) must be furthered even by enemies; and that Luther's book, without Luther's name but under that of his enemies, must be read. How could I avenge myself better?

But to return to the matter in hand! If your papist wants to make so much fuss about the word *sola* (alone) tell him this, "Dr. Martin Luther will have it so, and says that a papist and an ass are the same thing." *Sic volo, sic jubeo; sit pro ratione voluntas.*[21] We

---

[20] Duke George, "The Bearded," of Saxony (1471-1539), had affixed his name to the 1527 Preface to Emser's New Testament (see the text in *St. L.* 19, 494-501). However, Luther suspected that Emser was its real author; cf. his letter to Justus Jonas of December 10, 1527, in Smith and Jacobs, *Luther's Correspondence*, II, 426-427.

[21] "I will it; I command it; my will is reason enough" is line 223 from the famous sixth satire of the Roman poet Juvenal (*ca.* A.D. 60-140), directed against the female sex. Luther used the quotation when he wanted to characterize the capricious unlimited power of the pope.

are not going to be the pupils and disciples of the papists, but their masters and judges. For once, we too are going to be proud and brag with these blockheads; and as St. Paul boasts over against his mad raving saints [II Cor. 11:21ff.], so I shall boast over against these asses of mine. Are they doctors? So am I. Are they learned? So am I. Are they preachers? So am I. Are they theologians? So am I. Are they debaters? So am I. Are they philosophers? So am I. Are they dialecticians? So am I. Are they lecturers? So am I. Do they write books? So do I.

I will go further with my boasting. I can expound psalms and prophets; they cannot. I can translate; they cannot. I can read the Holy Scriptures; they cannot. I can pray; they cannot. And, to come down to their level, I can use their own dialectics[22] and philosophy better than all of them put together; and besides I know for sure that none of them understands their Aristotle.[23] If there is a single one among them all who correctly understands one *proemium* [preface] or chapter in Aristotle, I'll eat my hat.[24] I am not saying too much, for I have been trained and practiced from my youth up in all their science and am well aware how deep and broad it is. They are very well aware, too, that I can do everything they can. Yet these incurable fellows treat me as though I were a stranger to their field, who had just arrived this morning for the first time and had never before either seen or heard what they teach and know. So brilliantly do they parade about with their science, teaching me what I outgrew[25] twenty years ago, that to all their blatting

---

[22] The art of debate was highly developed in the later Middle Ages.

[23] For Luther's view of Aristotle, and for a bibliography on the subject, see Peter Petersen, *Geschichte der aristotelischen Philosophie im protestantischen Deutschland* (Leipzig: Meiner, 1921), pp. 33-38. Cf. also Luther's own judgment of Aristotle's several works in *To the Christian Nobility of the German Nation. SW* 1, 336-338.

[24] *So will ich mich lassen prellen.* The meaning may be roughly equivalent to a seriously intended, "I'll be hanged." Apparently derived from the sport of fox hunting, the expression was taken over by boisterous groups, such as students, for a certain hazing procedure: their victim was thrown roughly and repeatedly up into the air by means of a tightly stretched blanket or net. Cf. *WA* 17¹, 117, n. 1; Grimm, *Deutsches Wörterbuch*, VII, 2101, *MA³* 6, 432, n. 12, 26; and *BG* 7, 30, n. 2.

[25] *An den schuhen zu rissen.* Cf. Wander (ed.), *Deutsches Sprichwörter-Lexikon*, IV, 357-359, "*Schuh*," Nos. 184-229.

and shouting I have to sing, with the harlot, "I have known for seven years that horseshoe-nails are iron."[26]

Let this be the answer to your first question. And please give these asses no other and no further answer to their useless braying[27] about the word *sola* than simply this, "Luther will have it so, and says that he is a doctor above all the doctors of the whole papacy." It shall stay at that! Henceforth I shall simply hold them in contempt, and have them held in contempt, so long as they are the kind of people—I should say, asses—that they are. There are shameless nincompoops among them who have never learned their own art of sophistry—like Dr. Schmidt[28] and Doctor Snotty-Nose,[29] and their likes—and who set themselves against me in this matter, which transcends not only sophistry, but (as St. Paul says [I Cor. 1:19-25]), all the world's wisdom and understanding as well. Truly an ass need not sing much; he is already well known anyway by his ears.[30]

To you and to our people, however, I shall show why I chose to use the word *sola*—though in Romans 3[:28] it was not *sola*, but *solum* or *tantum* that I used,[31] so sharply do the asses look at my

---

[26] *Mit jhener metzen . . . Ich habs fur siben jaren gewist, das hüffnegel eysen sind.* This obscure expression may possibly derive from a popular folk song.

[27] *Unnütze geplerre.*

[28] This was Luther's name for Johann Faber of Leutkirch (1478-1541); once sympathetic and friendly toward the humanist cause, he had switched in 1520-1521 to become an energetic opponent of the Reformation. With this name a pun may have been intended since Faber's father was a *Schmied* or smith.

[29] *Rotzlöffel* was a widely current term of opprobrium for some young or inexperienced person. Grimm, *Deutsches Wörterbuch*, VIII, 1330. Luther frequently used it, as here, as an abusive name for Johann Cochlaeus (1479-1552), whose "productivity and zeal" in polemic against Luther "was unmatched by any other Catholic theologian of his time." His publications, however, "were written in haste and bad temper, without . . . theological thoroughness" (*The Catholic Encyclopedia*, IV, 79). Having won little recognition while he lived, several of them were put on the Index by Pope Paul IV (1555-1559) (*Schaff-Herzog*, III, 151). Again a pun was intended: while *Rotz* meant nasal mucus, *löffel* was the equivalent of the Latin *cochlear* meaning spoon. Both Faber and Cochlaeus had participated a few months earlier in preparing the first refutation of the *Augsburg Confession* (*Schaff-Herzog*, I, 362).

[30] Wander (ed.), *Deutsches Sprichwörter-Lexikon*, I, 860, "*Esel*," No. 150.

[31] Luther's point is that the adverb which he supplied in his German New Testament of 1522 (*WA*, DB 7, 38)—*allein* (alone)—would have presupposed in Latin not a *sola fide* but a *solum* or *tantum fide*, and should be referred to in Latin as an adverb rather than an adjective (*MA*[3] 6, 432, n. 13, 10). Luther did not himself emend the Latin text however (cf. above, p. 174, n. 3).

text! Nevertheless I have used *sola fide* elsewhere,[32] and I want both: *solum* and *sola*. I have constantly tried, in translating, to produce a pure and clear German, and it has often happened that for two or three or four weeks we have searched and inquired for a single word and sometimes not found it even then. In translating Job,[33] Master Philip,[34] Aurogallus,[35] and I labored so, that sometimes we scarcely handled three lines in four days. Now that it is translated and finished, everybody can read and criticize it. One now runs his eyes over three or four pages and does not stumble once—without realizing what boulders and clods had once lain there where he now goes along as over a smoothly-planed board. We had to sweat and toil there before we got those boulders and clods out of the way, so that one could go along so nicely. The plowing goes well when the field is cleared.[36] But rooting out the woods and stumps, and getting the field ready—this is a job nobody wants. There is no such thing as earning the world's thanks. Even God himself can earn no thanks, with the sun, indeed with heaven and earth, or with his own Son's death. It simply is and remains world, in the devil's name, because it just will not be anything else.

Here, in Romans 3[:28], I knew very well that the word *solum* is not in the Greek or Latin text; the papists did not have to teach me that. It is a fact that these four letters s o l a are not there. And these blockheads stare at them like cows at a new gate.[37] At the same time they do not see that it conveys the sense of the text; it belongs there if the translation is to be clear and vigorous. I wanted

---

[32] Cf. Luther's *Praefatio in epistolam Pauli ad Romanos* as published in his 1529 revision of the Vulgate: *Hinc et sola fides justificat, solaque legem implet. WA, DB* 5, 621.

[33] Luther mentions his difficulties with the translation of Job in a letter to Spalatin of February 23, 1524. Smith and Jacobs, *op. cit.,* II, 221. Cf. also Luther's Preface to the book of Job. *LW* 35, 251-253.

[34] Philip Melanchthon (1497-1560) had been professor of Greek at the University of Wittenberg since 1518.

[35] Matthew Aurogallus (1490-1543), teacher of Hebrew at Wittenberg since 1521, was one of Luther's chief assistants in translating the Old Testament. Cf. *LW* 35, 206.

[36] Wander (ed.), *Deutsches Sprichwörter-Lexikon,* III, 1334, "*Pflügen,*" No. 5.

[37] The proverb has reference to the silent amazement which unthinkingly gapes at something new. Wander (ed.), *Deutsches Sprichwörter-Lexikon,* I, 100, "*Ansehen,*" No. 37.

to speak German, not Latin or Greek, since it was German I had undertaken to speak in the translation. But it is the nature of our German language that in speaking of two things, one of which is affirmed and the other denied, we use the word *solum (allein)*[38] along with the word *nicht* [not] or *kein* [no]. For example, we say, "The farmer brings *allein* grain and *kein* money"; "No, really I have now *nicht* money, but *allein* grain"; "I have *allein* eaten and *nicht* yet drunk"; "Did you *allein* write it, and *nicht* read it over?" There are innumerable cases of this kind in daily use.

In all these phrases, this is the German usage, even though it is not the Latin or Greek usage. It is the nature of the German language to add the word *allein* in order that the word *nicht* or *kein* may be clearer and more complete. To be sure, I can also say, "The farmer brings grain and *kein* money," but the words "*kein* money" do not sound as full and clear as if I were to say, "The farmer brings *allein* grain and *kein* money." Here the word *allein* helps the word *kein* so much that it becomes a complete, clear German expression.

We do not have to inquire of the literal Latin, how we are to speak German, as these asses do. Rather we must inquire about this of the mother in the home, the children on the street, the common man in the marketplace. We must be guided by their language, the way they speak, and do our translating accordingly. That way they will understand it and recognize that we are speaking German to them.

For example, Christ says: *Ex abundantia cordis os loquitur* [Matt. 12:34, Luke 6:45]. If I am to follow these asses, they will lay the original before me literally and translate thus: "Out of the abundance of the heart the mouth speaks."[39] Tell me, is that speaking German? What German could understand something like that? What is "the abundance of the heart"? No German can say that; unless, perhaps, he was trying to say that someone was altogether too magnanimous or too courageous,[40] though even that

---

[38] This adverb would be rendered in idiomatic English by either "alone" or "only."

[39] *Aus dem uberfluss des hertzen redet der mund.* This was Emser's translation of the passage. *MA*[3] 6, 432, n. 14, 21.

[40] *Es sey das einer allzu ein gros hertz habe oder zu viel hertzes habe.*

would not yet be correct. For "abundance of the heart" is not German, any more than "abundance of the house," "abundance of the stove," or "abundance of the bench" is German. But the mother in the home and the common man say this, "What fills the heart overflows the mouth."[41] That is speaking good German, the kind that I have tried for—and unfortunately not always reached or hit upon. For the literal Latin is a great hindrance to speaking good German.

So, for example, Judas the traitor says, in Matthew 26[:8], *Ut quid perditio haec?*[42] and in Mark 14[:4], *Ut quid perditio ista unguenti facta est?*[43] If I follow these literalistic asses I would have to translate it thus: "Why has this loss of ointment happened?"[44] But what kind of German is that? What German says, "Loss of the ointment has happened"? If he understands that at all, he thinks that the ointment is lost and must be looked for and found again; though even that is still obscure and uncertain. Now if that is good German, why do they not come out and make us a fine, pretty, new German Testament like that, and let Luther's Testament lie? I think that would really bring their talents to light! But a German would say *Ut quid*, etc., thus: "Why this waste?"[45] Or, "Why this extravagance [*schade*]?" Indeed, "It's a shame about the ointment." That is good German, from which it is understood that Magdalene[46] had wasted the ointment that she poured out and been extravagant. That was what Judas meant, for he thought he could have used it to better advantage.

Again, when the angel greets Mary, he says, "Hail Mary, full

---

[41] *Wes das hertz vol ist, des gehet der mund über.* This was Luther's translation of the passage in both his 1522 and 1546 German Testaments (*WA*, DB 6, 58-59 and 238-239). Herman Haupt says this was a "truly popular" expression, current among the common people at the turn of the sixteenth century (*Zeitschrift für deutsche Philologie* [Halle: Waisenhaus, 1897], XIX, 109-110). The sense of the proverb, current in many languages, is that the nature or state of the heart or soul is disclosed through words (Wander [ed.], *Deutsches Sprichwörter-Lexikon*, II, 615, *"Herz,"* No. 341).
[42] "Why this waste?" (RSV).
[43] "Why was the ointment wasted?" (RSV).
[44] *Warumb ist dise verlierung der salben geschehen?*
[45] *Was sol doch solcher unrat?* This was Luther's translation of the Mark 14:4 passage in both his 1522 and 1546 German Testaments. *WA*, DB 6, 192-193.
[46] Tradition had so identified the woman in the house of Simon as the leper at Bethany.

of grace, the Lord is with you!"[47] [Luke 1:28]. Up to now that has simply been translated according to the literal Latin.[48] Tell me whether that is also good German! When does a German speak like that, "You are full of grace"? What German understands what that is, to be "full of grace"? He would have to think of a keg "full of" beer or a purse "full of" money. Therefore I have translated it, "Thou gracious one,"[49] so that a German can at least think his way through to what the angel meant by this greeting. Here, however, the papists are going wild about me, because I have corrupted the Angelic Salutation;[50] though I have still not hit upon the best German rendering for it. Suppose I had taken the best German, and translated the salutation thus: "Hello there, Mary"[51]—for that is

---

[47] *Gegruesset seistu, Maria vol gnaden, der Herr mit dir.*

[48] The Latin Vulgate reads: *Ave gratia plena.* A New Testament History Bible of the fifteenth century, for example, written in German, simply retains these three untranslated Latin words for the opening of Gabriel's address to Mary, and follows them with a literal German paraphrase: *Ave gratia plena, Maria, du pist vol aller genaden.* See the complete text of the Annunciation from this particular Bible in M. Reu, *Luther's German Bible* (Columbus: Lutheran Book Concern, 1934), p. 60°.

[49] *Du holdselige* was Luther's rendering of the Vulgate *gratia plena. WA, DB* 6, 210-211.

[50] Emser said that the first part of the Ave Maria or Hail Mary prayer had been rendered by Luther in lewd terms of vulgar familiarity (*auff gut bulerisch*). While admitting that *gratia* does at times mean the favor one has with other people, Emser insisted that in this context it must mean the favor Mary had with God—in order to preserve the idea that "the grace which Eve had lost has been won for us again by Mary, and the malediction (*maledeyung*) of Eve has been turned into the benediction (*benedeyung*) of Mary." *Annotationes,* p. XLV. He ascribes Luther's divergent rendering to Luther's "untenable distinction" between grace and gift made in the Preface to Romans (see *LW* 35, 369). *Annotationes,* pp. LXXVII-LXXVIII.

[51] The German *Gott grusse dich, du liebe Maria,* literally, "God greet you, you dear Mary," has no exact equivalent in English. "God greet you," used as a greeting on arrival, is comparable to the English "God be with you" (contracted to "good bye"), used as a parting salutation; in a sermon on the Annunciation, March 25, 1525, Luther held this same expression to be the equivalent of the Vulgate's *Dominus vobiscum* in Judg. 6:12 and Ruth 2:4, i.e., an informal Hebrew greeting. *WA* 17¹, 153, ll. 14-23. *Liebe* is frequently used quite formally in German modes of address without any connotations of the term's literal meaning of inner attachment, sympathy, and affection; it can be translated rather literally as "beloved," but also rather freely as "O" or "my"—or left untranslated, with the tone of voice alone conveying the particular connotation intended. What Luther here intended as a rather literal term of endearment, his critics construed as a meaningless formal term of common familiarity. Cf. Grimm, *Deutsches Wörterbuch,* VI, 896-898.

what the angel wanted to say, and what he would have said, if he had wanted to greet her in German. Suppose I had done that! I believe that they would have hanged themselves out of tremendous fanaticism for the Virgin Mary, because I had thus destroyed the salutation.

But what do I care if they rage or rave? I shall not prevent them from translating as they please. However I shall translate too, not as they please but as I please. Whoever does not like it can just leave it alone and keep his criticism to himself, for I shall neither look at nor listen to it. They do not have to answer for my translation, nor bear any responsibility for it. Listen well to this! I shall say "gracious [*holdselige*] Mary," and "dear [*liebe*] Mary," and let them say "Mary full of grace [*volgnaden*]." Whoever knows German knows very well what a fine, expressive [*hertzlich*] word that word *liebe* is: the dear Mary, the dear God, the dear emperor, the dear prince, the dear man, the dear child. I do not know whether this word *liebe* can be said in Latin or other languages with such fulness of sentiment, so that it pierces and rings through the heart,[52] through all the senses, as it does in our language.

I believe that with the Greek *kecharitomene* [Luke 1:28] St. Luke, a master of the Hebrew and Greek tongues, wanted to render and clarify the Hebrew word that the angel used. And I think that the angel Gabriel spoke with Mary as he speaks with Daniel, calling him *Chamudoth* and *Ish chamudoth, vir desideriorum,*[53] that is, "You dear Daniel";[54] for that is Gabriel's way of speaking as we see in the book of Daniel. Now if I were to translate the angel's words literally, with the skill of these asses, I should have to say this, "Daniel, thou man of desires."[55] That would be pretty German! A German would hear, of course, that *Man, Lueste,* and *begyrunge* are German words—though not altogether pure German words, for *lust* and *begyr* would be better. But when the words are thus put together: "thou man of desires," no German would know what is said. He would think, perhaps, that Daniel is full of evil desires.

---

[52] *Das also dringe und klinge ynns hertz.*
[53] Dan. 9:23, 10:11, 19, "Man greatly beloved."
[54] *Du lieber Daniel.*
[55] *Daniel, du man der begirungen oder: Daniel, du man der lüste.*

Well that would be fine translating! Therefore I must let the literal words go and try to learn how the German says that which the Hebrew expresses with *ish chamudoth*. I find then that the German says this, "You dear Daniel," "You dear Mary," or "You gracious maid," "You lovely maiden," "You gentle girl," and the like. For a translator must have a great store of words, so that he can have them on hand in the event that one word does not fit in every context.

And why should I talk so much about translating? If I were to point out the reasons and considerations back of all my words, I should need a year to write on it. I have learned by experience what an art and what a task translating is. Therefore I will tolerate no papal ass or mule to be my judge or critic, for they have never tried it. He who desires none of my translating may let it alone. If anyone dislikes it or criticizes it without my knowledge and consent, the devil repay him! If it is to be criticized, I shall do it myself. If I do not do it, then let them leave my translation in peace. Let each of them make for himself one that suits—what do I care?

This I can testify with a good conscience—I gave it my utmost in care and effort, and I never had any ulterior motives. I have neither taken nor sought a single penny for it, nor made one by it. Neither have I sought my own honor by it; God, my Lord, knows this. Rather I have done it as a service to the dear Christians and to the honor of One who sitteth above, who blesses me so much every hour of my life that if I had translated a thousand times as much or as diligently, I should not for a single hour have deserved to live or to have a sound eye. All that I am and have is of his grace and mercy, indeed, of his precious blood and bitter sweat. Therefore, God willing, all of it shall also serve to his honor, joyfully and sincerely. Scribblers[56] and papal asses may blaspheme me, but real Christians—and Christ, their Lord—bless me! And I am more than plentifully repaid, if even a single Christian acknowledges me as an honest workman. I care nothing for the papal asses; they are not worthy of acknowledging my work, and it would grieve me to the bottom of my heart if they blessed me. Their blasphemy is my

---

[56] Cf. above, p. 176, n. 16.

highest praise and honor. I shall be a doctor anyway, yes even a distinguished doctor; and that name they shall not take from me till the Last Day, this I know for certain.

On the other hand I have not just gone ahead anyway and disregarded altogether the exact wording of the original. Rather with my helpers[57] I have been very careful to see that where everything turns on a single passage, I have kept to the original quite literally and have not lightly departed from it. For example, in John 6[:27] Christ says, "Him has God the Father sealed [*versiegelt*]." It would have been better German to say, "Him has God the Father signified [*gezeichent*]," or, "He it is whom God the Father means [*meinet*]." But I preferred to do violence to the German language rather than to depart from the word.[58] Ah, translating is not every man's skill as the mad saints imagine. It requires a right, devout, honest, sincere, God-fearing, Christian, trained, informed, and experienced heart. Therefore I hold that no false Christian or factious spirit can be a decent translator. That becomes obvious in the translation of the Prophets made at Worms.[59] It has been carefully done and approaches my German[60] very closely. But Jews

[57] Cf. above, p. 180; cf. also *LW* 35, 206.

[58] The Greek *esphragisen* of John 6:27 means literally to seal, mark with a seal, or set a seal upon (in the sense of confirm, accredit, or stamp with approval). The Latin *signavit*, however, by which it was accurately rendered in the Vulgate, may mean in addition tropologically to signify, or designate. Luther's preference was always for the native *zeichen* over the foreign *versiegeln*, which was derived from the Latin legal term *sigillum* (cf. Grimm, *Deutsches Wörterbuch*, IV, 6920). However, *zeichen*, being the equivalent of the Latin *signare*, was broader in meaning than the Greek *sphragisein*; while *versiegeln* was its exact equivalent. What was at stake in Luther's rendering, besides fidelity to the original, was the conveying of a meaning which Luther did not want to lose or obscure, a meaning which he set down as a marginal gloss to John 6:27 in his German Testament, "Sealed means endowed with the Holy Spirit, so that whoever 'eats of this food' (as in the following verses) also receives the Spirit and shall live." *WA*, DB 6, 348.

[59] The first Protestant translation of the Prophets from the Hebrew, made by Ludwig Haetzer (1500-1529) and Hans Denk (1495-1527), was published by Peter Schöffer at Worms on April 13, 1527. The translators were not only Anabaptists but also antitrinitarians, Denk denying the atonement of Christ and Haetzer disputing even Christ's deity, which may in part account for Luther's allegation that "Jews had a hand in it." Albert Hauck (ed.), *Realencyklopädie für protestantische Theologie und Kirche* (3rd ed.; 24 vols.; Leipzig, 1896-1913), IV, 576-580; VII, 325-329.

[60] Luther's translation of the Old Testament first began to appear with the publication of Isaiah late in 1528. *BG* 7, 36, n. 7. See *LW* 35, 228-229.

had a hand in it, and they do not show much reverence for Christ. Apart from that there is plenty of skill and craftsmanship there. So much for translating and the nature of the languages!

Now I was not relying on and following the nature of the languages alone, however, when, in Roman 3[:28] I inserted the word *solum* (alone). Actually the text itself and the meaning of St. Paul urgently require and demand it. For in that very passage he is dealing with the main point of Christian doctrine,[61] namely, that we are justified by faith in Christ without any works of the law. And Paul cuts away all works so completely, as even to say that the works of the law—though it is God's law and word—do not help us for justification [Rom. 3:20]. He cites Abraham as an example and says that he was justified so entirely without works that even the highest work—which, moreover, had been newly commanded by God, over and above all other works and ordinances, namely circumcision—did not help him for justification; rather he was justified without circumcision and without any works, by faith, as he says in chapter 4[:2], "If Abraham was justified by works, he may boast, but not before God." But when all works are so completely cut away—and that must mean that faith alone justifies—whoever would speak plainly and clearly about this cutting away of works will have to say, "Faith alone justifies us, and not works." The matter itself, as well as the nature of the language, demands it.

"But," they say, "it has an offensive sound, and people infer from it that they need not do any good works." Land, what are we to say? Is it not much more "offensive" that St. Paul himself does not use the term "faith alone," but spells it out even more bluntly, and puts the finishing touches on it[62] by saying, "Without the works of the law"? And in Galatians 1[2:16] and many other places he says, "Not by the works of the law," for the expression "faith alone"

---

[61] Cf. *LW* 35, 373-374.

[62] *Schuttets wol gröber eraus, und stosset dem fass den boden aus.* The latter phrase was a common expression meaning to bring matters to a head or to destroy utterly that which one felt was beyond saving. See *LW* 35, 405, n. 85. Cf. Wander (ed.), *Deutsches Sprichwörter-Lexikon,* I, 933-934, *"Fass,"* Nos. 109, 114, *et al.*

is susceptible of another interpretation,[63] but the phrase "without the works of the law" is so blunt, offensive, and scandalous that no amount of interpreting can help it. How much more might people learn from this "that they need not do any good works," when they hear this preaching about the works themselves put in such plain, strong words, "No works," "without works," "not by works"! If it is not "offensive" to preach, "without works," "no works," "not by works," why should it be "offensive" to preach, "by faith alone"?

And what is still more "offensive," St. Paul is here rejecting not just ordinary works, but "works of the law." Now someone could easily take offense at that all the more and say that the law is condemned and accursed before God, and we ought to be doing nothing but evil—as they did in Romans 3[:8], "Why not do evil that good may come?" This is the very thing that one factious spirit[64] began to do in our time. Are we to deny Paul's word on account of such "offense," or stop speaking out freely about faith? Land, St. Paul and I want to give such offense; we preach so strongly against works and insist on faith alone, for no other reason than that the people may be offended, stumble, and fall, in order that they may learn to know that they are not saved by their good works but only by Christ's death and resurrection. Now if they cannot be saved by the good works of the law, how much less shall they be saved by bad works, and without the law! For this reason it does not follow that because good works do not help, therefore bad works do help, any more than it follows that because the sun cannot help a blind man to see, night and darkness must, therefore, help him to see.

I am amazed that anyone can take exception in a matter as evident as this. Just tell me: Is Christ's death and resurrection our work, that we do, or is it not? Of course it is not our work, nor the work of any law either. Now it is Christ's death and resurrection

---

[63] The inference referred to already in this very paragraph was early drawn by Luther's enemies, though he never intended to say that true faith is, or ever could be—much less should be—without good works. His point was not that faith is ever "alone," but that "only" faith without works—hence the term "faith alone"—is necessary for justification before God. Cf. the famous passage in his Preface to Romans. *LW* 35, 370.

[64] *Rottengeyst* in Luther's usage frequently meant Thomas Münzer, as *Tyrann* meant Duke George. *MA*³ 6, 433, n. 18, 28.

alone that saves us and makes us free from sin, as Paul says in Romans 4[:25], "He died for our sins and rose for our justification." Tell me, further: What is the work by which we lay hold of Christ's death and resurrection? It cannot be any external work, but only the eternal faith that is in the heart. Faith alone, indeed, all alone, without any works, lays hold of this death and resurrection when it is preached by the gospel. Why then this raging and raving, this making of heretics and burning them at the stake, when the matter itself at its very core is so clear and proves that faith alone lays hold of Christ's death and resurrection, without any works, and that his death and resurrection [alone] are our life and our righteousness? Since, then, the fact itself is so obvious—that faith alone conveys, grasps, and imparts this life and righteousness—why should we not also say so? It is no heresy that faith alone lays hold on Christ, and gives life; and yet it must be heresy, if anyone mentions it. Are they not mad, foolish, and nonsensical? They admit that the thing is right, but brand the saying of it as wrong, though nothing can be both right and wrong at the same time.

Moreover I am not the only one, or even the first, to say that faith alone justifies. Ambrose said it before me, and Augustine and many others. And if a man is going to read St. Paul and understand him, he will have to say the same thing; he can say nothing else. Paul's words are too strong; they admit of no works, none at all. Now if it is not a work, then it must be faith alone. What a fine, constructive, and inoffensive doctrine that would be, if people were taught that they could be saved by works, as well as faith! That would be as much as to say that it is not Christ's death alone that takes away our sins, but that our works too have something to do with it. That would be a fine honoring of Christ's death, to say that it is helped by our works, and that whatever it does our works can do too—so that we are his equal in strength and goodness! This is the very devil; he can never quit abusing the blood of Christ.

The matter itself in its very core, then, demands that we say, "Faith alone justifies." And the nature of our German language also teaches us to express it that way. I have in addition the precedent of the holy fathers. And the danger of the people also compels it, so that they may not continue to hang upon works and wander away from faith and lose Christ, especially in these days, for they have been accustomed to works so long they have to be torn away from them by force. For these reasons it is not only right but also highly necessary to speak it out as plainly and fully as possible, "Faith alone saves, without works." I am only sorry that I did not also add the words *alle* and *aller*, and say, "without *any* works of *any* laws," so that it would have been expressed with perfect clarity. Therefore it will stay in my New Testament, and though all the papal asses go stark raving mad they shall not take it from me.

Let this be enough for the present. If God gives me grace, I shall have more to say about it in the tract *On Justification*.[65]

Coming to the second[66] question, whether the departed saints intercede for us, I shall give you only a brief answer now, for I am thinking of publishing a sermon on the angels in which, God willing, I shall treat this point more fully.[67]

In the first place you know that under the papacy it is not only taught that the saints in heaven intercede for us—though we cannot know this, since the Scriptures tell us no such thing—but the saints have also been made gods, so that they have to be our patrons, on whom we are to call—some of whom never even existed. To each of these saints some particular power and might has been ascribed. One has power over fire, another over water, another over pestilence, fever, and all kinds of disease. Indeed God has had to be altogether idle, and let the saints work and act in his stead. The papists themselves are now aware of this abomination; they are quietly putting up their pipes, and presently preening and primping themselves with this teaching about the intercession of the saints. I shall defer this subject for the present, but you can bet I shall not forget it and allow their preening and primping to go unpaid for.

In the second place you know that there is not a single word

---

[65] This tract was never completed. Extant fragments of it in the form of notes and outlines give some indication of what Luther at the time intended. *WA* 30^{II}, 657-676.

[66] Cf. above, p. 174.

[67] The sermon on the angels preached September 29, 1530, at Coburg Castle, however, did not deal at all with the matter of venerating the saints. *WA* 32, 111-121.

of God commanding us to call on either angels or saints to intercede for us, and we have no example of it in the Scriptures. For we find that angels spoke with the fathers and the prophets, but none was ever asked to intercede for them. Even the patriarch Jacob did not ask the angel with whom he wrestled for any intercession, but merely took from him the blessing [Gen. 32:24-29]. Actually we find in the Apocalypse the very opposite: the angel would not allow himself to be worshiped by John [Rev. 22:9]. Thus the worship of saints shows itself to be nothing but human twaddle, man's own invention apart from the word of God and the Scriptures.

Since in the matter of divine worship, however, it is not proper for us to undertake anything without God's command—whoever does so is tempting God—it is therefore neither to be advised nor tolerated that one should call upon the departed saints to intercede for him or teach others to call upon them. Rather this is to be condemned, and men should be taught to avoid it. For this reason I, too, shall not advise it and so burden my conscience with other people's iniquities. It was exceedingly bitter for me to tear myself away from [the worship of] the saints, for I was steeped and fairly drowned in it. But the light of the gospel is now shining so clearly that henceforth no one has any excuse to remain in darkness. We all know very well what we ought to do.

Moreover this is in itself a dangerous and offensive way of worship, because people are easily accustomed to turning from Christ; they quickly learn to put more confidence in the saints than in Christ himself. Our nature is, in any case, all too prone to flee from God and Christ and to trust in men. Indeed it is exceedingly hard for one to learn to trust in God and Christ, though we have vowed [in baptism][68] and are in duty bound to do so. Therefore this offense is not to be tolerated, whereby those who are weak and of the flesh engage in idolatry, against the first commandment and against our baptism. Even if you attempt nothing else but to switch men's confidence and trust from the saints to Christ, by both teaching and practice, that will be difficult enough to accomplish—that men should come to him and lay hold on him aright. There is no

---

[68] Cf. *The Holy and Blessed Sacrament of Baptism* (1519). LW 35, 40-42.

need to paint the devil on the door; he will be on hand anyway.[69]

Finally we are certain that God is not angry with us, and that we are quite secure, even if we do not call upon the saints to intercede for us, for he has never commanded it. He says that he is a jealous God, visiting their iniquities on those who do not keep his commandments [Exod. 20:5-6]; but here there is no commandment, and hence no wrath to be feared either. Since, then, there is on this side security and on that side great danger and offense against God's word, why should we give ourselves over from security into danger, where we have no word of God to sustain, comfort, and save us in time of need? For it is written, "Whoever loves danger will perish by it" [Ecclus. 3:26], and God's command says, "You shall not tempt the Lord your God" [Matt. 4:7].

"But," they say, "that way you condemn the whole of Christendom, which till now has everywhere maintained this." I reply: I know very well that the priests and monks seek this cloak for their abominations. They want to impute to Christendom the damage wrought by their own negligence. Then when we say, "Christendom does not err," we shall be saying at the same time that they too do not err; that way they may not be accused of any falsehood or error, since Christendom holds it to be so. Thus no pilgrimage can be wrong, however manifestly the devil is a party to it; no indulgence can be wrong, however gross the lies that are involved—in a word, there is nothing there but holiness! Therefore to this you should reply, "It is not a question of who is and who is not condemned." They inject this extraneous subject in order to lead us away from the subject at hand. We are now discussing God's word. What Christendom is or does belongs elsewhere. The question here is: What is or is not God's word? What is not God's word does not make Christendom.

We read that in the days of Elijah the Prophet there was apparently no word of God and no worship of God in all Israel. For he says, "Lord, they have slain thy prophets and thrown down thy altars, and I am left completely alone" [I Kings 19:10, 14]. Here

---

[69] The sense of this popular proverb is that it is not necessary to ask for trouble—to entice the devil—since it comes of its own accord. Cf. Wander (ed.), *Deutsches Sprichwörter-Lexikon,* IV, 1087, *"Teufel,"* No. 650.

King Ahab and others might have said, "Elijah, with talk like that you condemn the whole people of God." However God had at the same time kept seven thousand [I Kings 19:18]. How? Do you not think that God could now also, under the papacy, have preserved his own, even though the priests and monks within Christendom have been mere teachers of the devil and gone to hell? Many children and young people have died in Christ. For even under Antichrist, Christ has forcibly preserved baptism, the simple text[70] of the gospel in the pulpit, the Lord's Prayer, and the Creed; whereby he preserved many of his Christians, and hence also his Christendom, and said nothing about it to these devil's teachers.

And even though Christians have done some bits of the papal abomination, the papal asses have not yet thereby proved that they did it gladly; still less does it prove that they did the right thing. All Christians can err and sin, but God has taught them all to pray in the Lord's Prayer for forgiveness of sins. And God could very well forgive the sins they had to commit unwillingly, unknowingly, and under the compulsion of Antichrist—without saying anything about it to the priests and monks! This, however, can easily be proved, that in all the world there has always been a lot of secret murmuring and complaining against the clergy, that they were not treating Christendom properly. And the papal asses have valiantly withstood such murmuring with fire and sword, down to the present day. This murmuring proves how happy Christians have been over these abominations, and how right they have been in doing them!

So come right out with it you papal asses and say that this is the teaching of Christendom: these stinking lies which you villains and traitors have imposed by force upon Christendom, and for the sake of which you arch-murderers have slain many Christians. Why every letter of every papal law bears witness to the fact that nothing has ever been taught by the counsel and consent of Christendom. There is nothing there but *districte precipiendo mandamus.*[71] That has been their Holy Spirit. This tyranny Christendom has had to

---

[70] *Den blossen text* means the bare text, devoid of corrupting glosses or explanations.

[71] "We teach and strictly command" is a common phrase in papal bulls. *CL 4*, 193, n. 7.

endure; by it, it has been robbed of the sacrament, and, through no fault of its own, been held in captivity.[72] And the asses would palm off on us this intolerable tyranny of their own wickedness, as a willing act and example of Christendom—and so clear themselves!

But this is getting too long. Let this be answer enough to your questions this time. More another time. Pardon this long letter. Christ our Lord be with us all. Amen.

MARTIN LUTHER,

Your good friend.

The Wilderness,[73] September 8, 1530.

---

[72] This is the theme of *The Babylonian Captivity*. SW 1, 355-478.
[73] This manner of dating is common in Luther's Wartburg letters, and it recurs in those written from Coburg castle in 1530.

ON THE COUNCILS
AND THE CHURCH

1539

Translated by Charles M. Jacobs

Revised by Eric W. Gritsch

INTRODUCTION

Luther's *On the Councils and the Church* represents his final judgment concerning the medieval church as well as the first broad
foundation for a new doctrine of the church within nascent Lutheranism. Luther presents his critique of papal and conciliar authority in three parts: Part I argues that the church cannot be
reformed according to the decrees of the councils and the church
fathers. Part II discusses the historical significance of the apostolic council at Jerusalem (Acts 15) and the first four ecumenical
councils—Nicaea (325), Constantinople (381), Ephesus (431), and
Chalcedon (451). Luther concludes from his analysis that although councils protect the church from error, they have no authority to create new articles of faith. Part III deals with the
true marks of the church according to Holy Scripture. Luther's
earlier proposal at the Leipzig Debate in 1519[1] that pope and
council be made subject to the word of God becomes an elabo-
rate argument for a radically new concept of the church.

Experience taught Luther to bury all hopes for any reconcilia-
tion with Rome—a sad lesson, climaxing in the conviction that "a
free, general, Christian council," once his dream, was never to become a reality. In his *Open Letter to the Christian Nobility*[2] of
1520 Luther had already called for such a council, but to no avail.
Rome would not listen to the German heretic. After all, the reform councils of the fifteenth century, whose aim it was to curb
papal authority, did not leave Rome with happy memories. First
through the excommunication of Luther in 1521, then through
tedious diplomacy, Rome therefore tried to rebuff all attempts to
call a council. And yet, pressure from Charles V (1519-1556) and
the German princes could not be endured forever. After years of
negotiations, diplomatic artistry, and futile attempts to assemble
it earlier, Paul III (1534-1549) finally called a council, which met
in 1545 at Trent. Luther, who died shortly after the first conciliar sessions in Trent, became more and more infuriated by

[1] *LW* 31, 313-325.
[2] *SW* 1, 251-353.

197

Rome's tactics of delay. Since the Diet of Augsburg in 1530 and the Peace of Nürnberg in 1532 it had become evident that the Protestant cause would not receive a real hearing by pope and emperor. Still, the adherents of the *Augsburg Confession* had declared in 1530 their willingness "to participate in a general, free, and Christian council,"[3] and so in the mid-1530's when papal emissaries, among them Paul Vergerio, papal nuncio to Germany,[4] began to appear in Germany to secure Protestant participation in the council, Protestants had to decide whether or not to attend. Members of the Smalcald League agreed in 1537 to Protestant participation in the council on four conditions: (1) it must be a free, not a papal council; (2) Protestants must be invited as full participants, not as heretics; (3) its decisions must be based upon the authority of Holy Scripture and not upon that of the pope; and (4) it must be held in Germany, if at all possible.[5]

Rome, of course, never accepted these conditions. Furthermore, the hostilities between Charles V and Francis I of France (1515-1547) led to one postponement of the council after another. In June, 1536, Paul III issued a call for a council to meet in Mantua in May, 1537; in April, 1537, he postponed it until November of that same year, then until May 1, 1538, naming Vicenza as the new meeting place. The prelates did not assemble, however, and finally on May 21, 1539, the council was postponed indefinitely because the emperor was at war with France on that date.

It was under these circumstances that Luther prepared *The Smalcald Articles*, published in 1538.[6] He began to write *On the Councils and the Church* at the same time. Since 1533 he had planned to deal extensively with the history of the councils and the church.[7] In 1535 he published a small tract on the Council of

---

[3] Theodore G. Tappert (ed.), *The Book of Concord*, pp. 26-27.
[4] Paul Vergerio (1497/98-1565) visited Wittenberg in November, 1535, and had a conversation with Luther. See the detailed account in Julius Köstlin, *Martin Luther* (3rd ed.; 2 vols.; Elberfeld, 1883), II, 378-384. There is a brief summary of the meeting in E. G. Schwiebert, *Luther and His Times* (St. Louis: Concordia, 1950), p. 740.
[5] *C.R.* 2, 962.
[6] Tappert (ed.), *Book of Concord*, pp. 287-318.
[7] Cf. *WA* 50, 495.

Constance (1415),[8] followed by a Latin edition of three letters of John Huss and several brief statements concerning conciliar authority in general.[9] Luther's concern for a clear position with regard to conciliar authority was accompanied by a growing interest in the history of the church.[10] In 1538 he published his edited versions of the Apostles' and Athanasian Creeds, the *Te Deum*, and the Nicene Creed,[11] as well as a letter written by Jerome dealing with papal authority.[12] Then he began to work his way through almost all the available sources dealing with the history of the early and medieval church. Most of these sources are used and quoted in the treatise *On the Councils and the Church:* they are the *Ecclesiastical History* of Eusebius of Caesarea, covering the period from the apostles to Constantine the Great (324);[13] its supplementation and elaboration to the year 395 by Rufinus, entitled *The Eleven Books of Ecclesiastical History* (*Historiae Ecclesiasticae Libri XI*);[14] the *Historia Tripartita* of Cassiodorus Senator, who edited and continued these earlier works until *ca.* 560, based upon excerpts from Theodoret of Kyros, Socrates, and Sozomenus of Constantinople;[15] and the collections of the fathers and canon law.[16] In addition, Luther used the newly published two-volume work of Peter Crabbe on the councils[17] and Bartolomeo Platina's *Lives of the Popes,* written between 1471 and 1481.[18] While working on

---

[8] *Theses Against the Council of Constance* (*Sprüche Wider das Concilium Constantiense*). WA 39[I], 13-38.

[9] *Three Letters of John Huss* (*Tres Epistolae Ioannis Hussii*), which includes Luther's brief comments on councils. WA 50, 23-34.

[10] On Luther's interest in church history, see Ernst Schäfer, *Luther als Kirchenhistoriker* (Gütersloh, 1897), and John M. Headley, *Luther's View of Church History* (New Haven, Conn.: Yale University Press, 1963).

[11] *The Three Symbols.* LW 34, 197-229.

[12] *Epistola Sancti Hieronymi ad Evagrium de potestate papae cum praefatione Lutheri.* Cf. WA 50, 339-343; PNF[2] 6, 288-289.

[13] Eusebius' *Ecclesiastical History* is contained in MPG 13, 29-374, and PNF[2] 1, 73-387.

[14] Rufinus' history is contained in MPL 21, 461-540.

[15] The *Historia Tripartita* was the standard Latin textbook on church history in the Middle Ages. It is contained in MPL 69, 879-1214, and PNF[2] 2, 1-178; 2, 236-427; 3, 25-159.

[16] They are contained in MPG, MPL, and CIC.

[17] Peter Crabbe (*ca.* 1470-1553), a Franciscan monk, published his two-volume *Concilia Omnia* with Peter Quentel in Cologne in 1538.

[18] Platina (1421-1481), humanist librarian of Sixtus IV (1471-1484), described the popes from St. Peter to Paul II (d. 1471). Entitled *Historia de Vitis Pon-*

the treatise he became convinced that the flow of reliable historical sources ended at the time of the fourth ecumenical council.[19]
For this reason he treated only the first five centuries.

On March 14, 1539, Luther reported to Philip Melanchthon
that he had finished the treatise, but was not quite happy with
the way it had turned out.[20] Three German editions appeared
during the same year; the first two were printed by Hans Lufft in
Wittenberg, the third by Crafft Müller in Strassburg. A Latin edition, produced by Justas Jonas and printed in 1557 in Basel, became well known during the sixteenth and seventeenth centuries.

Although *Von den Consiliis und Kirchen* was translated *On the
Councils and the Churches* before (*PE* 5, 127), the following reasons compelled the editor to translate *Kirchen* as "church": (1) Luther used the singular in a letter to Melanchthon on March 14,
1539 (*WA*, Br 8, 391, ll. 23-24), announcing that he had finished
the treatise "on the church" (*de ecclesia*). (2) Jonas' Latin edition, which he began immediately after the first German edition
was printed, used the singular (*WA* 50, 506-507). (3) The special
edition of Part III (*Sonderdruck*) in 1540 (*WA* 50, 507) used the
singular, *von der Kirche*, as did the Wittenberg Edition of Luther's
works in 1554. (4) Finally, Luther's doctrine of the church, as he
developed it in the treatise, consistently pointed to the one, ecumenical, Christian church which is represented by all believers
rather than by pope and councils.

I want to take this opportunity to express my appreciation for
the help given by Professor E. Gordon Rupp, who wrote the introduction to this volume. I also wish to thank Frederick C. Ahrens,
who prepared the indexes, and Martin Bertram, who helped re-
translate this treatise.

Two English translations precede this one: C. B. Smyth, *Martin Luther's Authority of Councils and Churches* (London, 1847),
and the one by Charles M. Jacobs in *PE* 5, 131-300, of which this
translation is a revision. The German text is in *WA* 50, 509-653.

E.W.G.

---

tificum, his work was incorporated into *Liber pontificalis,* the major source
book for the lives of the popes. Cf. *WA* 50, 502-504. Luther had already used
it against John Eck during the Leipzig Debate. Cf. *LW* 31, 315.
[19] See below, pp. 298-299.
[20] *WA,* Br 8, 391.

ON THE COUNCILS
AND THE CHURCH

I often joined in the general laughter when I saw someone offer a morsel of bread on the tip of a knife to dogs and then, as they snapped at it, slap their snouts with the knife handle, so that the poor dogs not only lost the bread but also had to suffer pain. That is a good joke. It never occurred to me at that time that the devil could also play his jokes on us and consider us such wretched dogs, until I learned how the most holy father, the pope, with his bulls, books, and daily practices plays the same kind of a dog's joke on Christendom. But, Lord God, with what great harm to the soul and with what mockery of divine majesty! It is just what he is doing with the council now: the whole world has been waiting and clamoring for it; the good emperor and his whole empire have been working to attain it for nearly twenty years;[1] and the pope has always made vain promises and put it off, offering the morsel of bread to the emperor, as to a dog, until, at the opportune moment, he slaps him on the snout while mocking him as his fool and dupe.

Now he is summoning the council for the third time;[2] but he first sends his apostles[3] into all lands to have kings and princes pledge their allegiance to the pope's doctrines. The bishops and their clergy concur in this strategy and absolutely refuse either to yield or to permit a reform, thus the [course of the] council is already determined, before it even convenes, namely, not to undertake any reforms, but to observe everything in accord with what has come to be present practice. Isn't that a splendid council?

---

[1] On November 28, 1518, Luther made his first appeal to a general council. Cf. WA 2, 34, and Schwiebert, *op. cit.*, p. 369. The emperor and various diets had been demanding one since 1523. Thus approximately twenty years had elapsed between these demands and the time Luther wrote this statement.
[2] On October 8, 1537, Pope Paul III called a general council to meet in Vicenza in May, 1538.
[3] Between 1533 and 1538 six papal nuncios appeared in Germany to prepare for the council, including Paul Vergerio. See the Introduction, p. 198, n. 4.

It has not yet convened, and already it has done what it was to do when it met, that is, to slap the emperor on the snout, and even more, to overtake the Holy Spirit and outstrip him by far! Yet I have feared, and often written and said, that they would not and could not hold a council unless they had first captured and controlled the emperor, kings, and princes, so as to have total freedom to decree whatever they pleased, to buttress their tyranny, and to oppress Christendom with far greater burdens than ever before.

In God's name, if you lords—emperor, kings, princes—like the way in which these accursed, damned people trample on your muzzles and rap your snouts, we have to let it happen and remember that they acted much worse in the past: they deposed kings and emperors, anathematized them, drove them out, betrayed them, murdered them, and vented their devilish malice on them, as history testifies; and they intend to go on doing that. Despite this, Christ will know how to find and preserve his Christendom, even against the gates of hell [Matt. 16:18], though emperors and kings neither would nor could help in any way. He can dispense with their help much better than they can do without his. How did he get along before kings and emperors were born? And how would he get along now if no emperor or king existed, even though a whole world of devils raged against him? He is not unused to bitter fare, and he, in turn, can cook up even bitterer fare. Woe to them who must eat it!

But we poor, weak Christians, who must endure being dubbed heretics by such saints, ought to be happy and of good cheer. We ought to praise and thank God the Father of all mercy with great joy for taking such good care of us and for smiting our murderers and bloodhounds with such Egyptian blindness and such Jewish madness that they are determined to yield on no point and to let Christendom perish rather than to allow the most trifling idolatry (with which they are stuffed full and overfull) to be reformed. Of this they boast, and this they do. Cheerful (I say) we ought to be; for thus they make our case better than we could ever have desired, and make theirs worse than they now might think. They know and admit that they are wrong on many points and on top of it have Scripture and God against them, and yet they want to butt their heads against God, and knowingly defend wrong as right. Thus consoled, a poor Christian should indeed be able to take the sacrament even without going to confession, and risk a hundred necks if he had them, when he sees, indeed, when he feels so palpably, that God rules on our side and the devil on theirs.

Thus we now have the final decree of the future council at Vicenza,[4] and the severe verdict of the latest (so estimable) council: the entire world is to despair of a reformation of the church, and there is to be no hearing. Instead (as they boast), they would let Christendom perish, that is, they would have the devil himself as god and lord, rather than have Christ and abandon even a small fraction of their idolatry. Not satisfied with that, they want to coerce us poor Christians with the sword to consciously worship the devil with them and to blaspheme Christ. Such defiance has neither been recorded nor heard of in all of history. Other tyrants at least have the dubious honor of crucifying the Lord of majesty unknowingly, as do the Turks, heathen, and Jews. But here they are, who in Christ's name and as Christians, indeed, as the most select Christians, boast and arm themselves against Christ, saying, "We know that Christ's words and deeds are against us; nevertheless, we refuse to tolerate or yield to his word. Indeed, he must yield to us and tolerate our idolatry; even so we want to be Christians and to be known as such."

So, since the pope, with his following, simply refuses to convoke a council and reform the church, or offer any advice or assistance toward that end, but boastfully defends his tyranny with crimes, preferring to let the church go to ruin, we, so shamefully forsaken by the pope, cannot go on and must seek counsel and help elsewhere and first of all seek and ask our Lord Jesus Christ for a reformation. These desperate tyrants, whose evil forces us to despair of a council and of a reformation, must not drive us also to despair of Christ or to leave the church without counsel and help; we must instead do what we can, and let them go to the devil as they wish.

---

[4] See the Introduction, p. 198.

Herewith they testify and cry, to their own perdition, that they are the true Antichrists and "autocatacrites"[5] who condemn themselves and obstinately insist on their own damnation. They thereby exclude themselves from the church and boast publicly that they want to be and to remain the church's most bitter foes. For he who says that he would rather let the church perish than mend his ways or yield on any point confesses clearly and publicly that he is not only no Christian desirous of being in the church (which he would rather allow to founder so that he might survive and not sink with the church), but that he is also willing to contribute to the church's destruction—as they prove so horribly with their deeds over and above their words, permitting hundreds of parishes to lie waste and churches to die without shepherd, sermon, and sacrament.

In times past the bishops, and indeed every Christian (even as at present), let themselves be tortured and went to their deaths gratefully and cheerfully for the dear church. Christ himself died for his church, to preserve and sustain it. But the pope and his following now boast that the church must die for them, so that they may be preserved in their tyranny, idolatry, knavery, and every villainy. What do you think of these fellows? They want to remain, so the church must go. How are we to know what's what? But if the church is to perish, then Christ, upon whom it is built as upon a rock against the gates of hell [Matt. 16:18], must perish first. If Christ is to perish, then God himself, who has established this rock and foundation, must perish first. Who could have suspected these lords to have such great power that the church, together with Christ and God himself, should perish so easily before their threats? They must be far, far mightier than the gates of hell and all devils, against whom the church has prevailed and must now prevail.

Thus they scream (I say) about themselves that they neither want to be the church nor be in the church, but that they want to be the church's worst enemies and help it go to ruin. Yet until now they have pestered and harassed us with the word, "Church! Church!" There has been no limit or end to their shouting and

---

[5] From the Greek *autokatakritos*, "self-condemned." See Titus 3:11.

spitting that they should be regarded as the church; and they charged us miserably with heresy, they cursed us and murdered us because we refused to hear them as the church. Now, I am sure, we are honestly and mightily absolved so that they will not and cannot call us heretics any longer, for they no longer wish to be glorified as the church, but as enemies of the church want to let it be destroyed, even lending a hand in its suppression. It is incongruous for them to be the church and, simultaneously, to let the church perish rather than perish themselves, indeed, to have a hairsbreadth of themselves perish. This is what the passage means, "I will condemn you out of your own mouth, you wicked servant" [Luke 19:22].

If the Last Day were not close at hand, it would be no wonder if heaven and earth were to crumble because of such blasphemy. However, since God is able to endure this, this day cannot be far off.[6] But they laugh about all that, forgetting that God has made them blind, mad, raving, and foolish, esteeming it as great wisdom and manliness. I, too, would feel as secure as they feel, if only their innocent blindness spoke in their actions; but the great wrath of God, revealed in them, terrifies me profoundly. It is high time for all of us to weep and to pray earnestly, as Christ wept over Jerusalem and commanded the women not to weep over him but to weep over themselves and their children [Luke 23:28]. For they do not believe that the time of their affliction is at hand, and they do not want to believe it, even though they can see it, hear it, smell it, taste it, touch it, and feel it.

How should one act in the future, now that the pope will neither accord us a genuine council nor tolerate any reform, but, together with his followers, is willing to let the church perish? He put himself out of the church to save himself and not perish in and with the church. - He is gone and has bidden the church farewell! So what (I say) should one do or undertake now that we are to be without a pope? For we are the church, or in the church, which the papists are willing to let go to ruin so that they might survive. We too would like to survive, and are resolved, together with our Lord Jesus and his Father, the God of us all, not

---

[6] On Luther's belief that the Last Day was close at hand, see SW 3, 318, n. 3.

to go under miserably before the defiance of the papists. We see the necessity for a council or a reformation in the church, for we see such gross abuses that even if we were oxen or asses—not to speak of human beings or Christians—and could not perceive these abuses with our eyes or ears, we should still have[7] to feel them with our paws and hoofs and stumble over them. What if we ourselves, the church destined to perish, were to hold a council against the abiding lords, without the pope and without their consent, and undertook a reformation which would appear quite transitory to these abiding squires, but which they nonetheless would have to put up with?[8] But we want to come to the point of our discussion, since we have now lost the most holy head, the pope, and have to take as much counsel with ourselves as our Lord may grant.

Part I

Many of the papists occupied themselves for years with the councils and the fathers, until they finally gathered all councils into one book, which appeals to me, since I never before found all the councils together.[9] Now there are (in my opinion) several good, pious souls who would have liked to see the church reformed on the pattern of these same councils and fathers, as they too are aware that the present position of the church in the papacy is woefully at variance (as is evident) with the ways of the councils and the fathers. But in this case their good opinion is of no avail, for they undoubtedly have the idea that the pope, with his following, would or should participate in such a reformation. That, however, is fruitless, for here stands the pope, with his abiding lords, declaring obstinately to them as well as to us that they would rather let the church perish than yield on one single point; that is, they would sooner let councils and fathers perish too than give in to them in any way. If councils and fathers were to be obeyed—for God's sake!—what would become of the pope and the present-day bishops? Indeed, they would have to become the church des-

---

[7] *Müsten.*
[8] John Frederick of Saxony (1532-1547) had suggested such a plan. Cf. *C.R.* 3, 141.
[9] I.e., the decisions of the councils, a reference to Peter Crabbe's work on the councils. See the Introduction, p. 199, n. 17.

tined to perish, and would no longer be the abiding lords.

I shall pass over the ancient years, the period encompassing a thousand or fourteen hundred years after the birth of Christ, in silence. It is not more than one hundred years ago that the pope adopted the holy practice of bestowing two benefices, such as canonries or parishes, on one priest,[10] about which the Parisian theologians and their associates grumbled and wrote many terrible things.[11] I am not yet sixty years old; nevertheless, I know that within my time it has become customary for a bishop to have more than one diocese.[12] But meanwhile the pope has devoured everything, stolen annates and everything else, distributed dioceses by threes, abbeys and prebends by tens and twenties. How can he regurgitate all this and dissolve his chancellory for the sake of the fathers and the councils? Yes, you say, it is an abuse. Very well, then, take your ancient councils and fathers to heart and reform all this; for it was not like this a hundred years ago, indeed, not even sixty years ago, before you were born.

Now of what use is your reformation according to the fathers and councils? You hear that the pope and the bishops will not tolerate it. And if they cannot tolerate the condition of the church as it existed fifty years ago, when you and I were children, my dear man, how will or can they tolerate our proposal to reform the church by restoring it to its condition of six hundred or a thousand or fourteen hundred years ago? Such a proposal is simply impossible, since the pope is in control and wants to remain unreformed. Therefore we must admit that councils and fathers are powerless in these matters, and so is anything we can say or think about them; for the pope is above councils, above fathers, above kings, above God, above angels. Let me see you depose him and

---

[10] Luther had listed such abuses in *To the Christian Nobility* (1520). See especially SW 1, 283-284.
[11] In the fourteenth and fifteenth centuries the University of Paris was the center of conciliarism. Luther may have been referring to John of Paris, who criticized papal authority in *On Regal and Papal Power* (*De Potestate Regia et Papalia*) at the beginning of the fourteenth century. J. Leclercq (ed.), *De Potestate Regia et Papalia* (Paris, 1942). Cf. Walter Ullmann, *The Growth of Papal Government in the Middle Ages* (2nd ed.; London, 1962), p. 385, n. 5.
[12] Cardinal Albrecht of Mainz (1490-1545) held two archbishoprics and one bishopric at the same time. Cf. SW 1, 47.

make the fathers and councils his masters! If you do that, I shall gladly join you and assist you. But as long as that does not happen, what is the use of your talking or writing much about councils and fathers? There is no one to take this matter to heart. If the pope, together with his abiding lords, cardinals, bishops, etc., is unwilling to participate in the reformation or to submit to the councils and the fathers with us, there is no use for a council, nor can we hope for a reformation from him, because he will knock down everything anyway and bid us to keep silent.

But do they desire that we, together with them, let ourselves be reformed according to the councils and fathers, and thus help the church, even though the pope with his followers would neither do it nor permit it? To this I give a double answer. Either they are hateful, poisonous, and evil, and do this with bad intent; or they are goodhearted and mean well (as far as this is possible for them). Let the former be told to first take themselves by the nose and remove the log from their own eye [Matt. 7:3-5], then, together with pope and cardinals, or without the pope and cardinals, etc., to grow fond of the councils and fathers and hold to them. When that happens we shall instantly be on hand to emulate such a holy example, and be much better than they are. We are not such accursed people (praise and thank God!) that we would let the church perish rather than yield even on major points, as long as they are not against God; on the contrary, if it depends on our knowledge and ability, we are prepared to perish leaving neither hide nor hair behind, rather than to see the church suffer harm or loss.

But when they themselves pay the fathers and councils no heed and yet would force us to do so, they go too far, and we have to say, "Physician, heal thyself!" [Luke 4:23], and, as Christ says, "They bind heavy burdens, hard to bear, and lay them on men's shoulders; but they themselves will not move them with their finger" [Matt. 23:4]. That leads to nothing, and we have ample reason for refusal, especially since they make such great claims for the sanctity of the fathers and councils, which we do not uphold; nor do they, except with words they speak and write only to flaunt before us. Yet we confess, and must confess, that we are very poor, weak Christians on many points.

First, we have so much to do in our faith, day and night, what with reading, thinking, writing, teaching, exhorting, and comforting both ourselves and others that there is indeed neither time nor space left even to wonder whether there ever were councils or fathers, much less to concern ourselves with such sublime things as crowns,[13] chasubles, long robes, etc., and with their profound sanctity. If they have risen so far that they have even become angels, and have so much faith that the devil must leave them alone and cannot let an error loose among them, or terrify a timid conscience, we weak Christians have not yet attained this, and fear that we never shall attain it on earth. That is why they should be gracious and merciful with us and not condemn us because we cannot match their holiness yet. If we should leave our work in matters of faith and, weak as we are, dare their great holiness in dress and food, we might forsake our weak holiness and still not attain their high and splendid holiness, thus sitting down between two chairs.[14]

But if they decline to be gracious and merciful with us, we shall have to let them be angels and dance among the flowers in Paradise as those who have long since mastered faith and no longer experience any temptation from devil, flesh, or world in their celestial sanctity. But we must plague ourselves and wallow in mire and filth, as poor abecedarians and beginners, unable to be such great doctors and masters in faith. For if we had as much faith as they imagine they have, we would bear and hold to crowns, chasubles, councils, and fathers more easily than they do. But this is not so; they bear them easily (for to bear nothing is to bear very easily), meanwhile boasting that we do not want to bear them.

Likewise, the Ten Commandments occupy us poor Christians so much that we are unable to attend to other exalted works that they praise as spiritual, conciliar, and patristic. With utmost diligence we urge and discipline both ourselves and our followers to love God above all things and our neighbor as ourselves, to be

---

[13] *Platten.* Cf. Luther's marginal notes in his edition of the *Donation of Constantine* (1537). WA 50, 72. Cf. also *LW* 41, 287, n. 58.

[14] A German proverb, *"Zwischen Zweien stülen nidersitzen,"* which means roughly "to fall on one's face." Cf. Ernst Thiele, *Luthers Sprichwörtersammlung,* No. 114.

humble and patient, merciful and kind, chaste and sober, neither covetous nor envious, and whatever else God's commandments enjoin. We should be happy if there were no pride, avarice, usury, envy, drunkenness, gluttony, adultery, or wantonness among our people. But there is so much weakness and imperfection among us that we induce but a few to do these good works. The masses remain unchanged and grow worse day by day. Now figure it out: if we are so unsuccessful in doing these necessary works commanded by God, how can we abandon these and devote ourselves to those sublime, splendid, unnecessary works of which they tell us?

If we had done these divine, insignificant, contemptible, or, as they disdainfully call them, "civil" works,[15] then, God willing, we would also begin to do their spiritual, ecclesiastical works having to do with eating meat, dress, certain days, etc.

But it is easy for them because they keep all of God's commandments, love God above all things, are neither avaricious nor usurious, neither adulterers nor whoremongers, neither boozers nor drunkards, neither proud nor envious, etc.; but they perform all these insignificant, good, divine works so easily they are downright idle. Therefore it is only right that they undertake, over and above our "civil" works, stronger and greater works in obedience to the church or the fathers, for they are far too strong to practice such insignificant, good works with us, having outstripped and outdistanced us by far. But according to their profound, great compassion and St. Paul's doctrine, they should nevertheless pity us weak, poor Christians and not condemn or mock us because we, like infants, learn to walk by toddling along holding on to chairs, indeed, we crawl in the mud and cannot skip and dance so nimbly over and around God's commandments as they do—these strong heroes and giants who can tackle greater and sublimer tasks than that of loving God above all things and one's neighbor as oneself, which St. Paul calls the fulfilment of the law in Romans 13 [:10], as Christ also does in Matthew 5 [:19].

But if they will not have pity on us, we nevertheless ask for a

---

[15] Cf. *The Augsburg Confession*, Art. XXVI. Tappert (ed.), *Book of Concord*, pp. 63-70.

time of grace until we have carried out God's commandments and the unimportant children's works. After that we will be glad to switch to their sublime, spiritual, knightly, and manly works. For what good would it do to force a child to work and keep pace with a strong man? It wouldn't work—a child is unable to do it. So we poor, weak Christians, who with regard to God's commandments and his insignificant good works totter along the chairs like children and at times can hardly crawl on all fours, indeed, even slide along the ground, and must be held by Christ on leading-strings as a mother or nurse holds a child—we simply cannot keep pace with their strong, manly gait and performance, and may God preserve us from it! Therefore we shall save the ecclesiastical and conciliar holiness (as they call it) until we have no more work to do on God's commandments and divine works, and not bear a reformation we cannot bear. May this be a sufficient answer to the former class of people who with bad intentions ask this reformation of us.

To the others, who mean well and hope, albeit vainly, that a fine reformation such as they have in mind might perhaps still be achieved on the basis of the councils and fathers, even despite an unwilling pope's attempt to thwart it, I reply, also with good intent, that I regard this as an impossible undertaking, and indeed do not know how to go about it. I, too, read the fathers, even before I opposed the pope so decisively. I also read them with greater diligence than those who now quote them so defiantly and haughtily against me; for I know that none of them attempted to read a book of Holy Scripture in school, or to use the writings of the fathers as an aid, as I did. Let them take a book of Holy Scripture and seek out the glosses[16] of the fathers; then they will share the experience I had when I worked on the letter to the Hebrews with St. Chrysostom's glosses, the letter to Titus and the letter to the Galatians with the help of St. Jerome, Genesis with the help of St. Ambrose and St. Augustine, the Psalter with all the writers available, and so on.[17] I have read more than they

---

[16] Comments on biblical passages.
[17] Luther refers here to the period between 1513 and 1517 when he was engaged in an intensive study of biblical and patristic literature. See Köstlin, *Martin Luther*, I, 107-122, and Schwiebert, *op. cit.*, pp. 278-302.

think, and have worked my way through all the books; this makes them appear impudent indeed who imagine that I did not read the fathers and who want to recommend them to me as something precious, the very thing that I was forced to devaluate twenty years ago when I read the Scriptures.

St. Bernard[18] declares that he learned his wisdom from the trees, such as oaks and pines, which were his teachers; that is, he conceived his ideas from Scripture and pondered them under the trees. He adds that he regards the holy fathers highly, but does not heed all their sayings, explaining why in the following parable: he would rather drink from the spring itself than from the brook, as do all men, who once they have a chance to drink from the spring forget about the brook, unless they use the brook to lead them to the spring. Thus Scripture, too, must remain master and judge, for when we follow the brooks too far, they lead us too far away from the spring, and lose both their taste and nourishment, until they lose themselves in the salty sea, as happened under the papacy.

But enough of that! We want to cite reasons such an undertaking is impossible. First, it is obvious that the councils are not only unequal, but also contradictory. The same is true of the fathers. If we should try to bring them into accord with one another, far greater discord and disputes would ensue than we have at present, and we would never get out of it. Since (in these matters) they are very unlike and often contradictory, we should first have to figure a way to cull out the best and let the rest drop. That would provoke an uproar. The one would say, "If we are going to keep them, then we must keep them in their entirety or not at all." The other would say, "Well, you pick out what you like and leave what you dislike." Who would be the judge here?

Look at the decree with which Gratian[19] had proposed to do

---

[18] Bernard of Clairvaux (1090-1153), Benedictine abbot and famed mystic. This passage could not be located in Bernard's works. On Luther's attitude toward Bernard, see Walther Köhler, *Luther und die Kirchengeschichte nach Seinen Schriften* (Erlangen, 1900), pp. 320-333.
[19] The *Decretum* of Gratian, a Benedictine canonist at the law school of the University of Bologna. It originated in *ca.* 1140 and represents the first part of Roman Catholic canon law (*CIC* 1), accepted as such by Pope Gregory IX (1228-1241) in 1234, whose *Decretalium* became the second part of canon law

this very thing—the book thus becoming known as *Concordantia Discordantiarum*—that is, he had wanted to compare the discordant statements of the fathers and the councils, to reconcile the contradictions, and to cull out the best. He succeeded, like a crab walks; he often cast aside the best and kept the worst, and yet he neither compared nor harmonized. As the jurists themselves say, it stinks of ambition and avarice, and a canonist is nothing but an ass.[20] How much worse then would we fare if we tried to harmonize all the words and deeds of fathers and councils! All our labor and trouble would be futile, and the evil would only be aggravated.[21] And I do not wish to become involved in such a dispute because I am well aware that it would be interminable and in the end we would be stuck with a vain, uncertain thing, at the expense of wasted time and labor. These young scribblers[22] are much too untried when they think that whatever they read and imagine must be so, and all the world must worship it, although they neither know the *a b c* of Scripture, nor are they versed in the councils and fathers. They shout and sputter without knowing what they are saying or writing.

I shall say no more of Gratian. St. Augustine writes to Januarius[23] that the church in his day, three hundred years after the birth of Christ (for in this year 1539 he has been dead for eleven hundred and two years),[24] was already so encumbered on all sides with the ordinances of the bishops that even the Jewish political system was more tolerable. And he continues clearly and plainly with the words, "*Innumerabilibus servilibus oneribus premunt ecclesiam*,"[25] that is, "They oppress the church with innumerable bur-

---

(*CIC* 2). Luther studied it during his stay in Erfurt and in preparation for the Leipzig Debate in 1519.

[20] The saying cannot be documented. Cf. the poem Luther composed about a similar saying in *WA* 39, 20.

[21] A German proverb, "*Übel erger machen*." Cf. Thiele, *Luthers Sprichwörtersammlung*, No. 478.

[22] *Papirklicker*, i.e., "paper-clippers."

[23] Augustine (354-430), bishop of Hippo, whose writings Luther esteemed. He often cites this letter to Januarius. *Epistola 82. MPL* 33, 221; *PNF*[1] 1, 315.

[24] Augustine died in 436 according to medieval chronology. Luther's chronological sources are not quite right. See below, p. 215, n. 36, and Schäfer, *op. cit.*, p. 103.

[25] Luther has added *innumerabilibus* and *ecclesiam* to the original text.

dens," while the Jews are burdened only by God and not by men, etc. He also states that Christ desired to have only a few easy ceremonies imposed on his church, namely, baptism and the sacrament;[26] he mentions no more than these two, as every one may read. The books are available, so no one can accuse me of inventing this.

But he also weakens this, saying in the same place, *"Hoc genus habet liberas observationes,"*[27] that is, "No one is obligated to keep all of these, but may ignore them without sin." If St. Augustine is not a heretic here, I never will be one. He who takes the statements of many bishops and many churches and throws the whole pile into the fire, pointing solely to baptism and sacrament, makes certain that Christ did not wish to impose any other burdens on the church—if that which is nothing but comfort and grace could be called a burden—when he says, "My yoke is easy, and my burden light" [Matt. 11:30], that is, my yoke is peace and my burden is joy.

Yet this fine, sensible man does the great, or (as they are called) universal or principal, councils the honor of differentiating them from the other councils and the ordinances of all bishops, saying that one should esteem them, and he writes in the same place that one should reasonably obey the decrees of these great principal councils, since much depends on them; if I may use his own words, *saluberrima autoritas*, that is, it is very useful to regard them as authoritative.[28] But he neither saw any of these great principal councils nor attended any of them, otherwise he would perhaps have written differently, or more, about them. For not more than four great principal councils are famous and well known in all the books. The Roman bishops compare these to the four gospels, as they loudly proclaim in their decretals.[29] The first is the Nicene council, held in Nicaea, in Asia, in the fifteenth year of the reign of Constantine the Great,[30] almost thirty-five years

---

[26] The eucharist. *MPL* 33, 200; *PNF*[1], 300.
[27] *MPL* 33, 200; *PNF*[1] 1, 300.
[28] *MPL* 33, 200; *PNF*[1] 1, 300.
[29] Cf. *Decreti Prima Pars*, dist. V, C. II. *CIC* 1, 35; *MPL* 187, 71-79.
[30] The year 325. Constantine the Great ruled from 306 to 337.

before Augustine's birth.[31] The second was held in Constantinople,[32] in the third year of the emperors Gratian and Theodosius I, who ruled jointly.[33] St. Augustine was still a pagan and no Christian at that time, a man approximately twenty-six years old, so he could not concern himself with these matters. He did not live to see the third council held at Ephesus,[34] still less the fourth one at Chalcedon.[35] All of this is reliable; it is based on history and a computation of the years.[36]

I had to say these things in order to make sure that the meaning of St. Augustine's statement that the great principal councils must be regarded as authoritative by reason of their importance is understood properly; namely, that he was speaking of only the two councils, held at Nicaea and Constantinople, which he had not attended, but about which he later learned from writings. At that time no bishop was superior to any other, for neither the Roman nor the other bishops could ever have brought such councils about if the emperor had not convoked them, as is well evidenced by the particular, or small, councils held now and then in the different countries by the bishops themselves, without a summons from the emperor. I judge, in my foolishness, that the great principal councils derive their name from the fact that the bishops were summoned from all the countries by the monarch, the great chief or universal ruler.[37]

History will have to bear me out, even though all the papists get mad, that if Emperor Constantine had not convoked the first council at Nicaea, the Roman bishop Sylvester[38] would have been obliged to leave it unconvoked. And what could the wretched

---

[31] Augustine was born in 361 according to medieval chronology. Cf. Schäfer, *op. cit.*, p. 103; p. 289, nn. 3, 4.
[32] In 381.
[33] Gratian (375-383) and Theodosius I (379-395).
[34] In 431.
[35] In 451.
[36] Luther's chronological computations are based upon the work of John Carion, a mathematician, who published a chronology of world history with the help of Philip Melanchthon in 1532 in Wittenberg. In 1541 Luther published his *Supputatio Annorum Mundi. WA* 53, 22-172; cf. Headley, *op. cit.*, pp. 109-111.
[37] Cf. Melanchthon's *Treatise on the Power and Primacy of the Pope.* Tappert (ed.), *Book of Concord*, pp. 329-330.
[38] Sylvester I (314-337).

bishop of Rome do, since the bishops in Asia and Greece were not subject to him? And even if he could have done it without the power of the emperor Constantine, he would not have had it meet in Nicaea, in Asia, so far across the sea, where no one respected his authority (as he well knew and had experienced), but in Italy, near Rome, or somewhere else nearby; and he would have forced the emperor to come there. I say the same about the other three councils (named above). If the emperors Gratian, Theodosius, Theodosius II,[39] and Marcian[40] had not assembled these three great councils, they would never have been held for the sake of the bishop of Rome or all the other bishops; for the bishops in other countries valued the Roman bishop just as little as the bishops of Mainz, Trier, and Cologne at present value each other in the matter of authority—indeed much less!

Yet one sees in the histories that the Roman bishops have from the first sickened, ailed, wheezed, and gasped for sovereignty over all the bishops, but could not achieve it because of the monarchs. For even before the Nicene council they wrote many letters,[41] sometimes to Asia, sometimes to Africa, and so on, demanding that nothing should be publicly decreed without the Roman See. But no one paid any attention to this at the time, and the bishops in Africa, Asia, and Egypt proceeded as though they had not heard it, although they addressed him with many fine words and humbled themselves, without, however, conceding anything. This is what you will find when you read the histories[42] and compare them diligently. But you must pay no heed to their clamor or that of their adulators; rather, keep eyes and mind fixed on the story and the text.

Since the word "council" now enjoyed the profound respect of Christians throughout the world—partly because of the above-mentioned letter of Augustine—and since these fine monarchs or emperors had died, the Roman bishops constantly strove to associate the name "council" with themselves so that all Christendom

[39] Theodosius II (408-450).
[40] Marcian (450-458). Theodosius II and Marcian ruled over the Eastern half of the Roman Empire.
[41] This is specifically mentioned in Peter Crabbe's work on the councils.
[42] The histories used by Luther. See above, p. 199.

would have to believe what they said, and so that they themselves might secretly become monarchs with the help of this fine name (I wager that I am here hitting the truth and also their own conscience, if they could have a conscience). And it has come to pass; they have brought it about with their ailing and gasping, so that they have now become Constantine, Gratian, Theodosius, Marcian, and much more than these four monarchs and their four great principal councils. For now the pope's councils mean, "I will it; I command it; my will is the reason for it."[43] But [this is not the case] in the entire world, nor in all of Christendom, [it is the case] only in that part of the Roman Empire over which Charles the Great[44] ruled, through whom they attained and accomplished very much, until possessed by all the devils they shamefully murdered, kicked, and in many ways betrayed several emperors—as they still do wherever they can.[45]

But this is enough for now about St. Augustine's comment on the councils. We also want to show what he thought of the fathers. In his letter to St. Jerome, also quoted by Gratian in dist. IX, he says about them: "I have learned to hold the Scriptures alone inerrant. Therefore I read all the others, as holy and learned as they may be, with the reservation that I regard their teaching true only if they can prove their statements through Scripture or reason."[46] Furthermore, in the same section of the *Decretum* is St. Augustine's statement from the preface to his book *On the Trinity:* "My dear man, do not follow my writing as you do Holy Scripture. Instead, whatever you find in Holy Scripture that you would not have believed before, believe without doubt. But in my writings you should regard nothing as certain that you were uncertain about before, unless I have proved its truth."[47]

---

[43] *Sic volo, sic iubeo, sit pro ratione voluntas.* A satirical proverb by Juvenal (*ca.* 60-*ca.* 135), a Roman poet. Cf. *Satura* VI, 223. G. G. Ramsey (trans.), *Juvenal and Persius* ("The Loeb Classical Library" [New York: Putnam, 1918]), p. 101.

[44] Charlemagne (768-814).

[45] A reference to the humiliations put upon the Holy Roman emperors by the popes.

[46] Jerome (*ca.* 345-420), translator of the Vulgate and renowned church father. The quotation is found in *MPL* 33, 277; *PNF*[1] 1, 350. Cf. also *Decreti Prima Pars,* dist. IX, C. V. *CIC* 1, 17.

[47] *On the Trinity* (*De Trinitate*), III, 2. *MPL* 42, 869; *PNF*[1] 3, 56.

Many more such statements are found in his other writings; as when he says, "As I read the books of others, so I wish mine read," etc.[48] I shall let the other sayings wait for now; the papists know very well that many similar passages appear here and there in Augustine's writings, and that several of these are contained in the *Decretum*. Yet against their conscience they ignore or suppress these sayings and set the fathers, the councils, indeed, even the bishops of Rome, who by and large were very unlearned men, above all of this. St. Augustine must have felt many a shortcoming in the fathers who preceded him, because he wants to be free, and have all of them, including himself, subjected to the Holy Scriptures. Why should he have needed to be so declinatory toward his forefathers, saying, ". . . as holy and learned as they may be"? He surely could have said, "Indeed, everything they write I put on a level with Holy Scripture because they are so holy and learned." However, he says no, as he also says in the other letter to St. Jerome, who was furious because St. Augustine disapproved of one point in his commentary on Galatians, "Dear brother" (for he was such a fine, friendly man), "I hope that you do not expect your books to be regarded as equal to those of the apostles and prophets," etc.[49] May a pious and good man never write letters to me like those St. Augustine addressed to St. Jerome, asking me not to regard my books as the equal of those of the apostles and prophets! I would be ashamed to death. But it is this with which we are dealing now, and which St. Augustine clearly observed: the fathers were occasionally very human, and had not overcome what is written in the seventh chapter of Romans. Therefore he does not want to trust either his predecessors the holy and learned fathers or himself, and undoubtedly his successors much less, who very likely would be less trustworthy; but instead he wants to have Scripture as master and judge, just as it was related earlier of St. Bernard, that oaks and pines were his masters and that he would rather drink from the spring than from the brook.[50] He would not have spoken like this

[48] In the letter to Jerome. *MPL* 33, 277; *PNF*[1] 1, 350.
[49] *MPL* 33, 277. Cf. *Preface to the Wittenberg Edition of Luther's German Writings. SW* 1, 9.
[50] Cf. above, p. 212.

if he had regarded the books of the fathers the equals of Holy Scripture and had found no flaw in them. Then he would have said instead, "It is the same whether I drink from the Scriptures or from the fathers." He does not do that, but rather lets the brooks flow and drinks from the spring.

What should we do now? If we should take the church back to the teaching and ways of the fathers and the councils, there stands St. Augustine to confuse us and thwart our plan because under no circumstances does he want reliance placed on the fathers, bishops, councils, as learned and holy as they may be, or on himself. Instead, he directs us to Holy Scripture. Outside of that, so he says, all is uncertain, lost, and in vain. But if we exclude St. Augustine, then it conflicts with our purpose, namely, to have a church according to the teachings of the fathers. For when St. Augustine is eliminated from the ranks of the fathers, the others are not worth much. Moreover, it would be senseless and intolerable not to consider St. Augustine one of the best fathers, since he is revered as the best by all of Christendom, and both schools and churches have preserved his memory above that of all others, as is clearly seen. And yet you force on us the endless trouble and labor of holding up councils and fathers against Scripture and living accordingly. Before that is done we shall all be dead and the Last Day will have long since come!

Well, we shall set aside St. Augustine, St. Bernard, and all others who write in the same vein, and take up the fathers and councils ourselves to see whether we can make our lives conform to them. But we shall take up the very best ones, lest we draw this out too long, particularly the first two principal councils praised by St. Augustine, namely, those of Nicaea and Constantinople, although he did not attend them, as we said above. Indeed, to play absolutely safe, and so that we cannot fail or worry, we shall take up the very first council of the apostles,[51] held in Jerusalem, of which St. Luke writes in Acts, chapters 15 [:1-29] and 16 [:4]. It is written there that the apostles boasted that the Holy Spirit had arranged this through them: *"Visum est Spiritui sancto et nobis,"* etc., "It has seemed good to the Holy Spirit and

---

[51] This apostolic council took place in *ca.* 44 or 45.

to us to lay upon you no greater burden than these necessary
things: that you abstain from what has been sacrificed to idols
and from blood and from what is strangled and from unchastity.
If you keep yourselves from these, you will do well" [Acts 15:28-
29].

There we hear that the Holy Spirit (as the preachers of councils boast) commands that we eat nothing that has been sacrificed to idols, no blood, and nothing that is strangled. Now if we
want to have a church that conforms to this council (as is right,
since it is the first and foremost council, and was held by the
apostles themselves), we must teach and insist that henceforth no
prince, lord, burgher, or peasant eat geese, doe, stag, or pork
cooked in blood, and that they also abstain from carp jelly, for
there is blood in them, or, as cooks call it, "color."[52] And burghers
and peasants must abstain especially from red sausage and blood
sausage, for that is not only fluid blood, but also congealed and
cooked blood, a very coarse-grained blood. Likewise we are forbidden to eat rabbits and birds, for these are all strangled (according to hunting customs),[53] even if they were only fried, not cooked
in blood.

Should we, in obedience to this council, refrain from blood,
then we shall let the Jews become our masters in our churches
and kitchens; for they have an especially large book on the subject of eating blood,[54] so large that no one could vault over it with
a pole. They look for blood so painstakingly that they will not
eat meat with any heathen or Christian—even if it is not strangled,
but butchered most meticulously (like oxen or calves), drained of
blood, and washed—preferring to die. For God's sake, what har-
ried Christians we would become because of that council, just with
the two items of eating blood and the meat of strangled animals!
Well then, begin, anyone who wants to or can, to bring Christendom into conformity with this council; I shall then be glad to fol-

---

[52] *Farbe.*
[53] A reference to snares.
[54] Luther probably read the Babylonian Talmud, which had been available
since 1523 in an edition printed by Daniel Bomburg in Venice. Cf. I. Epstein
(trans.), *The Babylonian Talmud* (34 vols.; London, 1935-1948). Examples
of the subject are in *Hullin*, chap. 2.

low. If not, I want to be spared the screams of "Councils! Councils! You neither heed the councils nor the fathers!" Or I will counter with the cry, "You yourselves do not heed the councils or the fathers, since you disdain even the supreme council and the supreme fathers, the apostles. Do you think I should or must heed councils and fathers you yourself do not as much as touch with one finger?" I would only say, as I said to the Sabbatarians,[55] that they should keep their Mosaic law first, and then we would keep it too. But now that they neither keep it nor are able to keep it, it is ridiculous that they expect us to keep it.

If you say it is impossible to carry out the decrees of such a council now because the contrary has spread too far, it is of no help, since we resolved to conform to the councils, and it says here that the Holy Spirit has so commanded it. Against the Holy Spirit no spreading or entrenching counts, and no conscience is safe with such a subterfuge. If we wish to be conciliar, we will have to keep this council above all others. If not, we need not keep any of the other councils either, and thus we are rid of all the councils. For in this council there were no ordinary bishops and fathers (as in the others), but the apostles themselves, assured of the Holy Spirit and the most exalted of the fathers. Furthermore, it is not so impossible for us not to eat blood and strangled animals. How would it be if we had to live solely on grain, cabbages, beets, apples, and all the other fruits of the earth and the trees, as our ancestors did before the Deluge, when the eating of meat was not yet permitted?[56] We would still not starve, even though we did not eat meat or fish. How many people have to live today on a diet rare in meat and fish! So the impossibility does not help us at all to strengthen our conscience against the Holy Spirit because we could quite well revert, without harm to body or soul, to a fare not only free of blood or strangled animals, in accordance with the teaching of Moses, but also fishless and meatless, as before the Deluge. I am very surprised anyway that the devil did not bring to light among so many quarrelsome

---

[55] Jews or Christians obeying only Jewish laws. Cf. *Against the Sabbatarians* (*Wider die Sabbather*) (1538). *WA* 50, 312-337.

[56] Gen. 7:11-24. Luther assumed that all animals were prohibited as food before the Flood.

spirits of today these beautiful ideas that have so many fine examples from Scripture on their side!

If we were to say that all these things are not only impossible, but also that they have fallen of themselves, either through disuse or nonuse, or, as I am wont to call the canons no longer applicable, *mortuos*,[57] it would not stand the test either. I know very well that the pope and his followers look for excuses like this to justify themselves, claiming that the church had the authority to alter such a council of the apostles. Yet they lie, for they cannot produce proof of any church that has done this or ordered any change. Therefore it does not behoove the church to alter the ordinances of the Holy Spirit, and it no longer does so.

Besides, these "blind leaders" [Matt. 15:14] do not see that they invite a switch for their own hide with such talk. For if we concede that man has the power to change the Holy Spirit's ordinance and commandment, we shall on the same day swiftly kick the pope with all his encyclicals and bulls, saying, "If the first decree of the apostles is not valid, though we are convinced that it was issued by the Holy Spirit, as they themselves boast, 'it is clear,'[58] how much less valid are the power and the decrees of the pope, since we are nowhere near as certain that the Holy Spirit is with them as he was with the apostles." For we will nevertheless have to grant the apostles some status too; and if they were not above the popes (as the heretic, Dr. Luther, believes), they should at least be assigned a seat next to the popes. And the popes often were truly vile scoundrels, repeatedly repudiating each other's decrees. As the Holy Spirit cannot contradict himself like this, and as the apostles could not have been such popes or scoundrels, it follows that we have to argue differently. Such rotten obscenities will not do it, unless one wished to say that the church is built upon a reed that the wind blows to and fro, depending on the whim of the pope or of other men. The church must not sway on a reed, but should stand on a rock and be firmly founded— Matthew 7 [:25] and 16 [:18].

---

[57] "Dead."

[58] *Visum est*. Luther's opponents often summed up their arguments against him by saying, "It is clear, it is clear."

But as we started to say, it fell of itself, with no changes by the church; that is why we don't have to keep it anymore. Well, dear friend, *Male*,[59] says the jurist—should one not keep a law or should it become invalid simply because it is no longer observed or because it has fallen into disuse? Then let us enjoy ourselves and disregard all laws! Let a whore say that she is right because the sixth commandment has fallen and is no longer in use among adulterers and adulteresses. Yes, we children of Adam shall, with the devils, convene and decree a council against God. Do you hear, God, all your commandments have fallen and are no longer in use among us men and devils, so we should no longer keep them, but must oppose them. You must approve this and not damn us, since there is no sin where the law has fallen. So robbers and arsonists may work out their own salvation too, saying, "We no longer owe you princes and lords obedience, but do right in fighting and robbing you; for your law has fallen into disuse among us," etc.

Now advise us here, what should we do? It does not help that the apostolic council has fallen (which is the truth) or that it has been changed by the church (which is a lie). What harm would it do to scratch out the word "Holy Spirit" and attribute the council's work solely to the apostles, without the Holy Spirit— would this help the matter? Is it ridiculous? Well then think of something better! For if the Holy Spirit is not scratched out of the council, one of two things must happen; either both we and the papists must study and obey such a council, or, if it is to be ignored and not obeyed, then we poor heretics should be spared the screams of "Councils! Councils! Councils!" For as already stated, if this council is not to be kept, then none of the others is to be kept either. Otherwise, they, in return, will have to hear the cry, "Physician, heal thyself" [Luke 4:23], "Hans, take hold of your own nose!"[60] Let those who scream like that obey the council first, and we shall be glad to follow in their footsteps. If not, it will be found that they do not cry and spew the word "Coun-

---

[59] "Wrong." It might be a pun on the Latin *male* in terms of a German proverb, *"Mal dir was!"* meaning approximately, "Fooled again!"

[60] I.e., simply a proverbial way of repeating, "Physician, heal thyself." Cf. *WA* 30III, 378.

cill Councill" sincerely, but slap people's snouts with it to treacherously and maliciously terrify poor consciences, and to destroy simple souls.

I am pointing out all this about this council because it was the first and foremost, and so that we might reflect on these matters before we permit the church to live or govern according to the councils. If this council confuses us so much, what would happen if we were to take up all the others? It is true, I admit, that the word "council" is easily spoken, and the sermon "one should keep the councils" is easily preached. But what should be our attitude on the question of reinstating their authority? What about that, dear friend? The pope, with his followers, is clever indeed; he extricates himself easily, and says that he is above all councils and may keep what he will and allow others to keep what he wills. Yes, if the problem can be solved in that way, then let us stop using the word "council" and stop preaching (that the councils should be observed) and, instead, scream, "Pope! Pope!" and, "One must obey the pope's doctrine!" Thus we too will all extricate ourselves easily and become as fine Christians as they are. What does the council matter to us if we cannot or will not keep it, but boast only of the name or the letter?

Or what seems even better to me (since we have thus gotten into this conversation, and must also jest a little in this Shrovetide season)[61]—since the letters in the word "council" are after all the main concern, not deeds or results—is to make the professional penmen[62] popes, cardinals, bishops, and preachers; for they could write such letters beautifully, large, small, black, red, green, yellow, and in any way desired. Then the church would be nicely governed in accordance with the councils, and there would be no need to obey what these councils had decreed; instead, the church would be content with the letters *c-o-u-n-c-i-l, c-o-u-n-c-i-l.* But if the penmen do not please us, then let us take painters, carvers, and printers, who will paint, carve, and print beautiful councils for us. Then the church will be excellently governed! And let us make the painters, carvers, and printers popes, cardinals, and bishops too.

---

[61] *Fastnacht.* In 1539 Shrove Tuesday was on February 19.
[62] *Stulschreiber.*

Why ask further how to keep the decrees of the council? Letters and pictures are enough!

But think a little further. What if all men were blind and could not see these written, painted, carved, or printed councils? How could the church then be governed through the councils? My advice is to take the choristers in Halberstadt and Magdeburg[63] and, instead of singing the *Quicunque*,[64] let them shout, *"Concilium! Concilium!"* until the church shakes to its rafters! We could hear them, even far across the Elbe,[65] though we were all blind. Then the church would be well governed, and these choristers would promptly be made vain popes, cardinals, and bishops, who could easily govern the church, which would otherwise have become impossible for the most holy fathers in Rome. But I shall say more about this council a little later; it is getting too much for me. I must not forget the Council of Nicaea either, which is the best and the first principal council after that of the apostles.

This council decreed, among other things,[66] that apostate Christians shall be readmitted, for seven years of penance.[67] If they died in the meantime, they were to be absolved and not denied the sacrament; today's council-screamers do not keep this, but transgress it and consign the dying Christians to purgatory, thus giving them more penance. If the pope were to observe this decree—the devil!—what poor beggars he and all the monasteries would become if this mine, treasure-trove, and trade, namely, purgatory, masses, pilgrimages, endowments, brotherhoods,[68] indul-

---

[63] The episcopal residences nearest to Wittenberg.

[64] The first word of the Athanasian Creed which, under the synonym *quicunque*, constituted a part of the Roman liturgy sung on Sundays not associated with a particular festival or saint. The creed is also found in Tappert (ed.), *Book of Concord*, pp. 19-21.

[65] The Elbe River is about fifty miles from Magdeburg and Halberstadt.

[66] Luther could find the decrees of Nicaea in several different versions. Besides the edition of Crabbe (see p. 199, n. 17, and *WA* 50, 531, n. *c*), Luther probably used the text preserved by Rufinus (*MPL* 21, 473-475). The decrees are translated in *PNF²* 14, 8-42, from canon law. The text does not always agree with *MPL* 21, 473-475. See, for example, p. 226, n. 70. Luther's citations are not always accurate. On Luther's judgment concerning the Council of Nicaea, see Headley, *op. cit.*, pp. 164-170.

[67] Canon XII in Rufinus' version. *MPL* 21, 474.

[68] *Bruderschafft.* A community of clergymen and laymen committed to works of charity (often in relationship to their "merits"). See, for example, "Hospitalers," *O.D.C.C.*, pp. 658-659.

gences, bulls, etc.,[69] would have to go to ruin. May the devil preserve the pope and all cardinals, bishops, monks, and nuns from having the church ruled according to this council. What would become of them? But since this decree pertains only to me, a man who has until now been agitating against the pope and who can well imagine how they would like to twist the council's words to direct them against me, I shall now drop this subject. I must now deal with matters that affect both parties, to the praise and honor of the council-screamers.

The same council decreed that those who give up warfare for the sake of religion and later go to war again are to spend five years among the catechumens and are then to be admitted to the sacrament after two more years. I am now taking the word "religion"[70] to mean the common Christian faith—but more about that later. In order not to get derailed or interrupted, I shall not argue about such incidental questions as whether the council forbade warfare, or whether it had the power and right to forbid or condemn war (so long as the soldiers do not otherwise deny the faith, to which the preceding statement refers).[71]

We want rather to investigate whether this article, that no soldier can be saved or be a Christian, had been kept before, or whether it can be kept on and on as a matter of law.[72] The pope himself and all his followers will have to testify that this article has fallen and can moreover never possibly be re-established, even less than the apostles' decree about blood sausage, black jelly, and the like, of which we spoke earlier. The council does not speak of murderers, robbers, enemies, but *de militia,* that is, "of regular

---

[69] All these practices were connected with the sacrament of penance and belief in purgatory.

[70] Canon XIII in Rufinus (*MPL* 21, 474). Luther confuses the number of years: Canon XIII states "thirteen years." Luther could easily have made the error by looking up Canon XII instead of Canon XIII. Moreover, Canon XIII does not contain the term "religion." The Latin, *religio,* appears only in canon law, which lists the decrees of Nicaea in various sections. Thus Luther might have used the text of Rufinus (*MPL* 21, 474) and that of *Decreti Secunda Pars, De Penitencia,* dist. V, C. IV (*CIC* 1, 1240-1241), where the term appears in C. V. The editors of *WA* assume that Luther confused the canons in Rufinus and looked up C. V instead of C. IV in canon law. See *WA* 50, 531, n. c.

[71] The "preceding statement" is Canon XII.

[72] Cf. *Whether Soldiers, Too, Can Be Saved* (1526). SW 3, 427-477.

wars," in which a prince, king, or emperor may under his banner take to the field, to whom God himself commanded us in Romans 13 [:1-7] to be subject and obedient (like St. Maurice[73] and many others), even if they be heathen, so long as they do not compel us to fight against God.

Well then, let us govern the church according to this council. First of all, we shall unbuckle the emperor's sword and then command the whole world to keep the peace, allowing no one to wage war or to tolerate it, for war is forbidden on pain of seven years' penance, in the Nicene council. What more do we want! The church is governed now; one needs no soldiers; the devil is dead; and all the years since the time of this council have been golden years,[74] indeed, they have been life eternal in profound peace, that is, if the council's statute is legal and enforcible.

But we would have to have unusually good painters here who could portray such churches for us so that we could see them; or if we were blind, we would have to have far greater criers than the choristers of Halberstadt[75] so that we could at least hear it. Perhaps the professional penmen could also write the letters in the word *concilium* because they have more colors available and can make better letters than we poor Christians. And yet, since the work itself is no longer there, we cannot attain salvation through letters, pictures, and shouts. We must speak differently about these things, and leave letters, pictures, and shouts to the papists. As long as we want to be Christians it might behoove us to live according to the councils and not merely to glorify the letters in the word "council."

You may say that the council's decree applies to those Chris-

---

[73] The commander of an Egyptian legion (Theban) which is said to have been exterminated under the Roman emperor Maximinian (286-305) because it would not participate in the persecutions of Christians. Thus sixty-six hundred died. The story of Maurice and the Theban legion is one of the most famous legends of the Middle Ages. Cf. *O.D.C.C.*, p. 877.

[74] "Golden" or "jubilee" years were instituted by Pope Boniface VIII (1294-1303) in 1300 for the purpose of granting special penance to pilgrims worshiping at the shrines in Rome. Though only every hundredth year was to be a jubilee year, the interval between such years was fixed at fifty in 1343, at thirty-three in 1389, and at twenty-five in 1473.

[75] See above, p. 225, n. 63.

tians who voluntarily run after war for the sake of money,[76] and that one should rightly condemn them. Otherwise, it would be utterly ridiculous for a council to denounce a regular war or obedience to government. For heaven's sake! I am willing to be a senseless fool and an ass, I who certainly also esteem councils very highly. Interpret it as well as you can, and I will be content with it. Only tell me, were you present at the Nicene council when this article was adopted, since you can repeat this interpretation with such certainty? If not, where else did you read this? The article simply says *militia*, "of war"; it says nothing of unjust wars,[77] which did not need to be condemned by councils since they are also thoroughly condemned, according to reason, by all the heathen, who were neither Christians nor councils.

If a king or a prince must fight and defend himself in a just war, he has to take whatever he can get. If, however, mercenaries are to be condemned, how are emperors, kings, and princes going to survive, since there are now only mercenaries available? Tell me, are those lords to fight alone, or are they to weave scarecrows to oppose the foe? Ask the council's advice on whether this could be done! Yes, my dear friend, it is easily said that the council has decreed this, if one looks at the letters like a cow stares at the gate, without reflecting on the implications and on how one should act and comply. And why didn't the popes and bishops later keep this decree themselves—they who have waged so many wars and shed so much blood throughout the world, and still do this unceasingly,[78] meanwhile constantly screaming, "Councils! Councils! Fathers! Fathers!" while reserving the freedom to act contrary to them and culling from them whatever they want us to do?

See here, Luther, this way you will cast the suspicion of sedition upon the Council of Nicaea. If we were now to teach that

[76] Cf. Canon XII. *MPL* 21, 1636.
[77] The differentiation between "just" and "unjust" wars grew out of Christian attitudes toward war and peace. Thus the "just war" was defined as an effort to restore peace. Cf. Roland H. Bainton, *Christian Attitudes Toward War and Peace* (New York and Nashville: Abingdon Press, 1960), pp. 89-100.
[78] Luther may have been thinking of the Catholic military league (*Bund*) formed at Nürnberg in 1538 against the Protestant Smalcald League.

the emperor and his soldiers (even though they had a just cause) were condemned, we should rightly be regarded as seditious on the basis of our own writings. I am now (I declare) and must be a good conciliarist; later I shall say more about it and explain myself. Now I repeat that the council cannot be speaking of anything but regular warfare, as it was being conducted at the time throughout the Roman Empire, under the same Emperor Constantine,[79] as well as previously under the heathen. The foot soldiers, called *milites*[80] at the time, were resident citizens then who drew permanent pay, so that whenever the father died or grew too old, his son was compelled to become a soldier in his stead, a custom the Turks still follow today. I am told that the king of France does practically the same thing in Switzerland and gives pay even to children.[81] If this is true, then, it is no lie.[82]

The horsemen, too, were professional and hereditary soldiers and served on salary, being called *equites*.[83] These horsemen were not unlike our noblemen, who must be equipped with mounts and armor, for which they have their fiefs. That the Roman Empire thus always had a certain number both of infantrymen and of cavalrymen receiving permanent pay, etc., I am mentioning to convey a proper understanding of the council, namely, that it cannot have referred to anything but regular warfare, since it had to speak about the Roman soldiery. According to St. Paul's teaching,[84] many Christians were duty-bound to obey orders therein—like St. Mau-

---

[79] Cf. p. 214, n. 30. Known for his wars of succession and his autonomous leadership in the church, Constantine was baptized on his deathbed. The sincerity of his faith, however, has been questioned. Cf. Herrmann Döries, *Das Selbstzeugnis Kaiser Konstantins* (Göttingen, 1954), pp. 397-424.

[80] The technical term for the Roman infantry. Although there were generations of soldiers among the imperial Praetorian guard, Rome's imperial armies had been secured by conscription and voluntary enlistment ever since Emperor Marius (120-70 B.C.).

[81] It was common practice in the late Middle Ages to hire Swiss citizens as soldiers. Occasionally, as among the Turks, entire families were involved. This system of "pensions" was bitterly assailed by Huldreich Zwingli (1484-1531). *LWZ* 1, 68-69.

[82] A proverbial German expression, "*Ists war, so sey es nicht erlogen.*" The origin of this proverb is not known.

[83] The technical term for the Roman cavalry.

[84] A reference to Rom. 13:1-7.

rice[85] with his comrades—also Jovian, Gratian, Valentinian, Theodosius, etc., before they became emperors.[86] But if it was right to
serve the pagan emperors in war before baptism, why should it
have been wrong to serve Christian emperors in the same way
after baptism?

Could it be that *religio*[87] here does not refer to the Christian
faith, but to monasticism? Then I would be trapped and would,
according to this council, have to crawl back into my cowl, even
if I wanted to do something else. Furthermore, I should not be
able to find St. Peter in heaven, because he was a fisherman before he became an apostle, and after his apostolic office he again
plied his trade as a fisherman, although he had left it for Christ's
sake.

But even if *religio* now would mean monasticism, the fact remains that neither religious orders nor monasteries or monks existed
at that time, although they arose very soon thereafter. St. Anthony
and his companions lived about that time; he is called the father
of all monks.[88] But at that time a monk was what we today call a
recluse or hermit, according to the Greek word *monachos,* [and the
Latin] *solitarius,* that is, a solitary person who lives alone, apart
from men, in a forest or wilderness or otherwise alone. I know of
no such monks today, nor have there been any like that for more
than a thousand years,[89] unless we were to call the poor prisoners
in towers and dungeons monks, who unfortunately are true monks,
for they sit alone, separated from their fellows. The monks of the
papacy are more among people and less alone than anyone else;
for what class or vocation in the world is more with and among

---

[85] Cf. above, p. 227, n. 73. Maurice represents an exception since he did not
obey his emperor.

[86] Jovian (363-364); Gratian was regent of the Western half of Constantine's
empire; he was preceded by Valentinian I (364-375). Theodosius I, who succeeded Valens (364-378) in the East, united the empire in 394. These rulers
all distinguished themselves as military leaders.

[87] Cf. above, p. 226, n. 70.

[88] Luther regarded the origin of monasticism as the end of apostolic times and
the beginning of postapostolic times. Anthony (d. 356) took up the life of a
hermit in *ca.* 270.

[89] This is correct in so far as there were no hermits, i.e., monks living completely by themselves. Occasionally, however, some monks lived a life of complete seclusion. Cf. *O.D.C.C.*, p. 631.

people and less separated from people than these monks? Unless it be claimed that the monasteries located in the cities and in the country are built neither near nor among people.

But let us forget about grammar, we want to talk about the matter at issue. Does *religio* here mean the monasticism existing at that time? Then why does this council condemn the military, that is, obedience to temporal government, and say that monks who show this obedience cannot be saved? We could still put up with praise of monasticism, but that the regular army is damned, as though St. Anthony could not in good conscience serve the emperor in war, is going too far. Where then would the emperor finally get his soldiers if everybody wanted to become a monk preaching that he was forbidden to serve in war? Tell me, my dear man, how close do you suppose this teaching comes to rebellion, especially if we were to teach it?—particularly since we know that this self-chosen monasticism is not commanded by God, but obedience is commanded. If the monks really wanted to escape from people, they should be honorable and honestly flee, not leave a stench behind them; that is, they should not by their fleeing give other vocations and offices a stench as though these were utterly damned and their own self-chosen monasticism were pure balsam. When a person flees from human society and becomes a monk it sounds as though he were saying, "Shame on you! How these people stink! How accursed is their vocation. I want to be saved and let them go to the devil!" If Christ had fled like this too and had become such a holy monk, who would have died for our sin or atoned for us poor sinners? Do you suppose it would have been the monks with their unsociable and austere mode of life?

True, John the Baptist was also in the wilderness, but he did not withdraw entirely from mankind, for he returned to be among people and preached after he had attained manhood. Christ dwelt (like Moses on Mount Sinai) for forty days in complete solitude among the beasts in the wilderness, and neither ate nor drank. But he too returned to the midst of people. Well then, if we like, let us regard them as hermits and monks. Still, neither condemns the vocation of mercenaries, even though they themselves were not soldiers. On the contrary, John addresses them, saying, "Rob no one by violence or by false accusation, and be content with your wages" [Luke 3:14]. Christ went to the centurion at Capernaum, who undoubtedly also served for wages, to help his servant. Yet Jesus did not bid him to forsake his vocation, but instead praised his faith above all Israel [Matt. 8:10]. And St. Peter allowed Cornelius of Caesarea to remain a centurion after his baptism, together with his troops, who were there in the pay of the Romans [Acts 10]. How much less, then, should St. Anthony and his monks have cast a stench on this order of God with his new and self-appointed holiness, simple layman that he was, wholly unlearned in the vocation of preacher and administrator in the church. To be sure, I do believe that he was a great man in the sight of God, as were many of his disciples; but his undertaking was offensive and dangerous, though he was preserved in it as the elect are preserved amid sin and other offenses. But the example and teaching of Christ and John is to be praised, not the example of his existence.

Now whether *religio* refers to faith or to monasticism, it follows from this council that military service, which at that time represented obedience to temporal government, is to be viewed either as disobedience to God or as stinking obedience to man-chosen monasticism. But the legend of St. Martin[90] indicates that *religio* meant Christian faith; for when he desired to become a Christian, he gave up his hereditary military service, in which his father had been and when his father became too old, had had his son enrolled in his stead—in conformity with the law and custom of the Roman Empire. This act was construed as cowardice and flight from the enemy, as though fear had moved him to become a Christian. We can read this in the legends about him. Thus it is apparent that the illusion had already taken root among the people at that time (not without the preachments of several bishops) that soldiering was an accursed vocation dangerous to the soul, to be eschewed by all who would serve God, for St. Martin lived not

---

[90] Martin of Tours (d. *ca.* 400), one of the most celebrated monks of the West. Luther's source is the legendary account, *The Life of St. Martin, Bishop of Tours* (*Vita S. Martini Episcopi Turonensis*), by Sulpicius Severus (*ca.* 340-410), a well-known early chronicler. MPL 20, 159-176.

long after the Council of Nicaea, since he was a soldier under Julian.[91]

Now if we wish to obey this council or to reinstate it, we have to emulate St. Anthony and flee into the wilderness and make monks of emperors and kings, or say that they can be neither Christians nor saved, or else proclaim that they live in a dangerous and stinking obedience and do not serve God. But if we choose to disobey this council, then we need obey none, for one is as good as another because the same Holy Spirit rules them all in equal measure. Moreover, we want to have councils in fact and consequences, not painted councils or the mere letters of the word "council."[92] But I cannot escape the suspicion that a fraud was committed and that the dear holy fathers never did set up such an article. Surely they would have spared the emperor Constantine this, he who had liberated them from the tyrants, not with St. Anthony's monkery, but with war and sword. It looks as though the other loose bishops pasted it in or smuggled it into the records later.[93]

The same council likewise decreed that the Roman bishop should, in accordance with an old custom, take charge of the suburbicarian churches, just as the bishop in Alexandria had charge of those in Egypt.[94] I cannot and will not explain the word *suburbicariae* because it is not my word; but it seems to mean the churches located up to that time in Italy[95] around the Roman churches, just as the churches in Egypt were adjacent to the churches in Alexandria. Let whoever wants to interpret it do so, but I still understand it to mean that this council gave the bishop of Rome no dominion over his surrounding churches, but en-

---

[91] Julian the Apostate (361-363), so called because he rejected Christianity. He was a nephew of Constantine the Great.

[92] Cf. above, p. 224.

[93] The acts of the Council of Nicaea, as of the ancient councils in general, had been handed down in various forms, into some of which forgeries had been inserted; there was no authentic text available in Luther's day. Today's modern texts have been established by methods of literary criticism of the kind Luther here employs. For an account of the history of these texts, see *PNF*[2] 14, XVI-XXI.

[94] Cf. Canon VI. *MPL* 21, 473.

[95] Included also were Sicily, Sardinia, and Corsica. Cf. Tappert (ed.), *Book of Concord*, p. 322.

trusted them to his care; and it did not do it as though it had to be done "by divine right,"[96] but because of an old custom. Custom, however, does not mean *scriptura sancta* or God's word. Furthermore, it took the churches of Egypt (also in keeping with an old custom) away from the bishop of Rome and entrusted them to the bishop of Alexandria. Likewise, it is to be assumed that the churches in Syria were entrusted to the bishop of Antioch or Jerusalem, since they are farther away from Rome than Alexandria or Egypt.

Now if this council is to be valid in our churches and go into effect, we must first condemn the bishop of Rome as a tyrant and burn all his bulls and decretals. There is no bull or decretal in which he does not boast vociferously and menacingly that he is the supreme head and lord of all the churches on earth, to whom everyone on earth must be subject, if they wish to be saved.[97] This is exactly as much as saying, "The Council of Nicaea is false, accursed, and damned for taking from me domination over all things and for making the bishop of Alexandria my peer." Anyway, the Turk and the sultan long ago so interpreted and invalidated this article by destroying Alexandria[98] that neither we nor the pope need concern ourselves with it. Thus we learn that the articles of the councils are not all to be kept forever, like articles of faith.

The council likewise decreed that those who emasculate themselves because of the great and unbearable lust of their flesh shall not be admitted to the clergy or to any other office in the church.[99] Furthermore, it decreed that the bishops are to have no women about them or living with them, except mother, sister, aunts (that is, a father's or mother's sister), or other near relative.[100] Here I

---

[96] *Iure divino.*
[97] This is a reference to the bull *Unam Sanctam,* issued in 1302 by Pope Boniface VIII, whose language Luther here imitates. See Ray C. Petry (ed.), *Readings in the Early and Medieval Church* ("A History of Christianity," Vol. I [Englewood Cliffs, N. J.: Prentice Hall, 1962]), pp. 505-506.
[98] Alexandria was destroyed in 641 by the Saracens.
[99] Cf. Canon I. *MPL* 21, 473.
[100] Canon III. *MPL* 21, 473. Luther misinterprets this canon. It does not refer to clerical marriage, but to the presence of women who were neither wives nor relatives. They were called "associates" (*subintroductae*) because they lived in spiritual marriage. On this term, see *O.D.C.C.,* p. 1300.

do not understand the Holy Spirit in this council at all. If those who emasculate themselves because of unbearable passion are not qualified for ecclesiastical office, and those who have a wife or take a wife to ward off such lust, according to St. Paul's suggestion in I Corinthians 7 [:2] are not qualified either, what will be the outcome? Should a bishop or a preacher be stuck in this unbearable passion, and be forbidden to rescue himself from this perilous state by either marriage or emasculation? Why should it be necessary to command a man who has a wife not to have any other women about him, which is, of course, unseemly even for laymen and husbands? Thus the matter of mother, sister, or aunt would take care of itself; if the bishop had a wife, there would be no need for a prohibition. Or does the Holy Spirit have nothing better to do in the councils than to bind and burden his servants with impossible, dangerous, and unnecessary laws?

The histories relate that St. Paphnutius, that excellent man, opposed the bishops in this council who proposed to forbid marriage even to those who had married before their ordination and who wanted to forbid them to discharge their conjugal duties with their own wives. He, however, advised against it, saying that discharging one's conjugal duties was also a mark of chastity.[101] It is recorded that he won out, but these two decrees sound as though the bishops had proceeded to forbid wives anyway, for there were also many incompetent, false bishops in the pious crowd and holy council, such as the Arians[102] and their gang (history clearly shows that), who perhaps contributed to this too. But more of that later. Let us stop talking about the councils for a while and take a look at the fathers—although St. Augustine confuses us because he wants none of them (as was said above)[103] believed, but wants them all held captive and subject to Scripture. We shall nevertheless take a look at them too.

---

[101] *Historia Tripartita*, II, 14. *MPL* 69, 933; *PNF*² 2, 256. See in this volume, p. 252. Little is known of Paphnutius (d. 360) save that he was an Egyptian bishop and a member of the Nicene council, and that he opposed the prohibition of clerical marriage.

[102] The Arians derived their name from Arius (d. 336), a presbyter in Alexandria condemned for his Christology. He asserted, contrary to the Nicene Creed, that Christ was not of the same substance with the Father.

[103] Cf. above, p. 217.

St. Cyprian,[104] one of the earliest fathers, since he lived long before the Council of Nicaea at the time of the martyrs, and was himself one of the outstanding martyrs, taught and staunchly insisted that those who were baptized by heretics had to be rebaptized.[105] He stuck to this until his martyrdom, although he was strongly admonished by other bishops, and St. Cornelius, bishop of Rome,[106] who was martyred at the same time, refused to support him. St. Augustine afterward had great difficulty in excusing him, and finally had to resort to saying that such an error had been washed away by his blood, shed for the love of Christ. Thus spoke St. Augustine, condemning St. Cyprian's doctrine of rebaptism, which has since been condemned again and again (and rightfully so). But we are well content with St. Cyprian, for in him Christ comforts us poor sinners mightily, showing that his great saints are after all still human—like St. Cyprian, this excellent man and dear martyr, who blundered in more serious matters, about which we lack the time to speak now.

But what will we do with the fathers who transmitted this doctrine to St. Cyprian? In the *Ecclesiastical History*, Book VII, pages 1 and 2,[107] you may read what that fine Bishop Dionysius of Alexandria[108] wrote about it to Bishop Sixtus of Rome,[109] saying that this policy had been followed by other great and prominent bishops before the bishops in Africa followed it, that it had been decided upon by the Council of Iconium,[110] and that therefore such important facts should be considered before condemning the practice. But in the Council of Nicaea is clearly written the article that one should rebaptize the heretics, the Paulianists or Photinians.[111] And if this article offends St. Augustine in his *On Here-*

---

[104] Cyprian became bishop of Carthage in 248, and was put to death in 258 because of his faith.

[105] Cf. *Epistola ad Ianuarium. Sententiae episcoporum LXXXVII de haereticis baptizandis; Epistola ad Iubaianum. MPL* 3, 1073-1082; 1089-1116; 1153-1174; *ANF* 5, 375-377; 565-572; 379-386.

[106] Cornelius I (251-253).

[107] Cf. *MPG* 13, 256; *PNF²* 1, 294.

[108] Dionysius (d. *ca.* 264) was involved in many controversies over rebaptizing schismatics.

[109] Sixtus II (257-258).

[110] Held in Phrygia, an ancient country of Asia Minor, in *ca.* 235.

[111] Cf. Canon XIX. *MPL* 21, 475; *PNF²* 14, 40. This canon is not genuine,

sies[112] because he had plagued himself for a long time with the Anabaptist Donatists,[113] he nevertheless extricates himself for the sake of the Nicene council's decree by saying it must be assumed that the Photinians did not employ the baptismal formula, which other heretics did. If only one could believe it, since there is no proof. For the Photinians did not have, nor did they create, a gospel different from that possessed by the whole church; it thus seems more plausible to assume that they used the common formula, for heretics always like to boast of possessing Scripture. Thus Anabaptism tries to justify itself against St. Augustine and us all, because the Nicene council and other earlier councils and fathers agreed with Cyprian.[114]

Furthermore, the *Constitutions of the Holy Apostles*,[115] the ordinances of the apostles, have now been printed in many editions so that the church may again be properly governed. Among them is this canon: "One should count the heretics' sacrament and baptism as nothing, but should instead rebaptize them."[116] And it can readily be inferred that if the apostles ordained this, it was transmitted (as Dionysius states)[117] by the earlier fathers and councils

---

but is a later addition to the acts of the council. The Paulianists and Photinians are the followers of the heretical bishops Paul of Samosata (d. 269) and Photinus of Sirmium (d. 376). Both rejected Nicene Christology. Cf. *O.D.C.C.*, pp. 1034, 1069.

[112] Cf. *MPL* 42, 34.

[113] A schismatic group named after Donatus (d. *ca.* 355), under whose leadership they established their own church in Carthage. Condemned by a synod in Carthage in 411, they spread throughout North Africa after a debate with St. Augustine, who recommended their persecution by the state. They also became known as Anabaptists (from the Greek "rebaptizers") because they rebaptized converts from the Roman church. Cf. W. H. C. Frend, *The Donatist Church* (Oxford, 1952).

[114] Luther assumes here that the Council of Nicaea settled the question of Anabaptism in favor of Cyprian's position. Yet the council simply acknowledged the Roman practice (with the exception of Paulianism). Cf. Schäfer, *op. cit.*, pp. 272-273.

[115] *Canones apostolorum.* A collection of alleged decrees of synods, claiming apostolic origin. The collection stems from the late fourth or early fifth century and is closely related to the *Apostolic Constitution*. *MPG* 1, 555-591; *ANF* 7, 387-505. In 1524 a new edition was published in Paris bv Jacques Merlin, which was followed by others. Cf. *WA* 50, 540, n. *d.* Luther could find them in Crabbe's work on the councils.

[116] Canon XXXVIII.

[117] Cf. above, p. 236.

to St. Cyprian, and by him to the Council of Nicaea, for Cyprian preceded this council. If the apostles actually decreed this, then St. Cyprian is right, and St. Augustine with all of Christendom and with us who share his view are defeated. For who would teach contrary to the apostles? If the apostles did not decree this, then one should drown and hang all such authors and teachers for circulating, printing, and advertising such books under the apostles' names. They also deserve not to be believed with regard to other books or utterances of theirs henceforth, because they are constantly producing books which they themselves do not believe but nevertheless foist on us, with the letters c-o-u-n-c-i-l, f-a-t-h-e-r-s. If it is only a matter of letters—and their one concern is to fool us with them—a chorister in Halberstadt could cry them out far better than they.

Now if St. Cyprian had such apostles' rules on his side, as well as the Nicene and other councils, how shall we compare the fathers? The apostles and St. Cyprian demand rebaptism; St. Augustine and the whole later church declare this to be wrong. Who is going to preach to Christians in the meantime until this dispute is adjusted and settled? Yes, it is fun to fool around with councils and fathers if one juggles with the letters or constantly postpones the council, as has now been done for twenty years,[118] and does not think of what happens meanwhile to the souls who must be fed with conscientious teaching, as Christ says, "Tend my sheep" [John 21:16].

I excuse St. Cyprian first to the extent that he was not an Anabaptist such as ours are today,[119] for he held that the heretics had no sacrament at all and that therefore they had to be baptized like other heathen. He was honestly mistaken in believing that he was not rebaptizing, but baptizing an unbaptized heathen; for he knows and holds not a rebaptism, but only one single baptism. But our Anabaptists admit that our baptism and that of the papacy is a true baptism, but since it is administered or received by unworthy people, it is no baptism at all. St. Cyprian would never have concurred in this, much less practiced it.

---

[118] Cf. above, p. 201, n. 1.
[119] Cf. Luther's *Concerning Rebaptism*. LW 40, 229-262.

I have a high regard for St. Cyprian's person and faith, and that is why I said the foregoing in his behalf; for doctrine is subject to the words of St. Paul, "Test everything," etc. [I Thess. 5:21]. But we are not interested here in what I may say, but in bringing the fathers into agreement with one another, so that we may become certain of what and how to preach to the poor Christians. Here the apostles and Cyprian are at odds with St. Augustine and the church over baptism. If we obey St. Augustine, then we have to condemn the apostles with their rules and the Nicene council with the earlier fathers and councils, including St. Cyprian. And on the other hand, if St. Cyprian and the apostles are right, then St. Augustine and the church are wrong. Meanwhile, who is going to preach and baptize until we reach an agreement? The papists boastfully quote the canons of the apostles and the councils together with the fathers against us. Some of these, for example, are incorporated in Gratian's canon law.[120] Now if the dam should break and some of these canons and councils were found to be heretical, as the one about rebaptism is, who could prevent the flood from bursting forth irresistibly and proclaiming with a roar, "You lie in everything you write, say, print, vomit, and shout. Not a word of yours can be believed, even though you quote councils, fathers, and apostles"?

However, while we both thus cull from the councils and the fathers, they what they like, and we what we like, and cannot reach an agreement—because the fathers themselves disagree as much as do the councils—who, my dear man, is going to preach to the poor souls who know nothing of such culling and quarreling? Is that tending the sheep of Christ, when we ourselves do not know whether what we are feeding them is grass or poison, hay or dung? And are they to dangle and hang until it is settled and the council arrives at a decision? Oh, how poorly Christ would have provided for the church if this is how things have to go on! No, there must be another way than proving things by means of councils and fathers, or there could have been no church since the days of the apostles—which is impossible, for it is writ-

---

[120] See for example, *Decreti Prima Pars,* dist. XXXV, C. I; dist. XLVII, C. I; dist. LXXXVIII, C. III. *CIC* 1, 131, 151, 307.

ten, "I believe one holy, Christian church,"[121] and, "I am with you always, to the close of the age" [Matt. 28:20]. These words must be the truth, even if all the fathers and councils were wrong! The Man must be called "I am the truth" [John 14:6]; fathers and councils should on the other hand be called "Every man is a liar" [Rom. 3:4] whenever they contradict each other.

I am not saying this for the sake of our people, to whom I will later show what councils, fathers, and church are, if they do not know it (from which God has protected them!), but I am saying this for the sake of the screamers who think that we have never read the fathers and the councils. Although I have not read all the councils—I do not intend to read them all; this would be too great a waste of time since I did read the four principal councils very thoroughly, much more so than any of them did I am sure—I shall also make bold to say that I hold, after the four principal councils, all the others to be of lesser value, even though I would regard several (understand me rightly), I say several, as equally good. I am more familiar with the fathers, I hope, than these screamers who tear out of context whatever they choose and discard the rest if it annoys them. Therefore we must approach the matter differently.

But why should we get excited? If we wish to harmonize the sayings of the fathers let us consult the master of the *Sentences*,[122] who is diligent beyond measure in this task and was way ahead of us, for he too felt this anguish[123] over the disagreement of the fathers and wanted to remedy these things. In my opinion, he did it better than we would, and you will find in no one council, nor in all of the councils, and in none of the fathers, as much as in the book *Sentences*. The councils and fathers deal with several points of Christian doctrine, but none of them deals with them all as this man does; at least, he deals with most of them. And yet, about the real articles, such as faith and justification, he speaks too undecidedly and weakly, even though he gives high

---

[121] The Nicene Creed.
[122] Peter Lombard (*ca.* 1100-1160). His *Four Books of Sentences* (*Sententiarum Libri Quatuor*) was the standard theological textbook of the Middle Ages. The work is contained in *MPL* 192.
[123] *Anfechtung.*

enough praise to the grace of God. Also, as was said above,[124] we might as well have let Gratian do the work of harmonizing the councils for us, something to which he gave much effort, but in which he is not as pure as the master of *Sentences,* for he concedes too much to the Roman bishop, and applies everything to him. Otherwise, he would perhaps have done a better job in harmonizing the councils than we could do now.

If any one wishes further proof that the dear, holy fathers were human beings, he should read the booklet of Dr. Pomer, our pastor,[125] on the four chapters to the Corinthians. He will indeed have to learn from this that St. Augustine was right when he wrote, "My dear man, do not," etc., as was quoted above,[126] namely, that he will believe none of the fathers unless he has Scripture on his side. Dear God, if the Christian faith depended on men or were based on the words of men, what need would there be then for Holy Scripture? Or why should God have given it? Then let us shove it under the bench and, in its stead, lay only the fathers and councils on the desk. Or if the fathers were not human beings, how then shall we human beings attain salvation? If they were human they would also at times have thought, spoken, and acted just as we think, speak, and act, but afterward they would speak (like us) the beloved prayer, "Forgive us our trespasses," etc., especially since they did not have the same promise of the Holy Spirit that the apostles had, but had to be the apostles' disciples.

If the Holy Spirit had been so foolish as to expect or trust that the councils or fathers would do everything well and make no mistakes there would have been no need for him to warn the church against them, saying in I Corinthians 4 [3:12] that one should examine all things and be on one's guard wherever men build with straw, hay, and wood on the foundation. In that way

---

[124] Cf. above, pp. 212-213.
[125] John Bugenhagen (1485-1528), known as Pomeranus from the place of his birth (Pommern), had been pastor at the town church in Wittenberg since 1523. His *Commentary on Four Chapters of the First Epistle to the Corinthians* (*Ioannis Bugenhagii Pomerani Commentarius, in quatuor capita prioris Epistolae ad Corinthios*) was published in 1530. For the text, see Georg Geisenhof (ed.), *Bibliotheca Bugenhagia* (Leipzig, 1908), No. 266.
[126] Cf. above, p. 217.

he foretold, not privately and feebly, but openly and mightily, that in the holy church there would be those who build with wood, straw, and hay, namely, teachers who would remain on the foundation and be saved, even though harmed by fire, which cannot be said of the heretics, for they lay a different foundation. The others, however, remain on the foundation, that is, in the faith in Christ, attain salvation, and are called God's saints, even though they too have hay, straw, and wood which must be consumed by the fire of Holy Scripture, albeit without injuring their salvation. As St. Augustine says of himself, *"Errare potero, hereticus non ero,"* "I may err, but I shall not become a heretic."[127] Reason: heretics not only err, but do not want to be corrected; they defend their error as though it were right, and fight against the recognized truth and their own conscience.

St. Paul says of them in Titus 3 [:10-11], "As for a man who is factious, after admonishing him once or twice, have nothing more to do with him, knowing that such a person is perverted and sinful; he is *autokatakritos,*"[128] that is, he wilfully and wittingly persists in remaining condemned in his error. But St. Augustine willingly confesses his error, and lets it be pointed out to him, so he cannot be a heretic even though he has erred. All the other saints do the same and gladly consign their hay, straw, and wood to the fire so that they may remain on the foundation of salvation, as we did too, and still do.

Therefore, because it cannot be otherwise with the fathers (I am speaking of the holy and good ones)—when they build without Scripture, that is, without gold, silver, and precious stones, then they will build with wood, straw, or hay—we must, according to St. Paul's verdict, know how to differentiate between gold and wood, between silver and straw, between precious stones and hay; and we must not be compelled by those obnoxious screamers to believe that wood and silver are the same, that silver and straw are the same, and that emeralds and hay are the same. Or we ought to ask them (if this could be done) first to become so clever themselves as to take wood for gold, straw for silver, and

---

[127] The passage could not be found in Augustine's works.
[128] "Self-condemned"; cf. above, p. 204, n. 5.

hay for pearls. Otherwise, they should justly spare us, and not expect such foolishness or childishness of us.

And all of us should also take note of this miracle of the Holy Spirit, namely, that he wanted to give the world all the books of Holy Scripture, of both the Old and the New Testaments, solely through Abraham's people and seed, and that he did not have a single book composed by us Gentiles, just as he did not intend to choose the prophets and apostles from among the Gentiles, as St. Paul says in Romans 3 [:2], the Jews enjoy a great advantage, since they "are entrusted with the oracles of God," and according to Psalm 147 [:19], "He declares his word to Jacob, his statutes and ordinances to Israel." And Christ himself says in John 4 [:22], "We worship what we know, for salvation is from the Jews," and Romans 9 [:4-5] says, "To them belong the covenants, the giving of the law, the patriarchs, and Christ."

Therefore we Gentiles must not value the writings of our fathers as highly as Holy Scripture, but as worth a little less; for they are the children and heirs, while we are the guests and strangers who have come to the children's table by grace and without any promise. We should, indeed, humbly thank God and, like the Gentile woman, have no higher wish than to be the little dogs that gather the crumbs falling from their masters' table [Matt. 15:27]. As it is, we proceed arrogantly and put our fathers and ourselves on a level with the apostles, never thinking that God could break us to pieces more easily, since he did not spare the natural branches and Abraham's seed or heirs for their unbelief, Romans 11 [:21]. And yet, that accursed abomination in Rome usurps the authority to change Scripture arbitrarily solely to suit himself, without any regard for apostles and prophets. That is why St. Augustine is right when he writes to St. Jerome (as related above), "Dear brother, I hope that you do not expect your books to be regarded as equal to those of the apostles and prophets. God forbid that you should desire such a thing."[129]

Moreover, there is neither a council nor a father in which one could find, or from whom one could learn, the whole of Christian doctrine. For example, the Nicene council deals only with the doc-

---

[129] Cf. above, p. 218, n. 49.

trine that Christ is truly God; the one at Constantinople, that the Holy Spirit is God; the one at Ephesus, that Christ is not two but one person; the one at Chalcedon, that Christ has not one but two natures, the human and the divine. These are the four great principal councils; they deal with no more than these four articles, as we shall hear. But this is still not the complete teaching of the Christian faith. St. Cyprian deals with how one must suffer and die in a firm faith; he rebaptizes heretics; and he also rebukes bad morals and women.[130] St. Hilary[131] defends the Nicene council, states that Christ is true God, and deals with a few psalms. St. Jerome[132] extols virginity and the hermits. St. Chrysostom[133] teaches prayer, fasting, almsgiving, patience, etc., and St. Ambrose[134] deals with many subjects; but St. Augustine treats the greatest number, and that is why the master of the *Sentences* has taken most of his material from him.

In summary, put them all together, both fathers and councils, and you still will not be able to cull from them all the teachings of the Christian faith, even if you culled forever. If it had not been for Holy Scripture, the church, had it depended on the councils and fathers, would not have lasted long. And in proof of this: where do the fathers and councils get what they teach or deal with? Do you think that they first invented it in their own day, or that the Holy Spirit always inspired them with something new? How was the church preserved prior to these councils and fathers? Or were there no Christians before councils and fathers came up? That is why we must speak differently about the councils and fathers and look not at the letters but at the meaning. May that

---

[130] See for example, *Exhortation to Martyrdom, Addressed to Fortunatus* (*MPL* 4, 678-702; *ANF* 5, 496-506), and *On the Dress of Virgins* (*MPL* 4, 451-478; *ANF* 5, 430-436).

[131] Hilary of Poitiers (*ca.* 315-367), famous for his defense of the Nicene council in his *Against the Emperor Constantius* (*Contra Constantium Imperatorem*). *MPL* 10, 577-606.

[132] In *Epistola* 22, *ad Eustachium*. *MPL* 22, 394-425; *PNF*² 6, 22-41.

[133] John of Constantinople (*ca.* 354-407), known since the sixth century as Chrysostom ("gold mouth") because of his preaching. See, for example, his *Six Books on the Priesthood*. *MPG* 26, 623-692; *PNF*¹ 9, 33-83.

[134] Ambrose (*ca.* 340-397) was bishop of Milan. His writings are in *MPL* 15–17; *PNF*² 10.

suffice for the first part of this book, so that we can catch our breath too.

Part II

First, concerning the councils, for the letters c-o-u-n-c-i-l afford us stupid people endless difficulty, even more than f-a-t-h-e-r-s and c-h-u-r-c-h. Yet I do not wish to set myself up as judge or master in this matter; I only wish to express my ideas. Grace and luck is wished to anyone who can do better. Amen.

I shall take to heart what St. Hilary says in *On the Trinity:* *"ex causis dicendis summenda est intelligentia dictorum,"*[135] that is, "He who wants to understand what is said must see why or for what reason it was spoken." In the same manner, actions are best understood by understanding that which motivates them.[136] Natural reason also teaches this. I shall illustrate it to make it simpler: if one peasant brings suit against another, saying, "Dear judge, this man calls me a rogue and a rascal," these words and letters, by themselves, convey the idea that the plaintiff has suffered a great wrong, and that they are false and sheer lies. But if the defendant appears and gives reasons for such words, saying, "Dear judge, he is a rascal and a rogue for he was flogged out of the city of N. for his rascality, and he was saved from hanging only through the great efforts and pleading of pious people, and now he wants to do violence to me in my own home," the judge will understand these letters differently than he had before—as daily experience in government shows. For before one learns the reason and the motive for what a man says, it is only letters, the shouts of choristers, or the songs of nuns.

Likewise, Christ says to Peter, "Whatever you bind on earth shall be bound in heaven, and whatever you loose on earth shall be loosed in heaven" [Matt. 16:19]. The pope takes the letters, rides into Never Never Land[137] with them, and interprets them as,

---

[135] Cf. *On the Trinity*, IX, 2. MPL 10, 282; PNF[1] 9, 156. Luther was apparently quoting from memory since his quotation differs from the text in MPL: *"Cum dictorum intelligentia, aut ex praepositis aut ex consequentibus expectatur."*

[136] Luther switches into Latin here: *Sic ex causis agendi cognoscuntur acta.*

[137] *Schlauraffenland*, from a German fairy tale.

"Whatever I do in heaven and on earth is right. I have the keys to bind and to loose everything and all." Indeed, if we had eaten beets, etc.!¹³⁸ But if one looks at the sense, one finds that Christ talks about binding and loosing sin, because these are keys to the kingdom of heaven, into which no one can enter unless his sins are forgiven, and from which no one is excluded except him around whom they have been tied because of his impenitent life. Thus these words have nothing to do with St. Peter's power, but apply to the needs of despondent or proud sinners. But the pope converts these keys into two skeleton keys to all the kings' crowns and treasures, to the purse strings, the life, the honor, and the goods of the entire world. For he, like a fool, looks at the letters and pays no heed to the sense.

There are many passages in Holy Scripture that are contradictory according to the letters; but when that which motivates them is pointed out, everything is all right. I should think that all jurists and medical men find a great deal of this in their books too, as I said earlier about the judge. And what is the entire being of man other than sheer antilogies and contradictions, until one hears the facts? That is why my antilogists¹³⁹ are admirable, fine, pious sows and asses, who collect my antilogies and discard that which motivates them, indeed, even diligently obscure them; just as though I, too, could not point out antilogies in their books, which cannot even be reconciled by any reason! But enough of this, for they do not deserve that many words.

We shall now take up the Council of Nicaea, which was undertaken for the following reasons: the praiseworthy Emperor Constantine had become a Christian and had given the Christians peace from tyrants and persecutors.¹⁴⁰ He was so filled with strong, earnest faith and sincerity that he warred even against his brother-

---

¹³⁸ An allusion to the German proverb, "*Versenge mir die ruben nicht!*" Cf. Thiele, *Luthers Sprichwörtersammlung*, No. 85.

¹³⁹ A reference to his opponents who, like John Eck, wrote *Obelisks* against him. Cf. *LW* 31, xvi.

¹⁴⁰ Eusebius, *Ecclesiastical History*, IX, 10. *MPG* 13, 335; *PNF*² 1, 366. The subsequent account is based on *Historia Tripartita*, beginning in I, 12. *MPL* 69, 901; *PNF*² 23, 251. The reference to the Persians, however, is not contained there. See Schäfer, *op. cit.*, pp. 291-294.

in-law Licinius,[141] to whom he had given his sister Constantia in marriage, and whom he had made co-emperor, and pushed him out of the empire because he would not stop shamefully persecuting Christians, even after several warnings. Now when the good emperor had established this peace for the Christians and done everything for their good, promoting the church in every way he could, all was secure, so he planned a war outside his empire, against the Persians. Into such a fair and peaceful paradise and into such happy days did the old serpent come and arouse Arius, a priest in Alexandria, against his bishop. He wanted to bring up something new against the old faith, and because he coveted fame, he assailed his bishop's doctrine, declaring that Christ was not God. Many priests and great and learned bishops rallied about him, and the malady grew rapidly in many lands, until Arius dared to boast that he was a martyr, having ·to suffer for the truth's sake at the hands of his bishop Alexander,[142] who did not let him get away with these things and wrote terrible letters against him to all the lands.[143]

When this came to the ears of the good emperor, he acted like a very wise prince; he wanted to douse the flames before the fire grew any bigger. He wrote a letter[144] to both bishop Alexander and priest Arius, admonishing them so kindly and so earnestly that it could not have been better written. He explained to them with what difficulty he had effected peace for the Christians in the empire and if they should now war among themselves it would be a great irritation to the heathen who would perhaps fall from the faith again (which then did happen and he himself complained), and he would thus be hindered from marching against the Persians. To sum up, it was a humble, Christian letter, written by this great emperor to these two men. To me it seems much too humble, for I know my own rough pen so that I could not have drawn such a humble missive from my inkwell, especially if I had been emperor, and an emperor like that!

But the letter did not help. Arius had now gained a large fol-

---

[141] Licinius ruled the Eastern half of the Roman Empire from 314 to 324.
[142] Alexander, bishop of Alexandria (ca. 313-328), who excommunicated Arius.
[143] *Historia Tripartita*, I, 14, 15. MPL 69, 914-915; PNF² 3, 41-42.
[144] *Historia Tripartita*, I, 19. MPL 69, 918-920; PNF² 2, 6-7.

lowing, and wanted to butt his head against his bishop. The pious emperor did not give up either. He sent a personal ambassador, an excellent, world-renowned bishop named Hosius of Cordova, from Spain,[145] to the two in Alexandria, and throughout Egypt, to settle the dispute. This did not help either, and meanwhile the fire kept spreading as though a forest burned. Then the good emperor Constantine made his final move and collected the best and most renowned bishops in every land, ordered that they be brought to Nicaea on the imperial asses, horses, and mules, and asked them to find a satisfactory solution to the matter. Many fine bishops and fathers really did come, especially the famous Jacob of Nisibis[146] and Paphnutius of Ptolemais, bishops who had suffered severe persecution under Licinius and who had performed miracles. But there were also several Arian bishops among them, like mouse-droppings in the pepper.[147]

The emperor was now in good spirits, and hoped for the good ending of the matter; he honored them all. Then several of them came along and handed the emperor a bill of complaint for what one bishop had against the other, and asked for the emperor's judgment. He declined to have anything to do with them, for he was not interested in the bishops' squabbles, but wanted to have this article about Christ judged, and he had not convoked the council for the sake of their bickering. But since they persisted, he bade them to bring him all the bills, and then he cast them, unread, into the fire. However, he sent them away with the kind words that he could not be their judge, they whom God had set as judges over him; and he exhorted them to deal with the main issue.[148] Now then! That is my idea of a wise, gentle, and patient prince. Someone else would have been so irritated by these bishops that he would have knocked the cask to pieces.[149] And

---

[145] *Historia Tripartita*, I, 20. *MPL* 69, 920; *PNF*² 2, 252. Hosius of Cordova (257-ca. 357) was Constantine's ecclesiastical adviser.

[146] A celebrated opponent of Arianism (d. 338); Nisibis is in Mesopotamia.

[147] A German proverb, "*Wie meuse dreck unter pfeffer.*" Cf. Thiele, *Luthers Sprichwörtersammlung*, No. 371.

[148] Here Luther used, besides the *Historia Tripartita*, II, 2 (*MPL* 69, 922-923), Rufinus' translation of Eusebius' *Ecclesiastical History*, I, 2 (*MPL* 21, 468).

[149] *Das fas in einen hauffen gestossen*, an intensification of the German proverb, "*Dem fas den boden ausstossen.*" Thiele, *Luthers Sprichwörtersammlung*, No. 335.

yet he did express his opinion clearly when he burned their complaints, without any regard for their episcopal dignity, thus reproving them for their childish conduct because they had been summoned for a far more important purpose.

Now when the council met, he sat down among the bishops, on a chair lower than theirs.[150] The bishop of Rome, Sylvester, was not present, but (as some say) he had sent two priests.[151] After the bishop of Antioch, Eustathius[152] (who chaired this council), had thanked and praised the emperor for his kindness, Arius' doctrine was publicly read (for it appears that Arius himself was not present, being neither a bishop nor a delegate);[153] it stated that Christ was not God, but was created and made by God, as the histories record at length. At this the holy fathers and bishops arose from their seats in indignation, tore the document to pieces, and declared it was not true; and so Arius was openly condemned by the furious council, so deeply did it hurt the fathers and so unbearable was it for them to hear this blasphemy of Arius. All the bishops signed this condemnation, the Arian bishops too, albeit hypocritically, as the future showed, except two bishops from Egypt who did not sign.[154] So the emperor dissolved the council on the same day, and he himself, and the council too, sent out a written report of this event throughout the world.[155] And the emperor Constantine, very happy that the matter was settled and disposed of, treated the bishops very kindly, especially those who had been persecuted.

This explains why the council met and what they had to do, namely, to preserve this ancient article of faith that Christ is true God against the new cleverness of Arius, who, on the basis of rea-

---

[150] *Historia Tripartita*, II, 5. *MPL* 69, 924-925; *PNF*[2] 3, 43-44.
[151] *Historia Tripartita*, II, 1. *MPL* 69, 920-921; *PNF*[2] 2, 253. In the *Tripartita* Julius, not Sylvester, is mentioned as bishop of Rome. On the basis of Crabbe's *Concilia Omnia*, Luther named Sylvester. Later scholarship confirmed Luther's historical judgment.
[152] Eustathius was bishop of Antioch from *ca.* 324 to *ca.* 330.
[153] A peculiar error by Luther. Both the *Historia Tripartita*, II, 5 (*MPL* 69, 924; *PNF*[2] 3, 43), and Rufinus, I, 5 (*MPL* 21, 472), record that Arius was present.
[154] *Historia Tripartita*, II, 15, 16. *MPL* 69, 934-935; *PNF*[2] 2, 14, 16. They were Secundus of Ptolemais and Theonas of Marmarica.
[155] *Historia Tripartita*, II, 12. *MPL* 69, 931-932; *PNF*[2] 2, 12-13.

son, wanted to falsify this article, indeed, to change it and condemn it; because of this he was himself condemned. The council did not invent this doctrine or establish it as something new as though it had not previously existed in the churches, but rather defended it against the new heresy of Arius. This was demonstrated by the fact that the fathers became upset and tore up the document, thus confessing that since the days of the apostles they had learned and taught differently in their churches. Otherwise, what would have happened to the Christians who for over three hundred years prior to this council, ever since the days of the apostles, had believed in and worshiped the name of Jesus in prayer as true God, who had died in this faith, and had suffered cruel persecution because of it?

I have to point this out in passing, for the pope's hypocrites have lapsed into such gross folly that they think that councils have the power and the right to set up new articles of faith and to alter the old ones. That is not true, and we Christians have to tear up documents like this too. No council ever did it or can do it; the articles of faith must not grow on earth through the councils, as from a new, secret inspiration, but must be issued from heaven through the Holy Spirit and revealed openly; otherwise, as we shall hear later, they are not articles of faith. Thus the Council of Nicaea (as was said) did not invent this doctrine or establish it as something new, namely, that Christ is God; rather, it was done by the Holy Spirit, who came openly from heaven to the apostles on the day of Pentecost, and through Scripture glorified Christ as true God, as he had promised the apostles. It remained unchanged since the days of the apostles until this council, and so on until our own day—it will remain until the end of the world, as he says, "Lo, I am with you always, to the close of the age" [Matt. 28:20].

If we had nothing with which to defend this article except this council we would be in a bad way. Then I myself would not believe the council either, but say, "They were human beings." But St. John, St. Paul, St. Peter, and the other apostles are reliable and offer us a firm foundation and defense; for it was revealed to them and through the Holy Spirit given to them openly from heaven. The churches prior to this council derived it from them and this council has it from them too. For before the council, when Arius first began, as well as in the council and after the council, they defended themselves vigorously with Scripture, especially with St. John's gospel, and disputed sharply, as the books of Athanasius[156] and Hilary testify.[157] The *Historia Tripartita* also says in Book V, chapter 29, "At Nicaea the faith was grounded on the writings of the apostles."[158] Otherwise, if there were no Holy Scripture of the prophets and apostles, the mere words of the council would be meaningless, and its decisions would accomplish nothing. Therefore this article on the deity of Christ was the chief business of this council; indeed, it was the whole council, for that is why it was called and (as I said before) why it was adjourned on the same day on which it was adopted.

But on another day, when the emperor Constantine is not reported to have been present, they met again and dealt with other matters pertaining to the temporal, external rule of the church; among these were undoubtedly also the papers Constantine had previously thrown into the fire when he refused to judge. That is why they had to meet alone to settle these things without the emperor. Most of this was sheer clerical squabbling: there were not to be two bishops in one city; no bishop of a small church was to covet a larger one; clerics or servants of a church were not to leave their own church to wander aimlessly about from one church to another; no one was to consecrate the people of another bishop without his knowledge or consent; no bishop was to accept a person who had been expelled by another bishop; the bishop of Jerusalem should retain his ancient prerogative of preeminence before others; and more of such silly prattle.[159] Who could regard such things as articles of faith? And what can one preach about these things to the people in the church? What does

---

[156] Athanasius (*ca.* 295-373), bishop of Alexandria and the most vigorous defender of Nicene theology. For his writings, see *MPG* 16; *PNF²* 4.

[157] Cf. above, p. 244, n. 131.

[158] *Hanc solam fidem, quae Nicaeae apostolorum auctoritate fundata est.*" *MPL* 69, 1007*a*; *PNF²* 3, 83.

[159] Luther's source here is Rufinus I, 6. *MPL* 21, 473-475. Luther lists the following canons of Nicaea: X, XVI, XVII, XVIII, V, VIII. On the difference in numbering, see *PNF²* 14, 43.

all this have to do with the church or the people—unless one wanted to learn from this, as from a history book, that at this time there were everywhere in the church self-willed, base, disorderly bishops, priests, clerics, and people who were more concerned with honor, power, and wealth than with God or his kingdom, and who in this way had to be held in check!

It is easy to figure out that Constantine did not summon the council for these matters; otherwise, he probably would have done it before Arius ushered in this misery. Why should he have bothered about how these things would be kept? The bishops themselves, each in his own diocese, had to govern his own church and had done so before, as the articles themselves report. Moreover, it would have been a sin and a shame to call such a great council into session for such trivial matters, since God-given reason is quite sufficient to regulate these external matters, and the Holy Spirit, whose mission is to reveal Christ and not to dabble in such matters as are subject to reason, is not needed for this—unless, of course, one would call every act of pious Christians, even their eating and drinking, the work of the Holy Spirit. But the Holy Spirit must have better things to do for the sake of doctrine than these works which are subject to reason.

Not all who were present at this council were pious men; not all were Paphnutiuses, Jacobs, and Eustathiuses, etc. One can count seventeen Arian bishops who were prominent men, although they had to bow and scrape before the others.[160] The history of Theodoret reports[161] that there were twenty articles; Rufinus speaks of twenty-three. Now I cannot say whether the Arians or others afterward added to or subtracted from this number, or whether they substituted others (for the article which St. Paphnutius is said to have had adopted, concerning the wives of priests, is not among them).[162] But I do know well that nearly all of them have long been dead, buried in the books and fallen into decay, never able to rise again, as Constantine indicated and foretold by his act of

---

[160] Rufinus, I, 5. *MPL* 21, 472b.
[161] Although Luther did not read Theodoret's account, he found it quoted in the *Historia Tripartita* (II, 10-30), which usually quotes its sources. See Rufinus, I, 6. *MPL* 21, 473-475. See also Schäfer, *op. cit.*, p. 126, nn. 2, 3.
[162] Cf. above, p. 235, n. 101.

throwing them into the fire and burning them.[163] They are not kept and cannot be kept. They were hay, straw, and wood (as St. Paul puts it)[164] built on the ground; that is why fire consumed them in time, just as other transitory things disappear. But if they had been articles of faith or commandments of God they would have survived, like the article concerning the divinity of Christ.

However, one ember from these wooden articles has kept on glowing, namely, the one about the date of Easter.[165] We do not observe this article quite correctly either (as the mathematicians and astronomers point out to us) because the equinox in our time is far different than in that time, and our Easter is often celebrated too late in the year.[166] Long ago, shortly after the days of the apostles, the quarrel about the date of Easter broke out; and over this trifling and unnecessary matter the bishops accused one another of heresy and excommunicated one another, which was a sin and a shame. Several advocated observing it on the same day as the Jews, according to the law of Moses; others, lest they be regarded as Jewish, wanted to observe it on the following Sunday.[167] The bishop of Rome, Victor,[168] who also became a martyr, excommunicated all the bishops and churches in Asia approximately one hundred and eighty years before this council for not

---

[163] Cf. above, p. 248.

[164] I Cor. 3:12.

[165] Rufinus, I, 5 (MPL 21, 475b) and Historia Tripartita, II, 12 (MPL 69, 932c; PNF² 2, 13); IX, 38 (MPL 69, 1153-1156: PNF² 2, 130-134).

[166] Luther is aware of the difference between the Julian calendar (adopted in 46 B.C.) and the solar year. By A.D. 325 the equinox had moved from March 25 to March 21, the date on which Easter was celebrated. Until the introduction of the Gregorian calendar the equinox was moving forward at the rate of one day in 129 years. Gregory XIII (1572-1585) omitted thirteen days (October 5 to 14) in 1582 and introduced the leap year to balance the Christian calendar with the solar year. The Greek church did not accept the Gregorian calendar, and thus its calendar differs from the Gregorian calendar by thirteen days. For a detailed account of the chronological calculations in the history of the Christian calendar, see O.D.C.C., p. 403; Allan Hauck, Calendar of Christianity (New York: Association Press, 1961), pp. 11-26; Albert Hauck (ed.), Realencyklopädie für protestantische Theologie und Kirche (3rd ed.; 24 vols.; Leipzig, 1896-1913), XXI, 914-945.

[167] This quarrel took place in 190-191 between the churches of Asia Minor, favoring the Jewish date (the 17th of Nisan), and Rome, advocating the Sunday following.

[168] Victor was bishop from 189 to 198.

adhering to the same Easter date as he did. So early did the Roman bishops make a grab for majesty and power! But Irenaeus,[169] bishop of Lyons, in France, who had known Polycarp,[170] a disciple of St. John the Evangelist, reprimanded him and settled the quarrel so that Victor had to leave the churches in peace.

That is why Constantine also had to take up this matter and help to settle it in the council. He decreed that the same Easter date should be observed throughout the world; read the *Tripartita,* Book IX, chapter 38.[171] I suppose that the present again calls for a reform and correction of the calendar in order to assign Easter its proper place. But no one should undertake that except the exalted majesties, emperors and kings, who would have to unanimously and simultaneously issue an order to all the world saying when Easter is henceforth to be celebrated. Otherwise, if one country were to start without the others, and worldly events, such as markets, fairs, and other business, were governed by the present date, the people of the country would appear at the markets of another country at the wrong time, which would result in wild disorder and confusion in everything. It would be very nice, and easy to do, if the high majesties would want to do it, since all the preparatory work has been done by the astronomers[172] and all that is needed is a decree or command. In the meantime we hold to the flickering ember from the Nicene council that Easter is to be kept on a Sunday; meanwhile the date may wobble back and forth, for they are called "movable festivals";[173] I call them wobbling festivals[174] since the Easter day, with its associated festivals, changes every year, coming early in one year, late in another, and not on a certain day like the other festivals.

This wobbling of the festivals is due to the fact that the an-

---

[169] An ancient church father, Irenaeus was a bishop in *ca.* 177.
[170] Polycarp, bishop of Smyrna, died as a martyr in 155.
[171] *MPL* 69, 1154*d*-1155*a*; *PNF²* 2, 131.
[172] The French theologian Peter of Ailly (1350-1420) and the Italian cardinal Nicholas of Cusa (1401-1464) had suggested striking a few days from the Julian calendar. Pope Sixtus IV then asked the astronomer Regiomontanus to undertake a calendar reform which was completed and went into effect under Gregory XIII in 1582.
[173] *Festa mobilia.*
[174] *Schückelfest.*

cient fathers (as was said) in the very beginning wanted to have Easter at the time established by Moses, namely, in the full moon of March, nearest the equinox; and yet they were unwilling to Judaize entirely, or to keep Easter with the Jews on the day of the full moon, so as Christians they dropped the law of Moses and took the Sunday after the March full moon. Thus it happened last year, 1538, that the Jews observed their Easter on the Saturday after Invocavit—as our church calls it—that is, about five weeks before we observed our Easter.[175] Now the Jews laugh about that and ridicule us Christians, saying that we do not keep Easter right and that we do not even know how to keep it right, thus hardening their unbelief. This then irritates our people, and they would gladly see the calendar corrected by the exalted majesties, for without their co-operation this is impossible to do and still less advisable.

In my opinion this experience with Easter is nicely described by Christ in Matthew 9 [:16-17], "No one puts a piece of unshrunk cloth on an old garment, for the patch tears away from the garment, and a worse tear is made. Neither is new wine put into old wineskins; if it is, the skins burst, and the wine is spilled, and the skins are destroyed." They want to retain a part of the old law of Moses, namely, to pay heed to the full moon of March—that is the old garment. Then (as Christians delivered from the law of Moses by Christ) they do not wish to be subject to that same day of the full moon, but, instead want to take the following Sunday—that is the new patch on the old garment. That is why the everlasting squabble and the constant wobbling have to date caused much mischief in the church, and it will have to, until the end of the world, with books appearing without measure or end on this subject. Christ has permitted this to go on for a special reason, as he always proves his strength in weakness and teaches us to recognize our own weakness.

How much better it would have been if they had let Moses' law regarding Easter die altogether and had retained nothing of the old garment. For Christ, to whom this law applied, has an-

---

[175] In 1538 Easter was celebrated on April 21. The Saturday after Invocavit Sunday, the first Sunday in Lent, was March 16.

nulled it completely, killed it, and buried it forever through his passion and resurrection. He rent the veil of the temple and subsequently broke up and destroyed Jerusalem with its priesthood, principality, law, and everything. They should instead have reckoned and noted the days of the passion, the burial, and the resurrection by the course of the sun and set a fixed date for these, as they did with Christmas, New Year's, the day of the Magi,[176] Candlemas,[177] the Annunciation of Mary,[178] the Feast of St. John,[179] and other festivals, which they call fixed, not wobbling festivals. Then one would know every year for certain when the day of Easter and its associated festivals must come, without such great difficulty and disputation.

Well, you say, Sunday should be held in reverence for the sake of Christ's resurrection—it is therefore called *dies Dominica*[180]—and Easter is assigned to that day, since Christ rose on the day after the Sabbath (which we now call Saturday). This is certainly an argument that moved them, but since *dies Dominica* does not mean Sunday, but the Lord's day, why shouldn't any day on which Easter had fallen be called *dies Dominica,* the Lord's day? Is not Christmas also *dies Dominica,* the Lord's day, that is, the day on which the Lord's special event, his birth, is celebrated, which does not fall on a Sunday every year? Yet it is still called Christ's day,[181] that is, the Lord's day, even if it falls on a Friday, because it has a fixed letter[182] in the calendar calculated by the course of the sun. Just so could Easter have a fixed letter in the calendar, whether it came on Friday or Wednesday, as happens with Christmas. That way we would be well rid of the law of Moses with its full moon of March, just as no one asks today whether the moon is full or not at Christmas, but we adhere to the days as calculated by the sun's course and ignore the moon.

---

[176] Epiphany, January 6.
[177] The Purification of Mary (or the Presentation of Our Lord), February 2.
[178] March 25.
[179] June 24.
[180] "The Lord's day."
[181] *Christag.*
[182] In the calendar of Luther's time, as well as in ancient Christian calendars, each day was signified by a letter. Beginning with January 1, the letters ran from *a* to *g* and were repeated on the eighth day.

One might argue that since the equinox (as the astronomers point out) is movable, and the years in the calendar move too slowly and so do not keep pace with it, and the more years go by the worse it is, after a while the equinox would move further and further from a fixed Easter day,[183] as it would also move further and further from the day of St. Philip and St. James,[184] and from other festivals. What does it matter to us Christians? Even if our Easter should coincide with the day of St. Philip and St. James (which, I hope, will not happen before the end of the world) and move still further, we still celebrate Easter daily with our proclamation of Christ and our faith in him. It is enough to celebrate Easter once annually on a special day as an obvious, public, and perceptible reminder, not only because it affords an opportunity to discuss more thoroughly the history of the resurrection before the common people, but also because it represents a definite season according to which people may arrange their various business affairs, such as the seasons of St. Michael,[185] St. Martin,[186] St. Catherine,[187] St. John,[188] SS. Peter and Paul,[189] etc.

But this has been neglected from the very beginning; we cannot make any changes because the fathers did not initiate a change. The old garment with its great tear has stayed on and on, and now it may as well stay until the Last Day, which is imminent anyhow. Since the old garment has endured being patched and torn for approximately fourteen hundred years, it may as well let itself be patched and torn for another hundred years; for I hope that everything will soon come to an end.[190] And if the Easters have wobbled back and forth for about fourteen hundred years now, they may as well continue to wobble for the short time still

---

[183] Cf. above, p. 253, n. 166.
[184] May 1.
[185] September 29.
[186] November 11.
[187] November 25.
[188] June 24.
[189] June 29.
[190] Luther's view is based upon the idea that the world would last for six thousand years, of which only a few were left at his time. He seems to have arrived at the number fourteen hundred on the basis of his estimate for the beginning of the Easter controversies in *ca.* 190 until 1539. See Hauck, *Realencyklopädie*, XXI, 924.

remaining, since no one will do anything about it anyway, and those who would like to do something cannot.

I am entering into this lengthy and needless chatter solely for the purpose of expressing my opinion, in case several sects[191] in the course of time dare arbitrarily to move the Easter festival to another date than that which we now observe. And I believe if the Anabaptists had been sufficiently versed in astronomy to understand these things, they would have rushed in headlong, and (as is characteristic of the sect) introduced something entirely new and observed Easter on a different day than the whole world. But since they were unlearned in the sciences, the devil was unable to employ them as that kind of instrument or tool. Therefore, I advise that one let Easter come as it now comes, and keep it as it is kept now, and let the old garment be patched and torn (as was said); and let Easter wobble back and forth until the Last Day, or until the monarchs, in view of these facts, unanimously and simultaneously change it.

For this is not going to kill us,[192] nor will St. Peter's bark suffer distress because of it, since it is neither heresy nor sin (though the ancient fathers in their ignorance regarded it as such and dubbed each other heretics and excommunicated each other over it), but only an error or solecism in astronomy, which serves temporal government rather than the church. If the Jews mock us, as though we were doing it out of ignorance, then we, in turn, mock them far more because they adhere so rigidly and vainly to their Easter, and do not know that Christ fulfilled, annulled, and destroyed all that fifteen hundred years ago. For we do it willingly, knowingly, not out of ignorance. We would know quite well how to keep Easter according to the law of Moses—far better than they know it. But we will not and must not do it, for we have the Lord over Moses and over all things, who says, "The Son of man is lord of the sabbath" [Matt. 12:8]. How much more

---

[191] *Rotten*, a term Luther used frequently to designate the Anabaptists and other opponents of his position. For a survey of the various religious movements opposing the major reformers, cf. George H. Williams, *The Radical Reformation* (Philadelphia: Westminster, 1962).
[192] A German proverb, *"Es bricht uns kein bein."* Cf. Thiele, *Luthers Sprichwörtersammlung*, No. 324.

is he the Lord over Easter and Pentecost, which, in the law of Moses, are less than the sabbath, which is on the tables of Moses,[193] while Easter and Pentecost are outside the tables of Moses? Furthermore, we have St. Paul, who flatly forbids any one to be bound to holidays, feasts, and anniversaries of Moses, Galatians 4 [:10] and Colossians 2 [:16].

We therefore have and must have the power and the freedom to observe Easter when we choose; and even if we made Friday into Sunday, or vice versa, it would still be right, as long as it were done unanimously by the rulers and the Christians (as I said before). Moses is dead and buried by Christ, and days or seasons are not to be lords over Christians, but rather Christians are lords over days and seasons, free to fix them as they will or as seems convenient to them. For Christ made all things free when he abolished Moses. However, we will let things remain as they now are, since no peril, error, sin, or heresy is involved, and we are averse to changing anything needlessly or at our own personal whim, out of consideration for others who observe Easter at the same time as we do. We know we shall attain salvation without Easter and Pentecost, without Friday and Sunday, and we know that we cannot be damned—as St. Paul teaches us—because of Easter, Pentecost, Sunday, or Friday.

But to get back to the council, I say that we make too much of this ember from the Nicene council. The pope and his church subsequently made of this not only gold, silver, and precious stones, but also a foundation, that is, an article of faith, without which we could not be saved; and they all call it a commandment of, and an act of, obedience to the church. That makes them far worse than the Jews, for the Jews do have the Mosaic text commanded by God at that time in their favor, while these have nothing but their own fancy on their side; they come along and want to make a new garment out of the old rags of Moses. They claim that they are obeying Moses, though their doctrine is sheer fantasy, a dream about Moses who has long been dead and, as Scripture declares, buried by the Lord himself [Deut. 34:6] (that is, by Christ), so no one has ever found his grave. They

---

[193] The Decalogue.

want to reproduce the living Moses by magic before our eyes, but they fail to see, as St. Paul says in Galatians 5 [:3], that if they wish to keep one part of Moses they must keep all of Moses. Consequently, if they regard it a part of Mosaic law to set the date of Easter according to the full moon in March, they must also keep the whole law concerning the paschal lamb and forthwith become Jews, keeping a bodily paschal lamb with them. If not, they must discard it all, the full moon too, with all the rest of Moses; or in any case not regard this as necessary for salvation like an article of faith, which is what I believe the fathers in this council (especially the best ones) did.

Thus we see that this council dealt primarily with the article that Christ was truly God, for which it was convoked and for which it is and is called a council. They also dealt with several nonessential, physical, external, temporal matters on the side, rightfully to be viewed as temporal and not to be compared with articles of faith; nor are they to be regarded as eternal law (for they are past and expired). But the council found it necessary to attend to such physical matters as were pertinent and needful in their time, which no longer concern us today, and which are neither possible nor profitable for us to observe. And in proof of this, the article prescribing the rebaptism of heretics is false and wrong, even if it was formulated by the true fathers themselves[194] and not patched together by the Arians or the other loose bishops. Thus the apostolic council in Jerusalem also found it necessary for their day to settle, after it had disposed of the important business, several nonessential, external articles, such as that dealing with blood, strangled animals, and the sacrifice to idols; but not with the intention of making this an eternal law in the church, to be kept as an article of faith, for it has fallen into disuse. And why should we not also examine how this council can be understood within the context of the reasons that made it necessary?

This is how it came into being: Gentiles, who had been converted by Barnabas and Paul, had received the Holy Spirit through the gospel just as well as the Jews, and yet they were not under the law like the Jews. Then the Jews insisted very strongly that

---

[194] Cf. above, pp. 236-238.

the Gentiles be circumcised and commanded to keep the law of Moses; otherwise they could not be saved. These were hard, harsh, and heavy words—no salvation without the law of Moses and circumcision. The Pharisees who had become believers in Christ were especially insistent on this, according to Acts 15 [:5]. Thereupon the apostles and elders met to discuss this matter, and after they had quarreled at length and sharply, St. Peter arose and delivered the powerful and beautiful sermon in Acts 15 [:7-11], "Brethren, you know that in the early days God made choice among you, that by my mouth the Gentiles should hear the word of the gospel and believe. And God who knows the heart bore witness to them, giving them the Holy Spirit just as he did to us; and he made no distinction between us and them, but cleansed their hearts by faith. Now therefore why do you make trial of God by putting a yoke upon the neck of the disciples which neither our fathers nor we have been able to bear? But we believe that we shall be saved through the grace of the Lord Jesus, just as they will."

This sermon sounds as though St. Peter were really angry and disgusted about the harsh words of the Pharisees, who said that those who did not circumcise themselves and keep the law of Moses could not attain salvation, as was said above. He counters with hard, decisive words and says, "You are well aware that the Gentiles heard the Word and were saved through me, like Cornelius and his family; in proof of this, you grumbled against me and chided me because I had gone to the Gentiles, had converted and baptized them"—Acts 10 and 11.[195] "Is it possible that you have forgotten this and are determined to impose burdens on the Gentiles that neither our fathers nor we could bear? What is it but tempting God if we impose impossible burdens on others which we ourselves can carry as little as they can, especially since you know that God has given them the Spirit without this burden, and made them equal to us, since we, together with our fathers, did not receive the same Spirit due to the merit of the burden, but by grace. For because we were unable to bear the

---

[195] Luther here paraphrases Acts 10:1—11:18.

burden, we merited wrath far more than grace, since we were obligated to bear it as we had pledged to do."

This is the substance and the main concern of this council, namely, that the Pharisees wished to establish works or merits of the law, over against the word of grace, as necessary for salvation; that would have nullified the word of grace, including Christ and the Holy Spirit. That is why St. Peter argued so determinedly against it, asserting that one is saved solely by the grace of Jesus Christ, without any works at all. Not satisfied with that, he also dared to say that all their previous fathers—the patriarchs, the prophets, and the entire holy church in Israel—had been saved by nothing but the grace of Jesus Christ, and he condemned as tempters of God everyone who had wanted or still wanted to attain salvation in any other way. I think this is real preaching, and knocks the bottom out of the cask.[196] Shouldn't one burn this heretic who forbids all good works and holds grace and faith alone to be sufficient for salvation—and this for all the saints and all ancestors since the beginning of the world? We must now hear ourselves dubbed heretics and devils, though we simply teach this sermon of St. Peter and the decree of this council, as all the world now knows better than the Pharisees did, whom St. Peter is here chiding.

But St. Peter is far beyond us; and it is weird that he not only preaches the grace of God unto salvation, which everyone is surely glad to hear, but that he also declares that neither they themselves nor their ancestors were able to bear such a burden. In plain German this means, "We apostles and whoever we might be, including our ancestors, patriarchs, prophets, and the whole of God's people, have not kept God's commandments; we are sinners and are damned." He is not just speaking of blood sausage and black jelly here, but of the law of Moses, saying that no one has obeyed it or wanted to obey it. As Christ says in John 7 [:19], "None of you keeps the law." That (it seems to me) is really preaching the law unto damnation and making a damned sinner of oneself too. How then does that self-styled heir to St. Peter's

---

[196] Cf. above, p. 248, n. 149.

throne dare to call himself "most holy"[197] and to elevate whatever saints he wants, by virtue of their works and not by the grace of Christ? And where are the monks who can bear a much heavier burden than that of the law so that they also sell their surplus holiness?[198] We do not have this strange Peter's mind, for we do not dare to regard the patriarchs, prophets, apostles, and holy church as sinners, but must also call the pope the "most holy," meaning "the saint of saints, that is, Christ"![199]

But St. Peter deserves a very gracious and honest absolution, and is no longer to be considered strange, for he preaches in this very great article: first, the law, that we are all sinners. Second, that solely the grace of Christ gives us salvation, including the patriarchs, prophets, apostles, and the entire holy church from its beginning, all of whom he makes and damns as sinners with himself. Third, long before the Nicene council comes into being he teaches that Christ is true God, for he says that all the saints must be damned if they are not saved by the grace of our Lord Jesus Christ. To bestow grace and salvation like a lord, one must be true God, who can remove sin by grace, and death and hell by salvation. No creature can do that, unless it be the "most holy" in Rome—but without harming St. Peter's sermon! Fourth, he who holds otherwise and teaches Christians to attain salvation or obtain mercy through the law or their own works is a tempter of God.

Anyone who will may interpret this burden only in terms of the law of Moses and of circumcision, and not the Ten Commandments or good works. I am satisfied with that; if you can keep the Ten Commandments more easily than the Mosaic ceremonies, go ahead and be holier than St. Peter and St. Paul! I am so weak in keeping the Ten Commandments that it seems to me all Mosaic ceremonies would be far easier for me to observe, if the Ten Commandments would not press me so hard. But there is no time to argue that now; it has been amply discussed in other ways

---

[197] *Sanctissimum.*
[198] A reference to the monastic works of supererogation and to the sale of indulgences based upon the superfluous merits of Christ and the saints. Cf. Luther's *Explanations of the Ninety-five Theses. LW* 31, 83-252.
[199] *Sanctum Sanctorum id est Christum.*

and in other places.[200] But even reason will have to decide and admit that the Ten Commandments or the works of the Ten Commandments neither are nor can be called the grace of Jesus Christ, but are and must be called something entirely different. Now St. Peter asserts here that we must be saved solely by the grace of Jesus Christ; but that grace cannot be received or kept with one's hands, much less with the works of one's hands, but with faith in one's heart, is most certainly true.

It is also strange to see that St. Peter, who as an apostle had the authority and the power, together with the other apostles, to reformulate this article—which is why they are called the cornerstone of the church—nevertheless falls back on the holy church of God in former times, that church of all the patriarchs and prophets from the beginning, and says in effect, "This is not a new doctrine; for this is what our ancestors and all the saints taught and believed. Then how dare we teach a different or a better one, without tempting God and confusing and burdening our brethren's conscience?" That, I say, is the substance or main concern of this council, for which it was convened or convoked; and with which it was settled and adjourned. But the papal ass does not see this main item, and disregards it; instead, he gapes at the other four items added by James,[201] about blood, strangled meat, sacrifices to idols, and fornication, for they want to strengthen their tyranny thereby and claim that since the church has changed such articles, they want to have the power to change the articles of faith and the councils; that is, "We are the church and can decree and do what we like." Listen, papal ass, you are a particularly crass ass, indeed, you are a filthy sow!

The article of this council has neither fallen nor been altered, but, as St. Peter says, has been and will remain in force until the end of the world, for there have always been godly people who were saved solely by the grace of Christ and not by the law.

---

[200] Probably a reference to the controversy with the Antinomians in 1537. This group, whose spokesman was Luther's old friend John Agricola (*ca.* 1499-1566) of Eisleben, taught that repentance was possible only through the knowledge of God in the gospel, not in the law. Cf. Luther's tract *Against the Antinomians* (*Wider die Antinomer*). WA 50, 461-477.

[201] Acts 15:13-21.

The text and the faith of the gospel, baptism, the sacrament, the office of the keys, the name of Jesus Christ, etc., have survived even under the devil of the papacy, although the pope ranted against them with his accursed lies and shamefully misled the world; just as has been said of the Nicene council, that its decree existed before it and remained after it. For the true conciliar decrees must always remain—as they indeed always have—especially the chief articles, for the sake of which the councils came into being and are called councils.

But what are we to say here about this apostolic council in which James singles out four items—blood, what is strangled, sacrifices to idols, and fornication? Doesn't the council contradict itself, and isn't the Holy Spirit at variance with himself? For these two speeches are plainly and palpably contradictory—not to impose the burden of the Mosaic law, and simultaneously to impose it. Play the sophist, if you will, and say that the council did not speak of the whole law of Moses, but only of portions, several of which might be imposed and others not imposed. But that will not do; for in Galatians 6 [5:3] St. Paul concludes, "He who keeps one part of the law is bound to keep it in its entirety." This is equivalent to acknowledging one's duty to keep the whole law—otherwise, one wouldn't need a part of it either. Here, too, the new patch would be found on an old garment, creating a worse tear [Luke 5:36]. Thus it is quite evident that these items are contained in the law of Moses and nowhere else in the law of the Gentiles, for what need would there be to impose these things on the Gentiles if they were already familiar with them from their native law? How then do we reconcile these two—no law and the whole law?

Well then, if we cannot make them agree, we must dismiss St. James with his article and retain St. Peter with his chief article, for the sake of which the council was held; for without St. Peter's article no one can attain salvation. But, as St. Peter preached in this council, Cornelius and the Gentiles whom St. Peter had baptized along with him in his house were sanctified and saved before St. James came along with his article, etc. I also touched on the question above of whether one may conscientiously let these items go, since the Holy Spirit rules this council and sets all this up. But the dispute on whether the council contradicted itself and disagreed with itself is much sharper. And so, just when they want to relieve us of one impossible burden, they impose a still more impossible one on us, that we do simultaneously nothing and everything. To be sure, now that this has been invalidated we do well to adhere to that one part, namely, to St. Peter's article, that is, to the genuine Christian faith.

Only the fourth item mentioned by St. James, the one regarding fornication, has not been invalidated. To be sure, about twenty years ago courtesans[202] and accursed lords were already beginning to consider fornication not a mortal sin but a venial sin, and advocated the saying, "Nature should have its way,"[203] to which the holiest people in Rome still hold. And, I suppose, those. blind leaders were led to this conclusion because St. James set fornication alongside the other three items that have fallen: if the prohibition of blood, strangled meat, and sacrifices to idols is no longer valid, the prohibition of fornication is no longer valid either, since it is listed with these three items, and is furthermore a natural and human act. Let them go their way, they do not deserve anything better.

I shall give my opinion about this; may someone else improve on it. It has now often been said that one should view and also keep the councils according to the chief article which has given the council its purpose; for that is, and in that consists, the real essence of the council, the true body of the council, to which everything else must be adjusted and fitted, like a garment is fitted to the person who wears it or is dressed in it. If the garment doesn't fit, one takes it off and throws it away; then it is no longer a garment. Nor can there be a council (or for that matter an assembly, even a diet or a chapter) after the main business is settled, unless one or two items of secondary importance are found needing to be patched up or settled, as in the Nicene council, when, after it was settled that Christ is true God, the external

---

[202] Members of the papal court. Cf. the *Gravamina* of 1521. *DRTA. JR* 2, 673. Cf. also *To the Christian Nobility* (1520). *SW* 1, 282-283.
[203] *Natura petit exitum.*

matters pertaining to the Easter date and the squabbles of the priests came up—so here St. James's articles come up after the chief article of St. Peter.

Thus the final opinion and verdict of all the apostles and the council was that men must be saved, without the law or the burden of the law, solely by the grace of Jesus Christ. When St. Peter, St. Paul, and their followers had reached this verdict, they were happy and quite satisfied, for they had worked and striven for such a decision against the Pharisees and Jews who had become believers, but still wanted to keep the law. Now when St. James submitted his article, they could put up with it, since it was not imposed as law or a burden of the law, as the council's letter also reports, "To lay upon you no greater burden than these necessary things: that you abstain from blood," etc. [Acts 15:28-29]. They might even have liked St. James to add more items, such as the rule about leprosy or the like, even though they do not affect the Ten Commandments. But these things should not be law or a burden (they say), but items otherwise necessary. Yet when a burden is no longer a burden, it is good to bear; and when a law is no longer law, it is good to keep, like the Ten Commandments. How much more is that true of ceremonies, especially if they are abolished or if very few are retained. But more about this later. For if the pope would relieve us of his burden, so that it need no longer be law, we should readily obey him, especially if he were to retain but a few of his ordinances and drop most of them. Thus St. James and his article must now be interpreted without prejudice to St. Peter's article concerning grace without law, which must remain pure and constant and must rule alone without the law.

However, to understand this council fully we want to take a look at the causes of these secondary issues of St. James. The law of Moses was (so to say) ingrained, born into, suckled into, worked into, and lived into the Jews from their youth, so that it had become almost a part of their nature, as St. Paul says in Galations 2 [:15], "We are Jews by birth," that is, we are born Mosaic. He is here speaking of the law and not merely of birth; this is why they could not tolerate the nature of the Gentiles or be equated with them when they were dispersed among Gentiles in other lands and saw these Gentiles eat blood, strangled meat, and meat sacrifices to idols and still boast that they were God's people or Christians. This moved St. James to guard against such offense, so that the Gentiles did not abuse their freedom too wilfully just to spite the Jews, but acted decently, so that the Jews, rooted so deeply in the law, would not be offended and spurn the gospel. For, dear God, one should have patience with sick and erring men. We drunken Germans too are wise at times and say, "A load of hay must give a wide berth to a drunken man; for no one can win his spurs against sick people, and no one can become an expert among ignoramuses."[204]

Now St. James nevertheless does it very moderately; he disregards the whole Mosaic law concerning sacrifice and all the other items that had to be observed in Jerusalem and in the country and takes up only the four items which offend the Jews dispersed among the Gentiles. These dispersed Jews could not but see the Gentiles' ways, live among them, and at times eat with them; so it was vexing, and also wrong, to place blood sausage, rabbits cooked in blood, blood jellies, and meat sacrifices to idols before a Jew, especially if one knew that he abhorred it and took it as an insult. It would be the same as if I said, "Listen, Jew! Even if I could bring you to Christ by refraining from eating blood sausage or from serving it to you, I would not do it. I would rather scare you away from accepting Christ and chase you to hell with blood sausage." Would that be kind, not to mention Christian? Must not everyone at times keep silent and refrain from an action for the benefit of another human being, when he sees and knows that words and deeds would work his neighbor's harm, especially if this silence does not offend God? Now, at that time, the Gentiles were very antagonistic to the Jews, and very proud because they were their masters. The Jews, on the other hand, were intolerant, believing that they alone were God's people—as many histories clearly testify.

---

[204] Three German proverbs: "*Einem truncken Man soll ein fuder hau weichen*"; "*an krancken Leuten kan niemand kein Ritter werden*"; "*an unverstendigen kann niemand kein meister werden.*" They are not contained in Thiele, *Luthers Sprichwörtersammlung.*

Therefore this good advice of St. James was the very best means to peace, indeed, even to the salvation of many; since the Gentiles had attained Christ's grace without law and merit, they should now, on their part, show themselves helpful in a few matters so that the Jews, as the sick and erring folk, might attain the same grace. For it did not harm the Gentiles before God to avoid the external custom of eating blood, strangled meat, and meat sacrifices to idols in public (since grace had liberated their conscience from all that) and to desist, for the benefit and salvation of the Jews, from giving wilful offense; besides, in the absence of the Jews they could eat and drink what they wished, without jeopardy to their conscience. And the Jews, too, would be equally free in their conscience, but could not change the old external customs so suddenly—"Custom is second nature,"[205] especially when it has grown from God's law. Thus fairness and reason also teach that one should not spite nor hinder, but rather serve and help them in accord with the command, "You shall love your neighbor," etc. [Matt. 22:39].

So these two articles, that of St. Peter and that of St. James, are contradictory and yet they are not. St. Peter's deals with faith, St. James's with love. St. Peter's article tolerates no law; it eats blood, strangled meat, meat sacrifices to idols, and the devil in the bargain, without paying much attention, for it feels responsible to God alone and not to man, and does nothing but believe in the gracious God. But St. James's article lives and eats with man; it also directs everything to St. Peter's article, carefully warding off any obstacle that might obstruct the way. Now the office of love is so constituted on earth that since whatever is loved and helped is changeable and transient, love cannot have the same object forever; the one passes away and is replaced by another which it must also love, until the end of the world. Now when the Jews had become upset or stiff-necked and the Gentiles no longer had so much love to give them, everything lapsed—not changed by the power of the church, as the papists lie, but be-

---

[205] *Consuetudo est altera natura.* A proverb preserved by Cicero (106-43 B.C.), famous Roman philosopher, in *De Finibus*, V, 25, 74. See H. Rackham (trans.), *Cicero: De Finibus Bonorum et Malorum* ("The Loeb Classical Library" [New York: Putnam, 1921]), p. 476.

cause the cause was removed. So the Christians freely ate blood and black jelly, from which they had abstained for a time out of consideration for the Jews, even though they had not been bound to abstain before God in accordance with their faith. For if St. James had intended to impose these items as law he would have had to impose the entire law, as St. Paul says in Galatians 5 [:3], "He who keeps one law must keep them all"; that would flatly contradict St. Peter's article, which St. James confirms.

But this, I believe, was the reason St. James added fornication, which has always been forbidden in the Ten Commandments, to the other items: fornication was regarded by the Gentiles as a light, indeed, as no sin at all, as one can read in the Gentiles' books and as I pointed out above, which twenty years ago the courtesans and worthless priests also began to say publicly and to believe. Thus among the Gentiles fornication was as great a sin as eating blood sausage, rabbits cooked in blood, blood jellies, or meat sacrifices to idols. Just read in Roman history how unwilling they were to take wives, so that the Emperor Augustus had to compel them to marry; for they thought fornication was right, and to be forced to marry was to suffer violence and injustice.[206] That is why St. James wants to teach the Gentiles that they should gladly abstain from fornication without being forced to by the authorities, and live purely and chastely in the state of marriage, as the Jews did, who were greatly offended by such license in fornication and who could not believe, because of this disparity in food and conduct, etc., that these Gentiles should attain God's grace and become God's people.

The apostles, therefore, did not impose the law on the Gentiles, and yet they permitted the Jews to retain it for some time, meanwhile vigorously preaching grace—as we note in St. Paul when he became a Jew among the Jews and a Gentile among the Gentiles, so that he might win them all, I Corinthians 12 [9:20], and when he circumcised his disciple Timothy, who was already a believer, not because this was prescribed, but, as St. Luke says, "because of the Jews that were in those places" [Acts 16:3], be-

---

[206] Augustus (30 B.C.-A.D. 14) issued this marriage law in A.D. 9 for the third time after two previous attempts (in 28 and 18 B.C.) had failed.

cause he did not want to offend them. Later, in Acts 21 [:26], he let himself be purified in the temple with the Jews and he sacrificed according to the law of Moses, which he did as St. Augustine expressed it in that fine and now famous saying, *"Oportuit synagogam cum honore sepelire,"* "One must give Moses or his church and law an honorable burial."[207]

But how this council and both St. Peter's and St. James's articles were subsequently kept, you can gather amply from St. Paul's epistles,[208] wherein he complains everywhere about the false apostles who insisted on the necessity of the law to the detriment of grace, and who seduced whole clans and countries away from Christ and back to the law, albeit in the name of Christ—just as things became much worse after the Council of Nicaea. After that knave Arius had humbled himself and had even pledged allegiance to the council before Emperor Constantine,[209] for which the emperor reinstated him, he fanned the flames even more. And the bishops of his party pursued the game so abominably, especially after Constantine's death, through his son the emperor Constantius[210] (whom they had won over), that Constantius expelled all true bishops throughout the world except two, Gregory and Basil.[211] Some say that Constantine, the father, had also become an Arian[212] before he died and had in his will commended an Arian priest, strongly recommended by his sister Constantia on her deathbed, to his son Constantius, and that it was through him that the Arians later became so powerful.

These histories admonish us to pray faithfully for great lords, for the devil seeks them out more than others since he can do the greatest damage through them. And they are also a warning to

---

[207] The passage could not be located in Augustine's works.
[208] See for example, I Cor. 1:10 ff.; II Cor. 10:2 ff.; Gal. 5:12.
[209] *Historia Tripartita*, III, 6. *MPL* 69, 950d; *PNF*² 2, 277. Arius presented a "confession of faith" (*Expositio*) to the emperor.
[210] Constantius was regent in the Orient (337-350) and then emperor (350-361). He supported the Arian party.
[211] *Historia Tripartita*, VII, 22. *MPL* 69, 1086b; *PNF*² 2, 99. Gregory of Nazianz (*ca.* 329-390), bishop of Constantinople, and Basil the Great, bishop of Caesarea (370-379). Together with Gregory of Nyssa (d. *ca.* 394) they defended the Nicene Creed against Arianism.
[212] This was recorded in the *Chronology* (*Chronicon*) of St. Jerome. See *MPL* 27, 499-500.

us to be careful and not readily believe the sectarian spirits,[213] even when they humble themselves deeply, as this knave Arius did, and as Saul did with David [I Sam. 24:16 ff.]. "Sometimes even the wicked are defeated" (one says).[214] But they keep in the background until they have enough air and room; then they, like Arius, go ahead and do anyway what they had in mind, so that it really does not surprise me very much that the fathers imposed such severe and long penances on apostate Christians. They must have discovered how false their humility was, and how rarely they sincerely and from the bottom of their hearts humbled themselves or repented—just as Sirach [Ecclus. 12:10] says, "Never trust your reconciled enemy," etc.

To sum up, I let anyone who does not know what *osculum Judae*, "Judas kiss" [Matt. 26:49], means read with me the story of Arius under Constantine, and he will have to say that Arius far outdid Judas. He deceived the good emperor Constantine with these nice words: "We believe in one God, the Father almighty, and in the Lord Jesus Christ, his Son, born of the Father before the whole world, one God, one Word, by whom everything was made," etc.[215] My dear man, what Christian could regard these words as heretical, or think that Arius still viewed Christ as a creature? And yet that he did became quite evident during the hearing. Auxentius,[216] the bishop of Milan, the immediate predecessor of Ambrose, later similarly fooled the people with such beautiful words that at first I really grew angry at St. Hilary when I read the words "Blasphemy of Auxentius" on the title page of Auxentius' *Confessions*.[217] I would have staked my body and soul on Auxentius' oath that he regarded Christ as true God. I also hope that despite such deceptive and crafty words many pious simple

---

[213] *Rottengeister*.

[214] *"Aliquando compunguntur et mali."* A Latin proverb of unknown origin.

[215] Quoted from Arius' *Confession of Faith (Expositio)*. See p. 271, n. 209.

[216] Deposed in 370 by Damasus I, the bishop of Rome (366-384), he kept his bishopric until his death (374).

[217] Auxentius stated his position in a letter to the emperor. Hilary of Poitiers added his *Book Against the Arians or Auxentius of Milano (Liber Contra Arianos vel Auxentium Mediolanensem)* and entitled the whole *An Example of Auxentius' Blasphemy (Exemplum Blasphemia Auxentii)*. See *MPL* 10, 617-618; *Historia Tripartita*, V, 29. *MPL* 69, 1006; *PNF*[2] 3, 83.

folk retained their former belief and were preserved in it, not understanding these words in any way other than that of the faith, as no one could understand them differently who is not informed of the hidden meaning given them by the Arians.

And because it is necessary for Christians to know such an illustration, and since the ordinary reader does not study history so closely and does not realize how useful it is as a warning against all other sectarian spirits whom the devil their god makes so slippery that one cannot catch or grasp them anywhere, I will relate this affair briefly in several items.

First, Arius had taught that Christ is not God, but a creature.[218] Then the good bishops exacted from him the confession that Christ is God; but this he did in a false sense, meaning that Christ was God just like St. Paul, St. Peter, and the angels, who are called "gods and sons of God" in Scripture.[219]

Second, when the fathers became aware of this they again pressed him and his adherents to admit that Christ was true and very God; he used these words for the sake of appearance because it had theretofore been taught like this in all the churches. But among themselves they, particularly Eusebius,[220] bishop of Nicomedia and Arius' highest patron, interpreted these words like this: *"Omne factum dei est verum,"*[221] "Whatever God creates or makes is true and real; for whatever is false God did not make. Therefore we are willing to confess that Christ is a real, true God (but according to us a created god, like Moses and all the saints)," etc. Here they conceded everything that we still confess in our hymns in church on Sunday and have ever since the Nicene council: "God of God, light of light, very God of very God."[222]

---

[218] *Historia Tripartita,* I, 12. *MPL* 69, 902*b*; *PNF²* 3, 34.

[219] See for example, Job 38:7; Ps. 82:6; John 10:34; I Cor. 8:5.

[220] Eusebius (*ca.* 260-*ca.* 340) was the leader of the middle party (over against orthodoxy and radical Arianism) at the Council of Nicaea. He granted Arius asylum, but did not change his position.

[221] This quotation is not found in the *Historia Tripartita.* Luther probably coined a phrase which may summarize the contents of a letter of Eusebius to Paul, bishop of Tyre, and the statements in a document ascribed to Athanasius; cf. *Historia Tripartita,* I, 16; II, 7. *MPL* 69, 915-916; 926-927; *PNF²* 3, 42-43, 44-46.

[222] The Nicene Creed was sung every Sunday following the reading of the gospel.

273

Third, when the trickery that they with these words still called Christ a creature became known, the dispute became sharper, so that they had to confess that Christ had existed prior to the whole world. Who could here believe otherwise than that Arius and his bishops were genuine Christians and had been unjustly condemned by the Nicene council? For they were playing these tricks soon after the Nicene council (which had made short work of them and formulated the creed as it still exists) because they wanted to ruin the Nicene council and assailed one after another of its points.[223]

Fourth, when this dodge was discovered too, that Christ was still to be and to be called a creature, with the understanding that he had indeed existed before the whole world—that is, that he had been created and made before the whole world or any other creature [Col. 1:15]—they were forced to acknowledge that the whole world, all things, were made by him, as John 1 [:3] declares. However, among their own people they interpreted this to mean that Christ was made first and then all things were made by him.[224]

Fifth, it was now easy for them to confess, "Begotten, not made," born of God, not made, born as all Christians, born of God, are children of God, John 1 [:12-13]; not made among other creatures, but before all creatures.

Sixth, when it came to the core of the matter, that Christ is homousius[225] with the Father, that is, that Christ is of one and the same divinity with the Father and has one and the same power with him, they could find no more subterfuges, loopholes, detours, or evasions. Homousius means "of one essence or nature" or "of the same and not of a second essence," as the fathers had decreed in the council and as is sung in Latin, consubstantialis, and as some afterward called it, coexistentialis, coessentialis. This they had accepted in the council at Nicaea, and this they still accepted when they had to speak before the emperor and the fathers; but they fought it bitterly before their own people

---

[223] Historia Tripartita, IV, 10. MPL 69, 961; PNF² 2, 38.
[224] Historia Tripartita, V, 7. MPL 69, 988-990; PNF² 2, 56-57.
[225] A Latin translation of the Greek "of one substance."

and asserted that such words were not used in Holy Scripture.[226] They held many councils, even during Constantine's lifetime, in order to weaken the Nicene council; they stirred up much trouble, and later frightened our people so much that St. Jerome, dismayed by it, wrote a distressing letter to Damasus, bishop of Rome, suggesting that the word *homousius* be stricken. "For," (he says) "I do not know what sort of poison there is in these letters that the Arians get so upset by them."[227]

A dialogue is still extant in which Athanasius and Arius argue about this word *homousius* before an officer called Probus.[228] When Arius pressed the point that no such word was to be found in Scripture and Athanasius countered in kind, saying that the words *"innascibilis, ingenitus Deus,"* that is, "God is unborn"—which the Arians had employed to prove that Christ could not be God since he was born, while God was unborn, etc.—were not to be found in the Bible either, the official Probus decided against Arius. It is certainly true that one should teach nothing outside of Scripture pertaining to divine matters, as St. Hilary writes in *On the Trinity,* Book I,[229] which means only that one should teach nothing that is at variance with Scripture. But that one should not use more or other words than those contained in Scripture—this cannot be adhered to, especially in a controversy and when heretics want to falsify things with trickery and distort the words of Scripture. It thus became necessary to condense the meaning of Scripture, comprised of so many passages, into a short and comprehensive word, and to ask whether they regarded Christ as *homousius,* which was the meaning of all the words of Scripture that they had distorted with false interpretations among their own people, but had freely confessed before the emperor and the council. It is just as if the Pelagians[230] were to try to embarrass

---

[226] *Historia Tripartita,* V, 8. *MPL* 69, 990-992; *PNF*[2] 2, 57-58.

[227] *Epistola 15. MPL* 22, 355-358; *PNF*[2] 6, 18-20.

[228] *Dialogue Against the Arians (Contra Arianos Dialogus). MPL* 62, 155-179. This dialogue passed in the sixteenth century as a work of Athanasius. The author, however, was Vigilius of Thapsus (d. *ca.* 500), whose exact role in the Arian controversy is unknown. Luther already knew of the dialogue during his stay in Erfurt. Cf. *WA* 30[III], 530.

[229] Chapter 18. *MPL* 10, 49; *PNF*[2] 9, 50-51.

[230] The followers of Pelagius (d. *ca.* 418), who opposed Augustine's doctrine

us with the term "original sin" or "Adam's plague" because these words do not occur in Scripture, though Scripture clearly teaches the meaning of these words, that we are "conceived in sin," Psalm 51 [:5], that we are "by nature children of wrath," Ephesians 2 [:3], and that we must all be accounted sinners "because of the sin of one man," Romans [5:12].

Now tell me, if Arius would still today come before you and confess to you the entire creed of the Nicene council, as we sing it today in our churches, could you regard him as heretical? I myself would say that he was right. And if he nevertheless would, like a knave, believe otherwise and subsequently interpret and teach these words differently, wouldn't I have been nicely duped? That is why I do not believe that Constantine became an Arian, but that he adhered to the Nicene council. What happened to him was that he was deceived and believed that Arius agreed with the Nicene council. He also had him take an oath (as was said above) and then demanded that Arius again be received in Alexandria. But as Athanasius refused to do this because he knew the false Arius better than Constantine did, he had to be expelled.[281] It probably occurred to Constantine, as a human being, that Arius, this pious Christian, had been condemned in Nicaea out of envy or jealousy, especially since the Arians, particularly Eusebius of Nicomedia, won the emperor over, filled his ears with gossip, and eulogized Arius. For great kings and lords, though they may be pious, are not always surrounded at court by angels and St. John the Baptist, but often by Satan, Judas, and Doeg, as the Book of Kings clearly testifies [I Kings 22:22; I Sam. 22:9]. It is a good sign that Constantine, before his death, recalled Athanasius, no matter how hard the Arians tried to prevent it, *Tripartita*, III, 11,[232] whereby he indicated that he did not want to have the Nicene council and its doctrines rejected, but that he would have liked to establish unity.

---

of original sin, teaching that sin is not a natural state, but an act of free will. Luther refers here to the Roman theologians who taught Pelagianism or Semi-Pelagianism.
[231] *Historia Tripartita*, III, 6. *MPL* 69, 950d; *PNF²* 2, 277.
[232] Actually *Historia Tripartita*, IV, 1-3. *MPL* 69, 957-958; *PNF²* 2, 283-284, 301.

That is just what some of our false papist scribblers[233] are doing now; they pretend to teach faith and good works in order to embellish themselves and to besmirch us, as though they had always taught thus and we had unjustly accused them of teaching otherwise, so that, adorned in this sheep's clothing [Matt. 7:15] as though they were exactly like us, they may nicely bring their wolf into the sheep pen again. They do not seriously mean to teach faith and good works; but since they (like the Arians) cannot retain their poison and wolfishness or re-establish it except in this sheepskin of faith and good works, they decorate and hide their wolfskin until they get back into the sheep pen. But one should do to them as they do to our people and demand that they recant their abominations and prove it by casting off all the abuses that have prevailed against faith and good works in their churches among their people, so that one could know them by their fruits [Matt. 7:16]. Otherwise, one cannot believe their mere words and gestures, that is, their sheepskins. Arius, too, should have recanted in the same way, confessed his error, and actually attacked his former doctrine and conduct, as St. Augustine did his Manichaeism,[234] as many people are now doing with their former popery and monkery, among whom, by the grace of God, I can number myself. But they deny that they erred and cannot give God the honor of confessing it, just as the Arians wanted to have their lies defended and did not want people to think that they had been expelled by the council.

We should remember such historical examples well, especially those of us who must be preachers and have the order to feed the flock of Christ, so that we may exercise care and be good bishops, as St. Peter says in I Peter 5 [:2]; for to be an *episcopus*, or bishop, means to be careful, to be alert, to watch diligently, so that the devil does not take us by surprise. Here we see that he is such a master of dissimulation, disguise, and pretense that he becomes far fairer than the "angels of light" [II Cor. 11:14]; and false bishops are holier than true bishops, and the wolf more

---

[233] Cf. above, p. 213, n. 22.
[234] Named after Manichaeus, a Persian religious philosopher who was executed in Persia in *ca.* 275. It was a syncretistic cult teaching the incompatibility of spirit and matter. Until 384 Augustine was a Manichaean.

pious than any sheep. We are not dealing now with the crude, black, papal poltergeists[235] outside of Scripture. They are now to be found in Scripture and in our doctrine; they want to be like us and yet tear us to pieces. But here only the Holy Spirit can help, and we must pray diligently; otherwise, we shall be badly beaten.

All of this explains quite clearly why the council was held, namely, not for the sake of outward ceremonies, but for the sake of the important article about the divinity of Christ. That was why the dispute arose and was dealt with in the council; afterward it was assailed by the unspeakable raging of the devil, while the other articles were ignored. And this misery lasted for approximately three hundred years among Christians,[236] so that St. Augustine believes that Arius' pain in hell grows worse from day to day as long as that error endures, for Mohammed has come out of this sect. And from what I have presented above one can see clearly that this council neither thought up nor established anything new, but only condemned Arius' new error against the old faith on the basis of Scripture—from which may be inferred that no council (much less the pope in Rome) is authorized to think up or establish new articles concerning faith or good works, as they so falsely boast. This should be enough for the time being about the first principal council of Nicaea.

The second principal council, of Constantinople, about fifty years after the Nicene council, convened under the emperors Gratian and Theodosius,[237] had the following causes: Arius had denied the divinity of Christ and of the Holy Spirit.[238] In the meantime a new heresy was formed—the Macedonians[239] (for one error

---

[235] *Polter Bapst geister.*
[236] The last Arians were converted to the Roman church under the Lombard king Grimoald (d. 671).
[237] Cf. above, p. 215, n. 33.
[238] The Jena edition of Luther's works (*Jenaer Ausgabe*), which appeared between 1555 and 1558, reads, "and not that of the Holy Spirit" (*und nicht des heiligen Geistes*) (VII, 245b). The doctrine of the Holy Spirit was not discussed in the Arian controversy, but was formulated in the sixth century. Cf. *"Filioque"* in *O.D.C.C.*, p. 504.
[239] Named after Macedonius (d. *ca.* 362), who opposed Bishop Paul of Constantinople (d. 350). Macedonius is linked with a semi-Arian party, later known as Pneumatomachi, from the Greek *pneumatomachoi*, "murderers of the spirit," i.e., those who refused to believe in the divinity of the Holy Spirit.

always begets another and one misfortune another, without end or cessation). They praised the decision of the Nicene council that Christ is true God and vigorously condemned Arius and his heresy; but they taught that the Holy Spirit is not true God, but a creature of God through whom God moves, enlightens, comforts, and strengthens the heart of man, and through whom he does all that Scripture says of him. This heresy also took strong root among many great, learned, and able bishops. This came about because Macedonius was bishop of Constantinople, the largest capital city of the entire Eastern empire and the residence of the imperial court. This same bishop started the heresy; it made quite an impression that the foremost bishop, in the imperial residence in Constantinople at that, taught this. Almost all the lands around Constantinople and those dependent on it hurried to support him, and Macedonius was not idle either; he agitated for his cause energetically, and would have liked to attract the whole world (as the devil is wont to do in all heresies).

Now the good bishops proved themselves too weak to withstand this bishop's heresies; for a bad priest in Alexandria, Arius, had previously aroused such confusion. But here it was not a priest, not even an ordinary bishop, but the bishop of the foremost city of the imperial palace of Constantinople who was arousing such confusion. Here the bishops had once again to call upon the emperor to assemble a principal council against such blasphemy, which the pious emperor Theodosius[240] did, convoking it in Constantinople,[241] in the parish and church in which Macedonius had been bishop, just as Constantine had earlier convoked the Nicene council in Nicaea, where Theogonius was bishop,[242] who had, together with Eusebius of Nicomedia, supported Arius and had later helped to reinstate him.

The next year Damasus, bishop of Rome, also held a council, and would have liked to deal with these matters in Rome so that the Roman See might acquire the authority to call councils and to judge all matters. It was to be known as a principal council, for

---

[240] Theodosius I.
[241] *Historia Tripartita,* IX, 12. *MPL* 69, 1128-1129; *PNF²* 2, 121-122.
[242] *Historia Tripartita,* II, 9. *MPL* 69, 928d; *PNF²* 2, 10.

as the foremost bishop of the world, he summoned the same fathers who a year before had met in council at Constantinople. But they did not want to come, although they wrote him a very nice Christian letter[243] telling him what they had dealt with in the Council of Constantinople; they informed him, among other things, of how they had condemned Macedonius' heresy and how they had appointed other bishops in Constantinople, Antioch, and Jerusalem. Oh, they should not have done that without the knowledge and consent of the bishop of Rome, who wanted the exclusive right and power to convoke councils (which he, in fact, was powerless to do), to sentence all heresies (which he could not do), and to change bishops (which he was not entitled to do).

They gave him, in addition, some good slaps in the face, telling him that in the new church in Constantinople (for the city had been built recently)[244] they had made Nectarius bishop, and Flavian bishop of Antioch, and Cyril bishop of Jerusalem.[245] These three items were very uncomfortable, indeed, intolerable for the bishop of Rome to hear and read: the first, that they call Constantinople a new church and appoint a bishop there, though no new church and new bishop should have been created without the knowledge and consent of the bishop of Rome; the second is even worse, that they call the church in Antioch the first and the oldest church, in which (as they proved through St. Luke in Acts 11 [:26]) the believers in Christ were called Christians for the first time, and in which St. Peter and St. Paul and many of the greatest apostles had proclaimed the gospel for more than seven years. That, in my German, would be like saying, "Listen, lord bishop of Rome! You are not the first or foremost bishop, but if any particular church should be it, it would more justly be the church in Antioch, which has the Scriptures of St. Luke and actual facts on its side, while Rome can claim neither Scripture nor facts in its behalf."

But these were fine and excellent people, who wished to check the arrogant spirit of Rome gently and mildly, with Christian love

---

[243] The letter is quoted in *Historia Tripartita*, IX, 14. *MPL* 69, 1130-1133; *PNF²* 3, 137-138.
[244] In 330 Constantine the Great dedicated the city as the "new Rome."
[245] *Historia Tripartita*, IX, 14. *MPL* 69, 1132c-1132d; *PNF²* 3, 138.

and humility, and, as Sirach teaches, "To spit on a spark" [Ecclus. 28:12], and to exhort the bishop of Rome to consider that since the gospel had not come to Antioch from Rome but to Rome from Antioch, the church of Antioch as the oldest church should reasonably enjoy precedence over Rome as the younger church; that is, if precedence was to be a question. This ambition (as the words show) rightfully incensed these fine and holy fathers against the Roman bishop (as was just), and if there had been a Dr. Luther in the council and he could have had his way, such a gentle letter would not have been addressed to the bishop of Rome. In a word, there were men in this council with whom all the bishops of Rome of all time could not compare in the least.[246]

The third is the worst, that they call the church in Jerusalem the mother of all churches because Christ the Lord himself had been bishop there, and in proof of this had sacrificed himself on the cross for the sins of the whole world; there the Holy Spirit had been given from heaven on the day of Pentecost; there all the apostles had afterward ruled the church together (not only Peter, of whom the bishop of Rome boasts). Not one of these events had occurred in Rome. Thus they gently admonished the bishop of Rome to consider that he was far from being the bishop of Jerusalem, of the mother church, but that his church in Rome was a daughter church which did not have Christ and the apostles and which did not bring Jerusalem to the faith; but rather, he and his church had been brought to the faith through the church in Jerusalem—so had St. Paul humbled the Corinthians, telling them that the gospel did not come from them, but from others to them [II Cor. 10:14].

But at the end they really overshot the mark and appointed a patriarch to the new church in Constantinople without the previous knowledge and consent of the bishop of Rome, just as though his co-operation in these matters did not matter at all. This is where the eternal quarreling and bickering started (as the pope's hypocrites themselves write)[247] between the bishops of Rome and Constantinople over primacy or supreme authority. When the

---

[246] Proverbial German, "*Nicht kundten das wasser reichen.*"
[247] It cannot be established which authors Luther had in mind.

bishop of Constantinople (though he was in a new city) was as patriarch the equal of the bishop of Rome, the one at Rome feared that the other would arrogate the primacy to himself—which afterward actually happened. The bishops of Constantinople asserted that the emperor had his residence or court in Constantinople and not in Rome and that Constantinople was known as "new Rome"; this is why he would have to be the supreme bishop because he was the bishop of the imperial city and court. On the other hand, the one in Rome asserted that Rome was the true Rome, and that the emperor was known as the Roman emperor and not the Constantinopolitan emperor, and that Rome had existed before Constantinople. They indulged in such childish, womanish, and foolish squabbles that it is a sin and a shame to hear and read.

The bickering went on until Phocas[248] became emperor. He had had the pious emperor Maurice (whom history calls a saint), his predecessor and lord (Phocas had been his captain) beheaded, together with his wife and children. This godly Cain confirmed the supremacy of bishop Boniface[249] of Rome over all other bishops. And this kind of supremacy could have been justly certified by no better man than by this shameful murderer of an emperor! So Rome had as good a beginning of papacy as its empire had previously had, when Romulus murdered his brother Remus so that he could rule alone and name the city after himself. Nevertheless, the bishops of Constantinople paid no attention to this, and the squabble continued on and on, although the Roman bishops meanwhile embellished the emperor Phocas' certification with fig leaves [Gen. 3:7], and screamed loudly with great bellowing, Revelation 12 [13:5], that the church of Rome was supreme, not by human command but by Christ's own institution, Matthew 16 [:18], "You are Peter." But the ones in Constantinople saw that

---

[248] In 602 Phocas headed a revolution in Constantinople which deposed the ruler of the Eastern half of the Roman Empire, Maurice I (Maurikios), who had been on the throne since 582. He and his entire family were put to death. Pope Gregory I (590-604) hailed the revolution as an act of God against a tyrant. Phocas was emperor until 610, when he was deposed and killed in another revolution, headed by Heraclius. Cf. Schäfer, *op. cit.*, p. 330, n. 3.

[249] Boniface III (607) was bishop for only eight months. He had been Rome's diplomatic representative at Constantinople and a friend of Phocas.

those in Rome were quoting the words of Christ falsely and senselessly, like uneducated people, and ignored them.

Thus the two churches, Rome and Constantinople, wrangled over the invalid primacy with vain, rotten, lame, and useless squabbles, until the devil finally devoured them both, the ones in Constantinople through the Turks and Mohammed,[250] the others in Rome through the papacy and its blasphemous decretals. I am relating all of this so that one can see what misery was caused by this fine council in Constantinople because the bishop of that city was made patriarch, which would have happened anyway, even if no patriarch of Constantinople had been appointed, for the ambitious devil's head in Rome had already begun to make all kinds of demands of the bishops (as we said above). And if the bishop of Constantinople had not crossed him, he would have rubbed against the bishops of Alexandria, Jerusalem, and Antioch, and he would not have tolerated the decree of the Council of Nicaea, which had made him the equal of the bishop of Alexandria and the inferior of the bishop of Jerusalem. He wants to be supreme without councils and fathers, "by divine right,"[251] instituted by Christ himself—as he bellows, blasphemes, and lies in his decretals.

Well then! There we have the second principal council in Constantinople; it did three things: first, it affirmed that the Holy Spirit is true God, simultaneously condemning Macedonius, who averred and taught that the Holy Spirit was a creature. Second, it deposed the heretical bishops and appointed true bishops, particularly in Antioch and Jerusalem. Third, it made the bishop Nectarius of Constantinople a patriarch, which enraged, incensed, and infuriated the bishops of Rome—although the dear fathers may have done it with the best of intentions. The first is the real, main item and the sole reason for holding the council, from which one can also understand the intention of the council, namely, that it was to do no more and did no more than to preserve the doctrine of the divinity of the Holy Spirit; and with this the council really had finished what it had been summoned to do. The second item, about the deposition

---

[250] A reference to the fall of Constantinople in 1453, when the Christian Byzantine Empire came to an end.
[251] *Iure divino.*

of bishops, is not an article of faith, but an external, tangible work, which reason, too, should and can perform and which does not require either the extraordinary action of the Holy Spirit (as do the articles of faith) or the summoning of a council; and that is why it probably occurred on another day, after the day of the council.

They did not re-establish the churches or bishoprics in Antioch and Jerusalem, but they let them remain as they had been from the beginning. They only put in different persons, which was necessary. These offices must have been in the church from the beginning, and they must remain until the end, but one must always put in different persons, like Matthias, who replaced Judas [Acts 1:26], and living bishops who replace those who die. This is not properly the business of the councils, but it may, indeed it must, be done before the councils, in between the councils, and after the councils, as the needs of the churches demand it. One cannot have councils every day, but one must have persons every day to fill the offices of the churches whenever these become vacant.

The third item is a new one, that they made a patriarch, out of human good intentions. But we have related above what came out of this—what disgraceful quarreling and backbiting these two bishops indulged in—so that one can clearly see that the Holy Spirit did not institute this, for it is not an article of faith, but an external and tangible work of reason, or of flesh and blood. What does the Holy Spirit care about which bishop goes first and which goes last? He has other things to do besides fooling in such worldly child's play! And from this one not only learns that the councils lack the power to create new good works, much less new articles of faith, but one also receives the warning that councils should not create or establish anything new at all. They should know that they did not meet to do this, but to defend the old faith against new teachers although they may put new persons (who cannot be called articles of faith or good works, since they are fallible mortal men) into the old existing offices, which one has to do in the churches, outside the councils, more often than in the councils, indeed, every day.

The fathers of this council themselves also confessed that they did not establish anything new when they (as was said) wrote

Damasus, the bishop of Rome, what among other things they had done in the council, "We know that this is the old true faith that conforms to baptism and teaches us to believe in the name of the Father, the Son, and the Holy Spirit," etc.[252] Indeed, they said nothing at all about the third item, the patriarchate of Constantinople.[253] Perhaps they thought that this was not the item for which they had assembled in the council, and that it would not be heresy if a Christian would not consider it an article of faith to regard the bishop as a patriarch, just as there are many people today who are neither heretics nor lost because they do not regard the pope as the head of the church, despite his councils, decretals, bulls, and bellowing. Or perhaps they did not do it unanimously, but the emperor Theodosius did it, for the other histories report that Theodosius, who had no power to set up articles of faith, suggested and urged it.[254]

Since they themselves now say and confess that it is the old true faith in which we were baptized and in which we were instructed, why should we concede to the councils the great power to establish new doctrines and to burn as heretics all who do not believe them? That would indeed mean misunderstanding the councils and not knowing at all what a council is or what its office and function are; it would be to look merely at the letters and to give the council complete power, even over God! More about that later. We still want to take a brief look at the other two principal councils.

The third principal council was held under Theodosius II,[255] whose grandfather was Theodosius I, mentioned in connection with the second council. This emperor summoned two hundred bishops to Ephesus.[256] And although the Latin writers wanted to weave the

---

[252] *Historia Tripartita*, IX, 14. MPL 69, 1131d; PNF² 3, 138.

[253] *Historia Tripartita*, IX, 13. MPL 69, 1129c; PNF² 2, 121. These records accord the bishop of Constantinople "the next prerogative honor after the bishop of Rome." See above, pp. 281–282.

[254] Rufinus (II, 19), the source Luther used in addition to the *Historia Tripartita*, records the involvement of Theodosius I in ecclesiastical affairs. MPL 21, 526.

[255] Cf. above, p. 216, n. 39. This was the Council of Ephesus in 431.

[256] *Historia Tripartita*, XII, 5. MPL 69, 1207–1208; PNF² 2, 172. The number of bishops is recorded by Crabbe, whom Luther may have regarded as one of the "Latin writers." See WA 50, 581, n. c.

pope into the story, it is nonetheless true that not the pope but the emperor had to summon this council. Now there was a patriarch in Constantinople of equal rank with the bishop of Rome,[257] so the Eastern bishops paid the bishop of Rome far less heed than before; that is why it was impossible for the bishop of Rome[258] to convoke such a council, especially in Ephesus, far across the sea in Asia. If he had had the power, he would surely have called it closer to Rome, as Damasus did with the former council, that of Constantinople. Yet it is said that he had his delegates there;[259] that may be, but they did not preside.

Here was the reason for this council:[260] the dear fathers and good bishops were gone—St. Ambrose, St. Martin, St. Jerome, St. Augustine (who died that very year), St. Hilary, St. Eusebius, and others like them.[261] In their stead fathers had come up who were not their equals so that even Emperor Theodosius no longer wanted to see a bishop of Constantinople chosen from the priests or clergy of that city because these were usually proud, ambitious, and unruly, managing to cause nothing but trouble. Even St. John Chrysostom was such a person, as the *Historia Tripartita* informs us.[262] Therefore the emperor sent for a "foreigner"[263] (that is what they called him) from Antioch, by the name of Nestorius,[264] who was a man of strict and chaste life, with a pleasing voice, eloquent, an outspoken foe of all heretics. He was to become patriarch and bishop of Constantinople. But here the emperor made a mistake; he tried to escape the rain and plunged into the water.[265]

---

[257] Cf. above, pp. 279-280, and Schäfer, *op. cit.*, p., 304, n. 1.

[258] Celestine I (422-432).

[259] This reference is contained only in Crabbe. For the exact quotation, see *WA* 50, 581, n. *e*.

[260] Luther's source for the following account is the *Historia Tripartita*, XII, 4. *MPL* 69, 1204-1207; *PNF²* 2, 169-172.

[261] Ambrose died in 397; Martin of Tours in *ca.* 400; Jerome in 420; Augustine in 430; Hilary in 367; and Eusebius of Caesarea in *ca.* 340.

[262] *Historia Tripartita*, X, 3. *MPL* 69, 1166*b*; *PNF²* 2, 139. See also *Historia Tripartita*, X, 13. *MPL* 69, 1176*b*; *PNF²* 2, 148.

[263] *Advena*. See *Historia Tripartita*, XII, 4. *MPL* 69, 1204*a*; *PNF²* 2, 169.

[264] Nestorius (d. *ca.* 451), regarded as the founder of the Nestorian heresy, according to which Christ consisted of two completely separate persons, one human and one divine.

[265] A German proverb, "*Wollt dem regen entlauffen und fiel ins wasser.*" Cf. Thiele, *Luthers Sprichwörtersammlung*, No. 478.

This man began to defend his priest Anastasius,[266] who had preached that one should not call the holy Virgin the mother of God, for since she was human she could give birth to no God. This offended all Christians; they understood it to mean that he regarded Christ, born of Mary, not as God but as a mere man, such as we all are. This created such unrest and disturbance that the emperor had to assemble a council to relieve the matter. Then the great bishops assembled (although slowly) in Ephesus, Nestorius with many others like Cyril of Alexandria[267] and Juvenal of Jerusalem.[268] And when John of Antioch[269] delayed his coming, Cyril (who was opposed to Nestorius) and Juvenal proceeded to condemn Nestorius, and he and his followers in turn condemned them. When John of Antioch arrived and found this split, he became furious with Cyril because he had so hotheadedly and hurriedly condemned Nestorius; and these two clashed over it, and each condemned the other and deposed the other from his bishopric.

When Nestorius saw the excitement that had arisen, he said, "Oh, let us remove the cause of this trouble and admit that Mary may be called the mother of God!" But this recantation did not help him; he had to remain under condemnation and in exile. To be sure, the two bishops of Antioch and Alexandria continued to condemn one another after their return home from the council, but in the end they again made peace.[270] It is quite irritating, indeed, saddening, to read that such important men behaved so womanishly and childishly; they really needed a Constantine who would have thrown their bickering letters into the fire too. But those who could have done that were gone.

Now if Nestorius really was in such error that he took Christ to be not God but a mere human being, then he was justly condemned, for his teaching was much worse than that of Arius or Macedonius.

This then is the third principal council; it dealt with no more

---

[266] Anastasius, a presbyter in Constantinople, was sympathetic to Nestorius, cause. He is mentioned only by Socrates in the *Historia Tripartita*, VII, 2.
[267] Cyril (412-414), the most vehement opponent of Nestorius.
[268] Juvenal, bishop of Jerusalem (422-458).
[269] John, bishop of Antioch (429-441).
[270] *Historia Tripartita*, XII, 6. *MPL* 69, 1208; *PNF*² 2, 172.

than this, and we still note that it set up no new doctrine, but defended the old true faith against the new doctrine of Nestorius, if that is really what he taught; thus we cannot grant the councils the power to establish new doctrines. That Christ is true God had been defended previously in the councils of Nicaea and Constantinople, as a true old article, kept from the beginning and proven and authenticated by Holy Scripture against the new heresy of Arius. The other decrees established there apply to bodily matters and are not articles of faith; these we drop.

In order to understand this council thoroughly we shall talk a little more about it. For awhile I myself could not understand just what Nestorius' error was; in any event, I thought that Nestorius had denied the divinity of Christ and had regarded Christ as no more than a mere man, as the papal decretals and all papal writers say.[271] But their own words, when I really looked at them, made me change my mind. They accuse Nestorius of making two persons out of Christ, namely, God and man. Some, who also failed to understand him, thought he had taught that Christ was first born of Mary as mere man and then led such a holy life that the Godhead merged with him, and he thus became God, and their writing is so confused that I think they still do not know today how and why they condemned Nestorius. Remember that they testify that Nestorius took Christ to be both God and man, only he is said to have made two persons of him. Thus it is certain that Nestorius did not take Christ to be a mere man, as we all assumed, for according to their own words he also took him to be God. The only knot that remains is that he is said to have regarded Christ, really and truly God and man, as a dual person, divine and human. That is one fact.

Now he who divides Christ and makes two persons of him fashions two Christs—one divine Christ who is altogether God and not a human being, and a human Christ, who is altogether man and no God at all; otherwise, there could not be two persons. Now it is certain that Nestorius did not believe in two Christs, but in only one single Christ, as their own words convey, that Nestorius re-

---

[271] See for example, *Decreti Tertia Pars, De Consecratione,* dist. V, C. XXXIX. *CIC* 1, 1423; *MPL* 187, 957. See also Crabbe (quoted in *WA* 50, 583, n. *c.*).

garded Christ, that is, the one, sole, same, true Christ and none other, as being two persons. So it must also be false and incorrect to say that Nestorius took Christ to be two persons, for it cannot be that Christ is two persons and yet remains the same one Christ; but rather, as said, if there are two persons, then there are two Christs and not one Christ. But Nestorius holds to no more than one Christ, so he could not have taken Christ to be two persons; otherwise, he would indeed have had to say both yes and no against himself in the same article. Nor do any histories record that Nestorius held Christ to be two persons—except that the pope and their histories imply it, although they themselves admit otherwise when they imputed to Nestorius the teaching that Christ had become God after he was born of Mary or had become united with God into one person. Their conscience or their confused mind forced them to say this, since they had to admit that Nestorius did not believe in more than the one single Christ.

Now the question is: what was it that was condemned about Nestorius and why was this third principal council convoked against him if he did not teach otherwise than that Christ is true God and true man, and one single Christ, not two Christs, that is, one person in two natures—as we all believe and as all Christendom has believed from the beginning? For it appears that the pope and his followers put the words into Nestorius' mouth that he viewed Christ as a mere man and not also as God, and that he took Christ to be two persons or two Christs. This appears (I say) not only from the histories, but also from the very words and documents of the popes and their writers.[272] Now in order to discover the reasons for this council we ask, what was really Nestorius' error?

You may read a page or two of the *Historia Tripartita*, Book XII, chapter 4,[273] which you can do in half of a quarter of an hour, wherein is written everything that one can really know about Nestorius and this council, and see if I hit the mark. The problem was this: Nestorius was a proud and unlearned man, and when he became such a great bishop and patriarch he supposed that he should be looked upon as the most learned man on earth, needing neither

---

[272] *Decreti Secunda Pars*, causa XXIV, ques. 3, C. XXXIX. *CIC* 1, 1005.
[273] *MPL* 69, 1204-1207; *PNF*[2] 2, 169-172.

to read the books of his predecessors and of other people, nor to
learn their way of speaking about these things. Instead, since he
was eloquent and endowed with a good voice, he wanted to be a
self-made doctor or master, and no matter how he expressed it or
pronounced something, it should be accounted correct. He ap-
proached the statement that Mary was God's mother or the bearer
of God with the same pride. Then he, in turn, encountered other
proud bishops, whom his pride displeased, especially Cyril of Alexandria; for there was no Augustine or Ambrose at hand. Now Nestorius had learned in the church of Antioch that Christ was true
God born of the Father in eternity, as the Nicene council had defended, and afterward born a true man of the Virgin Mary. Nestorius did not question these two items; he himself had preached
them for a long time. Indeed, he had even persecuted the Arians
at the Council of Nicaea, condemning them so vehemently that he
had also instigated many murders and much bloodshed, so
staunchly did he regard Christ as true God and man.

Moreover, he also conceded that Christ, God's Son, was born
of the Virgin Mary into his humanity, not into his divinity, which
we and all Christians also say. But here is where the problem
arose: he did not want Mary to be called the mother of God because of this, since Christ was not born of her into his divinity, or,
to express it plainly, since Christ did not derive his divinity from
her as he did his humanity. There we have the entire bone of contention: God cannot be born of a human being or have his divine
nature from one; and a human being cannot bear God or impart
the divine nature to a God. This unlearned, uncouth, and proud
man insisted on the literal meaning of the words, "God born of
Mary," and interpreted "born" according to grammar or philosophy,
as though it meant to obtain divine nature from the one who bore
him, and the *Tripartita* also says that he viewed these words as an
abomination[274]—as we, and all Christians (if that were to be the
sense of these words), do too.

One can see from this that Nestorius, as an ignorant, proud
bishop, adheres faithfully to Christ, but in his ignorance does not
know what and how he is speaking, like one who does not quite

---

[274] *Historia Tripartita*, XII, 4. MPL 69, 1206b; PNF² 2, 171.

know how to speak of such things, but still wants to speak as an expert. We too know very well that God did not derive his divinity from Mary; but it does not follow that it is therefore wrong to say that God was born of Mary, that God is Mary's Son, and that Mary is God's mother. I have to illustrate this with a plain example: if a woman bears a child, a rotten Nestorius (that is what the *Tripartita* calls him)[275] may be proud and ignorant and puzzle out, "This woman has given birth to the child, but she is not the child's mother because the child's soul is not derived from her nature or blood, but from elsewhere—for instance, from God. Thus this child is, to be sure, born of the woman according to the body; but since the soul is not from her body, she is not the child's mother, for she is not the mother of the child's soul."

A no-good sophist like this does not deny that the two natures, body and soul, are one person, nor does he say that there are two persons or two children, but admits that two natures, like body and soul, form one person or one child; also that the mother has not borne two children, but only one child. However, he fails to see what he is denying or what he is saying. Just such a man was Nestorius, who admits that Christ is God and man in one person; but because his divinity does not come from his mother Mary, she should not be called God's mother. This was rightly condemned in the council, and ought to be condemned. And although Nestorius has a correct view on one point of the principal matter, that Christ is God and man, one should nevertheless not tolerate his other point or mode of expression, that God was not born of Mary and was not crucified by the Jews just as one should not tolerate the sophist (who declares very correctly that a mother cannot bear or impart a child's soul) when he says that a child is not the mother's natural child and a mother is not the child's natural mother.

In summary, the proud, unlearned bishop instigated a bad Greek quarrel, or as the Roman Cicero said of the Greeks, "A controversy has long disturbed the little Greeks, who are fonder of ar-

---

[275] *Historia Tripartita*, XII, 4. *MPL* 69, 1207a; *PNF²* 2, 171: "*Non ergo mediocrem concussionem orbiterrarum tepidissima Nestorii ratiocinatio concitant*" ("This idle contention of his has produced no slight ferment in the religious world").

gument than of truth."[276] For whoever admits that a mother bore a child who has body and soul should admit and believe that the mother has borne the whole child and is the child's true mother, even though she is not the mother of the soul; otherwise, it would follow that no woman is the mother of any child, and the fourth commandment, "Honor thy father and thy mother," would have to be abolished. Thus it should also be said that Mary is the true natural mother of the child called Jesus Christ, and that she is the true mother of God and bearer of God, and whatever else can be said of children's mothers, such as suckling, bathing, feeding—that Mary suckled God, rocked God to sleep, prepared broth and soup for God, etc. For God and man are one person, one Christ, one Son, one Jesus, not two Christs, not two Sons, not two Jesuses; just as your son is not two sons, two Johns, two cobblers, even though he has two natures, body and soul, the body from you, the soul from God alone.

Thus Nestorius' error was not that he believed Christ to be a pure man, or that he made two persons of him; on the contrary, he confesses two natures, the divine and the human, in one person—but he will not admit a *communicatio idiomatum*.[277] I cannot express that in one word in German. *Idioma* means that which is inherent in a nature or is its attribute, such as dying, suffering, weeping, speaking, laughing, eating, drinking, sleeping, sorrowing, rejoicing, being born, having a mother, suckling the breast, walking, standing, working, sitting, lying down, and other things of that kind, which are called *idiomata naturae humanae*, that is, qualities that belong to man by nature, which he can and must do or even suffer; for *idioma* in Greek, *proprium* in Latin, is a thing—let us, for the time being, call it an attribute. Again, an *idioma deitatis*,

---

[276] In *De Oratione*, I, 11: "*Iam diu torquet controversia verbi homines graeculos contentionis cupidiores quam veritatis.*" See E. W. Sutton and H. Rackham (trans.), *Cicero: De Oratione, Book I and II* ("The Loeb Classical Library" [2 vols.; Cambridge: Harvard University Press, 1942]), I, 36.

[277] "Communion of the properties," a doctrine propounded by scholastic theology which states that while the two natures were separated in Christ, the attributes of the one may be predicated by the other, in view of their union in Christ. Luther reinterpreted the doctrine in the context of his own theology. Cf. Paul Althaus, *Die Theologie Martin Luthers* (Gütersloh, 1962), pp. 160-174.

"an attribute of divine nature," is that it is immortal, omnipotent, infinite, not born, does not eat, drink, sleep, stand, walk, sorrow, weep—and what more can one say? To be God is an immeasurably different thing than to be man; that is why the *idiomata* of the two natures cannot coincide. That is the opinion of Nestorius.

Now if I were to preach, "Jesus, the carpenter of Nazareth (for the gospels call him 'carpenter's son' [Matt. 13:55]) is walking over there down the street, fetching his mother a jug of water and a penny's worth of bread so that he might eat and drink with his mother, and the same carpenter, Jesus, is the very true God in one person," Nestorius would grant me that and say that this is true. But if I were to say, "There goes God down the street, fetching water and bread so that he might eat and drink with his mother," Nestorius would not grant me this, but says, "To fetch water, to buy bread, to have a mother, to eat and drink with her, are *idiomata* or attributes of human and not of divine nature." And again, if I say, "The carpenter Jesus was crucified by the Jews and the same Jesus is the true God," Nestorius would agree that this is true. But if I say, "God was crucified by the Jews," he says, "No! For crucifixion and death are *idiomata* or attributes not of divine but of human nature."

Now when ordinary Christians hear this they cannot but think that he regards Christ as a mere man and is separating the persons, which he does not intend to do, though his words lend the impression that he does. From this one can see that he was a very peculiar saint and an injudicious man, for after he concedes that God and man are united and fused into one person, he can in no way deny that the *idiomata* of the two natures should also be united and fused. Otherwise, what could God and man united in one person be? Thus his folly is exactly that against which one teaches in the schools, "One who admits the premise of a good conclusion cannot deny the conclusion."[278] In German we would say, "If the one is true, the other must also be true; if the second is not true, then the

---

[278] "*Qui concedit antecedens bonae consequentiae, non potest negare consequens*," a proposition that appears in various Roman works; see for example, *De Oratione*, II, 53, in Sutton and Rackham (trans.), *op. cit.*, II, 357. Cf. also *C.R.* 13, 617, 627.

first is not true either."²⁷⁹ Whoever admits that Greta is your wife cannot deny that her child (if she is pious) is your child. If one teaches these things in the schools, no one thinks that there could be such crude people; but ask the regents and jurists whether they are not often confronted by such parties, who admit something and still do not want to grant what follows from it.

One might, however, allege that Nestorius had dishonestly confessed that Christ was God and only one person. No, the proud man was not that clever; rather, he was in earnest,²⁸⁰ for in one of his sermons he cried (says the *Tripartita*), "No, dear Jew, you should not strut! You were not able to crucify God."²⁸¹ He means to say with this that Christ is indeed God, but God was not crucified. And in the council, before Bishop Cyril, he said, "Many confess that Christ is God, but I shall never say that God is 'double' or 'triple.' "²⁸² That is like saying, "Jesus is God, as many of us confess; but I will never teach that God was born two or three times." He had in mind (as the *Tripartita* indicates)²⁸³ that God and death are irreconcilable. It seemed terrible to him to hear that God should die. His meaning was that Christ, in his divinity, was immortal; but he lacked the intelligence to express this thought properly. To add to the trouble the other bishops, also proud men, gave no thought to how one could heal the wounds, but only to tearing them further open.

So although speaking logically it must follow from Nestorius' opinion that Christ is a mere man and two persons, this was not actually his opinion. This crude, unlearned man did not see that he was asserting the impossible when simultaneously he seriously took Christ to be God and man in one person and yet declined to

²⁷⁹ *Ist eines war, so muss das ander auch war sein, ist das ander nicht war, so ist das erst auch nicht war.*
²⁸⁰ *Historia Tripartita*, XII, 4: "*Nusquam enim Dei verbi subsistentiam perimit . . .*") ("In these discourses he nowhere destroys the proper personality of the Word of God"). *MPL* 69, 1207a; *PNF²* 2, 171.
²⁸¹ *Historia Tripartita*, XII, 4: "*Noli gloriari Iudace, non crucifixisti Deum . . . .*" *MPL* 69, 1206d.
²⁸² *Historia Tripartita*, XII, 5: *Et cum plurimi Deum confiteantur esse Iesum: Ego, inquit Nestorius, bimestrem et trimestrem nequaquam confiteor Deum.* *MPL* 69, 1207c; *PNF²* 2, 172.
²⁸³ *Historia Tripartita*, XII, 4: "*Sermonem tantumodo quasi metuendum exparisse.*" *MPL* 69, 1206b; *PNF²* 2, 171.

ascribe the *idiomata* of the natures to the same person of Christ. He wants to hold to the truth of the first, but what follows from the first should not be true—he thereby indicates that he himself does not understand what he is denying.

We Christians must ascribe all the *idiomata* of the two natures of Christ, both persons, equally to him. Consequently Christ is God and man in one person because whatever is said of him as man must also be said of him as God, namely, Christ has died, and Christ is God; therefore God died—not the separated God, but God united with humanity. For about the separated God both statements, namely, that Christ is God and that God died, are false; both are false, for then God is not man. If it seems strange to Nestorius that God dies, he should think it equally strange that God becomes man; for thereby the immortal God becomes that which must die, suffer, and have all human *idiomata*. Otherwise, what would that man be with whom God personally unites, if he did not have truly human *idiomata*? It would be a phantom, as the Manichaeans[284] had taught earlier. On the other hand, whatever is said of God must also be ascribed to the man, namely, God created the world and is almighty; the man Christ is God, therefore the man Christ created the world and is almighty. The reason for this is that since God and man have become one person, it follows that this person bears the *idiomata* of both natures.

O Lord God! We should always rejoice in true faith, free of dispute and doubt, over such a blessed, comforting doctrine, to sing, praise, and thank God the Father for such inexpressible mercy that he let his dear Son become like us, a man and our brother! Yet the loathsome devil instigates such great annoyance through proud, ambitious, incorrigible people that our cherished and precious joy is hindered and spoiled for us. May God have pity! We Christians should know that if God is not in the scale to give it weight, we, on our side, sink to the ground. I mean it this way: if it cannot be said that God died for us, but only a man, we are lost; but if God's death and a dead God lie in the balance, his side goes down and ours goes up like a light and empty scale. Yet he

---

[284] Manichaeism had a place for Jesus as the manifestation of light, which it held to be equivalent with good. Since, however, it regarded matter as evil, Jesus' humanity was denied.

can also readily go up again, or leap out of the scale! But he could not sit on the scale unless he had become a man like us, so that it could be called God's dying, God's martyrdom, God's blood, and God's death. For God in his own nature cannot die; but now that God and man are united in one person, it is called God's death when the man dies who is one substance or one person with God.

This council condemned far too little of Nestorius, for it dealt only with the one *idioma,* that God was born of Mary. Thus the histories relate that it was resolved in this council, in opposition to Nestorius, that Mary should be called *Theotokos,* "bearer of God,"[285] even though Nestorius denied to God in Christ all *idiomata* of human nature such as dying, the cross, suffering, and everything that is incompatible with the Godhead. This is why they should not just have resolved that Mary was *theotokos,* but also that Pilate and the Jews were crucifiers and murderers of God, and the like. That they later condemned him, covering all the *idiomata,* with the words, "Nestorius denies that Christ is God and one person," is certainly correct in effect or according to logic, but is expressed too clumsily and oddly because Nestorius could get no other idea from it than that he had been treated unjustly and wrongly, for he had never taught such words, but on the contrary had always said that Christ was true and very God and not two persons, having for this reason vehemently persecuted the Arians. Such crude people cannot syllogize or draw logical conclusions, namely, that he who denies the *idiomata* or attributes of a nature can be said to deny the substance or nature itself. So the verdict should have been, "Although Nestorius confesses that Christ, true God and true man, is one person, but does not ascribe the *idiomata* of human nature to the same divine person of Christ, he is in error, just as much as if he denied the nature itself." Furthermore, they should not have emphasized only the *idioma* of his mother Mary; then the cause of this council would have been that much easier to understand, which, I think, very few people have understood so far—it is impossible to understand it from Platina[286] and those who follow him.

---

[285] *Historia Tripartita,* XII, 5. *MPL* 69, 1208a; *PNF*² 2, 172.
[286] Cf. above, p. 199, n. 18, and quotations from Platina in *WA* 50, 583, n. *b.*

I too have been confronted by Nestorians who fought me very stubbornly, saying that the divinity of Christ could not suffer. For example, Zwingli too wrote against me concerning the saying, "The Word became flesh."[287] He would simply not have it that "became" should apply to "Word." He wanted it to read, "The flesh was made word,"[288] because God could not become anything. I myself did not know at that time that this resembled the notion of Nestorius because I did not understand the council either, but recognized it as error on the basis of Holy Scripture, Augustine, and the master of the *Sentences*.[289] Who knows how many Nestorians may still be in the papacy, praising this council greatly and not knowing what they praise? For reason wants to be clever here and not tolerate that God should die or have any human characteristics, even though it is used to believing, like Nestorius, that Christ is God.

Well then, this council too did not establish anything new in faith, as we said above, but only defended the old faith against the new notion of Nestorius, so one cannot take any examples from it, or give the councils authority to establish new or different articles of faith. This article was in the church from the very beginning and was not newly established by the council, but was preserved through the gospel or Holy Scripture, for it is written in Luke 1 [:32] that the angel Gabriel announced to the Virgin Mary that of her would be born "the Son of the Most High." And St. Elizabeth, "Why is this granted me, that the mother of my Lord should come to me?" [Luke 1:43]. And at Christmas all the angels, "To you is born this day a Savior, who is Christ the Lord" [Luke 2:11]. And in Galatians 3 [4:4] St. Paul, "God sent forth his Son, born of woman." These texts (I am convinced) hold firmly enough that Mary is the mother of God. Thus St. Paul states in I Corinthians 3 [2:8], "The rulers of this world crucified the Lord of glory." Acts 20 [:28], God obtained the church "with his own blood," although

---

[287] John 1:14. Cf. Ulrich Zwingli's tract *Friendly Exposition of the Eucharist Affair, to Martin Luther* (C.R. 92, 562 ff.) and Luther's *Confession Concerning Christ's Supper* (1528). LW 37, 161-372. On the entire controversy on the eucharist, see Walther Köhler, *Zwingli und Luther* (2 vols.; Leipzig, 1924; Gütersloh, 1953), and LW 37, 153-159.

[288] Luther quotes the Vulgate text, "*Verbum caro facta est.*"

[289] Peter Lombard in *Four Books of Sentences*, III, dist. XII. MPL 192, 1076-1077.

God, to judge by reason, has no blood! And Philippians 2 [:6-7], "Christ, though he was in the form of God, emptied himself, taking the form of a servant, being born in the likeness of men." And the Children's Creed, the Apostles' Creed, says, "I believe in Jesus Christ his only Son our Lord, who was conceived, born of Mary, suffered, was crucified, died, was buried," etc. Here are written, clearly enough, the *idiomata* of human nature, and yet they are ascribed to the only Son and Lord, in whom we believe as we do in the Father, and as in the true God. That should suffice about this council.

The fourth principal council was held in Chalcedon in Pontus or Asia (approximately twenty-two or twenty-three years after the third preceding principal council in Ephesus) through Emperor Marcian, who succeeded Emperor Theodosius II as emperor in Constantinople in the year 455.[290] Thus the four great councils were held within a span of about one hundred and thirty years, for the one at Nicaea was held in the year 327.[291] But many other councils were held previous to, and along with, as well as after them, convoked here and there by the bishops themselves, without the emperors. But these four could not have met without the action of the emperors; the holy fathers were far too weak for that, and one would not easily give way to another, as the histories unfortunately demonstrate. This adds to our special consolation—we should not despair, because the Holy Spirit dwelt in several of these fathers and they were holy and must be called holy, so we too shall be holy and attain salvation.

But I should be glad to learn from someone else why this council met, for no trustworthy history has been transmitted to us. The *Ecclesiastical History*[292] ends with the first council, of Nicaea; the *Tripartita* and Theodoret[293] with the third at Ephesus; and from

---

[290] Marcian actually was emperor from 450 to 457. The chronological difference is due to Luther's using the chronology of John Carion. See above, p. 215, n. 36.

[291] Luther's *Supputatio* (see above, p. 215, n. 36) places the Council of Nicaea in 326, that of Constantinople in 376, that of Ephesus in 437, and that of Chalcedon in 458. Accordingly, there is a span of 132 years between the first and the fourth councils. Modern chronology places them in 325, 381, 431, and 451.

[292] Eusebius' *Ecclesiastical History*. Luther read it in the translation of Rufinus. See above, p. 248, n. 148.

[293] Theodoret's *Ecclesiastical History* ends in 428. The Council of Ephesus was

then on we almost have to depend upon the pope and his histories, in which it is, for sound and obvious reasons, very difficult to believe, for until then they had related everything to themselves and invented their own majesty through such miserable lies, which they still continue to do, that no one's conscience can rely on them. Now advise me, how am I, who does not understand this council or know what it did, going to be saved? And what happened to the dear saints and Christians who throughout these many centuries did not know what this council established? For there must always be saints on earth, and when those die, other saints must live, from the beginning to the end of the world; otherwise, the article would be false, "I believe in the holy Christian church, the communion of saints," and Christ would have to be lying when he says, "I am with you always, to the close of the age" [Matt. 28:20]. There must (I say) always be living saints on earth—they are wherever they can be—otherwise, Christ's kingdom would come to an end, and there would be no one to pray the Lord's Prayer, confess the Creed, be baptized, take the sacrament, be absolved, etc.

Well then, Platina and others say[294] this was the reason: in Constantinople an abbot, or as they called it, an archimandrite, named Eutyches,[295] had advanced another doctrine against Nestorius and had taught that Christ was one person only in the divine nature, against which the fathers in the council resolved that Christ is one person and two natures. That is only right and the Christian faith. But the pope's histories write that he taught that after the deity had assumed humanity and so had become Christ in one person, not more than the deity remained, and that Christ is to be regarded solely as God and not as man.[296] If that is Eutyches' opinion, he is exactly another crude Nestorius, who is said to have

---

held in 431. Luther, who did not read Theodoret's account (cf. above, p. 252, n. 161), erred when he assumed that Theodoret recorded this council.

[294] For the section in Platina, see WA 50, 593, n. b. Since Pope Leo I (440-461) is mentioned there, "others" may refer to him. Luther refers to Leo's letters below, which had been available in print since 1470 and were contained in Crabbe. Leo's works are contained in MPL 54—56; PNF² 12, 1-216.

[295] Eutyches (ca. 378-454), archimandrite of a large monastery at Constantinople.

[296] The "pope's histories" refers to Corpus Iuris Canonici, which contains a catalogue of heresies. See Decreti Secunda Pars, causa XXIV, ques. 3, C. XXIX. CIC 1, 1005.

taught that Christ is two persons and yet only one person; thus this one must have taught simultaneously two natures, and yet only one nature, in Christ. For this is what Pope Leo cries in a letter,[297] that Eutyches and Nestorius teach contradictory heresies—and it is certainly true that they who teach that Christ is two and yet one person or nature, and again, that there are two natures and yet only one nature in Christ, surely do contradict each other; indeed, each one contradicts himself.

But if the papists knew that this was not the meaning of Nestorius and of Eutyches, they should, in all fairness, have refrained from such statements, and should have spoken a bit more clearly about the matter and in *terminis propriis,* that is, they should have quoted their own words; otherwise, the heretics will think they are being unjustly and violently attacked with false words and wrong interpretations of their own words, as I said earlier about Nestorius.

That Eutyches did not think there was but one nature in Christ is reflected by the papists' own words when they say that Eutyches confessed that there are two natures in Christ, namely, that the deity has assumed humanity. Whoever confesses this says that Christ has more than one nature. But they do not indicate what Eutyches meant when he said that afterward only the divine nature remained in Christ, not the human; and so they let it rest, as though Eutyches had believed that Christ had two natures, and yet not two, but only one nature. Therefore the later histories are uncertain and obscure too, so that no one can understand what Eutyches or the pope's histories mean, and thus one loses the council, including the reason it was held. Indeed, one can find out through the histories of the councils and the letters of the popes, but, on the other hand, the pope's historians ought not to write so awkwardly and clumsily, nor babble their own words to us; one thing we can certainly gather from this is that they have understood this council exactly as well as I!

I shall give you my ideas; if I hit the mark, good—if not, the Christian faith will not fall herewith. Eutyches' opinion is also (like that of Nestorius) in error regarding the *idiomata,* but in a dif-

---

[297] Leo I. *Epistola 119: ad Maximum Antiochenum episcopum.* MPL 54, 1041b; PNF² 12, 85,

ferent way. Nestorius does not want to give the *idiomata* of humanity to the divinity in Christ, even though he maintains that Christ is God and man. Eutyches, on the other hand, does not want to give the *idiomata* of divinity to the humanity, though he also maintains that Christ is true God and true man. It is as though I preached that the "Word," God's Son, is creator of heaven and earth, equal to the Father in eternity, John 1 [:3], and that the "Word," the same Son of God, is true man, John 1 [:14]—Eutyches would grant me that and not doubt it. But if I continue and preach that this same man Christ is creator of heaven and earth, then Eutyches takes offense and is outraged at the words, "A man created heaven and earth," and says, "No! Such a divine *idioma* (as creating heaven) does not appertain to man." But he forgets that he previously conceded that Christ is true God and man in one person and nevertheless refuses to admit the conclusion or "the premise for a good conclusion."[298]

For whoever confesses that God and man are one person must, by reason of such a union of the two natures in one person, also unquestionably concede that this man Christ, born of Mary, is creator of heaven and earth; for he has become this in one person, namely, God who created heaven and earth. Eutyches does not understand such a conclusion, and yet he firmly maintains that Christ is both God and man. Nor does he see that he must deny the human nature of Christ if he rejects the divine *idiomata* of the human nature; for that would divide the person, and Christ would not remain man. And this is what those who write about Eutyches intended to show: he did not allow the human nature in Christ to remain "in his conclusion," though he confesses "in his premise" that the divine and human natures are one Christ, one person, and two natures. To sum up, as was said earlier, whoever confesses the two natures in Christ, God and man, must also ascribe the *idiomata* of both to the person; for to be God and man means nothing if they do not share their *idiomata*. That is why both Nestorius and Eutyches were rightfully condemned because of their error and reason.

---

[298] *Consequens bonae consequentiae.* On the origins of these and other technical terms used by medieval schoolmen, cf. above, p. 293, n. 278.

It is probably true that Eutyches suffered more anguish[299] than Nestorius, for many of the human *idiomata* were left behind by Christ, such as eating, drinking, sleeping, sorrowing, suffering, dying, being buried, etc. He now sits at the right hand of God and eats, drinks, sleeps, sorrows, suffers, or dies no more in eternity, just as will happen to us when we pass from this life into the other life, I Corinthians 15 [:49, 53]. These are temporal and transient *idiomata;* but the natural ones remain, for instance, that he has body and soul, skin and hair, flesh and blood, marrow and bones, and all the limbs of an ordinary human. That is why one must say that this man Christ, the flesh and blood of Mary, is creator of heaven and earth, has vanquished death, abolished sin, broken hell, all of which are true divine *idiomata,* and yet are rightfully and Christianly ascribed to the person who is flesh and blood of Mary, because it is not two but one person.

It is just like your son Peter being called a scholar, although this *idioma* is only of his soul and not of his body. A Eutyches might quibble and say, "No! Peter is not a scholar; his soul is." And again, a Nestorius might say, "No! I did not flog your son, but his body." That sounds as though one wanted to make two persons out of Peter, or to retain but one nature, though it is not meant that way. It is ignorance and coarseness, and proves that they were bad logicians. Such ignorance, however, is not rare in the world in other matters too; one often admits one thing and yet denies that which must follow from it, as was said, "Admitting the premise and denying the conclusion."[300] There are now, for instance, many great lords and learned people[301] who acknowledge freely and firmly that our doctrine of faith, which justifies by pure grace and without merit, is true. But that one should therefore put an end to and scorn monasticism and the serving of saints and the like, offends them, although it is demanded by the conclusion and is the consequence. No one can be justified without faith; it follows from this that one cannot be justified by a monastic life. Why hold to it then? What good is it?

---

[299] *Anfechtung.*
[300] *Antecedente concessio, negare consequens.*
[301] Luther may have in mind those humanists who agreed with the premises of the Reformation, but were unwilling to agree with the conclusions.

But I shall take myself by the nose too,[302] lest I prove so un-grateful as to forget my own folly. Twenty years ago I taught—[303] as I still do—that faith alone, without works, justifies. But if some-one had arisen at that time and taught that monkery and nunning ought to be called idolatry and the mass a veritable abomination, I, though I would not have helped to burn him, would at least have said that it served him right. And I—thoughtless fool—could not see the conclusion that I would have had to concede, that if faith alone does it, then monkery and mass do not. And still worse, I knew that these were nothing but human works and doc-trine, and yet I did not ascribe such value to the good works commanded by God and performed in faith. Thus I surely proved myself a real Nestorius and Eutyches (albeit in different matters), for I granted one thing but denied the other that followed from it, just as Nestorius admits that Christ is God and man but will not agree that this same God was born and died, which, however, does follow from it.

Moreover, Luther scolds the papists for teaching neither the Christian faith, nor good works, and they on their part do not keep mum either, but in turn rebuke Luther even more vehe-mently for not teaching the Christian faith correctly and for for-bidding good works. What is the obstacle? Why are they not united, although they confess one and the same thing? I shall tell you: a Nestorius has gone astray here on the *idiomata*. Luther wants to have good works, but they should not bear the glorious divine *idiomata*, such as atoning for sin, reconciling God's wrath, and justifying sinners, for such *idiomata* belong to another whose name is "the Lamb of God, who takes away the sin of the world" [John 1:29]. Truly, such *idiomata* must be left to the blood and the death of Christ; good works should have other *idiomata*, other merit and reward. This the papists do not want; instead they give to good works the power to atone for sin and make people pious. Therefore they cry out that Luther does not teach good works, but rather forbids them; but they do not see the conclusion or conse-quence that if one teaches good works that atone for sin, it is tan-

---

[302] Cf. above, p. 208.
[303] Cf. above, p. 201, n. l. This could also be a reference to his *Lectures on Galatians, 1519. LW* 27, 153-410.

tamount to teaching no good works at all, for such good works are *nihil in rerum natura,* "nothing at all," and cannot be. Consequently, in as much as they so firmly and decisively teach and confess good works, they teach no good works at all.

Here you see Nestorius' logic which admits a "premise" and denies the "conclusion" and thus also falsifies the premise. If the one is true, the other must also be true in any real conclusion or consequence. On the other hand, if the last is false, the first must also be false. They not only admit but absolutely insist that good works atone for sin; yet they condemn that which follows, that such works are not good, indeed, are nothing and no works at all. Now it really follows irrefutably from the former, for good works that atone for sin are as much as no good works, just as this conclusion is irrefutable: *Qui docet id quod non est, docet nihil,* "He who teaches what is not, teaches as much as nothing." One may likewise say of faith, "He who teaches a faith that does not justify alone and without good works teaches as much as no faith at all." For a faith that justifies with or by good works is nothing at all.

I will make it still plainer. Several jurists concede that it is right for priests to marry, but they do not grant the conclusion that their children should be their heirs; that is the same as saying that a priest's marriage must be fornication. If there is a marriage, then the child must also be the heir; if it is not an heir, then there is no marriage. In the schools this is called "denying the conclusion of an admitted premise in a good syllogism" and "retaining the premise when the conclusion has been destroyed"—[304] that is impossible, and those who do it are called crude and ignorant people. But this was the lack in both Nestorius and Eutyches, as happens to many other people in other matters. They both were certainly sincere when they regarded Christ as God and man in one person—as the histories as well as the records of the councils indicate—and yet, they could not reconcile themselves to the conclusion or consequence that the person who is both God and man was really crucified and created heaven; God could not be crucified or man create heaven.

---

[304] *Negare consequens antecedentis concessi in bona consequentia* and *Destructo consequente, retinere antecedens.*

And what shall we say of ourselves? The apostles in Jerusalem, together with many thousands of Jews, had been justified by faith alone, that is, by the grace of Christ. They still had their Nestoriuses and Eutycheses in their system and did not see the conclusion that the laws of Moses did not and could not contribute anything to it, but wanted to ascribe to it the *idiomata* which belong only to the Lamb of God, saying (as we said above) that the Gentiles could not be saved if they were not circumcised and did not keep the law. That was virtually denying Christ with his grace, as St. Paul says in Galatians 2 [:21], "If justification were through the law, then Christ died to no purpose"; and in Romans 11 [:6], "But if it is by grace, it is no longer on the basis of works." But those in Jerusalem said this, "To be sure, it is grace alone, but it must also be works alone, for without the law one cannot be saved, even though one must be saved by grace alone without works." That is, in plain German, boxing one's own ears[305] and not understanding what one says. The schools (as we said) call that "granting the premise and denying the conclusion" or "destroying the conclusion and affirming the premise." No one should at the same time say yes and no about the same thing, unless he be an utter ignoramus or a desperate scoffer.

That is what my Antinomians,[306] too, are doing today, who are preaching beautifully and (as I cannot but think) with real sincerity about Christ's grace, about the forgiveness of sin and whatever else can be said about the doctrine of redemption. But they flee as if it were the very devil the consequence that they should tell the people about the third article,[307] of sanctification, that is, of the new life in Christ. They think one should not frighten or trouble the people, but rather always preach comfortingly about grace and the forgiveness of sins in Christ, and under no circumstances use these or similar words, "Listen! You want to be a Christian and at the same time remain an adulterer, a whoremonger, a drunken swine, arrogant, covetous, a usurer, envious,

---

[305] "*Sich selbs in die backen hauen.*" Cf. Thiele, *Luthers Sprichwörtersammlung,* No. 8.

[306] Cf. above, p. 264, n. 200.

[307] The third article of the Apostles' Creed. See Luther's *Large Catechism.* Tappert (ed.), *Book of Concord,* pp. 415-420.

vindictive, malicious, etc.!" Instead they say, "Listen! Though you are an adulterer, a whoremonger, a miser, or other kind of sinner, if you but believe, you are saved, and you need not fear the law. Christ has fulfilled it all!"

Tell me, my dear man, is that not granting the premise and denying the conclusion? It is, indeed, taking away Christ and bringing him to nought at the same time he is most beautifully proclaimed! And it is saying yes and no to the same thing. For there is no such Christ that died for sinners who do not, after the forgiveness of sins, desist from sins and lead a new life. Thus they preach Christ nicely with Nestorian and Eutychian logic that Christ is and yet is not Christ. They may be fine Easter preachers, but they are very poor Pentecost preachers, for they do not preach *de sanctificatione et vivificatione Spiritus Sancti,* "about the sanctification by the Holy Spirit," but solely about the redemption of Jesus Christ, although Christ (whom they extoll so highly, and rightly so) is Christ, that is, he has purchased redemption from sin and death so that the Holy Spirit might transform us out of the old Adam into new men—we die unto sin and live unto righteousness, beginning and growing here on earth and perfecting it beyond, as St. Paul teaches.[308] Christ did not earn only *gratia,* "grace," for us, but also *donum,* "the gift of the Holy Spirit," so that we might have not only forgiveness of, but also cessation of, sin. Now he who does not abstain from sin, but persists in his evil life, must have a different Christ, that of the Antinomians; the real Christ is not there, even if all the angels would cry, "Christ! Christ!" He must be damned with this, his new Christ.

Now see what evil logicians we are in sublime matters that are so far beyond or remote from us that we simultaneously believe and disbelieve something. But in lowly matters we are exceedingly keen logicians. No matter how stupid a peasant is, he soon understands and figures out this: he who gives me a groschen is not giving me a gulden. This follows as a matter of course, and he sees the logic of it clearly. But our Antinomians fail to see that they are preaching Christ without and against the Holy Spirit because they propose to let the people continue in their old ways

---

[308] In, for example, Romans 6 and 7.

and still pronounce them saved. And yet logic, too, implies that a Christian should either have the Holy Spirit and lead a new life, or know that he has no Christ. Nevertheless, these asses presume to be better logicians than Master Philip[309] and Aristotle—I must not mention Luther because the pope was made to feel only their logic—they soar far too high for me! Well, then, the logic of Nestorius and Eutyches is a common plague, especially with reference to Holy Scripture; but in other matters it acquits itself better, although it plagues jurists and rulers enough in subtle matters, where they have to hear a yes and no at the same time and have difficulty in distinguishing the two.

Now if Nestorius and Eutyches stubbornly and proudly clung to their opinion (as I neither can nor should judge from the histories I read) after the bishops had instructed them, they were justly condemned not only as heretics but also as silly fools. But if they did not stubbornly cling to their opinion, as the acts of the councils themselves report, especially about Eutyches,[310] and the bishops neglected to instruct in a spirit of gentleness those who erred—in conformity with St. Paul's teaching [Gal. 6:1]—they will one day have to answer to the true judge for their pride and rash action,[311] although they themselves may have judged the case aright (for by now the councils had acquired a great reputation, and there were, I suppose, all of six hundred and thirty bishops in attendance here).[312]

I remember how Master John Wesel,[313] who was pastor in Mainz and who with his books dominated the University of Erfurt, from which I also received my master's degree, had to be

---

[309] Philip Melanchthon (1479-1560).

[310] *Historia Tripartita*, XII, 5. *MPL* 69, 1208a; *PNF*[2] 2, 172.

[311] A reference to the actions of the Council of Ephesus in 449, labeled the "robbers' synod" by Pope Leo I, in which Bishop Dioscur of Alexandria condoned tyrannical procedures and mob action. Its decisions have never been accepted by the Roman Catholic Church.

[312] Recorded by Platina, but not by Rufinus. See *WA* 50, 600, n. *c.*

[313] John of Wesel (*ca.* 1400-1481), an ecclesiastical reformer who attacked indulgences on the basis of Holy Scripture. He was tried before a Dominican commission employed by the inquisition, accused of heresy, and condemned to life imprisonment in a monastery. The quotation Luther attributes to him does not appear in the records of the trial. Cf. Robert Menties (trans.), Karl Ullmann's *Reformers Before the Reformation* (2 vols.; Edinburgh, 1855), I, 217-276.

condemned by those accursed, arrogant murderers called "inquisitors of heretical depravity"[314] (I should say "inventors") the Dominicans, only because he would not say, "I believe that there is a God," but said, "I know that there is a God"; for all the schools held that "the existence of God is known of itself,"[315] as St. Paul also says in Romans 1 [:19]. And you will find related in the *Apology* how the murdering Franciscans dealt with John Hilten in Eisenach.[316]

Suppose that an honorable man would unexpectedly approach you and me, his coarse expression giving a peculiar cast to the matter, saying, "I must tell you that a new prophet has arisen who teaches that if a man becomes perfectly holy he is able not only to perform miracles but also to create heaven and earth, angels, and whatever inhabits heaven and earth, out of nothing"— as several scholastics have also argued, Book IV [of the *Sentences*][317]—and, what is even worse, he says, "The old true God had died," etc. Here you and I would say, "He must be the devil and his mother." Scripture says, "I the Lord do not change" [Mal. 3:6]; and St. Paul, "Who alone has immortality" [I Tim. 6:16]. Why waste many words? God alone lives, and he himself is life. Then he would begin, "Why, you yourself teach and say that Christ is a man, perfectly holy, the creator of heaven and earth, furthermore, true God, who died for you on the cross." Behold how suddenly we become blasphemous Nestoriuses and Eutycheses, confessing simultaneously that Christ is God and man, one person, that he died for us, that he created heaven and earth, though we have just said it must be the devil and his mother who say that a man created heaven and earth and that God died! And yet, logical consistency compels us to believe that Christ is God and man in one person. Here you see how the *idiomata* can take unthinking people unawares and confuse and perplex them. In such an instance one should proceed with gentle instruction and

---

[314] "*Haereticae pravitatis inquisitores,*" the official title for those Dominicans who were employed by the inquisition, instituted by Pope Gregory IX in 1232.

[315] "*Deum esse, per se notum sit.*"

[316] The story is told in Philip Melanchthon's *Apology of the Augsburg Confession,* Art. XXVII. Tappert (ed.), *Book of Concord,* pp. 268-269.

[317] Book IV deals with the seven sacraments and with the last things. Cf. *MPL* 192, 839-962.

refrain from any arrogant condemnation of those who err. May God grant that I lie; but I fear that on the Last Day some of the heretics will be the judges, condemning the bishops who sat in judgment over them. God is strange and inscrutable in his judgments [Rom. 11:33]. However, we know that he "opposes the proud, but gives grace to the humble" [I Pet. 5:5]. Especially in the councils and in the church one should never act from *zelos*,[318] that is, from envy and pride, for that is intolerable to God.

That is my opinion about Eutyches. If I did not hit the mark, I missed it,[319] and it is their fault. Why did they not give a better account of the matter and report on it with greater care, so that it might be clearly understood? And what should we do if the acts of this council were lost? The Christian faith would not have to perish because of that! Other and far more useful things than the acts of this council have been lost. St. Augustine himself bemoans the fact that he could find but very little in his predecessors to aid him against Pelagius, though such an important subject must have been much discussed.[320] I have formed my opinions on the basis of the words of the Roman bishop Leo, who writes that the heresies of Nestorius and Eutyches are inconsistent or contradictory and in opposition to one another.[321] Now the *Tripartita* leaves no doubt that Nestorius confessed that Christ is true God and true man, very emphatically so, and that he was not an Arian, simply denying the divinity of Christ.[322] On the contrary, he banished and persecuted the Arians, even to the point of murder and slaughter. But his heresy consists in that he, confused and led astray by the *idiomata,* could not understand how God could be born of a woman and be crucified. Therefore Eutyches' heresy must be regarded contradictory because he regards Christ as God and man, but refuses to ascribe the *idiomata* of the divine nature to the human-nature; just as Nestorius, on the other hand,

---

[318] From the Greek for "zeal."

[319] A German proverb of unknown origin, *"Hab ichs nicht troffen, so hab ich gefeilet."*

[320] The passage could not be located in Augustine's writings. Cf. Schäfer, *op. cit.,* p. 314, n. 3.

[321] Leo I. *Epistola 165: ad Leonem Augustum,* C. II. *MPL* 54, 1155-1157; *PNF²* 12, 107-108.

[322] *Historia Tripartita,* XII, 4. *MPL* 69, 1204-1205; *PNF²* 2, 169.

would not ascribe the *idiomata* of the human nature to God in the one person of Christ. That is what is meant by saying that the two are in opposition to one.another or contradictory.

If, however, it was his intention simply to deny the human nature in Christ, then his heresy does not contradict that of Nestorius; then he must have been raving mad to believe that the divinity is united with humanity in Christ, and that at the same time only one nature, namely, the divine, remained or came into being. That would not only be opposed to Nestorius, but also to all believers and unbelievers, to all heretics and true Christians, to all heathen and all of mankind, for no man ever taught a thing like that. But since they gave such an account of this matter and themselves testified that Eutyches had admitted that divinity and humanity are merged into one person in Christ, and yet also made the other statement, as though they intended that no one should understand it, we will not understand it either. Why should we care, since we ourselves have a better conception of it? In the council Eutyches says that he had not stated his position in the words of which they accused him, namely, that he had denied the human nature in Christ.[323] From this one can infer that he was in error and that he did not want to deny the humanity in Christ. But if I were Dr. Luther, I would like to hear from these popish writers how they could believe their own words when they made bold to say that Nestorius held that there were two persons in Christ and yet only one person, and that Eutyches held that there were two natures in Christ and yet only one nature. I surely believe that they, too, are Nestorian and Eutychian dialecticians. I say nothing of their theology; perhaps they are compelled to be antilogicians.

But to return to the council—we find that this council too did not establish any new article of faith; again it furnishes no proof that councils are vested with the authority to foist new doctrines on Christendom, for this article is far more abundantly and firmly grounded in Scripture, John 5 [:27], "The Father has given him authority to execute judgment, because he is the Son of man." If Christ had adapted himself to Eutyches' opinion, he would have

---

[323] *Historia Tripartita*, XII, 4. *MPL* 69, 1208a; *PNF*² 2, 172.

been obliged to say, "because he is the Son of God," for to execute judgment is an *idioma* of divine, not of human, nature. Christ, however, imputes this power to his human nature, namely, to the Son of man, that is, the Son of the Virgin Mary. And in Matthew 22 [:43-45] Christ asks the Pharisees how they explain the fact that David calls Christ his Lord, though he had to be his Son and seed. If he is David's Son or seed, how then can he sit at the right hand of God? Here Eutyches would have had to say that not David's seed, but only God's Son can sit at the right hand of God. And yet he confesses that God's Son and David's Son are one person; but where the person sits, there sits God's Son and David's. Eutyches did not see this conclusion; therefore it was inferred that he did not regard Christ as man, but only as a divine person and nature, though this was not what he meant.

In summary, all the prophets, all of Scripture, ascribing to Christ or the Messiah an everlasting kingdom, redemption from sin, death, and hell, oppose Eutyches, for they all say that the seed of the woman shall bruise the serpent's head, Genesis 3 [:15], that is, shall vanquish sin, death, devil, and hell; these too are *idiomata* of divine nature and not of the woman's seed. And all the world is to be blessed through the seed of Abraham, Genesis 22 [:18], that is, sin, death, hell, the curse of God, are to be removed. These too are *idiomata*, not of Abraham's seed, but of divine nature. And later there followed the glorious and mighty prophecies of David, Isaiah, Jeremiah, and all the other prophets declaring that David's seed shall establish eternal righteousness, that is, abolish sin, death, and hell.[324] All of these are clearly *idiomata* of divine majesty and nature, yet are ascribed throughout Holy Scripture to the Son of David, Christ, the Son of the Virgin Mary. Even if I do not have this council or any proper understanding of it, I still have Scripture and a proper understanding of it. The council too is bound to hold to it; and for me Scripture is far more reliable than all councils.

Whoever is thus disposed may read more of the history of the councils; I read myself into a bad humor with it. Such bickering, confusion, and disorder prevailed there that I am really inclined

---

[324] For example, Jer. 23:5.

to believe Gregory of Nazianz, the teacher of St. Jerome, who, having lived before this time and having witnessed better councils and fathers, still wrote, "To tell the truth, I believe it advisable to flee all the councils of bishops; for I saw nothing good resulting from the councils, not even the abolition of evil, but rather sheer ambition and quarreling over precedence," etc.[325] I am surprised that they, in view of these words, did not long ago brand him as the worst heretic. But he speaks the truth when he says that the bishops are ambitious, haughty, quarrelsome, and vehement in the councils; you will find that corroborated in this council. By the same token, not all who teach correctly or uphold the true doctrine are necessarily holy. For Balaam also is a true prophet [Num. 24:16], and Judas is a true apostle [Matt. 10:4], and the Pharisees occupy the seat of Moses and teach the truth [Matt. 23:2-3]. Thus we too must have something else and something more reliable for our faith than the councils. That "something else" and "something more" is Holy Scripture.

The truth of his statement that he saw no good results come from the councils is strongly borne out by the histories. For before the Council of Nicaea the heresy of Arius was a jest compared with the misery evoked after the council, as was said above. The same applies to the other councils, as in the cases of Macedonius and Nestorius; for the faction that was condemned held together all the more firmly, trying to justify itself and to be exonerated. They fanned the flames more vigorously than before against the councils that had not understood them rightly. That is the way we Germans fared at the Council of Constance:[326] there the pope was made subject to the council and was deposed, and his tyranny and simony[327] were strongly condemned. Yet ever since that time he is possessed by seven more devils [Matt. 12:45] and his tyranny and simony have gotten off to an even better start. He devours, robs, and steals all convents, cloisters, churches; he sells indulgences, grace, law, God, Christ, the Holy Spirit; he betrays,

---

[325] *Epistola 130: ad Procopium. MPG* 37, 225-226.
[326] This council was held from 1414 to 1418. For more of Luther's reactions to this council, see Headley, *op. cit.,* pp. 225-228.
[327] Simony, meaning the sale of spiritual things for money, gets its name from Acts 8:18-24. Ecclesiastical offices frequently were bought in the Middle Ages.

ruins, confuses emperors and kings; he wages wars, sheds blood, assassinates body and soul, so that it becomes quite evident what god it is that keeps house in Rome. That is the reward we Germans have for deposing and reforming the popes at the Council of Constance. Indeed, I think that this was the appropriate end for this council. If seven devils do not suffice for them, then depose and reform more popes the next time, and you may have seventy-seven legions warring against you—provided there is still room for even more devils to inhabit them and they are not already full of them. Such was the reformation of the Council of Constance.

These then are the four principal councils and the reasons they were held. The first, in Nicaea, defended the divinity of Christ against Arius; the second, in Constantinople, defended the divinity of the Holy Spirit against Macedonius; the third, in Ephesus, defended the one person of Christ against Nestorius; the fourth, in Chalcedon, defended the two natures in Christ against Eutyches. But no new articles of faith were thereby established, for these four doctrines are formulated far more abundantly and powerfully in St. John's gospel alone, even if the other evangelists and St. Paul and St. Peter had written nothing about it, although they, together with the prophets, also teach and bear convincing witness to all of that. Since these four principal councils (which the bishops of Rome, according to their decretals, put on a level with the four gospels, as though these matters together with all articles of faith were not contained far more richly in the gospels, or as if the councils had not taken them from there—so nicely do these episcopal asses understand the essence of the gospels and of the councils) neither intended nor were able to create and establish anything new in matters of faith, as they themselves confess, how much less then can one assign such power to the other councils, which are to be regarded lower, if these four are and are to be called principal councils.

All the other councils too must be viewed in this way, be they large or small. Even though there were many thousands of them, they do not introduce anything new either in matters of faith or of good works; but they defend, as the highest judges and greatest bishops under Christ, the ancient faith and the ancient good works in conformity with Scripture. To be sure, they may also deal with temporal, transient, and changeable things in order to meet the need of their particular time; this, however, must also be done outside the councils in every parish and school. But if they establish anything new with regard to faith or good works, you may rest assured that the Holy Spirit had no hand in it, but only the unholy spirit with his angels. For in that instance they must act without and outside of Holy Scripture, indeed, in opposition to it, as Christ says, "He who is not with me is against me" [Matt. 12:30]. The Holy Spirit can neither know nor do anything more than St. Paul when he says in I Corinthians 2 [:2], "I decided to know nothing among you except Jesus Christ and him crucified." The Holy Spirit has not been given to teach or instill in us anything except Christ, but he is to teach and remind us of all that is in Christ "in whom are hid all the treasures of wisdom and knowledge" [Col. 2:3]. He is to make him clear to us, as Christ says [John 16:13], and not exalt our reason and notions or make an idol of these.

This is why these councils are outside Scripture and are councils of Caiphas, Pilate, and Herod; as the apostles say in Acts 4 [:26], "They were gathered against the Lord." They take counsel, or hold councils, against God and his Christ [Ps. 2:2]. And all the evangelists relate[328] that the chief priests and Pharisees conferred, or assembled councils, deliberating how they might kill Christ—as David had foretold in Psalm 2 [:2-3] that they would take counsel together against God and his anointed, calling Christ's preaching "bonds" and "cords" which they would burst asunder and cast from them. Such are the majority of the pope's councils, in which he sets himself up in Christ's stead as head of the church, makes Holy Scripture subject to himself, and tears it asunder. His decretals show how he condemned the sacrament in both kinds at Constance[329] after he had already rent marriage asunder, forbidden it and condemned it, and virtually crucified and buried Christ.

---

[328] Matt. 26:4; Mark 14:1-2; Luke 22:2; John 11:47-53.
[329] Cf. Luther's treatment of the decrees of the Council of Constance in WA 39^I, 13-39.

This brings us to the main question prompting me to write this booklet: what, then, is a council? Or, what is its task? If it is not the function of a council to establish new articles of faith, then all the world has to date been fooled terribly because it neither knows nor believes anything other than that a decision of a council is an article of faith or at least a work necessary for salvation, so that he who does not keep the decree of a council cannot be saved because he does not obey the Holy Spirit, the council's master. Well then, I think that my conscience is clear when I say that no council (as I said before) is authorized to initiate new articles of faith, because the four principal councils did not do that. Consequently, I will state my opinion here and reply to this main question as follows.

First, a council has no power to establish new articles of faith, even though the Holy Spirit is present. Even the apostolic council in Jerusalem introduced nothing new in matters of faith, but rather held that which St. Peter concludes in Acts 16 [15:11], and which all their predecessors believed, namely, the article that one is to be saved without the laws, solely through the grace of Christ.

Second, a council has the power—and is also duty-bound to exercise it—to suppress and to condemn new articles of faith, in accordance with Scripture and the ancient faith, just as the Council of Nicaea condemned the new doctrine of Arius, that of Constantinople the new doctrine of Macedonius, that of Ephesus the new doctrine of Nestorius, and that of Chalcedon the new doctrine of Eutyches.

Third, a council has no power to command new good works; it cannot do so, for Holy Scripture has already abundantly commanded all good works. What good works can one think of that the Holy Spirit does not teach in Scripture, such as humility, patience, gentleness, mercy, faithfulness, faith, kindness, peaceableness, obedience, self-discipline, chastity, generosity, readiness to serve, etc., and in summary, love? [Gal. 5:22-23]. What good work could one imagine that is not included in the commandment of love? What sort of a good work would it be if it were not motivated by love? For love, according to St. Paul's teaching, is the fulfilment of the whole law [Gal. 5:14]—as Christ himself says in Matthew 5.

315

Fourth, a council has the power—and is also duty-bound to exercise it—to condemn evil works that oppose love, according to all of Scripture and the ancient practice of the church, and to punish persons guilty of such works, as the Nicene council's decree rebuked the ambition and other vices of bishops and deacons. But here one should speak of two kinds of evil works: some that are, and are called clearly wicked, such as greed, murder, adultery, ambition, and the like. These we find condemned by the councils, as they are also condemned, outside the councils, in Holy Scripture and are, moreover, also punished by civil law. But besides these there are other, new good works which are not called evil, but are seemingly good, refined vices, holy idolatries invented by strange saints, or even mad saints; in summary, they are the white devil and a glittering Satan. Such evil, I should say new, good works should be condemned by the councils most sharply and severely, for they pose a danger to the Christian faith and an offense to Christian life and are a caricature or mockery of both.

For instance, when a weak Christian hears or sees a holy hermit or monk leading a special kind of life, more austere than that of the ancient, ordinary Christian way and vocation, he stumbles over this and supposes that the life of all the ancient Christians was nothing, or even worldly and dangerous, in comparison with that of this new saint. That gave rise to the abomination throughout the world of a Christian burgher or peasant who believes in Christ with a true and pure faith and practices the genuine, ancient good works commanded by God in Holy Scripture—such as humility, gentleness, patience, chastity, charity, and faithfulness toward his neighbor, industry, and application to his work, office, calling, and station—thinking such a man a true old saint and Christian, whereas he himself is a stench and a cipher compared to the new saint with his special garb, food, fasting, bed, mien, and other similar new good works, who is a conceited, ambitious, angry, impatient, hateful, lustful, presumptuous, false Christian. St. Paul himself calls such people arrogant and egotistic saints who choose a new mode of life for themselves and a new way of serving God not commanded by God, over and above the Christian church's old, true, common way of life and service to God, ordained and commanded by him.

The elect may have been preserved amid these offensive new works, but they had to shed this new skin and be saved in the old Christian skins, just as happened to St. Anthony[330] when he had to learn that a cobbler or tanner in Alexandria was a better Christian than he was with his monkery. He also conceded that he had not advanced as far as this cobbler had. So it was with the great St. John too, the "first hermit,"[331] who was also a prophet for the emperor Theodosius and highly lauded by St. Augustine.[332] When the people, among them St. Jerome, admired the severity of his life, he replied, "Why do you look for anything extraordinary among us? After all, you are more fortunate in your parishes, where the writings and the precepts of apostles and prophets are preached to you." That is what I call taking off the cowl and subjecting oneself to Holy Scripture, praising solely the ordinary Christian way of life. Paphnutius[333] too had to learn that he was on the same level with a fiddler who had been a murderer, and with two wives who had lain with their husbands that same night. Thus he was constrained to remark, "Alas! One must not despise any estate." The same thing also happened to St. Bernard, to Bonaventure,[334] and undoubtedly to many other pious men. In the end, when they realized that their new holiness and monkery could not stand the test against sin and death, they crawled and were saved in the ancient Christian faith, without such new holiness— as the words of St. Bernard testify in many places.[335]

In none of the councils, especially not in the four principal councils, do we find these new good works condemned, except that one or two small councils—for instance, the one that met at Gangra and was composed of twenty bishops (the proceedings of

---

[330] This story is recorded in the *Lives of the Fathers* (*Vitae Patrum*), III, 130, which passed as the work of Jerome, but is now ascribed to Rufinus. See *MPL* 73, 785.

[331] *Primus Eremita*, known as John the Hermit. See Rufinus, II, 20, 32. *MPL* 21, 526c; 538c.

[332] Augustine's praise is found in *The City of God* (*De Civitate Dei*), V, 26. *MPL* 41, 172; *PNF*¹ 2, 105.

[333] Cf. p. 235, n. 101. Paphnutius was a disciple of Anthony. See Rufinus, *History of the Monks* (*Historia Monachorum*), XVI. *MPL* 21, 436.

[334] Bonaventure (1221-1274), a Franciscan theologian known as "the seraphic doctor" because of his mysticism. He taught at the University of Paris.

[335] Cf. Schäfer, *op. cit.*, pp. 441 ff.

which recently appeared in print)[336]—did do something about it. On the contrary, they let the new holiness get the upper hand until the Christian church was hardly recognizable any longer. They acted like lazy gardeners who permit the vines to grow so rampant that the old true tree has to suffer or perish. Even before St. Anthony's day monasticism had made such headway that by the time of the fourth council there was an abbey near Constantinople, of which the aforementioned Eutyches was abbot—although the monasteries of that day were not such imperial castles of stone as they afterward became. For they called him *Archimandrita*.[337] *Mandrae* is said to mean a fence or hedge, made of bushes, shrubs, and boughs, used as an enclosure for animals or as a fold for sheep. And Eutyches, as the head of it, lived with his followers in such an enclosure and led a secluded life. From this one can gather what a monastery was like at the time, before it was enclosed with walls. But just as happens in a garden, where the weeds grow much higher than the true fruit-bearing shoots, so it also happens in the garden of the church: these new saints, who sprout and grow out from the side and yet want to be Christians, nourished by the sap of the tree, grow far better than the true old saints of the Christian faith and life. And since I have touched on the subject, I must relate what I noticed in the histories. St. Bernard was an abbot for thirty-six years, during which time he founded one hundred and sixty monasteries of his order.[338] Now, one knows what kind of monasteries the Cistercians have. At that time, perhaps, they may have been smaller, but today they are regular principalities. And I will say even more: at that time, that is, under the reign of the emperors Henry III, IV, and V,[339] within the span of twenty years, four different princely monastic orders

---

[336] The little synod of Gangra, in Paphlagonia, held in 343, adopted a series of canons directed against extreme asceticism. John Kymaeus, pastor in Homberg, used these canons in 1530 in an attack on the Anabaptists. The book was published in 1537 with a preface by Luther (WA 50, 46-47). The canons to which Luther here refers are noted in WA 50, 609, n. c.

[337] This term means "sheep-tender"; cf. John 21:16.

[338] Cf. Luther's *Supputatio*. WA 53, 156. Cf. also the analysis of his sources in WA 53, 9-15.

[339] Henry III (1039-1056); Henry IV (1065-1106); Henry V (1106-1125).

came into being—the Grandmontines,[340] the Reformed Regular Canons,[341] the Carthusians,[342] and the Cistercians.[343] And what do you suppose happened in the four hundred years since then? I truly believe that one could well say it rained and snowed monks— and it would be no wonder if there were no city or village today without a monastery or two, or at least a terminary or stationary.[344] The histories chide Emperor Valentinian[345] because he used the monks for service in war. Alas, my dear man, these idle folks were multiplying too fast. One also reads that several kings of France forbade men, especially serfs, to become monks, for everybody flocked to the monasteries in search of freedom under the cowl.

The world wants to be fooled. If you wish to catch many robins and other birds, you must place an owl or a screech owl on the trap or lime-rod, and you will succeed. Similarly, when the devil wants to trap Christians, he must put on a cowl, or (as Christ calls it) a sour, hypocritical expression [Matt. 6:16]. Thus we stand in greater awe of such owls and screech owls than of the true suffering, blood, wounds, death, and resurrection, which we see and hear of in Christ, our Lord, endured because of our sin. So we fall, in throngs and with all our might, away from our Christian faith and into the new holiness, that is, into the devil's trap and lime-rod. For we always must have something new. Christ's death and resurrection, faith and love, are old and just ordinary things; that is why they must count for nothing, and so

---

[340] The Order of Grandmont, originally located in Normandy, was formed in 1073. It disappeared after the French Revolution in 1789.

[341] The Augustinian Canons, founded after 1059. They are to be distinguished from the Augustinian Eremites, the order Luther joined in 1505. See *O.D.C.C.*, p. 109.

[342] Founded by Bruno of Cologne in 1084 in the mountainous region near Grenoble in France. They were known for their almost total seclusion from the world.

[343] Founded at Cîteaux in 1098 by Robert of Molesme. A more radical form of Benedictine monasticism, the Cistercian Order became famous through Bernard of Clairvaux.

[344] Terms originally used to designate the houses of mendicant orders and later applied to other monasteries.

[345] Luther confuses Valentinian I with his brother Valens; see p. 230, n. 86. It was Valens who, according to Platina, compelled Egyptian monks to enter the army and to return to the civic duties they had abandoned through their decision to become monks.

we must have new wheedlers (as St. Paul says). And this serves us right since our ears itch so much for something new that we can no longer endure the old and genuine truth, "that we accumulate,"[346] that we weigh ourselves down with big piles of new teachings. That is just what has happened and will continue to happen. For the subsequent councils, especially the papal ones (for afterward they are almost all papal), did not merely refrain from condemning these new good works, but exalted them throughout the world far above the good old works, so that the pope canonized or elevated many saints from the monastic orders.

At first it was rather nice to look at—and still is—but in the end it becomes an abominable, monstrous thing, since everyone adds to it from day to day. Thus, the beginning of St. Francis' order[347] looked fine, but now it has become so crude that they even put cowls on the dead so that the dead might be saved in them. Isn't it terrible to hear that? Well, that is the way it goes: if one starts to fall away from Christ and gets into the habit of falling, one can no longer stop. That has happened in our own time in the Netherlands, when Madame Margaret[348] ordered that she be made a nun after her death. It was done; she was dressed in a nun's garb, placed at a table, and offered food and drink served as for a true princess. Thus she atoned for her sin and became a holy nun. But after this had lasted a few days, the pious Emperor Charles heard of it, and he had it stopped. Had he not done that, I believe such an example would have flooded the whole world. That is what the new holiness does and must do because it wants to do better than the true, old Christian holiness, which does not fool like this, but remains constant and always exercises itself in faith, love, humility, discipline, patience, etc.; one sees in it nothing abominable, but only lovely, charming, peaceful, kind, and useful examples that please God and man. But the new holiness blusters with a peculiar, new demeanor to entice unsteady

---

[346] *Ut acervemus*, II Tim. 4:3.
[347] Francis of Assisi (*ca.* 1182-1226), whose real name was Giovanni Bernardone. Originally a mendicant order, the Franciscans had gained so much wealth by the thirteenth century that the debate about it resulted in a schism within the order in 1250.
[348] Margaret of Austria (1507-1530), aunt of Charles V and regent of the Netherlands.

souls to itself. It makes a great ado, but there is nothing to it,[349] as St. Peter writes [II Pet. 2:14-22].

Likewise, Gerson writes that the Carthusians are right when they apply their rule so rigorously that they eat no meat even if they should have to die.[350] Well then, if a pious physician here notices that the sick man could be helped by nothing but chicken broth or a bite of meat, then one does not obey the physician, but rather the sick man must die. There I praise St. Augustine, who writes in his Rule[351] that one should ask the physician's advice saying, "Not all people have the same capability, hence one should not regard all as equal." This is a true and beautiful "meekness";[352] moreover, it does not force them to remain forever, for the monastery was not a prison but a voluntary association of a few priests. Dr. Staupitz[353] once told me that he had heard from the bishop of Worms, who was a Dahlberg,[354] that if St. Augustine had written nothing but the Rule, one would still have to say that he was an excellent, wise man. This is certainly true; for he would have utterly condemned those Carthusians as murderers, and their monasteries as veritable, physical dens of murderers (which in truth they are). I myself saw a sick man, who was still young, walking with a crutch in the Carthusian monastery in Erfurt;[355] I asked him whether he was excused from the choir and the watch. "No," he replied sadly, "I must perish."

But we got our just desserts. God sent us his Son to be our teacher and savior. Not satisfied with that, he himself preaches from his high, heavenly throne to us all, saying, *"Hunc audite,"*

---

[349] A German proverb, *"Ist doch nichts dahinden."* Cf. Thiele, *Luthers Sprichwörtersammlung,* No. 6.

[350] John Gerson (1363-1429), a professor at the University of Paris and a cardinal. He asserted the authority of the general council over the pope at the various "reform councils" held in the beginning of the fifteenth century. See *Concerning the Carthusians' Abstention from Meat (De non esu carnium Carthusiensium)* in *Gersonis Opera* (2nd ed.; 4 vols.; Basel, 1488), II, 39.

[351] *The Rule of St. Aurelius Augustine (Regula S. Aurelii Augustini),* IX. *MPL* 32, 1383.

[352] *Epieikeia* in Greek. Cf. II Cor. 10:1.

[353] John von Staupitz, Luther's superior in the monastery; *LW* 31, xvi.

[354] John of Dahlberg, bishop of Worms (1482-1503).

[355] Luther stayed in Erfurt as a student and as a monk in the Augustinian monastery there, from 1501 until 1508, and was undoubtedly familiar with the nearby Carthusian monastery.

"Listen to him" [Matt. 17:5]. Thus we should drop to our knees with the apostles and believe that we hear nothing else in the whole world. But we let the Father and the Son preach in vain, do things on our own, and invent our own sermon. This then is the way it goes, as Psalm 81 [:11-12] says, "My people did not listen to my voice; so I gave them over to their stubborn hearts." Thence come such fine *etelothreskiae* and *apheidiae*, Colossians 2 [:23], "self-chosen spirituality" and "merciless severity to the body," so that we kill ourselves despite God's command that one should care for, not kill, the body. Don't you think that if in accordance with St. Augustine's *Rule* and St. Paul's teaching, one had let the physicians give advice about the bodies of those in the religious orders, especially the women, many a fine person would have been helped who otherwise has had to go mad or has died—as daily experiences have indeed taught us? However, this was the time of wrath, when the new and mad holiness had to reign for the punishment of the world.

Fifth, a council has no power to impose new ceremonies on Christians, to be observed on pain of mortal sin or at the peril of conscience—such as fast days, feast days, food, drink, garb. But if they do this, St. Augustine confronts them with the words addressed to Januarius, "Observance of these things is free. Christ instituted few ceremonies."[356] Because they have the power to command them, we have the power to ignore them; indeed, we are forbidden to observe them by St. Paul in Colossians 2 [:16], "Let not your conscience be troubled over certain days, over fasting, food, or drink," etc.

Sixth, a council has the power and is bound to condemn such ceremonies in accordance with Scripture; for they are un-Christian and constitute a new idolatry or worship, which is not commanded by God, but forbidden.

Seventh, a council has no power to interfere in worldly law and government, etc.; for St. Paul says, "He who wants to serve God in spiritual warfare should refrain from engaging in civilian pursuits" [II Tim. 2:4].

Eighth, a council has the power and is bound to condemn

---

[356] *Epistola 54. MPL* 33, 200; *PNF*[1] 1, 300.

such arbitrary ways or new laws, in accordance with Holy Scripture, that is, to throw the pope's decretals into the fire.

Ninth, a council has no power to create statutes or decretals that seek nothing but tyranny, that is, statutes on how the bishops should have the power and authority to command what they will and everybody should tremble and obey; but it has the power and is bound to condemn this in accordance with Holy Scripture, I Peter 5 [:3], "Not as domineering over those in your charge," and as Christ says, "But not so with you; rather let the leader become as one who serves" [Luke 22:26].

Tenth, a council has the power to institute some ceremonies, provided, first, that they do not strengthen the bishops' tyranny; second, that they are useful and profitable to the people and show fine, orderly discipline and conduct. Thus it is necessary, for example, to have certain days, and also places where one can assemble; also certain hours for preaching and for the public administration of the sacraments, for praying, singing, praising and thanking God, etc.—as St. Paul says, I Corinthians 14 [:40], "All things should be done decently and in order." Such items do not serve the bishops' tyranny, but only the people's need, profit, and order. In summary, these must and cannot be dispensed with if the church is to survive.

But if someone is occasionally hindered by some emergency, sickness, or whatever it may be from observing this, it need not be sin. For it is done for his benefit and not for the bishops'. If he is a Christian, he thereby will not harm himself. What difference does it make to God if someone does not want to belong to such a group or participate in this way? Everyone will find out for himself. In summary, he who is a Christian is not bound to such order; he would rather do it than let it go if he is not forced into it. Here, therefore, no law can be laid down for him; he would want to do and would prefer to do more than such a law demands. But he who haughtily, proudly, and wilfully despises it—let him go his way, for such a person will also despise a higher law, be it divine or human.

Perhaps you might say here, "What do you finally want to make of the councils if you clip them so close? At that rate a pastor, indeed a schoolteacher (to say nothing of parents), would have greater power over his pupils than a council has over the church." I answer: Do you think then that the offices of the pastor and the schoolteacher are so low that they cannot be compared with the councils? How could one assemble a council if there were no pastors or bishops? How could we get pastors if there were no schools? I am speaking of those schoolteachers who instruct the children and the youth not only in the arts, but also train them in Christian doctrine and faithfully impress it upon them; I also speak in the same manner of pastors who teach God's word in faithfulness and purity. For I can easily prove that the poor, insignificant pastor at Hippo, St. Augustine, taught more than all the councils (to say nothing of the most holy popes in Rome, whom I fear to mention). I will go further than that: there is more in the Children's Creed[357] than in all the councils. The Lord's Prayer and the Ten Commandments also teach more than all the councils. Moreover, they not only teach, but also guard against anything new that opposes the ancient doctrine. For heaven's sake! How the papists will pluck these words of mine from their context, shout them to bits, torture them to death, and prove them illogical; but meanwhile they will not mention the reasons I have spoken in this manner. For they are pious and honest people, who cannot do anything but calumniate and lie, something I should indeed be afraid of! But may God forgive me, I really cannot do it; I would rather let them go on with their slander and their lies.

But let us, you and me, discuss this subject together. What then can a council do, or what is its task? Listen yourself to their own words. *Anathematizamus* is the name of their office—"We condemn." Indeed, they speak even more humbly and do not say, "We condemn," but *anathematizat ecclesia,* "The holy Christian church condemns." The council's condemnation would not terrify me, but the holy church's condemnation would slay me in an instant because of the Man who says, "I am with you always, to the close of the age" [Matt. 28:20]. Oh, this Man's condemnation is not to be endured. But the councils, since they appeal to the holy Chris-

---

[357] The Apostles' Creed.

tian church as to the true and supreme judge on earth, testify that they cannot judge according to their own discretion, but that the church, which preaches, believes, and confesses Holy Scripture, is the judge—as we shall hear. Just as a thief or a murderer would be secure from the judge as far as his person is concerned, but law and country are united in the judge, their servant, and of these two he must be afraid.

A council, then, is nothing but a consistory, a royal court, a supreme court,[358] or the like, in which the judges, after hearing the parties, pronounce sentence, but with this humility, "For the sake of the law," that is, "Our office is *anathematizare,* 'to condemn'; but not according to our whim or will, or newly invented law, but according to the ancient law, which is acknowledged as the law throughout the entire empire." Thus a council condemns a heretic, not according to its own discretion, but according to the law of the empire, that is, according to Holy Scripture, which they confess to be the law of the holy church. Such law, empire, and judge must surely be feared on pain of eternal damnation. This law is God's word, the empire is God's church; the judge is the official or servant of both.

Not only the council, but every pastor and schoolteacher is also the servant or judge of this law and empire. Moreover, a council cannot administer this judicial office forever without intermission; for the bishops cannot forever remain assembled together, but must gather only in times of certain emergencies and then anathematize, or be judges. Thus, if an Arius in Alexandria grows too strong for his pastor or bishop, attracts the people, and also urges other pastors and people in the country to join him, so that the pastor in Alexandria is defeated and his judicial office can no longer defend the law of the empire, that is, the true Christian faith—in such an emergency and at such a time the other pastors and bishops should rally with all their might around the pastor of

---

[358] *Consistorium, Hofegericht, Camergericht.* These terms were borrowed from Roman law and represent names for courts in sixteenth-century Germany. The first Protestant *Consistorium,* not unlike a modern denominational synod, was formed in Saxony in 1539. The *Consistorium* was originally the supreme court in ancient Rome, and later the highest ecclesiastical court within the medieval church.

Alexandria and help him defend the true faith against Arius and condemn Arius to save the others, so that this misery does not get the upper hand. And if the pastors are unable to come, the pious Emperor Constantine should add his power to help assemble the bishops. It is just like when a fire breaks out; if the man of the house cannot extinguish it alone, all the neighbors should hurry over and help quench it. And if they do not hurry over, the government should help and command that they must gather to anathematize or condemn the fire, in order to save the other houses.

Thus the council is the great servant or judge in this empire and law. Yet when the emergency has passed, it has done its duty—just as, in temporal government, the supreme, great judges have to help when the lower, secondary courts prove too weak to cope with an evil, until the case is at last brought before the highest, greatest court, the diet, which cannot meet forever either, but must adjourn after the emergency is over and again leave matters to the lower courts. At the diet, however, it happens that occasionally new or additional laws have to be enacted, or that old laws have to be amended, improved, or even abolished; justice cannot forever be administered according to an eternal law, for this is a temporal government which rules over temporal, changeable, and variable things. Therefore the laws that are made for these changeable things must also change. If that for which the law was made no longer exists, then the law no longer represents anything, just as the city of Rome no longer has institutions and ways of life it had had before; and therefore the laws that were passed for these are also dead and invalid. Transient things have transient laws.

But in this empire of the church the rule is, "The word of our God will stand for ever" [Isa. 40:8]. One has to live according to it and refrain from creating new or different words of God and from establishing new and different articles of faith. That is why pastors and schoolteachers are the lowly, but daily, permanent, eternal judges who anathematize without interruption, that is, fend off the devil and his raging. A council, being a great judge, must make old, great rascals pious or kill them, but it cannot produce any others. A pastor and a schoolteacher deal with small, young rascals and constantly train new people to become bishops and councils, whenever it is necessary. A council prunes the large limbs from the tree or extirpates evil trees. But a pastor and a schoolteacher plant and cultivate young trees and useful shrubs in the garden. Oh, they have a precious office and task, and they are the church's richest jewels; they preserve the church. Therefore all the lords should do their part to preserve pastors and schools. For if indeed we cannot have councils, the parishes and schools, small though they are, are eternal and useful councils.

One can see quite well how earnestly the ancient emperors regarded parishes and schools,[359] since they endowed the monasteries so richly. That they were primarily schools is evidenced by these names: provost, dean, *scholasticus,* cantor, *canonici,* vicars, custodians, etc.[360] But what has become of these? O Lord God! If they were at least willing to do something, remain what they were, keep what they had, were princes and lords, and again introduced hours of study and compelled the canons, vicars, and choir pupils to listen to a daily lesson from Holy Scripture so that they would again, in some sense, look like a school, and so that one could have pastors and bishops and thus help to rule the church. O Lord God, what immeasurable benefit they could be to the church! And God would not begrudge them their wealth or power, but let them have them, if they but amended their shameful lives. But all our sighs and complaints are in vain. They neither hear nor see; they allow the parishes to lie waste and the people to become rude and wild without the word of God. I have heard it from people whom I must believe that in many dioceses there are two, three, and four hundred good parishes vacant. Isn't it dreadful and terrible to hear of such conditions among Christians? May God in heaven have mercy and give ear to our pitiable sighs and lamentations. Amen.

And to finish this matter of the councils at last, I hold that one should now be able to understand what a council is, its rights, power, office, and task; also, which councils are genuine and which false: namely, that they should confess and defend the ancient faith,

---

[359] Luther refers here to the educational reforms of Charlemagne. Cf. *WA* 50, 7.
[360] Cf. *The Smalcald Articles,* Part II, Art. III. Tappert (ed.), *Book of Concord,* pp. 297-298.

and not institute new articles of faith against the ancient faith, nor institute new good works against the old good works, but defend the old good works against the new good works—because he who defends the old faith against the new faith also defends the old good works against the new good works. For as the faith is, so are also the fruits or good works, though the two councils[361] did not see this conclusion. Otherwise, they would have condemned the archimandrite Eutyches not only because of the faith (which they did in earnest), but also because of his monkery (which they did not); on the contrary, they affirmed it, thereby proving that they were poor logicians, stating a premise but not drawing the conclusion—a common evil throughout the world. They just made the error with regard to good works that Nestorius and Eutyches made with regard to faith. That is to say: God not only wants to make us children in the faith, but also wants to show us up as fools in logic and regards us as simple Nestoriuses and Eutycheses, in order to humble us. For even if the theology of Nestorius and Eutyches is condemned, their rotten logic still remains in the world for all time, as it was there from the beginning, namely, that one states the premise, but does not draw the conclusion. How much can one say about it? If you have all the councils you are still no Christian because of them; they give you too little. If you also have all the fathers, they too give you too little. You must still go to Holy Scripture, where you find everything in abundance, or to the catechism, where it is summarized, and where far more is found than in all the councils and fathers.

Finally, a council should occupy itself only with matters of faith, and then only when faith is in jeopardy. For public evil works can be condemned and the good ones maintained at home by the temporal government and by pastors and parents. But the false good works also belong to matters of faith, since they vitiate the true faith. Therefore they too are part of the business of a council, if the pastors are too weak to deal with them. The councils (as was already said) did not pay any attention to them, with the exception of one or two small councils, such as that of Gangra mentioned above.[362] Ceremonies ought to be completely disre-

---

[361] Ephesus (431) and Chalcedon (451).
[362] Cf. above, p. 318, n. 336.

garded by the councils and should be left at home in the parishes, indeed, in the schools so that the schoolmaster, along with the pastor, would be "master of ceremonies."[363] All others will learn these from the students, without any effort or difficulty. For instance, the common people will learn from the pupils what, when, and how to sing or pray in church; they will also learn what to sing by the bier or at the grave. When the pupils kneel and fold their hands as the schoolmaster beats time with his baton during the singing of "And was made man,"[364] the common people will imitate them. When they doff their little hats or bend their knees whenever the name of Jesus Christ is mentioned, or whatever other Christian discipline and gestures they may exercise, the common people will do afterward without instruction, moved by the living example. Even under the pope all the ceremonies originated in the schools and the parishes, except where the pope was bent on exercising his tyranny with measures regarding food, fasts, feasts, etc. However, here too moderation must be applied, so that there do not get to be too many ceremonies in the end. Above all, one must see to it that they will not be considered necessary for salvation, but only serve external discipline and order, which can be changed any time and which must not be commanded as eternal laws in the church (as the popish ass does) and embodied in books with tyrannical threats, for this is something entirely external, bodily, transitory, and changeable.

Accordingly, we would have enough matters today that are sufficiently important and weighty to warrant the summoning of a council. For we poor, wretched Christians of small faith and, unfortunately, real *Misergi*,[365] that is, Christians who hate work—those of us who are still left—would have to put the pope on trial, together with his followers, because of the aforementioned article of St. Peter which says that it is tempting God if one encumbers the faithful with unbearable burdens "which neither we nor our forefathers have been able to bear" [Acts 15:10] (and which especially the pope and his ilk will not touch with one finger). St.

---

[363] *Magister Ceremoniarum.*
[364] *"Et homo factus est."* From the Nicene Creed.
[365] A Latin term meaning "those who feel miserable about work."

Peter indeed speaks of the law of Moses, which God himself commanded; but the papal ass oppressed us with his own filthy, foul, and stinking burdens, so that the holy church was forced to be his privy—and whatever issued from him above and below, we had to worship as God. Furthermore, he set fire to and burned down not one or two churches, as Arius and his kind did, but the whole Christian church when he destroyed, as far as he could, St. Peter's ancient, true article of faith; for that we must be saved by the grace of God alone (as St. Peter testifies [Acts 15:11]), as all of Christendom since the beginning of the world was saved, all the patriarchs, prophets, kings, saints, etc.—this he calls heresy, and he has consistently condemned this same article from the beginning, and cannot desist from doing so.

At this point we ask and cry for a council, requesting advice and help from all of Christendom against this arch-arsonist of churches and slayer of Christians, so that we can again have this article of St. Peter. But we also demand that no Nestorian or Eutychian logic be employed in it, which states or confesses one point but denies the conclusion or other point. We demand the whole article, full and pure, as it was instituted by St. Peter and taught by St. Paul, namely, that everything be condemned whose condemnation follows from this article—or, as St. Peter calls it, "the unbearable, impossible burden," and St. Augustine, "the countless burdens imposed on the church by the bishops."[366] What good does it do to admit the truth of the first part, that we are to be truly justified and saved solely by the grace of Christ, and still not let the second part, its necessary conclusion, follow? Thus St. Paul says, "But if it is by grace, it is no longer on the basis of works; otherwise, grace would no longer be grace" [Rom. 11:6], and St. Peter, "If it is grace, it is not the intolerable burden; if it is the intolerable burden, then it is not the grace of Christ, and it is tempting God."[367] St. Augustine, too, says, "Since Christ did not wish to burden the church with many ceremonies—indeed, wanted it to be free—it was not his will to have it oppressed by the innumerable

---

[366] In the frequently quoted letter to Januarius. *Epistola 54. MPL* 33, 201; *PNF*[1] 1, 300.

[367] Luther's own translation of Acts 15:10-11.

burdens of the bishops, making the lot of the church worse than that of the Jews, who were burdened with God's laws and not (like the church) with human, presumptuous, arbitrary ordinances."[368]

This dialectic of St. Peter, St. Paul, and St. Augustine is what we want to have, for it is the logic of the Holy Spirit, a logic which treats matters in their entirety rather than breaking them up in Nestorian fashion, allowing one thing alone to be true, but not the other that must also be true because it follows from the first. Otherwise, it would be like the stories recorded about several kings of Israel and Judah, who, to be sure, re-established the worship of God, but failed to do away with the high places or other altars and worship. This the prophet Elijah called "limping with two different opinions" [I Kings 18:21]. We Germans call it "trying to make two brothers-in-law with one sister."[369] Thus they tried to give one nation two different gods—or, even if they did institute any reforms at all, they still permitted a strange, different god to remain alongside the true one. They too were stupid Nestorian logicians who confessed that only one God should be worshiped and yet did not see and did not permit the logical conclusion that all other gods had to be removed; otherwise, they could not have the one God either. That is why we will not tolerate in the council which we demand a Nestorius, who gives us one thing, yet takes another from us, with whom we cannot even retain the one thing given to us. He is a regular Indian giver.[370] If the council grants us that the grace of Christ alone saves us and does not also grant us the conclusion and deduction that works do not save us, but maintains that works are necessary for satisfaction or for righteousness, then the first that was granted to us is thereby again taken from us, namely, that grace alone, without works, saves us. Thus we keep nothing, and the evil is made worse.

I will speak German:[371] the pope should not only abolish his tyranny of human ordinances in the council, but also hold with us that even the good works performed in accordance with God's com-

---

[368] *Epistola 54. MPL* 33, 200; *PNF*[1] 1, 300.

[369] *Zween schweger mit einer schwester machen wollen.* Cf. Thiele, *Luthers Sprichwörtersammlung,* No. 9.

[370] *Gebers Nemers.* Cf. *ibid.,* No. 290.

[371] I.e., frankly.

mandments cannot help to achieve righteousness, to blot out sin to attain God's grace—only faith can do this, faith in Christ, who is a king of righteousness in us through his precious blood, death, and resurrection, with which he blotted out our sin for us, made satisfaction, reconciled God, and redeemed us from death, wrath, and hell. Therefore he should condemn and burn all his bulls, decretals, books on indulgence, purgatory, monasteries, saint worship, and pilgrimages, together with all his countless lies and idolatries, since they rant directly against this article of St. Peter. He should also return everything he bought, stole, robbed, plundered, or acquired through it, especially his false primacy, which he extols as being so necessary that no one can be saved who is not subject to him. The pope's hat did not die for my sin, nor is its name Christ—and all Christians before and under him were sanctified and saved without his hat.

This, I think, is indeed an important enough matter about which to hold an impressive, decisive, and mighty council. The emperor and kings should lend a hand here and force the pope into it, if he is unwilling, as the emperors did in the four principal councils. But not all the bishops, abbots, monks, doctors, and worthless riffraff, or the large number of hangers-on, should come to it. Otherwise, it will be a council that spends its first year in arriving and in quarreling over who shall sit at the head, and who is to walk ahead of whom; the second year in reveling, banqueting, racing, and fencing; the third year in other matters and also in burning, perhaps a John Huss[372] or two—and meanwhile incurring expenses so vast that one could indeed finance a campaign against the Turks.[373] On the contrary, it would be necessary to summon from all lands people who are thoroughly versed in Holy Scripture and who are also seriously and sincerely concerned with God's honor, the Christian faith, the church, the salvation of souls, and the peace of the world. Among them there should also be a few intelligent and reliable laymen (for this is also a matter that con-

---

[372] John Huss (ca. 1369-1415), reformer of Bohemia who was martyred during the Council of Constance.
[373] Pope Paul III issued a bull on June 15, 1537, De Indulgentiis Contra Turcam, asking for assistance against the Turks. Cf. Luther's comments on the bull in The Bull of Paul III (Bulla Papae Pauli III). WA 50, 113-116.

cerns them). For instance, if Sir Hans von Schwarzenberg[374] were living, he and men like him could be trusted. And it would suffice if there were a total of three hundred select men to whom the fate of the country and the people could be entrusted—just as the first council[375] had only three hundred and eighteen members, summoned from all the lands the Turks and our monarchs now rule, and seventeen of them were false and Arians anyway. The second at Constantinople had one hundred and fifty; the third at Ephesus, two hundred; the fourth at Chalcedon, six hundred and thirty, almost as many as the others combined, and yet these men were quite unlike the fathers in Nicaea and Constantinople.[376]

Moreover, the affairs of all countries that no one else can or cares to judge, as well as old, superannuated, and bad quarrels should not be unearthed and dumped into the lap of the council. A Constantine should be there to rake up all these matters and cast them into the fire, ordering that they be judged and decided at home in the respective countries; he should order them to attack instead the questions at issue and dispose of these as quickly as possible. Then the pope's heresies, indeed, abominations, would be read in public, one by one, and all would be found in opposition to St. Peter's article and to the ancient, true Christian faith of the church, which has adhered to St. Peter's doctrine from the beginning of the world; and they would be promptly condemned, etc.

"Well," you say, "it is futile to hope for such a council." I myself think so too. But if one wants to talk about it and asks and wishes for a council, one would have to wish for a council like that, or forget about it completely, desire none, and say nothing at all. For the first council in Nicaea, and the second one in Constantinople, were councils like that—whose examples could indeed be easily followed. And I point this out to show that it would be the duty of emperors and kings, since they are Christians, to summon such a council for the salvation of the many thousands of souls

---

[374] John Freiherr von Schwarzenberg (1463-1528), a supporter of the Reformation, was imperial chamberlain in 1521 and later an adviser of Margrave George of Ansbach. He was an influential adviser of the emperor during the diets in Nürnberg in 1522 and 1524.

[375] Nicaea (325).

[376] Luther derived this information from the work of Crabbe. Cf. WA 50, 605, n. b.

that the pope, with his tyranny and avoidance of a council (as far as he is concerned), allows to perish, even though they all could be restored to St. Peter's article and to the true, ancient Christian faith. Otherwise, they would have to be lost, for they cannot obtain this doctrine of St. Peter's because they neither hear nor see anything of it.

And even if other monarchs declined to do anything toward a principal council, emperor Charles and the German princes could still hold a provincial council in Germany. Some think that this would result in a schism, but who knows? If we did our part in it and sincerely sought God's honor and the salvation of souls, God might yet touch and turn the hearts of the other monarchs so that they would, in time, approve and accept the judgment of this council. It could not happen suddenly; but if Germany were to accept it, it would also have an echo in other countries, whither it cannot or can hardly reach without a great preacher such as the council is, and without a strong voice heard from afar.

Well then, if we must despair of a council let us commend the matter to the true judge, our merciful God. Meanwhile we shall promote the small and the young councils, that is, parishes and schools, and propagate St. Peter's article in every way possible, preserving it against all the accursed new articles of the faith and of the new good works with which the pope has flooded the world. I shall comfort myself when I see the children wearing bishop's masks, thinking that God makes and will make genuine bishops of these play-bishops; on the other hand, I shall regard as play-bishops and mockers of God's majesty those who, according to their title, ought to be real bishops—as Moses says, "They have stirred me to jealousy with what is no god. . . . So I will stir them to jealousy with those who are no people; I will provoke them with a foolish nation" [Deut. 32:21]. It will not be the first time that he repudiates bishops. In Hosea he threatened, "Because you have rejected knowledge, I reject you from being a priest to me" [Hos. 4:6]. And so it came, and so it comes to pass.[877]

May that suffice regarding the councils. In conclusion, we shall now also speak about the church.

---

[877] Et factum est ita, et fit ita.

Part III

Just as they scream about the fathers and the councils, without knowing what fathers and councils are, only to drown out our voices with mere letters, so they also scream about the church. But as for saying what, who, and where the church is, they do not render either the church or God even the service of asking the question or thinking about it. They like very much to be regarded as the church, as pope, cardinals, bishops, and yet to be allowed, under this glorious name, to be nothing but pupils of the devil, desiring nothing more than to practice sheer knavery and villainy.

Well then, setting aside various writings and analyses of the word "church," we shall this time confine ourselves simply to the Children's Creed, which says, "I believe in one holy Christian church, the communion of saints." Here the creed clearly indicates what the church is, namely, a communion of saints, that is, a crowd[378] or assembly of people who are Christians and holy, which is called a Christian holy assembly, or church. Yet this word "church" [379] is not German and does not convey the sense or meaning that should be taken from this article.

In Acts 19 [:39] the town clerk uses the word *ecclesia* for the congregation or the people who had gathered at the market place, saying, "It shall be settled in the regular assembly." Further, "When he said this, he dismissed the assembly" [vs. 41]. In these and other passages the *ecclesia* or church is nothing but an assembly of people, though they probably were heathens and not Christians. It is the same term used by town councilmen for their assembly which they summon to the city hall. Now there are many peoples in the world; the Christians, however, are a people with a special call and are therefore called not just *ecclesia*, "church," or "people," but *sancta catholica Christiana*, that is, "a Christian holy people" who believe in Christ. That is why they are called a Christian people and have the Holy Spirit, who sanctifies them daily, not only through the forgiveness of sin acquired for them by Christ (as the Antinomians foolishly believe), but also through the abolition,

---

[378] *Hauffe.*
[379] *Kirche.*

the purging, and the mortification of sins, on the basis of which they are called a holy people. Thus the "holy Christian church" is synonymous with a Christian and holy people or, as one is also wont to express it, with "holy Christendom," or "whole Christendom." The Old Testament uses the term "God's people."

If the words, "I believe that there is a holy Christian people," had been used in the Children's Creed, all the misery connected with this meaningless and obscure word ("church") might easily have been avoided. For the words "Christian holy people" would have brought with them, clearly and powerfully, the proper understanding and judgment of what is, and what is not, church. Whoever would have heard the words "Christian holy people" could have promptly concluded that the pope is no people, much less a holy Christian people. So too the bishops, priests, and monks are not holy, Christian people, for they do not believe in Christ, nor do they lead a holy life, but are rather the wicked and shameful people of the devil. He who does not truly believe in Christ is not Christian or a Christian. He who does not have the Holy Spirit against sin is not holy. Consequently, they cannot be "a Christian holy people," that is, *sancta et catholica ecclesia.*

But since we use this meaningless word "church" in the Children's Creed, the common man thinks of the stone house called a church, as painted by the artists; or, at best, they paint the apostles, disciples, and the mother of God, as on Pentecost, with the Holy Spirit hovering over them. This is still bearable; but they are the holy Christian people of a specific time, in this case, the beginning. *Ecclesia,* however, should mean the holy Christian people, not only of the days of the apostles, who are long since dead, but to the end of the world, so that there is always a holy Christian people on earth, in whom Christ lives, works, and rules, *per redemptionem,* "through grace and the remission of sin," and the Holy Spirit, *per vivificationem et sanctificationem,* "through daily purging of sin and renewal of life," so that we do not remain in sin but are enabled and obliged to lead a new life, abounding in all kinds of good works, as the Ten Commandments or the two tables of Moses' law command, and not in old, evil works. That is St. Paul's teaching. But the pope, with his followers, has applied both the name and the image of the church to himself and to his vile, accursed mob, under the meaningless word *ecclesia*, "church," etc.

Nevertheless, they give themselves the right name when they call themselves *ecclesia* (that is, if we interpret this term to agree with their way of life), either *Romana* or *sancta*, but do not add (as, indeed, they cannot) *catholica*. For *ecclesia* means "a people"; that they are, just as the Turks too, are *ecclesia*, "a people." *Ecclesia Romana* means "a Roman people"; that they are too, and indeed much more Roman than the heathen of ancient times were. *Ecclesia Romana sancta* means "a holy Roman people"; that they are too, for they have invented a holiness far greater than the holiness of Christians, or than the holy Christian people possess. Their holiness is a Roman holiness, *Romanae ecclesiae*, a holiness "of the Roman people," and they are now even called *sanctissimi, sacrosancti,* "the most holy," as Virgil speaks of a "holy thirst for gold,"[380] and Plautus of "the most holy one of all";[381] for they cannot stand Christian holiness. Therefore they are not entitled to the name "Christian church" or "Christian people," if for no other reason than that "Christian church" is a name and "Christian holiness" an entity common to all churches and all Christians in the world; therefore it is called "catholic." But they have little, if any, regard for this common name and holiness; instead, they invented a special, higher, different, better holiness than that of others. This is to be known as *sanctitas Romana et ecclesiae Romanae sanctitas,* that is, "Roman holiness and the holiness of the Roman people."

For Christian holiness, or the holiness common to Christendom, is found where the Holy Spirit gives people faith in Christ and thus sanctifies them, Acts 15 [:9], that is, he renews heart, soul, body, work, and conduct, inscribing the commandments of God not on tables of stone, but in hearts of flesh, II Corinthians 3 [:3]. Or, if I may speak plainly, he imparts true knowledge of God, accord-

---

[380] *Sacra fames, sacra hostia.* Virgil (70-19 B.C.), a Roman poet, in *Aeneid,* III, 57. See H. Rushton Fairclough (trans.), *Virgil: Eclogues, Georgics, Aeneid I-III* ("The Loeb Classical Library" [2nd ed., rev.; Cambridge: Harvard University Press, 1956]), p. 352. Luther, quoting from memory, leaves out the term "gold" (*auri*).

[381] *Omnium sacerrumus.* Plautus (d. 184 B.C.), another Roman poet, in *Mostellaria,* IV, 2, 67. Henry T. Riley (trans.), *The Comedies of Plautus* (2 vols.; London, 1884), II, 500.

ing to the first table, so that those whom he enlightens with true faith can resist all heresies, overcome all false ideas and errors, and thus remain pure in faith in opposition to the devil. He also bestows strength, and comforts timid, despondent, weak consciences against the accusation and turmoil of sin, so that the souls do not succumb or despair, and also do not become terrified of torment, pain, death, and the wrath and judgment of God, but rather, comforted and strengthened in hope, they cheerfully, boldly, and joyfully overcome the devil. He also imparts true fear and love of God, so that we do not despise God and become irritated and angry with his wondrous judgments, but love, praise, thank, and honor him for all that occurs, good or evil. That is called new holy life in the soul, in accordance with the first table of Moses. It is also called *tres virtutes theologicas,* "the three principal virtues of Christians,"[382] namely, faith, hope, and love; and the Holy Spirit, who imparts, does, and effects this (gained for us by Christ) is therefore called "sanctifier" or "life-giver."[383] For the old Adam is dead and cannot do it, and in addition has to learn from the law that he is unable to do it and that he is dead; he would not know this of himself.

In accordance with the second table, He also sanctifies the Christians in the body and induces them willingly to obey parents and rulers, to conduct themselves peacefully and humbly, to be not wrathful, vindictive, or malicious, but patient, friendly, obliging, brotherly, and loving, not unchaste, not adulterous or lewd, but chaste and pure with wife, child, and servants, or without wife and child. And on and on: they do not steal, are not usurious, avaricious, do not defraud, etc., but work honorably, support themselves honestly, lend willingly, and give and help wherever they can. Thus they do not lie, deceive, and backbite, but are kind, truthful, faithful, and trustworthy, and do whatever else the commandments of God prescribe. That is the work of the Holy Spirit, who sanctifies and also awakens the body to such a new life until it is perfected in the life beyond. That is what is called "Christian

---

[382] They became principal topics in scholastic theology after Augustine. Cf. I Cor. 13:13.

[383] *Sanctificator* or *vivificator.*

holiness." And there must always be such people on earth, even though it may be but two or three, or only children. Unfortunately, only a few of them are old folks. And those who are not, should not count themselves as Christians; nor should they be comforted with much babbling about the forgiveness of sins and the grace of Christ, as though they were Christians—like the Antinomians do.

For they, having rejected and being unable to understand the Ten Commandments, preach much about the grace of Christ, yet they strengthen and comfort only those who remain in their sins, telling them not to fear and be terrified by sins, since they are all removed by Christ. They see and yet they let the people go on in their public sins, without any renewal or reformation of their lives. Thus it becomes quite evident that they truly fail to understand the faith and Christ, and thereby abrogate both when they preach about it. How can he speak lightly about the words of the Holy Spirit in the first table—about comfort, grace, forgiveness of sins—who does not heed or practice the works of the Holy Spirit in the second table, which he can understand and experience, while he has never attempted or experienced those of the first table? Therefore it is certain that they neither have nor understand Christ or the Holy Spirit, and their talk is nothing but froth on the tongue, and they are as already said, true Nestoriuses and Eutycheses, who confess or teach Christ in the premise, in the substance, and yet deny him in the conclusion or *idiomata*; that is, they teach Christ and yet destroy him through their teaching.

All this then has been said about Christian holiness, which the pope does not want. He has to have one that is much holier, namely, that found in the prescription of chasubles, tonsures, cowls, garb, food, festivals, days, monkery, nunning, masses, saint-worship, and countless other items of an external, bodily, transitory nature. Whether one lives under it without faith, fear of God, hope, love, and whatever the Holy Spirit, according to the first table, effects, or in misbelief, uncertainty of heart, doubts, contempt of God, impatience with God, and false trust in works (that is, idolatry), not in the grace of Christ and his merit, but in the atonement by works, even selling the surplus ones to others and taking in exchange all the goods and wealth of the world as well earned—all that is of no consequence because a man may be holier than Christian holiness itself.

Thus, in the second table it matters not that they teach disobedience toward parents and rulers, that they even murder, make war, set people against each other, envy, hate, avenge, are unchaste, lie, steal, are usurious, defraud, and indulge in every villainy to the utmost. Just throw a surplice over your head and you are holy in accordance with the Roman church's holiness, and you can indeed be saved without the Christian holiness. But we will pay no attention to these filthy people, for any effort expended on them will be futile. "God's wrath has come upon them at last," as St. Paul says [I Thess. 2:16]. Instead, we shall discuss the church among ourselves.

Well then, the Children's Creed teaches us (as was said) that a Christian holy people is to be and to remain on earth until the end of the world. This is an article of faith that cannot be terminated until that which it believes comes, as Christ promises, "I am with you always, to the close of the age" [Matt. 28:20]. But how will or how can a poor confused person tell where such Christian holy people are to be found in this world? Indeed, they are supposed to be in this life and on earth, for they of course believe that a heavenly nature and an eternal life are to come, but as yet they do not possess them. Therefore they must still be in this life and remain in this life and in this world until the end of the world. For they profess, "I believe in another life"; thereby they confess that they have not yet arrived in the other life, but believe in it, hope for it, and love it as their true fatherland and life, while they must yet remain and tarry here in exile—as we sing in the hymn about the Holy Spirit, "As homeward we journey from this exile. Lord, have mercy."[384] We shall now speak of this.

First, the holy Christian people are recognized by their possession of the holy word of God. To be sure, not all have it in equal measure, as St. Paul says [I Cor. 3:12-14]. Some possess the word in its complete purity, others do not. Those who have the pure word are called those who "build on the foundation with

---

[384] The fourth line of a pre-Reformation hymn adapted by Luther in 1524, "Now Let Us Pray to the Holy Ghost." *LW* 53, 263-264.

gold, silver, and precious stones"; those who do not have it in its purity are the ones who "build on the foundation with wood, hay, and straw," and yet will be saved through fire. More than enough was said about this above. This is the principal item, and the holiest of holy possessions,[385] by reason of which the Christian people are called holy; for God's word is holy and sanctifies everything it touches; it is indeed the very holiness of God, Romans 1 [:16], "It is the power of God for salvation to every one who has faith," and I Timothy 4 [:5], "Everything is consecrated by the word of God and prayer." For the Holy Spirit himself administers it and anoints or sanctifies the Christian church with it rather than with the pope's chrism, with which he anoints or consecrates fingers, garb, cloaks, chalices, and stones. These objects will never teach one to love God, to believe, to praise, to be pious. They may adorn the bag of maggots,[386] but afterward they fall apart and decay with the chrism and whatever holiness it contains, and with the bag of maggots itself.

Yet this holy possession is the true holy possession, the true ointment that anoints unto life eternal, even though you cannot have a papal crown or a bishop's hat, but must die bare and naked, just like children (in fact, all of us), who are baptized naked and without any adornment. But we are speaking of the external word, preached orally by men like you and me, for this is what Christ left behind as an external sign, by which his church, or his Christian people in the world, should be recognized. We also speak of this external word as it is sincerely believed and openly professed before the world, as Christ says, "Every one who acknowledges me before men, I also will acknowledge before my Father and his angels" [Matt. 10:32]. There are many who know it in their hearts, but will not profess it openly. Many possess it, but do not believe in it or act by it, for the number of those who believe in and act by it is small—as the parable of the seed in Matthew

---

[385] *Heiligthum* or *Heilthum*. These words recur continually in the following section. The term "holy possession" (used in *PE* 5, 270) conveys both the meaning of "sanctuary" and "relic." Luther plays constantly on the idea of wonder-working objects of reverence when he speaks of the marks of the church.

[386] *Madensack*, i.e., the body that goes to decay.

13 [:4-8] says that three sections of the field receive and contain the seed, but only the fourth section, the fine and good soil, bears fruit with patience.

Now, wherever you hear or see this word preached, believed, professed, and lived, do not doubt that the true *ecclesia sancta catholica*, "a Christian holy people" must be there, even though their number is very small. For God's word "shall not return empty," Isaiah 55 [:11], but must have at least a fourth or a fraction of the field. And even if there were no other sign than this alone, it would still suffice to prove that a Christian, holy people must exist there, for God's word cannot be without God's people, and conversely, God's people cannot be without God's word. Otherwise, who would preach or hear it preached, if there were no people of God? And what could or would God's people believe, if there were no word of God?

This is the thing that performs all miracles, effects, sustains, carries out, and does everything, exorcises all devils, like pilgrimage-devils, indulgence-devils, bull-devils, brotherhood-devils, saint-devils, mass-devils, purgatory-devils, monastery-devils, priest-devils, mob-devils, insurrection-devils, heresy-devils, all pope-devils, also Antinomian-devils, but not without raving and rampaging, as is seen in the poor men mentioned in Mark 1 [:23-26] and 9 [:17-29]. No, he must depart with raving and rampaging as is evidenced by Emser,[387] Eck,[388] Snot-nose,[389] Schmid,[390] Wetzel,[391]

---

[387] Jerome Emser (1478-1527), a humanist who became an adviser to Duke George of Saxony, Catholic ruler of Saxony and an enemy of Luther. Cf. Luther's polemic tract *To the Leipzig Goat* (1521). PE 3, 275-286.

[388] John Eck (1486-1543), known for his debate with Luther at Leipzig in 1518. Cf. LW 31, 309-325.

[389] *Rotzleffel*, a German term for "impudent young rascal" and Luther's name for John Cochlaeus (1479-1522), a Catholic theologian who was a fanatic opponent of the Reformation and the author of *Memoirs on the Actions and Writings of Martin Luther* (*Commentaria de Actis et Scriptis M. Lutheri*) (1549), a polemic biography of Luther. See Adolf Herte, *Die Lutherkommentare des Johannes Cochlaeus* ("Religionsgeschichtliche Studien und Texte," Vol. XXXIII [Münster, 1935]).

[390] John Faber (1478-1541), the son of a smith (*faber* in Latin) and bishop in Vienna. He had been writing polemic tracts against Luther since 1521.

[391] Used as a name for dogs and as a pun on George Wetzel (1501-1573), who was originally a follower of Luther, but since 1533 had been an opponent of the Reformation and a protege of Duke George of Saxony.

Bumpkin, Boor, Churl, Brute, Sow, Ass,[392] and the rest of his screamers and scribes. They all are the devil's mouths and members, through whom he raves and rampages. But it does them no good. He must take his leave; he is unable to endure the power of the word. They themselves confess that it is God's word and Holy Scripture, claiming, however, that one fares better with the fathers and the councils. Let them go their way. It is enough for us to know how this chief holy possession purges, sustains, nourishes, strengthens, and protects the church, as St. Augustine also says, "The church is begotten, cared for, nourished, and strengthened by the word of God."[393] But those who persecute and condemn it identify themselves by their own fruits.

Second, God's people or the Christian holy people are recognized by the holy sacrament of baptism, wherever it is taught, believed, and administered correctly according to Christ's ordinance. That too is a public sign and a precious, holy possession by which God's people are sanctified. It is the holy bath of regeneration through the Holy Spirit [Titus 3:5], in which we bathe and with which we are washed of sin and death by the Holy Spirit, as in the innocent holy blood of the Lamb of God. Wherever you see this sign you may know that the church, or the holy Christian people, must surely be present, even if the pope does not baptize you or even if you know nothing of his holiness and power—just as the little children know nothing of it, although when they are grown, they are, sad to say, estranged from their baptism, as St. Peter laments in II Peter 2 [:18], "They entice with licentious passions of the flesh men who have barely escaped from those who live in error," etc. Indeed, you should not even pay attention to who baptizes, for baptism does not belong to the baptizer, nor is it given to him, but it belongs to the baptized. It was ordained for him by God, and given to him by God, just as the word of God is not the preacher's (except in so far as he too hears and believes it) but belongs to the disciple who hears and believes it; to him is it given.

---

[392] Probably names suggested by the sound of "Wetzel," which lose their force in translation.

[393] *Ecclesia verbo dei generatur, alitur nutritur, roboratur.* The saying could not be located in Augustine's writings.

Third, God's people, or Christian holy people, are recognized by the holy sacrament of the altar, wherever it is rightly administered, believed, and received, according to Christ's institution. This too is a public sign and a precious, holy possession left behind by Christ by which his people are sanctified so that they also exercise themselves in faith and openly confess that they are Christian, just as they do with the word and with baptism. And here too you need not be disturbed if the pope does not say mass for you, does not consecrate, anoint, or vest you with a chasuble. Indeed, you may, like a patient in bed, receive this sacrament without wearing any garb, except that outward decency obliges you to be properly covered. Moreover, you need not ask whether you have a tonsure or are anointed. In addition, the question of whether you are male or female, young or old, need not be argued—just as little as it matters in baptism and the preached word. It is enough that you are consecrated and anointed with the sublime and holy chrism of God, with the word of God, with baptism, and also this sacrament; then you are anointed highly and gloriously enough and sufficiently vested with priestly garments.

Moreover, don't be led astray by the question of whether the man who administers the sacrament is holy, or whether or not he has two wives.[394] The sacrament belongs to him who receives it, not to him who administers it, unless he also receives it. In that case he is one of those who receives it, and thus it is also given to him. Wherever you see this sacrament properly administered, there you may be assured of the presence of God's people. For, as was said above of the word, wherever God's word is, there the church must be; likewise, wherever baptism and the sacrament are, God's people must be, and vice versa. No others have, give, practice, use, and confess these holy possessions save God's people alone, even though some false and unbelieving Christians are secretly among them. They, however, do not profane the people of God because they are not known; the church, or God's people, does not tolerate known sinners in its midst, but reproves them and also makes them holy. Or, if they refuse, it casts them out from

---

[394] Cf. below, pp. 346-356.

the sanctuary by means of the ban and regards them as heathen, Matthew 18 [:17].

Fourth, God's people or holy Christians are recognized by the office of the keys exercised publicly.[395] That is, as Christ decrees in Matthew 18 [:15-20], if a Christian sins, he should be reproved; and if he does not mend his ways, he should be bound in his sin and cast out. If he does mend his ways, he should be absolved. That is the office of the keys. Now the use of the keys is twofold, public and private. There are some people with consciences so tender and despairing that even if they have not been publicly condemned, they cannot find comfort until they have been individually absolved by the pastor. On the other hand, there are also some who are so obdurate that they neither recant in their heart and want their sins forgiven individually by the pastor, nor desist from their sins. Therefore the keys must be used differently, publicly and privately. Now where you see sins forgiven or reproved in some persons, be it publicly or privately, you may know that God's people are there. If God's people are not there, the keys are not there either; and if the keys are not present for Christ, God's people are not present. Christ bequeathed them as a public sign and a holy possession, whereby the Holy Spirit again sanctifies the fallen sinners redeemed by Christ's death, and whereby the Christians confess that they are a holy people in this world under Christ. And those who refuse to be converted or sanctified again shall be cast out from this holy people, that is, bound and excluded by means of the keys, as happened to the unrepentant Antinomians.

You must pay no heed here to the two keys of the pope, which he converted into two skeleton keys to the treasure chests and crowns of all kings. If he does not want to bind or reprove sin, whether it be publicly or privately (as he really does not), let it be reproved and bound in your parish. If he will not loose, or forgive it, let it be loosed and forgiven in your parish, for his retaining or binding, his remitting or releasing, makes you neither holy nor unholy, since he can only have skeleton keys, not the true

---

[395] Luther had previously discussed this subject at length in his treatise *The Keys* (1530). *LW* 40, 325-377.

keys. The keys belong not to the pope (as he lies) but to the church, that is, to God's people, or to the holy Christian people throughout the entire world, or wherever there are Christians. They cannot all be in Rome, unless it be that the whole world is there first—which will not happen in a long time. The keys are the pope's as little as baptism, the sacrament, and the word of God are, for they belong to the people of Christ and are called "the church's keys"[396] not "the pope's keys."[397]

Fifth, the church is recognized externally by the fact that it consecrates or calls ministers, or has offices that it is to administer. There must be bishops, pastors, or preachers, who publicly and privately give, administer, and use the aforementioned four things or holy possessions in behalf of and in the name of the church, or rather by reason of their institution by Christ, as St. Paul states in Ephesians 4 [:8], "He received gifts among men . . ."[398]—his gifts were that some should be apostles, some prophets, some evangelists, some teachers and governors, etc. The people as a whole cannot do these things, but must entrust or have them entrusted to one person. Otherwise, what would happen if everyone wanted to speak or administer, and no one wanted to give way to the other? It must be entrusted to one person, and he alone should be allowed to preach, to baptize, to absolve, and to administer the sacraments. The others should be content with this arrangement and agree to it. Wherever you see this done, be assured that God's people, the holy Christian people, are present.

It is, however, true that the Holy Spirit has excepted women, children, and incompetent people from this function, but chooses (except in emergencies) only competent males to fill this office, as one reads here and there in the epistles of St. Paul that a bishop must be pious, able to teach, and the husband of one wife[399]—and in I Corinthians 14 [:34] he says, "The women should keep silence in the churches." In summary, it must be a competent and chosen man. Children, women, and other persons are not qualified for this

[396] *Claves Ecclesiae.*
[397] *Claves Papae.*
[398] Luther is as usual quoting from memory, and confuses Eph. 4:8 with Ps. 68:18, from which the Ephesian passage quotes.
[399] For example, I Tim. 3:2; Titus 1:6.

office, even though they are able to hear God's word, to receive baptism, the sacrament, absolution, and are also true, holy Christians, as St. Peter says [I Pet. 3:7]. Even nature and God's creation makes this distinction, implying that women (much less children or fools) cannot and shall not occupy positions of sovereignty, as experience also suggests and as Moses says in Genesis 3 [:16], "You shall be subject to man." The gospel, however, does not abrogate this natural law, but confirms it as the ordinance and creation of God.

Here the pope will object through his loudmouths and brawlers of the devil, saying, "St. Paul does not speak only of pastors and preachers, but also of apostles, evangelists, prophets, and other high spiritual vocations; that is why there must be higher vocations in the church than those of pastors and preachers. What, Sir Luther, do you have to say now?" What do I have to say now? This is what I have to say: if they themselves would become apostles, evangelists, prophets, or would show me at least one among them—oh, what nonsense I am talking!—who is worth as much as a schoolboy or who is as well versed in Holy Scripture and in Christian doctrine as a seven-year-old girl, I shall declare myself caught. Now I know for certain that an apostle, an evangelist, a prophet knows more, or indeed as much, as a seven-year-old girl. (I am speaking about Holy Scripture and about faith.) For I thoroughly believe, more firmly than I believe in God, that they are acquainted with more human doctrine, and also with more villainy, because they are proving it before my very eyes by the things they are doing, and so they are apostles, evangelists, and prophets just as little as they are the church; that is to say, they are the devil's apostles, evangelists, and prophets. The true apostles, evangelists, and prophets preach God's word, not against God's word.

Now, if the apostles, evangelists, and prophets are no longer living, others must have replaced them and will replace them until the end of the world, for the church shall last until the end of the world [Matt. 28:20]. Apostles, evangelists, and prophets must therefore remain, no matter what their name, to promote God's word and work. The pope and his followers, who persecute God's word while admitting that it is true, must be very poor apostles, evangelists, and prophets, just like the devil and his angels. But why do I keep coming back to these shameful, filthy folk of the pope? Let them go again, and bid them not to return, or etc.

Just as was said earlier about the other four parts of the great, divine, holy possession by which the holy church is sanctified, that you need not care who or how those from whom you receive it are, so again you should not ask who and how he is who gives it to you or has the office. For all of it is given, not to him who has the office, but to him who is to receive it through this office, except that he can receive it together with you if he so desires. Let him be what he will. Because he is in office and is tolerated by the assembly, you put up with him too. His person will make God's word and sacraments neither worse nor better for you. What he says or does is not his, but Christ, your Lord, and the Holy Spirit say and do everything, in so far as he adheres to correct doctrine and practice. The church, of course, cannot and should not tolerate open vices; but you yourself be content and tolerant, since you, an individual, cannot be the whole assembly or the Christian holy people.

But you must pay no attention to the pope,[400] who bars any married man from being called to such an office. With Nestorian logic he declares that all must be chaste virgins; that is to say, all the clergy must be chaste, while they themselves may, of course, be unchaste. But look here! You bring up the pope again, and yet I did not want you any more. Well then, unwelcome guest that you are, I will receive you in Luther-like fashion.

The pope condemns the marriage of bishops or priests; that is now plain enough. Not content with that, he condemns bigamy[401] even more severely. Indeed, to express myself clearly, he distinguishes four, if not five, kinds of bigamy.[402] I will now call one who marries twice or who takes another's widow to wife a biga-

---

[400] This whole section repeats the ideas of a sermon preached by Luther on March 2, 1539. Cf. *WA* 47, 671-678.

[401] Luther calls it *digamia* (from the Greek *digamos*).

[402] See *Decreti Prima Pars*, dist. XXVI, C. I-III (*CIC* 1, 95-96); dist. XXXIII, C. II (*CIC* 1, 123); dist. XXXIV, C. IX-XVIII (*CIC* 1, 128-130); *Decretalium D. Gregorii Papae IX*, lib. i, tit. XXI (*CIC* 2, 146-148).

mist. The first kind of bigamist is one who marries two virgins successively; the second, one who marries a widow; the third, one who marries the betrothed whose deceased groom left her a virgin. The fourth acquires the name shamefully because he is the one who marries a "virgin," unknowingly or unwillingly, and later discovers that she is not at all pure or a virgin. And yet, in the pope's judgment this person must be more of a bigamist than the third type who married the virgin bride. All of these men stink and have an evil smell in canon law. They are not allowed to preach, baptize, administer the sacrament, or hold any office in the church, even if they were holier than St. John and their wives holier than the mother of God. So marvelously holy is the pope in his decretals!

However, if someone had ravished a hundred virgins, violated a hundred honorable widows, and lain with a hundred whores before that, he may become not only pastor or preacher but also bishop or pope. And even if he were to continue this kind of life, he would nonetheless be tolerated in those offices. But if he marries a bride who is a virgin, or a make-believe virgin, he cannot be a servant of God. It makes no difference that he is a true Christian, learned, pious, competent. He is a bigamist; thus, he must leave his office and never return to it. What do you think of that? Is that not a higher holiness than that of Christ himself, together with that of the Holy Spirit and his church? Christ spurns neither men with one wife or two successive wives, nor women with one husband or two successive husbands, if they believe in him. He lets them remain members of his holy, Christian people. He also make use of them for whatever work they are adapted. Scripture uses the term "bigamist" for one who, like Lamech, has two wives living at the same time [Gen. 4:19]. The pope, however, is more learned and calls one who marries two women successively a bigamist. He applies the same rule to women, for he is far more learned than God himself.

Better still, the pope himself admits that a bigamous marriage is a true marriage and does not constitute a sin against God, nor against the world or the church,[403] and that such a marriage is a

---

[403] *Decreti Prima Pars*, dist. XXVI, C. II. *CIC* 1, 95; *MPL* 187, 149c.

sacrament of the church; and yet such a man must be barred from holding an ecclesiastical office—as must the third or fourth type of bigamists, who really should be called husbands of one wife or husbands of virgins. Why? Well, here is the rub: such a marriage cannot be a sacrament or an image of Christ and his church, for Christ had but one bride, the church, and this bride has but one husband, Christ, and both remain virgins. So much sheer nonsense has been talked about this subject that it is impossible to relate it at all. The canonists should rightly be called lawyers for asses. First, if marriage is to be a sacrament of Christ and his church, then no marriage can be a sacrament unless both bridegroom and bride remain virgin, for Christ and the church remain virgins. But how will we get children and heirs under those conditions? What will become of the estate of marriage, instituted by God? In summary, there will be no marriage, other than that of Mary and Joseph and others like it. All the remaining marriages cannot be a sacrament, and may perhaps even be harlotry.

Second, who taught or decreed this, that we must keep it? St. Paul says (they say) in Ephesians 4 [5:31-32] that husband and wife are a great sacrament. I say, "Yes, in Christ and the church." My dear man, can you gather from these words of St. Paul that marriage is the kind of a sacrament of which they speak? He says that husband and wife are one body, which is a great sacrament. Then he interprets himself, saying, "I speak of Christ and the church, not of husband and wife." But they say that he is speaking of husband and wife. Paul envisages Christ and the church as a great sacrament or "mystery";[404] so they say that husband and wife are a great sacrament. Why then do they regard it as virtually the least of the sacraments, indeed, as sheer impurity and sin, in which one cannot serve God? Moreover, can you also deduce from St. Paul's words that men and women in bigamous marriages are not husband and wife or one body? If they are one body, why then are they not a sacrament of Christ and the church? After all, St. Paul is speaking generally about husbands and wives who become one body, whether they were single or widowed be-

---

[404] *Mysterium* (from the Greek *mysterion* used in Eph. 5:32).

fore, and calls them a sacrament (as you understand "sacrament"). Whence then are you so clever as to differentiate in marriage, taking only the single marriage as a sacrament of Christ and the church—that is, the marriage of a man with a virgin—and excluding all others? Who ordered you to martyr and force St. Paul's words in this manner?

Furthermore, you do not even call such a marriage a sacrament. For bridegrooms do not let their brides remain virgins, nor do the latter marry men in order that they may stay virgins; this they could do far better without husbands. No, they want and should bear children, for which God created them. What now becomes of the sacrament of Christ and the church, both of whom remained virgins? Is this the best argument "from image to historical fact or, conversely, from historical fact to image?"[405] Where did you learn such logic? Christ and the church are married, but remain virgins in the body; therefore husband and wife shall also remain virgins in the body. Furthermore, Christ is married to only one virgin; therefore a Christian or a priest shall also be married to only one virgin; otherwise, you say, there is no sacrament. Why, then, do you admit and say that the marriage of a widow is also a sacrament because it is a marriage, and again it is not a sacrament because the wife was not a virgin? Are you not mad, and crazy, and crass Nestorians, not knowing when you say yes and when you say no, stating one thing in the premise and another in the conclusion? Away with you stupid asses and fools!

Another crass error stemmed from the fact (unless, indeed, the former grew out of this) that they called and regarded bishops and popes as the bridegrooms of the church.[406] In verification of this view they cite the saying of St. Paul, "A bishop must be the husband of one wife" [I Tim. 3:2], that is to say, he must be the bishop of one church, as Christ is the bridegroom of one church; therefore they should not be bigamists. Popes and bishops, indeed,

---

[405] *A figura ad historiam, vel econtra, ab historia ad figuram.* A reference to the "dialectical" method of exegesis. Cf. Philip Melanchthon, *Dialectical Questions* (*Erotemata Dialectices*) (1527), VII, 653, 705. *C.R.* 13, 734. See also Clyde L. Manschreck, *Melanchthon* (New York and Nashville: Abingdon Press, 1958), p. 151.

[406] *Decreti Prima Pars*, dist. XXVI, C. II. *CIC* 1, 95; *MPL* 187, 149c.

are fine fellows to be bridegrooms of the church—yes, if she were a brothel-keeper or the devil's daughter in hell. True bishops are servants of this bride, and she is lady and mistress over them. St. Paul calls himself *diaconus*, a "servant of the church" [I Cor. 3:5]. He does not claim to be the bridegroom or the lord of this bride, rather, the true and only bridegroom of this bride is called Jesus Christ, God's Son. St. John does not say, "I am the bridegroom," but, "I am the friend of the bridegroom, who stands and hears him, and who rejoices greatly at the bridegroom's voice," for "he who has the bride" (he says) "is the bridegroom" [John 3:29]. One should gladly give ear to such speech and then conduct oneself as a servant.

But how nicely they themselves keep even this crass asininity and folly. A bishop may have three bishoprics, and yet he must be called husband of one wife. And even if he has but one bishopric, he still has one hundred, two hundred, five hundred, or more parishes or churches; yet he is the bridegroom of one church. The pope claims to be the bridegroom of all churches, both large and small, yet he is called the husband of one church. They are not bigamists or men with two wives, though they have all these brides at the same time. But he who marries a virgin who was betrothed to another is a bigamist. God will inflict gross, monstrous folly like this on us if we despise his word and want to do everything better than he commanded.

Indeed, they have an *acutius*[407] in their *Decretum,* in which St. Augustine holds, against St. Jerome, that he who had a wife before baptism and also one after baptism had two wives. Dear asses, does it therefore follow that St. Augustine, even though he views such a man as the husband of two wives (something Scripture does not do), wishes to have him condemned and barred from serving God, as you do? And even though this should follow, do you not have a strong *noli meis*[408] in dist. IX against it? How is it that you hold so fast to the *acutius* (though it is against Scripture) and pass so lightly over the *noli meis* and other chapters?

---

[407] A quotation from Augustine in *Decreti Prima Pars,* dist. XXVI, C. II: *Acutius intelligunt . . . . CIC* 1, 95; *MPL* 187, 149c.

[408] Augustine, *On the Trinity,* III, 2. *MPL* 42, 869; *PNF*[1] 3, 57. Cf. also above, p. 217.

This is, of course, your idea: you want to be lords of the church; whatever you say should be accepted as right. Marriage shall be right and a sacrament, if you will it so; on the other hand, marriage shall be an impurity, that is, a defiled sacrament that cannot serve God, if you will it so. Marriage shall bear children, and yet the wife shall remain a virgin or it is not a sacrament of Christ and the church, if you will it so. The bigamists are blameless and have a true marriage and sacrament, if you will it so; on the other hand, they are condemned and barred from serving God and have no sacrament of Christ and the church, if you will it so. Behold how the devil, who teaches you this nonsense, makes you reel and sway back and forth.

Why should I regard St. Augustine's statement as an article of faith if he himself does not wish to do so and if he himself does not even want to accept the sayings of his predecessors as articles of faith? Suppose that the dear fathers' opinion and teaching about a bigamist was such (as described)—what does it matter to us? It does not obligate us to hold and to teach that view. We must found our salvation on the words and works of man as little as we build our houses of hay and straw. But the canonists are such stupid asses and fools, with their idol in Rome, that they convert the words and deeds of the dear fathers into articles of faith against their will and without their consent. It should be proved by Scripture that such men may be called bigamists or trigamists; then their exclusion from the ministry of the church would be right and stand approved by St. Paul's instruction in I Timothy 3 [:2], "A bishop shall be the husband of one wife." But this frequently happened to the fathers—they sewed old patches on new cloth.[409] This is the case here: no bigamist shall be a servant of the church; that is right and that is the new cloth. But that this or that man is really a bigamist, that is the old patch of their own opinion because Scripture does not say it. Scripture regards the man who has two wives living at the same time as a bigamist; and it is assumed that St. Paul had had a wife, Philippians 4 [:3],[410] and that she died. So he too must have been a

---

[409] Cf. above, p. 255.
[410] Luther interprets the term "yokefellow" as an indication of Paul's marriage

man with two wives, obliged to give up his apostolic office; for in I Corinthians 7 [:8] he counts himself among the widowed, and yet in I Corinthians 9 [:5] he, along with Barnabas, claims the right to be accompanied by a wife. Who will assure us that the poor fishermen, Peter, Andrew, and James, were married to virgins and not to widows, or that they did not have two wives in succession?

These blockheads do not have the same idea of chastity that the fathers had, but would like to confuse the poor souls and jeopardize them, if only their stinking and filthy book[411] is regarded as right and their "science" is not found to err or to have erred. Otherwise, they would indeed see what chastity is—since, with regard to other "opinions"[412] (and what is their best and foremost but a matter of mere opinion?), they can say nicely, "It is not held; but hold this."[413] Why can they not do it here, especially since they do not hesitate to repudiate not only one father, but all of them, in "the cases to be decided,"[414] as their idol sputters and bellows? But they would like to rule the church, not with trustworthy wisdom, but with arbitrary opinions, and again confuse and perplex all the souls in the world, as they have done before. But just as they reject all the fathers and theologians in their petty canons, so do we, in turn, reject them in the church and in Scripture. They shall neither teach us Scripture nor rule in the church; they are not entitled to it, nor do they have the competence for it. But they shall attend to their trifling canons and squabbles over prebends—that is their holiness. They have cast us poor theologians, together with the fathers, from their books; for this we thank them most kindly. Now they propose to throw us out of the church and out of Scripture; and they themselves are not worthy to be in them. That is too much, and rips the bag

---

and assumes (on the basis of I Cor. 7:8) that he became a widower. Modern biblical scholarship does not agree. Cf., for example, George A. Buttrick *et al.* (eds.), *The Interpreter's Bible* (12 vols.; New York and Nashville: Abingdon, 1952-1957), IX, 107-108; X, 78-79.

[411] Canon law.

[412] *Opiniones.*

[413] *Non tenetur; hoc tene.*

[414] *Causis decidendis.* Here Luther mocks the slogans of medieval canonists who were frequently involved in court cases concerning ecclesiastical property.

wide open.[415] And furthermore, we shall not put up with it.

I truly believe that in accordance with their wisdom no man could marry a virgin and, after her death, become a priest among them, for who can guarantee or vouch that he is actually getting a virgin? "The road runs past the door"[416] (as they say). Now if he would find her not a virgin—and that is a chance he must take—he would, through no fault of his own, be a stinking bigamist. And if he wants to be certain that he can become a priest, he dare not marry a virgin either, for what assurance does he have that she is one? However, he may ravish virgins, widows, and wives, have many whores, commit all sorts of secret sins—he is still worthy of the priestly office. The sum and substance of it all is that the pope, the devil, and his church are averse to the estate of matrimony, as Daniel [11:37] says; therefore he wants it viewed as such a defilement that a married man cannot fill a priest's office. That is as much as to say that marriage is harlotry, sin, impure, and rejected by God. And even though they say, at the same time, that marriage is holy and a sacrament, that is hypocrisy and a lie, for if they would sincerely regard it as holy and a sacrament they would not forbid a priest to marry. But since they do prohibit it, it follows that they consider it impure and a sin—as they plainly say, "You must be clean, who bearest [the vessels of the lord]"[417] or (if some really are that pious) they must be stupid Nestorians and Eutychians, affirming a premise and denying the conclusion. May this be the reception that we, for the time being, accord the papal ass and the asinine papists, as we return to our own people.

Therefore do not worry (as was said) about the papists' talk concerning the personal qualifications for an ecclesiastical office, for these asses do not understand St. Paul's words, nor do they know what St. Paul's language calls a sacrament. He says [Eph. 5:31-32] that Christ and the church are a sacrament, that is, Christ and the church are one body, as husband and wife are, and that

---

[415] A German proverb, "Das zurreisset den sack." Cf. Thiele, Luthers Sprich-wörtersammlung, No. 39.

[416] Another proverb, "Der weg gehet fur der thür ruber." Cf. ibid., No. 10.

[417] Mundamini, qui fertis [vasa Domini]. A reference to the formula used at the ordination of priests.

this is a great mystery, to be apprehended by faith. It is not visible or tangible; therefore it is a sacrament, that is, something secret, a mystery, invisible, hidden. But since not only virginal but also widowed people entering matrimony are one body, every marriage is a figure or symbol of this great sacrament or mystery in Christ and the church. St. Paul speaks of neither virgins nor widows; he speaks of marriage, in which husband and wife are one body. Now wherever you find these offices or officers, you may be assured that the holy Christian people are there; for the church cannot be without these bishops, pastors, preachers, priests; and conversely, they cannot be without the church. Both must be together.

Sixth, the holy Christian people are externally recognized by prayer, public praise, and thanksgiving to God. Where you see and hear the Lord's Prayer prayed and taught; or psalms or other spiritual songs sung, in accordance with the word of God and the true faith; also the creed, the Ten Commandments, and the catechism used in public, you may rest assured that a holy Christian people of God are present. For prayer, too, is one of the precious holy possessions whereby everything is sanctified, as St. Paul says [I Tim. 4:5]. The psalms too are nothing but prayers in which we praise, thank, and glorify God. The creed and the Ten Commandments are also God's word and belong to the holy possession, whereby the Holy Spirit sanctifies the holy people of Christ. However, we are now speaking of prayers and songs which are intelligible and from which we can learn and by means of which we can mend our ways. The clamor of monks and nuns and priests is not prayer, nor is it praise to God; for they do not understand it, nor do they learn anything from it; they do it like a donkey, only for the sake of the belly and not at all in quest of any reform or sanctification or of the will of God.

Seventh, the holy Christian people are externally recognized by the holy possession of the sacred cross. They must endure every misfortune and persecution, all kinds of trials and evil from the devil, the world, and the flesh (as the Lord's Prayer indicates) by inward sadness, timidity, fear, outward poverty, contempt, illness, and weakness, in order to become like their head, Christ.

And the only reason they must suffer is that they steadfastly adhere to Christ and God's word, enduring this for the sake of Christ, Matthew 5 [:11], "Blessed are you when men persecute you on my account." They must be pious, quiet, obedient, and prepared to serve the government and everybody with life and goods, doing no one any harm. No people on earth have to endure such bitter hate; they must be accounted worse than Jews, heathen, and Turks. In summary, they must be called heretics, knaves, and devils, the most pernicious people on earth, to the point where those who hang, drown, murder, torture, banish, and plague them to death are rendering God a service. No one has compassion on them; they are given myrrh and gall to drink when they thirst. And all of this is done not because they are adulterers, murderers, thieves, or rogues, but because they want to have none but Christ, and no other God. Wherever you see or hear this, you may know that the holy Christian church is there, as Christ says in Matthew 5 [:11-12], "Blessed are you when men revile you and utter all kinds of evil against you on my account. Rejoice and be glad, for your reward is great in heaven." This too is a holy possession whereby the Holy Spirit not only sanctifies his people, but also blesses them.

Meanwhile, pay no heed to the papists' holy possessions from dead saints, from the wood of the holy cross. For these are just as often bones taken from a carrion pit as bones of saints, and just as often wood taken from gallows as wood from the holy cross. There is nothing but fraud in this. The pope thus tricks people out of their money and alienates them from Christ. Even if it were a genuine holy possession, it would nonetheless not sanctify anyone. But when you are condemned, cursed, reviled, slandered, and plagued because of Christ, you are sanctified. It mortifies the old Adam and teaches him patience, humility, gentleness, praise and thanks, and good cheer in suffering. That is what it means to be sanctified by the Holy Spirit and to be renewed to a new life in Christ; in that way we learn to believe in God, to trust him, to love him, and to place our hope in him, as Romans 5 [:1-5] says, "Suffering produces hope," etc.

These are the true seven principal parts of the great holy possession whereby the Holy Spirit effects in us a daily sanctification and vivification in Christ, according to the first table of Moses. By this we obey it, albeit never as perfectly as Christ. But we constantly strive to attain the goal, under his redemption or remission of sin, until we too shall one day become perfectly holy and no longer stand in need of forgiveness. Everything is directed toward that goal. I would even call these seven parts the seven sacraments, but since that term has been misused by the papists and is used in a different sense in Scripture, I shall let them stand as the seven principal parts of Christian sanctification or the seven holy possessions of the church.

In addition to these seven principal parts there are other outward signs that identify the Christian church, namely, those signs whereby the Holy Spirit sanctifies us according to the second table of Moses; when he assists us in sincerely honoring our father and mother, and conversely, when he helps them to raise their children in a Christian way and to lead honorable lives; when we faithfully serve our princes and lords and are obedient and subject to them, and conversely, when they love their subjects and protect and guard them; also when we bear no one a grudge, entertain no anger, hatred, envy, or vengefulness toward our neighbors, but gladly forgive them, lend to them, help them, and counsel them; when we are not lewd, not drunkards, not proud, arrogant, overbearing, but chaste, self-controlled, sober, friendly, kind, gentle, and humble; when we do not steal, rob, are not usurious, greedy, do not overcharge, but are mild, kind, content, charitable; when we are not false, mendacious, perjurers, but truthful, trustworthy, and do whatever else is taught in these commandments—all of which St. Paul teaches abundantly in more than one place. We need the Decalogue not only to apprise us of our lawful obligations, but we also need it to discern how far the Holy Spirit has advanced us in his work of sanctification and by how much we still fall short of the goal, lest we become secure and imagine that we have now done all that is required. Thus we must constantly grow in sanctification and always become new creatures in Christ. This means "grow" and "do so more and more" [II Pet. 3:18].

However, these signs cannot be regarded as being as reliable as those noted before since some heathen too practice these works and indeed at times appear holier than Christians; yet their actions do not issue from the heart purely and simply, for the sake of God, but they search for some other end because they lack a real faith in and a true knowledge of God. But here is the Holy Spirit, who sanctifies the heart and produces these fruits from "an honest and good heart," as Christ says in the parable recorded in Matthew 13 [Luke 8:15]. Since the first table is greater and must be a holier possession, I have summarized everything in the second table. Otherwise, I could have divided it too into seven holy possessions or seven principal parts, according to the seven commandments.

Now we know for certain what, where, and who the holy Christian church is, that is, the holy Christian people of God; and we are quite certain that it cannot fail us. Everything else may fail and surely does, as we shall hear in part. Men should be selected from this people to form a council; that might be a council ruled by the Holy Spirit. Thus Lyra, too, writes that the church is not to be assessed by the high or spiritual vocations in it, but by the people who truly believe.[418] I am surprised that he was not burned at the stake for these words, for denying that popes, cardinals, bishops, and prelates compose the church; this amounts to abominable heresy, intolerable and offensive to the holy Roman church. More about this elsewhere.[419]

Now when the devil saw that God built such a holy church, he was not idle, and erected his chapel beside it, larger than God's temple. This is how he did it: he noticed that God utilized outward things, like baptism, word, sacrament, keys, etc., whereby he sanctified his church. And since the devil is always God's ape,

---

[418] Nicholas of Lyra (1270-1340), a Franciscan theologian and famous interpreter of the Bible. Luther frequently quotes him, as does Melanchthon, who quoted this statement of Lyra's in the *Apology of the Augsburg Confession*, Arts. VII, VIII. Tappert (ed.), *Book of Concord*, p. 172. The quotation Luther cites is found in *Comments on Matthew XVI* (*Annotationes in Matth. XVI*). See *WA* 50, 644, n. *a*. Five volumes of Lyra's works were published in 1471-1472 in Rome. *O.D.C.C.*, p. 957.

[419] Cf. *The Smalcald Articles*, Art. IV. Tappert (ed.), *Book of Concord*, pp. 298-301.

trying to imitate all God's things and to improve on them, he also tried his luck with external things purported to make man holy— just as he tries with rain-makers, sorcerers, exorcists of devils, etc. He even has the Lord's Prayer recited and the gospel read over them to make it appear a great holy possession. Thus he had popes and papists consecrate or sanctify water, salt, candles, herbs, bells, images, *Agnus Dei*,[420] pallia,[421] chasubles, tonsures, fingers, hands—who can tell it all?—finally the monks' cowls to a degree that many people died and were buried in them, believing that thereby they would be saved. Now it would have been fine indeed if God's word or a blessing or a prayer were spoken over these created things, as children do over their food or over themselves when they go to bed and when they arise. St. Paul says of this, "Everything created by God is good, and is consecrated by the word of God and prayer" [I Tim. 4:4-5]. The creature derives no new power from such a practice, but is strengthened in its former power.

But the devil has a different purpose in mind. He wants the creature to derive new strength and power from his aping tomfoolery. Just as water becomes baptism by the power of God, a bath unto eternal life, washing away sin and bringing salvation, a power which is not inherent in water; just as bread and wine become the body and blood of Christ; just as sins are remitted by the laying on of hands in accordance with God's institution—so the devil too wants his mummery and aping tomfoolery to be strong and imbued with supernatural power. Holy water is to blot out sin, exorcise devils, fend off evil spirits, protect women in childbed, as the pope teaches us in the *Aquam sale, de pe*;[422] consecrated salt is to have the same effect. An *Agnus Dei* consecrated by the pope is to do more than God himself can do, as this is described in verses that I should some day publish with marginal

---

[420] Luther refers to amulets usually made of wax and stamped with the image of a lamb.

[421] A woolen shoulder cape with the insignia of the archbishop's office on it.

[422] *Aquam sale*, a section in canon law dealing with consecration, according to which holy salt is used in rites of purification. *De pe* is either a slip of the pen for *de co* (*de consecratione*) or Luther's abbreviation for *de poenitentia*, the title of the chapter on penitence. Cf. *Decreti Tertia Pars: De Consecratione*, dist. III, C. XX. *CIC* 1, 1358; *MPL* 187, 1787c.

notes.[423] Bells are to drive away devils in thunderstorms. St. Anthony's knives stab the devil; consecrated herbs expel venomous worms; some blessings heal cows, keep off milk thieves,[424] and quench fire; certain letters give security in war and at other times against iron, fire, water, wild beasts, etc.;[425] monasticism, masses, and the like are said to confer more than ordinary salvation. Who can tell it all? There was no need so small that the devil did not institute a sacrament or holy possession for it, whereby one could receive advice and help. In addition, he had prophetesses, soothsayers, and sages able to reveal hidden things and to retrieve stolen goods.

Oh, he is far better equipped with sacraments, prophets, apostles, and evangelists than God, and his chapels are much larger than God's church; and he has far more people in his holiness than God. One is also more inclined to believe his promises, his sacraments, and his prophets than Christ. He is the great god of the world. Christ calls him "ruler of the world" [John 12:31; 14:30; 16:11] and Paul "the god of this world" [II Cor. 4:4]. With this aping tomfoolery he estranges men from faith in Christ and causes the word and the sacraments of Christ to be despised and almost unrecognizable because it is easier to perceive such things than to blot out sin, help in time of need, receive salvation through the devil's sacraments rather than through Christ's. For it is Christ's will to make people holy and pious in body and soul through the Holy Spirit and not let them remain in unbelief and sin. This is too hard for those who do not wish to be pious or to desist from sin. They can readily dispense with this work of the Holy Spirit after they learn how they can be saved more easily without him—for example, by holy water, *Agnus Dei*, bulls and breves, masses and cowls—thus making it unnecessary to seek or heed anything else.

But not only that! The devil has armed himself with these

---

[423] Cf. Luther's notes *On the Blessed Water and the Agnus Dei of the Pope* (*Von dem Geweihtem Wasser und des Papstes Agnus Dei*) (1539). WA 50, 668-673.

[424] I.e., witches who make cows go dry.

[425] In 1518 Luther dealt with these ecclesiastical customs more favorably. Cf. for example, *The Decalog, Preached to the People of Wittenberg* (*Decem Praecepta, Wittenbergensi Praedicata Populo*) (1518). WA 1, 401.

things in order to abolish God's word and sacraments with them. This is his line of thought: if someone arises to attack my church, sacraments, and bishops, saying that external things do not save, then God's word and sacraments shall perish with them, for these too are external signs and his church and bishops are also human beings. If mine do not stand approved, his will stand approved even less, especially because my church, bishops, and sacraments work promptly and help now and in this life, visibly and tangibly, for I am present in them and help quickly, as soon as it is desired. Christ's sacraments, however, work spiritually and invisibly and for the future so that his church and bishops can only be smelled, as it were, faintly and from afar, and the Holy Spirit behaves as though he were absent, permitting people to endure every misfortune and making them appear as heretics in the eyes of my church. Meanwhile, my church is not only so close that one can actually grasp it, but also my works follow very quickly; so everyone assumes that it is the true church of God. This is the advantage I have.

And that is what happened. When we began to teach, on the basis of the gospel, that these external things do not save, since they are merely physical and creatural and are often used by the devil for the purpose of sorcery, people, even great and learned people, concluded that baptism, being external water, that the word, being outward human speech, that Scripture, being physical letters made with ink, that the bread, being baked by the baker, and the wine were nothing more than outward, perishable things. So they devised the slogan, "Spirit! Spirit! The Spirit must do it! The letter kills!" So Münzer[420] called us Wittenberg theologians scribes of Scripture and himself the scribe of the Holy Spirit, and many others followed his example. There you see how the devil had armed himself and built up his barricades. If anyone were to attack his outward doctrine and sacraments (which afford quick, visible, and mighty aid), then the outward words and sacraments

---

[420] Thomas Münzer (1489-1525), labeled the "restless spirit of Allstedt" by Luther, became a leader of the rebellious peasants in the Peasants' War of 1525. The passage is found in Hans J. Hillerbrand, "Thomas Münzer's Last Tract Against Martin Luther," *The Mennonite Quarterly Review*, XXXVIII (1964), 26.

of Christ (attended by tardy or, at least, by invisible and feeble help) must go down to far worse destruction along with them.

Therefore the *ecclesia*, "the holy Christian people," does not have mere external words, sacraments, or offices, like God's ape Satan has, and in far greater numbers, but it has these as commanded, instituted, and ordained by God, so that he himself and not any angel will work through them with the Holy Spirit. They are called word, baptism, sacrament, and office of forgiveness, not of angels, men, or any other creature, but of God; only he does not choose to do it through his unveiled, brilliant, and glorious majesty, out of consideration for us poor, weak, and timid mortals and for our comfort, for who could bear such majesty for an instant in this poor and sinful flesh? As Moses says, "Man shall not see me and live" [Exod. 33:20]. If the Jews could not endure even the shoes of his feet on Mount Sinai, that is, the thunder and the clouds, how could they, with their feeble eyes, have endured the sight of the sun of his divine majesty and the clear light of his countenance? No, he wants to work through tolerable, kind, and pleasant means, which we ourselves could not have chosen better. He has, for instance, a godly and kind man speak to us, preach, lay his hands on us, remit sin, baptize, give us bread and wine to eat and to drink. Who can be terrified by these pleasing methods, and wouldn't rather delight in them with all his heart?

Well then, that is just what is done for us feeble human beings, and in it we see how God deals with us as with beloved children and not, as he surely would have a right to, in his majesty. And yet, in this guise he performs his majestic, divine works and exercises his might and power, such as forgiving sin, cleansing from sin, removing death, bestowing grace and eternal life. Indeed, these things are missing in the devil's sacraments and churches. No one can say there, "God commanded it, ordered it, instituted it, and ordained it; he himself is present and will do everything himself"; but one must say, "God did not command, but forbade it, that man, or rather that ape of God, invented it and misled the people with it." For he effects nothing except that which is temporal, or, if it purports to be spiritual, it is sheer fraud. He cannot forgive sin eternally and save, as he lyingly claims, by means of holy water, masses, and monkery, even though he may restore a cow's milk which he had first stolen from her by his prophetesses and priestesses. Among Christians these are called the devil's harlots and, when apprehended, are rightfully burned at the stake, not because of the theft of milk, but because of the blasphemy with which they fortify the devil, his sacraments, and his churches against Christ.

In summary, if God were to bid you to pick up a straw or to pluck out a feather with the command, order, and promise that thereby you would have forgiveness of all sin, grace, and eternal life, should you not accept this joyfully and gratefully, and cherish, praise, prize, and esteem that straw and that feather as a higher and holier possession than heaven and earth? No matter how insignificant the straw and the feather may be, you would nonetheless acquire through them something more valuable than heaven and earth, indeed, than all the angels, are able to bestow on you. Why then are we such disgraceful people that we do not regard the water of baptism, the bread and wine, that is, Christ's body and blood, the spoken word, and the laying on of man's hands for the forgiveness of sin as such holy possessions, as we would the straw and feather, though in the former, as we hear and know, God himself wishes to be effective and wants them to be his water, word, hand, bread, and wine, by means of which he wishes to sanctify and save you in Christ, who acquired this for us and who gave us the Holy Spirit from the Father for this work?

On the other hand, what good would it do you even if you went to St. James,[427] clad in armor, or let yourself be killed by the severe life of the Carthusians, Franciscans, or Dominicans in order to be saved, and God had neither commanded nor instituted it? He still knows nothing about all this, but you and the devil invented them, as special sacraments or classes of priests. And even if you were able to bear heaven and earth in order to be saved, it would still all be lost; and he who would pick up the straw (if this were commanded) would do more than you, even if you

---

[427] I.e., to the shrine of St. James of Compostella in Spain, where according to Spanish tradition the apostle was martyred in 44. See Acts 12:2.

could carry ten worlds. Why is that? It is God's will that we obey his word, use his sacraments, and honor his church. Then he will act graciously and gently enough, even more graciously and gently than we could desire; for it is written, "I am the Lord your God; you shall have no other gods before me" [Exod. 20:2-3]. And, "Listen to him and to no other" [Matt. 17:5]. May that suffice on the church. More cannot be said unless each point is elaborated further. The rest must deal with different ideas, about which we want to speak too.

Besides these external signs and holy possessions the church has other externals that do not sanctify it either in body or soul, nor were they instituted or commanded by God; but, as we said at length above, they are outwardly necessary or useful, proper and good—for instance, certain holidays and certain hours, forenoon or afternoon, set aside for preaching or praying, or the use of a church building or house, altar, pulpit, baptismal font, candlesticks, candles, bells, priestly vestments, and the like. These things have no more than their natural effects, just as food and drink accomplish no more by virtue of the grace the children say at the table,[428] for the ungodly or rude folk who don't say it, that is, who neither pray to God nor thank him, grow just as fat and strong from food and drink as Christians do. To be sure, Christians could be and remain sanctified even without these items, even if they were to preach on the street, outside a building, without a pulpit, if absolution were pronounced and the sacrament administered without an altar, and if baptism were performed without a font—as happens daily that for special reasons sermons are preached and baptisms and sacraments administered in the home. But for the sake of children and simple folk, it is a fine thing and conducive to good order to have a definite time, place, and hour to which people can adapt themselves and where they may assemble, as St. Paul says in I Corinthians 14 [:40], "All things should be done decently and in order." And no one should (as no Christian does) ignore such order without cause, out of mere pride or just to create disorder, but one should join in observing such order for the sake of the multitude, or at least should not disrupt or hinder

---

[428] These prayers are called *Benedicite* and *Gratias*.

it, for that would be acting contrary to love and friendliness.

Nevertheless, there should be freedom here: for instance, if we are unable, because of an emergency or another significant reason, to preach at six or seven, at twelve or one o'clock, on Sunday or Monday, in the choir or at St. Peter's, one may preach at a different hour, day, or place, just as long as one does not confuse the people, but properly apprises them of such a change. These matters are purely external (as far as time, place, and persons are concerned) and may be regulated entirely by reason, to which they are altogether subject. God, Christ, and the Holy Spirit are not interested in them—just as little as they are interested in what we wish to eat, drink, wear, and whom we marry, or where we want to dwell, walk, or stand; except that (as was said) no one should, without reason, adopt his own way and confuse or hinder the people. Just as at a wedding or other social event no one should offend the bride or the company by doing something special or something that interferes, but one should join the rest, and sit, walk, stand, dance, eat, and drink with them. For it is impossible to order a special table for each individual, and also a special kitchen, cellar, and servant. If he wants anything, let.him leave the table without disturbing the others. Thus here too everything must be conducted peacefully and in order, and yet there must be freedom if time, person, or other reasons demand a change; then the masses will also follow harmoniously, since (as was said) no Christian is thereby made any more or less holy.

The pope, to be sure, has scribbled the whole world full of books about these things and fashioned them into bonds, laws, rights, articles of faith, sin, and holiness so that his decretal really deserves, once again, to be consigned to the fire.[429] For we could do well without this book[430] that has caused so much great harm. It has pushed Holy Scripture aside and practically suppressed Christian doctrine; it has also subjected the jurists, with their imperial law, to it. Thus it has trodden both church and emperor underfoot; in their stead it presented us with these stupid asses, the canonists, these will-o'-the-wisps who rule the church with it

---

[429] On December 10, 1520, in Wittenberg, Luther burned copies of the canon law along with the bull, *Exsurge, Domine,* excommunicating him.
[430] I.e., canon law.

and, still more deplorable, left the best parts in it and took the worst out, foisting them on the church. Whatever good there is in it, one can find much better and more richly in Holy Scripture, indeed, also in St. Augustine alone, as far as teaching Christendom is concerned; and then, as far as temporal government is concerned, also in the books of the jurists. For the jurists themselves once contemplated throwing this book out of jurisprudence and leaving it to the theologians. However, it would have been far better to throw it into the fire and reduce it to ashes, although there is something good in it, for how could sheer evil exist unless there was some good with it? But there is too much evil, so much that it crowds out the good, and (as was said) a greater measure of good is to be found in Scripture and also in the fathers and among the jurists. Of course, it might be kept in the libraries as evidence of the folly and the mistakes of the popes, some of the councils, and other teachers. That is why I am keeping it.

We will regard these externals as we do a christening robe[431] or swaddling clothes in which a child is clad for baptism. The child is not baptized or sanctified either by the christening robe or by the swaddling clothes, but only by the baptism. And yet reason dictates that a child be thus clothed. If this garment is soiled or torn, it is replaced by another, and the child grows up without any help from swaddling clothes or christening robe. Here too one must exercise moderation and not use too many of these garments, lest the child be smothered. Similarly, moderation should also be observed in the use of ceremonies, lest they become a burden and a chore. They must remain so light that they are not felt, just as at a wedding no one thinks it a chore or a burden to conform his actions to those of the other people present. I shall write on the special fasts when I write about the plague of the Germans, gluttony and drunkenness, for that properly belongs in the sphere of temporal government.[432]

---

[431] *Westerhemd* (from the Latin *vestis*, meaning "garment"). The robe was usually white (in accordance with Rev. 6:11) and was used in the early church to dress those to be baptized. Cf. WA 50, 651, n. *a*.
[432] Luther wrote about this in 1518 in his *Explanations of the Ninety-five Theses. LW* 31, 86-88.

Above and elsewhere[433] I have written much about the schools, urging firmness and diligence in caring for them. Although they may be viewed as something external and pagan, in as much as they instruct boys in languages and the arts, they are nevertheless extremely necessary. For if we fail to train pupils we will not have pastors and preachers very long—as we are finding out. The school must supply the church with persons who can be made apostles, evangelists, and prophets, that is, preachers, pastors, and rulers, in addition to other people needed throughout the world, such as chancellors, councilors, secretaries, and the like, men who can also lend a hand with the temporal government. In addition, if the schoolteacher is a godly man and teaches the boys to understand, to sing, and to practice God's word and the true faith and holds them to Christian discipline, then, as we said earlier, the schools are truly young and eternal councils, which perhaps do more good than many other great councils. Therefore the former emperors, kings, and princes did well when they showed such diligence in building many schools, high and low, monastic schools and convents, to provide the church with a rich and ample supply of people; but their successors shamefully perverted their use. Thus today princes and lords should do the same, and use the possessions of the cloisters for the maintenance of schools and provide many persons with the means for study.[434] If our descendants misuse these, we at least have done our duty in our day.

In summary, the schools must be second in importance only to the church, for in them young preachers and pastors are trained, and from them emerge those who replace the ones who die. Next, then, to the school comes the burgher's house, for it supplies the pupils; then the city hall and the castle, which must protect the schools so that they may train children to become pastors, and so that these, in turn, may create churches and children of God (whether they be burghers, princes, or emperors). But God must be over all and nearest to all, to preserve this ring or circle against

---

[433] Cf. Luther's *To the Councilmen of All Cities in Germany that They Establish and Maintain Christian Schools* (SW 3, 31-70) and *A Sermon on Keeping Children in School* (above, pp. 115-166).

[434] Cf. *The Smalcald Articles*, Art. III. Tappert (ed.), *Book of Concord*, pp. 297-298.

the devil, and to do everything in all of life's vocations, indeed, in all creatures. Thus Psalm 127 [:1] says that there are only two temporal governments on earth, that of the city and that of the home, "Unless the Lord builds the house; unless the Lord watches over the city." The first government is that of the home, from which the people come; the second is that of the city, meaning the country, the people, princes and lords, which we call the secular government. These embrace everything—children, property, money, animals, etc. The home must produce, whereas the city must guard, protect, and defend. Then follows the third, God's own home and city, that is, the church, which must obtain people from the home and protection and defense from the city.

These are the three hierarchies ordained by God, and we need no more; indeed, we have enough and more than enough to do in living aright and resisting the devil in these three. Just look only at the home and at the duties it alone imposes: parents and landlords must be obeyed; children and servants must be nourished, trained, ruled, and provided for in a godly spirit. The rule of the home alone would give us enough to do, even if there were nothing else. Then the city, that is, the secular government, also gives us enough to do if we show ourselves really obedient, and conversely, if we are to judge, protect, and promote land and people. The devil keeps us busy enough, and with him God gave us the sweat of our brow, thorns and thistles in abundance [Gen. 3:18-19], so that we have more than enough to learn, to live, to do, and to suffer in these two governments. Then there is the third rule and government. If the Holy Spirit reigns there, Christ calls it a comforting, sweet, and light burden [Matt. 11:30]; if not, it is not only a heavy, severe, and terrible task, but also an impossible one, as St. Paul says in Romans 8 [:3], "What the law could not do," and elsewhere, "The letter kills" [II Cor. 3:6].

Now why should we have the blasphemous, bogus law or government of the pope over and above these three high divine governments, these three divine, natural, and temporal laws of God? It presumes to be everything, yet is in reality nothing. It leads us astray and tears us from these blessed, divine estates and laws. Instead, it dresses us in a mask or cowl, thereby making us the devil's fools and playthings, who are slothful and no longer know these three divine hierarchies or realms. That is why we no longer want to put up with it, but acting in conformity with St. Peter's, St. Paul's, and St. Augustine's teaching, want to be rid of it and turn the words of Psalm 2 [:3] against them, "Let us burst their bonds asunder, and cast their cords from us." Indeed, we shall sing with St. Paul, "Even if an angel from heaven should preach a gospel contrary to that, let him be accursed" [Gal. 1:8]; and we shall say with St. Peter, "Why do you make trial of God by putting such a yoke upon the neck?" [Acts 15:10]. Thus we shall again be the pope's masters and tread him underfoot, as Psalm 91 [:13] says, "You will tread on the lion and the adder, the young lion and the serpent you will trample under foot." And that we shall do by the power and with the help of the woman's seed, who has crushed and still crushes the serpent's head, although we must run the risk that he, in turn, will bite us in the heel [Gen. 3:15]. To this blessed seed of the woman be praise and honor, together with the Father and the Holy Spirit, to the one true God and Lord in eternity. Amen.

PREFACES TO
THE BIBLE

1545-1546

Translated by Charles M. Jacobs
Revised by E. Theodore Bachmann

INTRODUCTION

"The Holy Scriptures are a vast and mighty forest, but there is not a single tree in it that I have not shaken with my own hand," said Luther.[1] The publication of his translation of the entire Bible into German in 1534 remains one of the celebrated events of the Reformation. Luther's achievement of providing the people with a trustworthy and highly readable rendition of the Bible from the original languages has received fitting attention elsewhere.[2] Here it is enough to note that while Luther's translation was by no means the first to appear in German,[3] it was by all standards the best and most widely influential. Indeed, prior to the publication of his own complete version in 1534, portions of his translation of the Old Testament had already been embodied in the editions of the first complete Protestant Bibles appearing in 1529 in Zurich and Worms.[4]

The ready availability of the Bible in the language of the people was, in the deepest sense of the term, an integral part of the Reformation. One of the devices that helped to facilitate the new reader's understanding of the Bible was the provision of prefaces for most of its books. These prefaces came out with the books themselves, in the irregular sequence of published instalments, for Luther's work of translation extended over many years, from the first appearance of his German New Testament in 1522 to the complete Bible in 1534. Nor was this all. Simultaneously with the production of new translation, Luther and his colleagues revised and improved upon such as had already been published. In many instances the prefaces, too, underwent a corresponding process of revision.

In providing prefaces for the books in the German Bible, Luther was simply following a traditional practice. The inclusion of a prologue illuminating the main thoughts of a treatise was a practice associated with the best in scholarly exposition as far back as

---

[1] *WA*, TR 1, No. 674, from the early 1530's.
[2] For a discussion of the subject, see Michael Reu, *Luther's German Bible* (Columbus, 1934); Willem J. Kooiman, *Luther and the Bible* (Philadelphia, 1961); and *WA*, DB 6, xvii-lxxxix.
[3] Reu, *op. cit.*, pp. 19-53.
[4] *Ibid.*, p. 207.

Aristotle. Jerome's Vulgate had prefaces to almost every book in the Bible, plus others for groups of books, such as Paul's epistles and the seven catholic epistles.[5] However, in the second century Marcion seems to have been the church's trailblazer in this direction with his prologues to the letters of Paul.[6] The second edition of Erasmus' New Testament in 1518 began with one hundred twenty folio pages of introductory material.[7]

Luther's prefaces, however, introduced something new by means of which he revealed his understanding of the Scriptures, namely, a set of value judgments and a ranking of the books into categories. For him the Gospel of John and the epistles of Paul, as well as I Peter, rank as "the true kernel and marrow of all the books."[8] As books of secondary rank come Hebrews, James, Jude, and Revelation.[9] While Luther's assigning of a standard of value to the New Testament books may have been simply an act of religious devotion, it proved to be also, as Holl points out, a pioneering step toward modern biblical scholarship.[10] Luther's prefaces are thus more than simply popular introductions for lay readers. They reveal a theological position of Christocentricity which inevitably affects his understanding of the New Testament canon.[11]

Included here are only the prefaces to the Old Testament and the New Testament, not the prefaces to individual books of the Bible. The translation is a revision of that by Charles M. Jacobs in *PE* 6, 367-489.

E. T. B.

---

[5] See below, p. 396, n. 9.
[6] Karl Holl, *Gesammelte Aufsätze zur Kirchengeschichte*, Vol. I, Luther (6th ed.; Tübingen: Mohr, 1932), p. 572.
[7] *WA,* DB 6, 535; *WA,* DB 7, 555.
[8] See below, p. 398.
[9] See *LW* 35, 394-398, especially p. 394, n. 43.
[10] Holl, *op. cit.,* p. 561.
[11] See Jaroslav Pelikan, *Luther the Expositor* (companion volume to *LW* 1-30), pp. 86-88.

PREFACES TO
THE BIBLE

Preface to the Old Testament[1]

1545 (1523)

There are some who have little regard for the Old Testament. They think of it as a book that was given to the Jewish people only and is now out of date, containing only stories of past times. They think they have enough in the New Testament and assert that only a spiritual sense[2] is to be sought in the Old Testament. Origen,[3] Jerome,[4] and many other distinguished people have held this view. But Christ says in John 5[:39], "Search the Scriptures, for it is they that bear witness to me." St. Paul bids Timothy attend to the reading of the Scriptures [I Tim. 4:13], and in Romans 1[:2] he declares that the gospel was promised by God in the Scriptures, while in I Corinthians 15[5] he says that in accordance with the Scriptures Christ came of the seed of David, died, and was raised from the dead. St. Peter, too, points us back, more than once, to the Scriptures.

They do this in order to teach us that the Scriptures of the Old

---

[1] Luther finished translating the five books of Moses by the middle of December, 1522. They were published as a group by Melchior Lotther in Wittenberg by early summer, 1523, and revised six times by 1528. In contradistinction to the New Testament, the Psalter, Jesus Sirach, and the Books of Solomon, the Pentateuch was never published in separate edition after its incorporation into the complete Bible of 1534 (WA, DB 8, xix-xxi). This preface, composed after completion of the translation of the Pentateuch and first published with the Pentateuch in 1523, was retained almost intact in the 1534 and later versions of the complete Bible. It has reference, of course, primarily to the first five books of the Old Testament (WA, DB 8, xli). Our translation is based on the 1545 text as given in WA, DB 8, 11-31. See LW 35, 227-232 for a general introduction to all of Luther's biblical prefaces.

[2] *Geistliche sinn.* The allegorical sense of Scripture was differentiated from its literal sense and its moral sense by the early exegetes.

[3] Origen (*ca.* 185-*ca.* 254) at Alexandria was the principal exponent of allegorical exegesis.

[4] Jerome (*ca.* 343-420) sought to combine the literal and the allegorical methods of interpretation, giving somewhat greater emphasis to the former than to the latter.

[5] I Cor. 15:3-4; cf. Rom. 1:3 and II Tim. 2:8.

Testament are not to be despised, but diligently read. For they themselves base the New Testament upon them mightily, proving it by the Old Testament and appealing to it, as St. Luke also writes in Acts 17[:11], saying that they at Thessalonica examined the Scriptures daily to see if these things were so that Paul was teaching. The ground and proof of the New Testament is surely not to be despised, and therefore the Old Testament is to be highly regarded. And what is the New Testament but a public preaching and proclamation of Christ, set forth through the sayings of the Old Testament and fulfilled through Christ?

In order that those who are not more familiar with it may have instruction and guidance for reading the Old Testament with profit, I have prepared this preface to the best of the ability God has given me. I beg and really caution every pious Christian not to be offended by the simplicity of the language and stories frequently encountered there, but fully realize that, however simple they may seem, these are the very words, works, judgments, and deeds of the majesty, power, and wisdom of the most high God. For these are the Scriptures which make fools of all the wise and understanding, and are open only to the small and simple, as Christ says in Matthew 11[:25]. Therefore dismiss your own opinions and feelings, and think of the Scriptures as the loftiest and noblest of holy things, as the richest of mines which can never be sufficiently explored, in order that you may find that divine wisdom which God here lays before you in such simple guise as to quench all pride. Here you will find the swaddling cloths and the manger in which Christ lies, and to which the angel points the shepherds [Luke 2:12]. Simple and lowly are these swaddling cloths, but dear is the treasure, Christ, who lies in them.

Know, then, that the Old Testament is a book of laws, which teaches what men are to do and not to do—and in addition gives examples and stories of how these laws are kept or broken—just as the New Testament is gospel or book of grace,[6] and teaches where one is to get the power to fulfil the law. Now in the New Testament there are also given, along with the teaching about grace, many other teachings that are laws and commandments for the control of the flesh—since in this life the Spirit is not perfected and grace alone

---

[6] Cf. below, p. 394.

cannot rule. Similarly in the Old Testament too there are, beside the laws, certain promises and words of grace, by which the holy fathers and prophets under the law were kept, like us, in the faith of Christ. Nevertheless just as the chief teaching of the New Testament is really the proclamation of grace and peace through the forgiveness of sins in Christ, so the chief teaching of the Old Testament is really the teaching of laws, the showing up of sin, and the demanding of good. You should expect this in the Old Testament.

We come first to the books of Moses. In his first book [Genesis] Moses teaches how all creatures were created, and (as the chief cause for his writing) whence sin and death came, namely by Adam's fall, through the devil's wickedness. But immediately thereafter, before the coming of the law of Moses, he teaches whence help is to come for the driving out of sin and death, namely, not by the law or men's own works (since there was no law as yet), but by "the seed of the woman," Christ, promised to Adam and Abraham, in order that throughout the Scriptures from the beginning faith may be praised above all works and laws and merits. Genesis,[7] therefore, is made up almost entirely of illustrations of faith and unbelief, and of the fruits that faith and unbelief bear. It is an exceedingly evangelical book.

Afterward, in the second book [Exodus], when the world was now full and sunk in blindness so that men scarcely knew any longer what sin was or where death came from, God brings Moses forward with the law and selects a special people, in order to enlighten the world again through them, and by the law to reveal sin anew. He therefore organizes this people with all kinds of laws and separates it from all other peoples. He has them build a tent, and begins a form of worship. He appoints princes and officials, and provides his people splendidly with both laws and men, to rule them both in the body before the world and in the spirit before God.

The special topic of the third book [Leviticus] is the appointment of the priesthood, with the statutes and laws according to which the priests are to act and to teach the people. There we see that a priestly office is instituted only because of sin, to disclose sin to the people and to make atonement before God, so that its entire

---

[7] Luther uses the name "First Book of Moses." Cf. *LW*, 35, 161, n. 1.

function is to deal with sin and sinners. For this reason too no temporal wealth is given to the priests; neither are they commanded or permitted to rule men's bodies. Rather the only work assigned to them is to care for the people who are in sin.

In the fourth book [Numbers], after the laws have been given, the princes and priests instituted, the tent and form of worship set up, and everything that pertains to the people of God made ready, then the whole thing begins to function; a test is made as to how well the arrangement operates and how satisfactory it is. This is why this very book says so much about the disobedience of the people and the plagues that came upon them. And some of the laws are explained and the number of the laws increased. Indeed this is the way it always goes; laws are quickly given, but when they are to go into effect and become operative, they meet with nothing but hindrance; nothing goes as the law demands. This book is a notable example of how vacuous it is to make people righteous with laws; rather, as St. Paul says, laws cause only sin and wrath.[8]

In the fifth book [Deuteronomy], after the people have been punished because of their disobedience, and God has enticed them a little with grace, in order that by his kindness in giving them the two kingdoms[9] they might be moved to keep his law gladly and willingly, then Moses repeats the whole law. He repeats the story of all that has happened to the people (except for that which concerns the priesthood) and explains anew everything that belongs either to the bodily or to the spiritual governing of a people. Thus Moses, as a perfect lawgiver, fulfilled all the duties of his office.[10] He not only gave the law, but was there when men were to fulfil it. When things went wrong, he explained the law and re-established it. Yet this explanation in the fifth book really contains nothing else than faith toward God and love toward one's neighbor, for all God's laws come

---

[8] Cf. Rom. 5:20; 7:7-9; 4:15.

[9] Cf. LW 35, 164, 289-290.

[10] Throughout this preface with but two exceptions we have rendered the German word Amt by its closest English equivalent, "office." We have done so for the sake of preserving the continuity in Luther's discussion of the law, even though Amt in various contexts is really susceptible of numerous more felicitous English renderings which may or may not be implied in the term "office," such as work, ministry, function, and even dispensation (the RSV term in II Cor. 3:7, which we have retained on p. 382). Cf. the use of the same term in LW 35, 348, l. 19, in connection with the gospel as well as the law.

to that. Therefore, down to the twentieth chapter, Moses, in his explanation of the law, guards against everything that might destroy faith in God; and from there to the end of the book he guards against everything that hinders love.

It is to be observed in the first place that Moses provides so exactly for the organization of the people under laws as to leave human reason no room to choose a single work of its own or to invent its own form of worship. For Moses not only teaches fear, love, and trust toward God, but he also provides so many ways of outward worship—sacrifices, thanksgivings, fasts, mortifications, and the like —that no one needs to choose anything else. Besides he gives instructions for planting and tilling, marrying and fighting, governing children, servants, and households, buying and selling, borrowing and repaying, and for everything that is to be done both outwardly and inwardly. He goes so far that some of the prescriptions are to be regarded as foolish and useless.

Why, my friend, does God do that? In the end, because he has taken this people to be his own and has willed to be their God. For this reason he would so rule them that all their doings may surely be right in his eyes. For if anyone does anything for which God's word has not first given warrant, it counts for nothing before God and is labor lost. For in Deuteronomy 4[:2] and 12[:32] he forbids any addition to his laws; and in 12[:8] he says that they shall not do merely whatever is right in their own eyes. The Psalter, too, and all the prophets lament that the people are simply doing good works that they themselves have chosen to do and that were not commanded by God. He cannot and will not permit those who are his to undertake anything that he has not commanded, no matter how good it may be. For obedience, which depends on God's word, is of all works the noblest and best.

Since this life, however, cannot be without external forms of worship, God put before them all these forms and included them in his commandment in order that if they must or would do God any outward service, they might take one of these and not one they themselves had invented. They could then be doubly sure that their work was being done in obedience to God and his word. So they are prevented on every hand from following their own reason and free will in doing good and living aright. Room, place, time, person, work, and form are all more than adequately determined and prescribed, so that the people cannot complain and need not follow simply the example of alien worship.

In the second place it should be noted that the laws are of three kinds. Some speak only of temporal things, as do our imperial laws. These are established by God chiefly because of the wicked, that they may not do worse things. Such laws are for prevention rather than for instruction,[11] as when Moses commands that a wife be dismissed with a bill of divorce [Deut. 24:1] or that a husband can get rid of his wife with a "cereal offering of jealousy" [Num. 5:11-31] and take other wives besides. All these are temporal laws. There are some, however, that teach about the external worship of God, as has already been mentioned.

Over and above these two are the laws about faith and love. All other laws must and ought to be measured by faith and love. That is to say, the other laws are to be kept where their observance does not conflict with faith and love; but where they conflict with faith and love, they should be done away entirely. For this reason we read that David did not kill the murderer Joab [I Kings 2:5-6], even though he had twice deserved death [II Sam. 3:27; 20:10]. And in II Samuel 14[:11][12] David promises the woman of Tekoa that her son shall not die for having slain his brother. Nor did David kill Absalom [II Sam. 14:21-24]. Moreover David himself ate of the holy bread of the priests, I Samuel 21[:6]. And Tamar thought the king might give her in marriage to her stepbrother, Amnon [II Sam. 13:13]. From these and similar incidents one sees plainly that the kings, priests, and heads of the people often transgressed the laws boldly, at the demand of faith and love. Therefore faith and love are always to be mistresses of the law and to have all laws in their power. For since all laws aim at faith and love, none of them can be valid, or be a law, if it conflicts with faith or love.

Even to the present day, the Jews are greatly in error when they hold so strictly and stubbornly to certain laws of Moses. They

---

[11] *Nur Wehrgesetz, mehr denn Leregesetz.*
[12] Where Luther cites correctly the Vulgate, in which the four books of I and II Samuel and I and II Kings were numbered as I, II, III, and IV Kings, we have given the corresponding RSV reference.

would rather let love and peace be destroyed than eat and drink with us, or do things of that kind. They do not properly regard the intention of the law; but to understand this is essential for all who live under laws, not for the Jews alone. Christ also says so in Matthew 12,[13] that one might break the sabbath if an ox had fallen into a pit, and might rescue it. Now that was only a temporal necessity and injury. How much more ought one boldly to break all kinds of laws when bodily necessity demands it, provided that nothing is done against faith and love. Christ says that David did this very thing when he ate the holy bread, Mark 3[2:25-26].

But why does Moses mix up his laws in such a disordered way? Why does he not put the temporal laws together in one group and the spiritual laws in another and the laws of faith and love in still another? Moreover he sometimes repeats a law so often and reiterates the same words so many times that it becomes tedious to read it or listen to it. The answer is that Moses writes as the situation demands, so that his book is a picture and illustration of governing and of living. For this is the way it happens in a dynamic situation: now this work has to be done and now that. No man can so arrange his life (if he is to act in a godly way) that on this day he uses only spiritual laws and on that day only temporal. Rather God governs all the laws mixed together—like the stars in the heavens and the flowers in the fields—in such a way that at every hour a man must be ready for anything, and do whatever the situation requires. In like manner the writing of Moses represents a heterogeneous mixture.

That Moses is so insistent and often repeats the same thing shows also the nature of his office. For one who is to rule a people-with-laws [Gesetzuolck] must constantly admonish, constantly drive, and knock himself out struggling with the people as [he would] with asses. For no work of law is done gladly and willingly; it is all forced and compelled. Now since Moses is a lawgiver, he has to show by his insistence that the work of the law is a forced work. He has to wear the people down, until this insistence makes them not only recognize their illness and their dislike for God's law, but also long for grace,[14] as we shall show.

---

[13] Matt. 12:11; cf. Luke 14:5.
[14] Cf. Luther's *Brief Explanation of the Ten Commandments, the Creed, and the Lord's Prayer.* PE 2, 354-355.

In the third place the true intention of Moses is through the law to reveal sin and put to shame all presumption as to human ability. For this reason St. Paul, in Galatians 2[:17], calls Moses "an agent of sin," and his office "a dispensation of death," II Corinthians 3[:7]. In Romans 3[:20] and 7[:7] he says, "Through the law comes nothing more than knowledge of sin"; and in Romans 3[:20], "By works of the law no one becomes righteous before God." For by the law Moses can do no more than tell what men ought to do and not do. However he does not provide the strength and ability for such doing and not doing, and thus lets us stick in sin. When we then stick in sin, death presses instantly upon us as vengeance and punishment for sin. For this reason St. Paul calls sin "the sting of death" [I Cor. 15:56], because it is by sin that death has all its right and power over us. But if there were no law, there would be no sin.[15] Therefore it is all the fault of Moses, who by the law precipitates and stirs up sin; and then upon sin death follows with a vengeance. Rightly, then, does St. Paul call the office of Moses a dispensation of sin and death [II Cor. 3:7], for by his lawgiving he brings upon us nothing but sin and death.

Nevertheless this office of sin and death is good and very necessary. For where there is no law of God, there all human reason is so blind that it cannot recognize sin. For human reason does not know that unbelief and despair of God is sin. Indeed it knows nothing about man's duty to believe and trust in God. Hardened in its blindness, it goes its way and never feels this sin at all. Meanwhile it does some works that would otherwise be good, and it leads an outwardly respectable life. Then it thinks it stands well and the matter has been satisfactorily handled; we see this in the heathen and the hypocrites, when their life is at its best. Besides reason does not know either that the evil inclination of the flesh, and hatred of enemies, is sin. Because it observes and feels that all men are so inclined, it holds rather that these things are natural and right, and thinks it is enough merely to guard against the outward acts. So it goes its way, regarding its illness as strength, its sin as virtue, its evil as good; and never getting anywhere.

See, then! Moses' office is essential for driving away this blindness and hardened presumption. Now he cannot drive them away

---

[15] Cf. Rom. 4:15.

unless he reveals them and makes them known. He does this by the law, when he teaches that men ought to fear, trust, believe, and love God; and that, besides, they ought to have or bear no evil desire or hatred for any man. When human nature, then, catches on to this, it must be frightened, for it certainly finds neither trust nor faith, neither fear nor love to God, and neither love nor purity toward one's neighbor. Human nature finds rather only unbelief, doubt, contempt, and hatred to God; and toward one's neighbor only evil will and evil desire. But when human nature finds these things, then death is instantly before its eyes, ready to devour such a sinner and to swallow him up in hell.

See, this is what it means for sin to bring death upon us and kill us. This is what it means for the law to stir up sin and set it before our eyes, driving all our presumption into despondency and trembling and despair, so that a man can do no more than cry with the prophets, "I am rejected by God," or, as we say in German, "The devil has me; I can never be saved." This is to be really cast into hell. This is what St. Paul means by those short words in I Corinthians 15[:56], "The sting of death is sin, and the power of sin is the law." It is as if he were saying, "Death stings and slays us because of the sin that is found in us, guilty of death; sin, however, is found in us and gives us so mightily to death because of the law which reveals sin to us and teaches us to recognize it, where before we did not know it and felt secure."

Notice with what power Moses conducts and performs this office of his. For in order to put human nature to the utmost shame, he not only gives laws like the Ten Commandments that speak of natural and true sins, but he also makes sins of things that are in their nature not sins. Moses thus forces and presses sins upon them in heaps. For unbelief and evil desire are in their nature sins, and worthy of death. But to eat leavened bread at the Passover [Exodus 12–13] and to eat an unclean animal [Leviticus 11, Deuteronomy 14] or make a mark on the body [Lev. 19:28, Deut. 14:1], and all those things that the Levitical priesthood deals with as sin—these are not in their nature sinful and evil. Rather they became sins only because they are forbidden by the law. This law can be done away. The Ten Commandments, however, cannot be done away, for here there really is sin, even if there were no commandments, or if they were not known—just as the unbelief of the heathen is sin, even though they do not know or think that it is sin.

Therefore we see that these many laws of Moses were given not only to prevent anyone from choosing ways of his own for doing good and living aright, as was said above,[16] but rather that sins might simply become numerous and be heaped up beyond measure. The purpose was to burden the conscience so that the hardened blindness would have to recognize itself, and feel its own inability and nothingness in the achieving of good. Such blindness must be thus compelled and forced by the law to seek something beyond the law and its own ability, namely, the grace of God promised in the Christ who was to come. Every law of God is good and right [Rom. 7:7-16], even if it only bids men to carry dung or to gather straw. Accordingly, whoever does not keep this good law—or keeps it unwillingly—cannot be righteous or good in his heart. But human nature cannot keep it otherwise than unwillingly. It must therefore, through this good law of God, recognize and feel its wickedness, and sigh and long for the aid of divine grace in Christ.

For this reason then, when Christ comes the law ceases, especially the Levitical law which, as has been said, makes sins of things that in their nature are not sins. The Ten Commandments also cease, not in the sense that they are no longer to be kept or fulfilled, but in the sense that the office of Moses in them ceases; it no longer increases sin [Rom. 5:20] by the Ten Commandments, and sin is no longer the sting of death [I Cor. 15:56]. For through Christ sin is forgiven, God is reconciled, and man's heart has begun to feel kindly toward the law.[17] The office of Moses can no longer rebuke the heart and make it to be sin for not having kept the commandments and for being guilty of death, as it did prior to grace, before Christ came.

St. Paul teaches this in II Corinthians 3[:7-14], where he says that the splendor in the face of Moses is taken away, because of the glory in the face of Jesus Christ. That is, the office of Moses, which makes us to be sin and shame with the glare of the knowledge of

---

[16] Cf. above, pp. 379-380.

[17] Separate editions of the Pentateuch prior to the 1534 complete Bible here read, "For through the grace of Christ the heart has now become good, loving the law and satisfying it." WA, DB 8, 24, n. 25/26.

our wickedness and nothingness, no longer causes us pain and no longer terrifies us with death. For we now have the glory in the face of Christ [II Cor. 4:6]. This is the office of grace, whereby we know Christ, by whose righteousness, life, and strength we fulfil the law and overcome death and hell. Thus it was that the three apostles who saw Moses and Elijah on Mount Tabor were not afraid of them, because of the tender glory in the face of Christ [Luke 9:32]. Yet in Exodus 34[:29-35], where Christ was not present, the children of Israel could not endure the splendor and brightness in the face of Moses, so that he had to put a veil over it.

For the law has three kinds of pupils. The first are those who hear the law and despise it, and who lead an impious life without fear. To these the law does not come. They are represented by the calf worshipers in the wilderness, on whose account Moses broke the tables of the law [Exod. 32:19]. To them he did not bring the law.

The second kind are those who attempt to fulfil the law by their own power, without grace. They are represented by the people who could not look at the face of Moses when he brought the tables of the law a second time [Exod. 34:34-35]. The law comes to them but they cannot endure it. They therefore put a veil over it and lead a life of hypocrisy, doing outward works of the law. Yet the law makes it all to be sin where the veil is taken off. For the law shows that our ability counts for nothing without Christ's grace.

The third kind of pupils are those who see Moses clearly, without a veil. These are they who understand the intention of the law and how it demands impossible things. There sin comes to power, there death is mighty, there Goliath's spear is like a weaver's beam and its point[18] weighs six hundred shekels of brass, so that all the children of Israel flee before him unless the one and only David—Christ our Lord—saves us from all this [I Sam. 17:7, 24, 32]. For if Christ's glory did not come alongside this splendor of Moses, no one could bear the brightness of the law, the terror of sin and death. These pupils fall away from all works and presumption and learn from the law nothing else except to recognize sin and to yearn for

---

[18] *Stachel*, meaning a sharp point such as the head of a spear, has additional overtones in this context, for it was also the word Luther had used in I Cor. 15:56 to speak of the "sting" of death (cf. p. 383). WA, DB 7, 134.

Christ. This is the true office of Moses and the very nature of the law.

So Moses himself has told us that his office and teaching should endure until Christ, and then cease, when he says in Deuteronomy 18[:15-19], "The Lord your God will raise up for you a prophet like me from among your brethren—him shall you heed," etc. This is the noblest saying in all of Moses, indeed the very heart of it all. The apostles appealed to it and made great use of it to strengthen the gospel and to abolish the law [Acts 3:22; 7:37]. All the prophets, as well, drew heavily upon it. For since God here promises another Moses whom they are to hear, it follows of necessity that this other one would teach something different from Moses; and Moses gives up his power and yields to him, so that men will listen to him. This [coming] prophet cannot, then, teach the law, for Moses has done that to perfection; for the law's sake there would be no need to raise up another prophet. Therefore this word was surely spoken concerning Christ and the teaching of grace.

For this reason also, St. Paul calls the law of Moses "the old testament" [II Cor. 3:14], and Christ does the same when he institutes "the new testament" [I Cor. 11:25].[19] It is a testament because in it God promised and bequeathed to the people of Israel the land of Canaan, if they would keep it. He gave it to them too, and it was confirmed by the death and blood of sheep and goats. But since this testament did not stand upon God's grace, but upon men's works, it had to become obsolete and cease, and the promised land had to be lost again—because the law cannot be fulfilled by works. And another testament had to come which would not become obsolete, which would not stand upon our deeds either, but upon God's words and works, so that it might endure for ever. Therefore it is confirmed by the death and blood of an eternal Person, and an eternal land is promised and given.[20]

Let this be enough about the books and office of Moses. What, then, are the other books, the prophets and the histories? I answer: They are nothing else than what Moses is. For they all propagate the office of Moses; they guard against the false prophets, that they

---

[19] Cf. Heb. 8:13: "In speaking of a new covenant he treats the first as obsolete." In Luther's Bible, as in the Vulgate, the adjective "new" appeared also in the synoptic accounts of the Last Supper, Matt. 26:28, Mark 14:24, and Luke 22:20.
[20] Cf. Heb. 9:11-12.

may not lead the people to works, but allow them to remain in the true office of Moses, the knowledge of the law. They hold fast to this purpose of keeping the people conscious of their own impotence through a right understanding of the law, and thus driving them to Christ, as Moses does. For this reason they also explicate further what Moses says of Christ, and furnish two kinds of examples, of those who have Moses right and of those who do not, and also of the punishments and rewards that come to both. Thus the prophets are nothing else than administrators[21] and witnesses of Moses and his office, bringing everyone to Christ through the law.

In conclusion I ought also to indicate the spiritual meaning[22] presented to us by the Levitical law and priesthood of Moses. But there is too much of this to write; it requires space and time and should be expounded with the living voice. For Moses is, indeed, a well of all wisdom and understanding, out of which has sprung all that the prophets knew and said. Moreover even the New Testament flows out of it and is grounded in it, as we have heard[23] It is my duty, however, to give at least some little clue[24] to those who have the grace and understanding to pursue the matter further.

If you would interpret well and confidently, set Christ before you, for he is the man to whom it all applies, every bit of it. Make the high priest Aaron, then, to be nobody but Christ alone, as does the Epistle to the Hebrews [5:4-5], which is sufficient, all by itself, to interpret all the figures of Moses. Likewise, as the same epistle announces [Hebrews 9–10], it is certain that Christ himself is the sacrifice—indeed even the altar [Heb. 13:10]—who sacrificed himself with his own blood. Now whereas the sacrifice performed by the Levitical high priest took away only the artificial sins,[25] which in their nature were not sins, so our high priest, Christ, by his own sacrifice and blood, has taken away the true sin, that which in its very nature is sin. He has gone in once for all through the curtain to God to make atonement for us [Heb. 9:12]. Thus you should

---

[21] *Handhaber* has the sense of uphold, support, or defend as well as of perform or execute. *WA*, DB 8, 29, n. 22; cf. Grimm, *Deutsches Wörterbuch*, IV, 393-396.

[22] *Geistliche Deutung;* cf. above, p. 375, n. 2.

[23] Cf. above, p. 375.

[24] *Grifflin* means a trick, device, or stratagem. Grimm, *Deutsches Wörterbuch*, IV, 312; cf. *WA*, DB 8, 29, n. 30.

[25] *Die gemachten sunde.* See above, pp. 383-384.

apply to Christ personally, and to no one else, all that is written about the high priest.

The high priest's sons, however, who are engaged in the daily sacrifice, you should interpret to mean ourselves. Here on earth, in the body, we Christians live in the presence of our father Christ, who is sitting in heaven; we have not yet passed through to him except spiritually, by faith. Their office of slaughter and sacrifice signifies nothing else than the preaching of the gospel, by which the old man is slain and offered to God, burned and consumed by the fire of love, in the Holy Spirit. This sacrifice smells really good before God; that is, it produces a conscience that is good, pure, and secure before God. This is the interpretation that St. Paul makes in Romans 12[:1] when he teaches that we are to offer our bodies to God as a living, holy, and acceptable sacrifice. This is what we do (as has been said) by the constant exercise of the gospel both in preaching and in believing.

Let this suffice for the present as a brief suggestion for seeking Christ and the gospel in the Old Testament.[26]

Whoever reads this Bible should also know that I have been careful to write the name of God which the Jews call "Tetragrammaton"[27] in capital letters thus, LORD [*HERR*], and the other name which they call *Adonai*[28] only half in capital letters thus, LOrd [*HErr*].[29] For among all the names of God, these two alone are

[26] In editions of the complete Bible from 1534 on, the preface ended at this point. The paragraphs which follow were found only in the earlier editions.
[27] Tetragrammaton, literally "four letters," is the technical term for the four-consonant Hebrew word for the name God, which is now commonly thought to be represented in English by the word "Yahweh." When the Hebrews came to this name in speaking or reading, they avoided uttering it because of its sacred character, pronouncing instead the word Adonai (Lord) unless (as at Gen. 15:2) it immediately followed the word "Adonai" in the text, in which case "Elohim" (God) was read. In written Hebrew texts the vowel-points of Adonai were given to the consonants of the Tetragrammaton with the resultant rendering in English, "Jehovah."
[28] Adonai literally means "my lord," but by usage it was in effect a proper name.
[29] While the Hebrew *YHWH* always had reference to God alone, *ADN* could mean either the divine Lord, or a lord or ruler who was not divine. Luther distinguished clearly between the two words by rendering *HERR* for *YHWH* and either *HErr* or *herr* for *ADN* (cf. *LW* 12, 99-101 and *LW* 13, 230). The distinction between the divine and human within *ADN*, however, was not consistently maintained in translation by the use of *HErr* and *herr* (cf. *WA*, DB 6, 538-539, note on Matt. 1:20). Cf. Luther's *HERR-HERR* in Jer. 23:5-6 with the RSV LORD-LORD, Luther's *HERR-herr* in Gen. 24:12 with the RSV LORD-

applied in the Scriptures to the real, true God; while the others are often ascribed to angels and saints. I have done this in order that readers can thereby draw the strong conclusion that Christ is true God. For Jeremiah 23[:6] calls him LORD, saying, "He will be called: 'The LORD, our righteousness.'" The same thing is to be found in other passages. Herewith I commend all my readers to Christ and ask that they help me get from God the power to carry this work through to a profitable end. For I freely admit that I have undertaken too much, especially in trying to put the Old Testament into German.[30] The Hebrew language, sad to say, has gone down so far that even the Jews know little enough about it, and their glosses and interpretations (which I have tested[31]) are not to be relied upon. I think that if the Bible is to come up again, we Christians are the ones who must do the work, for we have the understanding of Christ without which even the knowledge of the language is nothing. Because they were without it, the translators of old, even Jerome,[32] made mistakes in many passages. Though I cannot boast of having achieved perfection, nevertheless, I venture to say that this German Bible is clearer and more accurate at many points than the Latin. So it is true that if the printers do not, as usual, spoil it with their carelessness, the German language certainly has here a better Bible than the Latin language—and the readers will bear me out in this.

And now, of course, the mud will stick to the wheel,[33] and there will be no one so stupid that he will not try to be my master in this work, and criticize me here and there. Let them go to it. I figured from the very beginning that I would find ten thousand to criticize my work before I found one who would accomplish one-twentieth

---

master, and Luther's *HERR-HErr* in Ps. 110:1 (1545 version only, the earlier versions being both *HERR-HERR* and *HERR-herr*, *WA*, DB 10[I], 476-477) with the RSV LORD-lord. In Luther's Matt. 22:44 rendering of the first "Lord" of the Psalm quotation he went from *Gott* in 1522 through *Herr* and *HErr* to *HERR* in 1539 and later editions (*WA*, DB 6, 100, note). See Gen. 15:2, 8 where Luther translates *ADN YHWH* as *HErr HERR* (*WA*, DB 8, 73). Cf. also *WA*, DB 10[II], xxiii, n. 26.

[30] Cf. Luther's statement, "It was necessary for me to undertake the translation of the Bible, otherwise I would have died under the mistaken impression that I was a learned man." *WA* 10[II], 60, ll. 13-15; cf. also *WA*, Br 2, 423, ll. 48-50.

[31] Cf. Luther's *Defense of the Translation of the Psalms* (1531). *LW* 35, 203-223.

[32] Jerome (*ca.* 342-420), the foremost biblical scholar of the ancient church, translated the Bible into popular Latin (Vulgate). Cf. *LW* 35, 117, n. 1.

[33] Cf. Wander (ed.), *Sprichwörter-Lexikon*, II, 1556, "Koth," Nos. 4 and 16.

of what I have done. I, too, would like to be very learned and give brilliant proof of what I know by criticizing St. Jerome's Latin Bible; but he in turn could also defy me to do what he has done. Now if anyone is so much more learned than I, let him undertake to translate the whole Bible into German, and then tell me what he can do.[34] If he does it better, why should he not be preferred to me? I thought I was well educated—and I know that by the grace of God I am more learned than all the sophists in the universities—but now I see that I cannot handle even my own native German tongue. Nor have I read, up to this time, a book or letter which contained the right kind of German. Besides no one pays any attention to speaking real German. This is especially true of the people in the chancelleries, as well as those patchwork preachers and wretched writers.[35] They think they have the right to change the German language and to invent new words for us every day, such as *behertzigen,*[36] *behendigen,*[37] *ersprieslich,*[38] *erschieslich,*[39] and the like. Yes, my dear fellow, there are [and this is] also *bethoret* and *ernarret.*[40]

In a word, if all of us were to work together, we would have plenty to do in bringing the Bible to light, one working with the meaning, the other with the language. For I too have not worked at this alone,[41] but have used the services of anyone whom I could

---

[34] Cf. above, pp. 175-176; cf. also *LW* 35, 221-223.

[35] *Lumpen prediger und puppen schreyber.*

[36] Deriving largely from Swabian origin, the term had been used frequently by Emser. Friedrich Kluge, *Etymologisches Wörterbuch der deutschen Sprache* (17th ed.; Berlin: de Gruyter, 1957), p. 61.

[37] In a letter from Luther and Karlstadt to Duke Frederick of Saxony dated August 18, 1519, Luther—or perhaps his co-author—had himself used the term *Behendigkeit.* *WA,* Br 1, 477, l. 410. The use of *behendigen* is documented as early as 1484 in Wetterau. Moritz Heyne, *Deutsches Wörterbuch* (3 vols.; Leipzig: Hirzel, 1890-1895), I, 324.

[38] Meaning originally to spring forth or sprout, *erspriessen* early came to be used in New High German in the sense of "be useful, profitable, advantageous." The adjective too was given this derived meaning from about the beginning of the sixteenth century. Kluge, *op. cit.,* p. 173.

[39] Luther apparently was unaware that the intransitive verb *erschiessen* was used rather extensively in a sense synonymous with that of *erspriessen.* Grimm, *Deutsches Wörterbuch,* III, 962.

[40] *Bethören* means to make a fool of, in the sense of infatuate, seduce, or deceive. *Ernarren* means to play the fool, in the sense of be silly, astonish, or amaze. The construction of Luther's sentence conveys a double meaning: not only that these words too are recent innovations, but also that all such innovating is sheer folly.

[41] Cf. the Introduction in *LW* 35, 229.

get. Therefore I ask everyone to desist from abuse and leave the poor people undisturbed, and help me, if he can. If he will not do that, let him take up the Bible himself and make a translation of his own. Those who do nothing but abuse and bite and claw are actually not honest and upright enough to really want a pure Bible, since they know that they cannot produce it. They would prefer to be Master Know-it-all[42] in a field not their own, though in their own field they have never even been pupils.

May God bring to completion his work that he began [Phil. 1:6]. Amen.

---

[42] Cf. above, p. 176, n. 14.

Preface to the New Testament[1]

1546 (1522)

[It would be right and proper for this book to go forth without any prefaces or extraneous names attached and simply have its own say under its own name. However many unfounded [*wilde*] interpretations and prefaces[2] have scattered the thought of Christians to a point where no one any longer knows what is gospel or law, New Testament or Old. Necessity demands, therefore, that there should be a notice or preface, by which the ordinary man can be rescued from his former delusions, set on the right track, and taught what he is to look for in this book, so that he may not seek laws and commandments where he ought to be seeking the gospel and promises of God.

Therefore it should be known, in the first place, that the notion must be given up that there are four gospels and only four evangelists.[3] The division of the New Testament books into legal, historical, prophetic, and wisdom books is also to be utterly rejected. Some make this division,[4] thinking thereby (I know not how) to compare

---

[1] Prior to the 1534 edition of the complete Bible this preface—intended perhaps as a preface to the entire New Testament or at least to the first part of the New Testament including the gospels and Acts (see *WA*, DB 7, xxxi)—carried as a title the single word, "Preface." We have based our translation on the version which appeared in the 1546 edition of the complete Bible, noting significant variations from earlier versions, particularly from the first version as it appeared in the September Testament of 1522. *WA*, DB 6, 2-11. See *LW* 35, 227-232 for a general introduction to all of Luther's biblical prefaces.

[2] On the ancient practice of providing prefaces, see the Introduction, pp. 373-374. On the prefaces which appeared in early printed German Bibles, including the text of that to the book of Romans in the Mentel Bible—the first printed Bible in High German published by Johann Mentel in Strassburg about 1466—see Reu, *Luther's German Bible*, p. 35 and p. 305, n. 71.

[3] Limiting the number of gospels to four was an ancient practice going back at least to Jerome, who based his position on the existence of but four living creatures in Ezekiel 1 and Revelation 4—the man, lion, ox, and eagle. Migne 30, 531-534. *WA*, DB 6, 536, n. 2, 12. Cf. below, p. 396.

[4] This division had been made, e.g., in the 1509 Vulgate printed at Basel, which Luther had probably used. *WA*, DB 6, 537, n. 2, 14.

the New with the Old Testament. On the contrary it is to be held firmly that][5]

Just as the Old Testament is a book in which are written God's laws and commandments, together with the history of those who kept and of those who did not keep them,[6] so the New Testament is a book in which are written the gospel and the promises of God, together with the history of those who believe and of those who do not believe them.[7]

For "gospel" [Euangelium] is a Greek word and means in Greek a good message, good tidings, good news, a good report, which one sings and tells with gladness. For example, when David overcame the great Goliath, there came among the Jewish people the good report and encouraging news that their terrible enemy had been struck down and that they had been rescued and given joy and peace; and they sang and danced and were glad for it [I Sam. 18:6].

Thus this gospel of God or New Testament is a good story and report, sounded forth into all the world by the apostles, telling of a true David who strove with sin, death, and the devil, and overcame them, and thereby rescued all those who were captive in sin, afflicted with death, and overpowered by the devil. Without any merit of their own he made them righteous, gave them life, and saved them, so that they were given peace and brought back to God. For this they sing, and thank and praise God, and are glad forever, if only they believe firmly and remain steadfast in faith.

This report and encouraging tidings, or evangelical and divine news, is also called a New Testament. For it is a testament when a dying man bequeaths his property, after his death, to his legally

---

[5] The portions here set in brackets did not appear in any editions of the complete Bible, nor in editions of the New Testament after 1537. Divergences from the original 1522 text were due primarily to Luther's desire to accommodate the text of the New Testament prefaces to that of the Old Testament prefaces with which they were—in the 1534 complete Bible—to appear for the first time, rather than to criticism on the part of Emser or other opponents. That these divergences were not taken into account in the 1534-1537 separate editions of the New Testament was probably due to the carelessness of the printer, Luther having likely given no personal attention to these particular editions. *WA, DB* 6, 536.

[6] Cf. above, p. 376.

[7] The editions prior to the 1534 complete Bible here add, "Thus one may be sure that there is only one gospel, just as there is only one book—the New Testament—one faith, and one God who gives the promise" (Eph. 4:4-6).

defined heirs.[8] And Christ, before his death, commanded and ordained that his gospel be preached after his death in all the world [Luke 24:44-47]. Thereby he gave to all who believe, as their possession, everything that he had. This included: his life, in which he swallowed up death; his righteousness, by which he blotted out sin; and his salvation, with which he overcame everlasting damnation. A poor man, dead in sin and consigned to hell, can hear nothing more comforting than this precious and tender message about Christ; from the bottom of his heart he must laugh and be glad over it, if he believes it true.

Now to strengthen this faith, God has promised this gospel and testament in many ways, by the prophets in the Old Testament, as St. Paul says in Romans 1[:1], "I am set apart to preach the gospel of God which he promised beforehand through his prophets in the holy scriptures, concerning his Son, who was descended from David," etc.

To mention some of these places: God gave the first promise when he said to the serpent, in Genesis 3[:15], "I will put enmity between you and the woman, and between your seed and her seed; he shall bruise your head, and you shall bruise his heel." Christ is this woman's seed, who has bruised the devil's head, that is, sin death, hell, and all his power. For without this seed, no man can escape sin, death, or hell.

Again, in Genesis 22[:18], God promised Abraham, "Through your descendant shall all the nations of the earth be blessed." Christ is that descendant of Abraham, says St. Paul in Galatians 3[:16]; he has blessed all the world, through the gospel [Gal. 3:8]. For where Christ is not, there is still the curse that fell upon Adam and his children when he had sinned, so that they all are necessarily guilty and subject to sin, death, and hell. Over against this curse, the gospel now blesses all the world by publicly announcing, "Whoever believes in this descendant of Abraham shall be blessed." That is, he shall be rid of sin, death, and hell, and shall remain righteous, alive, and saved forever, as Christ himself says in John 11[:26], "Whoever believes in me shall never die."

Again God made this promise to David in II Samuel 7[:12-14] when he said, "I will raise up your son after you, who shall build

---

[8] Cf. LW 35, 87-90.

a house for my name, and I will establish the throne of his kingdom forever. I will be his father, and he shall be my son," etc. This is the kingdom of Christ, of which the gospel speaks: an everlasting kingdom, a kingdom of life, salvation, and righteousness, where all those who believe enter in from out of the prison of sin and death.

There are many more such promises of the gospel in the other prophets as well, for example Micah 5[:2], "But you, O Bethlehem Ephrathah, who are little to be among the clans of Judah, from you shall come forth for me one who is to be ruler in Israel"; and again, Hosea 13[:14], "I shall ransom them from the power of hell and redeem them from death. O death, I will be your plague; O hell, I will be your destruction."

The gospel, then, is nothing but the preaching about Christ, Son of God and of David, true God and man, who by his death and resurrection has overcome for us the sin, death, and hell of all men who believe in him. Thus the gospel can be either a brief or a lengthy message; one person can write of it briefly, another at length. He writes of it at length, who writes about many words and works of Christ, as do the four evangelists. He writes of it briefly, however, who does not tell of Christ's works, but indicates briefly how by his death and resurrection he has overcome sin, death, and hell for those who believe in him, as do St. Peter and St. Paul.

See to it, therefore, that you do not make a Moses out of Christ, or a book of laws and doctrines out of the gospel, as has been done heretofore and as certain prefaces put it, even those of St. Jerome.[9] For the gospel does not expressly demand works of our own by which we become righteous and are saved; indeed it condemns such works. Rather the gospel demands faith in Christ: that he has overcome for us sin, death, and hell, and thus gives us righteousness, life, and salvation not through our works, but through his own works, death, and suffering, in order that we may avail ourselves of his death and victory as though we had done it ourselves.

To be sure, Christ in the gospel, and St. Peter and St. Paul besides, do give many commandments and doctrines, and expound the law. But these are to be counted like all Christ's other works and

---

[9] Each of the four gospels had its own preface in Jerome's Vulgate. Luther's concern for the "one gospel" kept him from ever writing four such separate prefaces. Indeed at the beginning it seems likely that he envisioned but one preface for the entire New Testament. WA, DB 6, 537, n. 8, 5; WA, DB 7, xxi. LW 35, 117-124.

good deeds. To know his works and the things that happened to him is not yet to know the true gospel, for you do not yet thereby know that he has overcome sin, death, and the devil. So, too, it is not yet knowledge of the gospel when you know these doctrines and commandments, but only when the voice comes that says, "Christ is your own, with his life, teaching, works, death, resurrection, and all that he is, has, does, and can do."

Thus we see also that he does not compel us but invites us kindly and says, "Blessed are the poor," etc. [Matt. 5:3]. And the apostles use the words, "I exhort," "I entreat," "I beg," so that one sees on every hand that the gospel is not a book of law, but really a preaching of the benefits of Christ, shown to us and given to us for our own possession, if we believe. But Moses, in his books, drives, compels, threatens, strikes, and rebukes terribly, for he is a lawgiver and driver.

Hence it comes that to a believer no law is given by which he becomes righteous before God, as St. Paul says in I Timothy 1[:9], because he is alive and righteous and saved by faith, and he needs nothing further except to prove his faith by works. Truly, if faith is there, he cannot hold back; he proves himself, breaks out into good works, confesses and teaches this gospel before the people, and stakes his life on it. Everything that he lives and does is directed to his neighbor's profit, in order to help him—not only to the attainment of this grace, but also in body, property, and honor. Seeing that Christ has done this for him, he thus follows Christ's example.

That is what Christ meant when at the last he gave no other commandment than love, by which men were to know who were his disciples [John 13:34-35] and true believers. For where works and love do not break forth, there faith is not right, the gospel does not yet take hold, and Christ is not rightly known. See, then, that you so approach the books of the New Testament as to learn to read them in this way.

[Which are the true and noblest books of the New Testament][10]
[From all this you can now judge all the books and decide among them which are the best. John's Gospel and St. Paul's epis-

---

[10] Cf. above, p. 394, n. 5.

tles, especially that to the Romans, and St. Peter's first epistle are the true kernel and marrow of all the books. They ought properly to be the foremost books, and it would be advisable for every Christian to read them first and most, and by daily reading to make them as much his own as his daily bread. For in them you do not find many works and miracles of Christ described, but you do find depicted in masterly fashion how faith in Christ overcomes sin, death, and hell, and gives life, righteousness, and salvation. This is the real nature of the gospel, as you have heard.

If I had to do without one or the other—either the works or the preaching of Christ—I would rather do without the works than without his preaching. For the works do not help me, but his words give life, as he himself says [John 6:63]. Now John writes very little about the works of Christ, but very much about his preaching, while the other evangelists write much about his works and little about his preaching. Therefore John's Gospel is the one, fine, true, and chief gospel, and is far, far to be preferred over the other three and placed high above them. So, too, the epistles of St. Paul and St. Peter far surpass the other three gospels, Matthew, Mark, and Luke.

In a word St. John's Gospel and his first epistle, St. Paul's epistles, especially Romans, Galatians, and Ephesians, and St. Peter's first epistle are the books that show you Christ and teach you all that is necessary and salvatory for you to know, even if you were never to see or hear any other book or doctrine. Therefore St. James' epistle is really an epistle of straw,[11] compared to these others, for it has nothing of the nature of the gospel about it. But more of this in the other prefaces.][12]

---

[11] On the term "straw" cf. Luther's reference in *LW* 35, 395, to I Cor. 3:12. Luther's sharp expression may have been in part a reaction against Karlstadt's excessive praise of the letter of James. Cf. *WA, DB* 6, 537, n. 10, 6-34, and the literature there listed.

[12] See especially the Preface to James in *LW* 35, 395-398. Cf. also Luther's negative estimate of the letter of James as early as 1520 (*Babylonian Captivity of the Church* in SW 1, 470). Cf. his *Resolutiones* of 1519 in *WA* 2, 425.

INDEX

INDEX